IMPERIAL DEBRIS

IMPERIAL DEBRIS   *On Ruins and Ruination*

EDITED BY **ANN LAURA STOLER**

Duke University Press Durham and London 2013

© 2013 Duke University Press

All rights reserved

Printed in the United States of
America on acid-free paper ♾

Typeset in Quadraat by Tseng
Information Systems, Inc.

Chapters 1, 2, 3, and 9 are
reproduced by permission of
the American Anthropological
Association from *Cultural Anthropology* 23, no. 2 (2008). Not for
sale or further reproduction.

Frontispiece:
photo by John Collins.

Library of Congress Cataloging-in-Publication Data

Imperial debris : on ruins and ruination / edited by
Ann Laura Stoler.

p. cm.

Includes bibliographical references and index.

ISBN 978-0-8223-5348-5 (cloth : alk. paper)

ISBN 978-0-8223-5361-4 (pbk. : alk. paper)

1. Postcolonialism. 2. Postcolonialism—Social
aspects. I. Stoler, Ann Laura.

JV152.I474 2013

325′.3—dc23

2012044772

This volume is dedicated to
IMOGEN BUNTING,
who died suddenly of heart failure
at the age of twenty-five, in
the midst of work on this project.

A brilliant graduate student in
anthropology at the New School
for Social Research, Imogen was
a fearlessly ethical being, an
incandescent soul, and a political
activist who infused us all with
the vital demands she made on our
intellectual and quotidian lives.

CONTENTS

It would be hard to write about ruins today without acknowledging Walter Benjamin's imprint on the politicized readings we bring to them. When this volume was still in early formation in 2005, his writings on ruins had long made them a productive and privileged site of critical historical inquiry. Benjamin and Susan Buck-Morss's enabling reading of his Arcades project in *The Dialectics of Seeing*, fifteen years earlier, had helped turn many of us away from the nostalgic European gaze upon ruins, to treat them as symptom and substance of history's destructive force, to take the measure of the "fragility" of capitalist culture from the decaying structures left scattered across our urban and rural geographies, to attend to the force of these fragments and the traces of violence left in its wake. He would seem to be an obvious reference for what follows, and in sundry ways contributions to this volume build on his reflections.

But, strangely perhaps, because of the nature of the conversations that elicited this project (and the convergence of persons and concerns it joined), it was not Benjamin's treatment of ruins that served as this volume's inspiration. It is around processes of "ruination" as much as imperial ruins that this volume turns. Ruination was neither Benjamin's focus nor the process he sought to explicitly name. Our centering on ruination shifts the emphasis from the optics of ruins to the ongoing nature of imperial process. The latter joins psychological disablements to the imperial genealogies of dislocation and dispossession.

Our sights from the beginning were set on the search for a vocabulary and analytics that might speak to the stark and occluded durabilities of imperial effects, to their tangible and intangible effects. At a moment when "ruins theory" had not yet been named, Adriana Petryna, Vyjayanthi Rao, and I— from the varied places and problematics with which we each worked—set our sights on something more than ruins per se. We sought to identify neither the political aesthetics of ruins nor the aftermaths of catastrophic destruction, but rather the deeply saturated, less spectacular forms in which colonialisms leave their mark. Our attention has been on the lives of those whose sensibilities have been marked by the ruins in which they live, and on the possibilities foreclosed by how they have had to live in them.

In the process of conceptualizing our project, language choice has been key. Nietzsche may have been right that concepts are dead metaphors, but they can also be generative sites for concept formation. Or in the absence of concepts, metaphors speak to the nonspoken, to the nonconceptual sensibilities that escape consolidated conceptualized forms. As Hans Blumberger suggests, metaphors are anything but seamless similarity. They are "disturbances." They can be disruptive, suggest new analytic space and new associations, even as they seem smoothly to line up with that to which they refer. Metaphors can be political actors when they stretch our visions to new domains. Metaphors are never precise, as Blumberger reminds us. This gap is where their traction lies.

In the initial conference for this volume, in 2006, "scarred landscapes" shared a place with "imperial debris" in our conversations. But it was Derek Walcott's figurative language that seemed to offer the analytic capacity to join the waste of bodies, the degradation of environment, and the psychic weight of colonial processes that entangle people, soil, and things. "Rot," "debris," and "detritus" held us fast. In identifying colonialism as the "rot" that "remains," Walcott's metaphors take on a living valence. "Rot" opens to the psychic and material eating away of bodies, environment, and possibilities. "Rot" contains an active substance. It is hard to wipe out. Like debris, it is not where one always expects it to be. Nor is it always immediately visible. Such references have more than poetic purchase; they hold tight to the ongoing work of debris-making that we have sought to retain.

Like ruins, debris is constructed, ruination is made. Debris speaks to something else. Leftovers are assigned as detritus because they are rendered into neglect or valorized for insistent remembrance. The effort to make visible colonial processes that escape that naming has been enhanced by many who helped us think this project as it was forming. At the initial conference on "Scarred Landscapes and Imperial Debris," Claudia Baracchi, Jacqueline Brown, Faisal Devji, Diane Fox, Beatriz Jaguaribe, Hugh Raffles, Claudio Lomnitz, Karolina Szmagalska-Follis, Jonathan Veitch, Hylton White, and Gary Wilder each pushed the conversations in new directions. The anthropology graduate students David Bond, Imogen Bunting, and Joe Stefano intellectually fueled our deliberations. Julia Hell and George Steinmetz were valued interlocutors early on. Anonymous readers for the special issue that appeared in *Cultural Anthropology* were as well. Readers from Duke University Press offered enabling challenges to our formulations. I thank Kim and Mike Fortun for their incisive work as editors of *Cultural Anthropology*, and Ken Wissoker for encouraging us from start to end.

Graduate students at the New School for Social Research were extraordinary contributors to this venture. Vasiliki Touhoulitis brought the volume together for its initial submission to Duke University Press. Charles McDonald copyedited the revised contributions, offered substantially important revisions, submitted the final manuscript, and crafted the index. Katie Detwiler offered her insights throughout to its formulation. Students in my seminar "The Colonial and Postcolonial Order of Things" offered acute assessments of what worked and what did not. Most important, they kept me alert to what I remind them of all the time: namely, that books should be read not as new truths but as interventions in an ongoing conversation — often animated and redirected by the assumptions those students challenge and the questions they think to ask.

"The Rot Remains"

From Ruins to Ruination

A green lawn, broken by low walls of stone,
Dipped to the rivulet, and pacing, I thought next
Of men like Hawkins, Walter Raleigh, Drake,
Ancestral murderers and poets, more perplexed
In memory now by every ulcerous crime.
The world's green age then was a rotting lime
Whose stench became the charnel galleon's text.
The rot remains with us, the men are gone.
But, as dead ash is lifted in a wind
That fans the blackening ember of the mind,
My eyes burned from the ashen prose of Donne.
—DEREK WALCOTT, "Ruins of a Great House,"
Collected Poems 1948–1984

Derek Walcott's searing eulogy to empire and its aftermath as an "ulcerous crime" captures something that seems to elude colonial histories of the present again and again. His verbs shift between multiple tenses. If the insistence is on a set of brutal finite acts in the distant slave-trading past, the process of decay is ongoing, acts of the past blacken the senses, their effects without clear termination. These crimes have been named and indicted across the globe, but the eating away of less visible elements of soil and soul more often has not. Walcott's caustic metaphors slip and mix, juxtaposing the corrosive degrading of matter and mind. Most critically, Walcott sounds a warning to the distracted reader too easily lost in a receding past: proceed with caution, stay alert, for the "rot remains" long after murderous men like Drake have perished, rapacious planters have turned to ash, colonial officials have returned "home," and anxious white settlers have relinquished hold on what was never theirs—and are gone. His cadence joins the acidic stench of "rotting lime" with an "ulcerous crime," a sensory regime embodied, gouged deep in sensibilities of the present.

One could read Walcott's fierce phrasing as the hyperbolic, enraged words of a gifted poet in a "quarrel with history," whose metaphoric might weighs heavily against the sixteenth-century slave trade, its lucrative spoils and ruinous effects.[1] One could lament the verbosity of scholarly depictions, pale and placid next to Walcott's spare and piercing prose. But in first reading his poem several years ago, I approached his choice of language as something more, as a harsh clarion call and a provocative challenge to name the toxic corrosions and violent accruals of colonial aftermaths, the durable forms in which they bear on the material environment and on people's minds. Riveted on the "rot" that remains, Walcott refuses a timeframe bounded by the formal legalities of imperial sovereignty over persons, places, and things. His positioning struck me as a summons and an invitation to pursue that which poems ordinarily cannot. E. Valentine Daniel's "Epic in Verse," on the destruction of Sri Lanka, included here, is one notable exception. It, too, disrupts facile distinction between political history and poetic form, urging us to think differently about both the language we use to capture the tenacious hold of imperial effects and their tangible if elusive forms. In this volume we attempt to track the *uneven temporal sedimentations* in which imperial formations leave their marks. Most important, we seek to ask how empire's ruins contour and carve through the psychic and material space in which people live and what compounded layers of imperial debris do to them.

There is nothing uniform in how the volume's contributors broach the relationship between ruin and ruination—either the opacities in which these histories reside or the visceral reckoning with landscapes and lives in which they may be traced. Gastón Gordillo, for example, takes as his very subject the uncertain political imaginaries that underwrote the disappearance and reemergence of Spanish ruins in the Chaco region of Argentina, which obscure the parallel ruination of indigenous people and the history of their refusals to succumb to colonial conquest. John F. Collins explores how a Brazilian World Heritage program confuses colonial buildings and their occupants, and thus the redemption of people and the restoration of things, in ways that spur those who inhabit the ruins of Portugal's South Atlantic empire to tie together seemingly disparate strands of contemporary imperial formations and the improvement of ostensibly problematic populations. Nancy Rose Hunt rejects "mutilation photographs" to mark the durabilities of the Belgian Congo rubber regime. She explicitly turns away from the visual field toward those of hearing and sound. Ariella Azoulay, on the other hand, fiercely embraces the visual as she attends to the concerted work of the Israeli state to create invisibilities in the visual field of Palestinian dispossession. Her analysis wrestles with the task of seeing, with acts of violation for which there are no photographs able to document bodily exposures and intrusions of space. Here, debris is the built environment of Palestinian habitation, shorn of the private, as Azoulay argues, unprotected by the boundaries of what the privileged get to call home. What joins these efforts are tactical methodologies keenly attentive to the occluded, unexpected sites in which earlier imperial formations have left their bold-faced or subtle traces and in which contemporary inequities work their way through them.

A Counterpoint to Emergency

Scholarship is produced in uneven waves of reaction and anticipation, sometimes prescient about that which has not yet entered the public domain, at other times struggling to keep up with seismic shifts and unanticipated events that render our observations belabored and late. Studies of empire share something of both. In the United States, reactions to 9/11, to the invasion of Iraq, and to public revelations about the treatment of detainees at Guantánamo and Abu Ghraib have moved students of colonial and imperial history to counter with unusual urgency the resurgent assertions of imperial priorities expressed through both familiar and new rationales of rule that such terms as "benevolent empire," "humanitarian imperialism," and the "new liberal empire" were coined to convey. In response, scholars have marshaled their expertise to argue that targeted humiliations of subject populations, humanitarian intervention as offensive strategy, prolonged states of emergency, and preemptive military assault in the name of peace are neither aberrant nor exceptional tactics of imperial regimes, but fundamental to their governing grammar.

Empires past have long served arguments about how Euro-American geopolities could and should comport themselves in contemporary political predicaments.[2] But recent writing on empire does more than treat colonial history as a lesson plan in an analogic mode. What is striking about the current turn is how swiftly it has produced provocative and deep imperial genealogies of the present, pointed assaults on the common keywords and political concepts so often called on today: torture in the name of truth, displacement of targeted populations in the name of security, states of emergency to sanction violent intervention, and states of exception that justify the suspension of legal constraints and the expansion of new imperial sovereignties.

Such counterhistories have withered the conceit that the politics of compassion and humanitarianism make for "empire-lite": they have tracked the emergence of the U.S. "surveillance state" as one forged on the experimental terrain of counterinsurgency projects in the early-twentieth-century colonial Philippines; they have demonstrated that "empires of intelligence" have provided the architecture of British imperial pursuits throughout the Middle East and French empire's "structural imperative" for militarized terror in North Africa.[3] These revisions have been predicated in part on reassessing what constitutes contemporary colonial relations, what counts as an imperial pursuit, and which geopolities rest on residual or reactivated imperial practices—or have abandoned their imperious ambitions all together. Seasoned students of colonial history have been joined by a new cohort of commentators and scholars from a range of disciplines who ask about the lessons of empire and what should be garnered from them.[4]

Not all colonial and postcolonial scholarship works in such a pressing mode, of course. If some have turned to the current immediacies of empire, there are as many that labor to revise what constitutes the archives of imperial pursuit, to reanimate "arrested histories," to rethink the domains of imperial governance and the forms of knowledge that evaded and refused colonial mandates to succumb, "civilize," and serve.[5]

Still, academic debates about the lessons of empire—which first crescendoed and then diminished as the war on Iraq receded into the public's everyday—have taken a very particular direction. In the rush to account for the nature of imperial practices today and their similarities or differences from earlier European and U.S. imperial interventions, a restrictive conceptual apparatus has come to occupy dominant analytic space. Its vocabulary is aptly sharp and critical, bound by the keywords of our moment and the urgent themes to which they speak: security, disaster, defense, preparedness, states of emergency and exception.

This volume does not so much turn away from these concerns as it seeks to work through the less perceptible effects of imperial interventions and their settling into the social and material ecologies in which people live and survive. This is rarely, as Achille Mbembe insists, a matter of wholesale adaptations of colonial technologies. It is instead about reformulations and deformations of the crafts of governance in the management of people's lives.[6] We thus start from the observation that the less dramatic durabilities of duress that imperial formations produce as ongoing, persistent features of their ontologies have been set aside as if less "at hand," less pressing, and less relevant to current global priorities and political situations than their more attention-grabbing counterparts. We attempt to broach, albeit indirectly, a set of questions not often addressed: What conditions the possibilities by which some features of colonial relations remain more resilient, persistent, and visible than others? If "violent environments" are made so not by a scarcity of resources but by grossly uneven reallocation of access to them, the dispossessions and dislocations that accompany those violences do not always take place in obvious and abrupt acts of assault and seizure, but in more drawn out, less eventful, identifiable ways.[7] Our focus is on the more protracted imperial processes that saturate the subsoil of people's lives and persist, sometimes subjacently, over a longer durée.

But the challenge is directed more broadly at a deeper set of assumptions about the relationship between colonial pasts and colonial presents, the residues that abide and are revitalized—if in different working order today. In question is whether postcolonial studies has too readily assumed knowledge of the multiple forms in which colonial pasts bear on the present, and has been too quick to assert what is actually postcolonial in current situations. We take the opportunity to consider more carefully the physical structures, objects, and dispositions in which those histories are carried and conveyed, and not least to attend, as Daniel Miller more generally advocates, to the "unexpected capacity of objects to fade out of focus" as they "remain peripheral to our vision" and yet potent in marking partitioned lives.[8] Rethinking and expanding how to approach the "tangible" effects of ruination is key. If the "tangible" most commonly refers to that which is "capable of being touched," it equally refers to that which is substantial and capable of being perceived. One way to parse what motivates this venture might be its effort to identify new ways to discern and define what constitutes the tangibilities of colonial pasts and imperial presence.

Imperial Tangibilities

At issue is more than that long-contested term *postcolonialism*, which may be "thinly" employed to mark a sequential moment, or the fact that people and places that have been colonized are no longer, or thickly applied to reflect critically on when a present political reality, a set of social representations, a physical or psychological environment is considered to be shaped directly by a prior set of colonial relations. How those relations do so is sometimes precisely specified, though critics contend that they are often not—that the age of empire is over, that imperial regimes are defunct, that colonialisms have been long abandoned, and that political analysis and scholarship should move on as well. Some argue that an analytics committed to searching for colonial effects has dulled what once appeared as postcolonial studies' critical edge, that its accounts of the present are inadequate and partial, that its agents and subjects are long dead, and that its political charge is increasingly irrelevant.[9] Others argue that postcolonialism's consolidation as an academic specialization concertedly removed from the analysis of imperialism ensured that it "had always-already lost the plot."[10] Meanwhile, conservative constituencies in Canada, France, Australia, and the United States often take that argument elsewhere, insisting that colonial histories matter far less than they are contrived to do, that they are called on strategically by specific disenfranchised populations to register (unreasonable) political demands. In this view, an insistent return to colonialism's effects is seen to foster unfounded claims for redemption, apology, and retribution.[11]

The essays collected here defy these distorted assessments. Far more has emerged in the call to rewrite colonial histories, in the debates over old and new forms of imperial venture, and in the acrimonious exchanges over what counts as a colonial "legacy" and what does not. The fact that imperial forms have changed should provide a challenge, not render study of their obscured entailments obsolete. On the contrary, we take these obscured entailments and subjacent durabilities as objects of inquiry, not as given or fully understood facts. Their examination provides opportunities to unsettle well-worn formulations of imperial attributes, to consider an alternative vocabulary, and in so doing to redirect our questions. Why, for example, are Palestinian-Israeli relations, so long marginal to the dominant postcolonial scholarship, now so explicitly articulated in these terms? Why is it only now that students of Korean history are rewriting colonial accounts of the Japanese imperium and Korea's subjugation to it? Why has the domestic history of the United States, so long sequestered as that of a nation without empire, been exploded over the last decade by a new generation tracing policies of containment, enclosure, and segregation that inextricably link the internal and external techniques of colonial rule to imperial patterns across the globe? And why have these all occurred when in some quarters something called postcolonial studies is deemed so poorly equipped to speak to the present?

Given these discrepancies, it may be more productive to embrace the uncomfortable tenor of a contemporary malaise. One might think of mal-*aise* here in its multiple senses of embodied disquiet, a lethargy borne of vague ill-ease. To posit that colonial situations bear on the present is not to suggest that the contemporary world can be accounted for by colonial histories alone. It is rather to understand how those histories, despite having been so concertedly effaced, yield new damages and renewed disparities. While sources of this malaise may be overdetermined, some of them impinge on the very issues we seek to examine here: for one, as I have argued for some time, the quintessential Victorian Indian model of empire may offer a distracting and constricted guide to imperial sovereignties of differential breadth and historical depth. Two, we might note an overly expansive sense of what we imagine to know about the tenacious qualities of empire, and what new forms of authority they tether to and inhabit. If at times colonial studies has taken the relationship between colonial pasts and postcolonial presents as self-evident, this volume does not. Finally, we question whether a skewed attentiveness to colonial memorials and recognized ruins may offer less purchase on where these histories lodge and what they eat through than does the cumulative debris which is so often less available to scrutiny and less accessible to chart. What joins colonial pasts and imperial presence seems to escape some of the bald-faced rubrics on which students of the colonial have come to rely. Our focus is less on the noun *ruin* than on "ruination" as an active, ongoing process that allocates imperial debris differentially and *ruin* as a violent verb that unites apparently disparate moments, places, and objects.

Postcolonial scholarship has sometimes embraced a smug sense that the nature of colonial governance is a given and that we can now effortlessly move on to the more subtle complexities of the postcolonial present.[12] The literary critic Terry Eagleton concurs, suggesting that postcolonial studies suffers from an "increasingly blunted" historical sense.[13] Frederick Cooper, too, points to a flattening of time, to analyses "unmoored" from specific relations between colonial policy and postcolonial political structures.[14] What precipitates and sustains such historical "blunting" is worth pursuing further. Here we take the charge to be a vital one: to refocus on the *connective tissue* that continues to bind human potentials to degraded environments, and degraded personhoods to the material refuse of imperial projects—to the spaces redefined, to the soils turned toxic, to the relations severed between people and people, and between people and things. At issue are the political lives of imperial debris and the uneven pace with which people can extricate themselves from the structures and signs by which remains take hold. Rubrics such as "colonial legacy" offer little help. They fail to capture the evasive space of imperial formations past and present as well as the perceptions and practices by which people are forced to reckon with features of those formations in which they remain vividly and imperceptibly bound. They also gloss over the creative, critical, and sometimes costly measures people take to become less entangled—or to make something new of those entanglements.

Ruinous Processes in Imperial Formations

To look at "imperial formations" rather than at empire per se is to register the ongoing quality of processes of decimation, displacement, and reclamation. Imperial formations are relations of force. They harbor those mutant, rather than simply hybrid, political forms that endure beyond the formal exclusions that legislate against equal opportunity, commensurate dignities, and equal rights. Working with the concept of imperial formation rather than empire per se shifts emphasis from fixed forms of sovereignty and its denials to *gradated forms* of sovereignty and what has long marked the technologies of imperial rule—sliding and contested scales of differential access and rights.[15] Imperial formations are defined by racialized relations of allocations and appropriations. Unlike empires, they are processes of becoming, not fixed things. Not least, they are states of deferral that mete out promissory notes that are not exceptions to their operation, but constitutive of them: imperial guardianship, trusteeships, delayed autonomy, temporary intervention, conditional tutelage, military takeover in the name of humanitarian works, violent intervention in the name of human rights, and security measures in the name of peace.

Raymond Williams's notion of a "formation" calls attention to those "tendencies," with "variable and often oblique relations to formal institutions."[16] Our interest, too, is in those oblique relations, in dissociated and dislocated histories of the present, in those sites and circumstances of dispossession that imperial architects disavow as not of their making, in violences of disenfranchisement that are shorn of their status as imperial entailments and that go by other names. As Edouard Glissant once noted, a population "whose domination by an Other is concealed . . . must search elsewhere for the principle of domination . . . because the system of domination . . . is not directly tangible."[17] Our concern is with the opacities that imperial formations produce between the elusive vectors of accountability and the lasting tangibilities in which ruination operates—and on which such formations thrive. A richer sense of the nature of "tangibility" is critical to this venture.

To Ruin: A Virulent Verb

In its common usage, *ruins* indicates privileged sites of reflection—of pensive rumination. Portrayed as enchanted, desolate spaces, large-scale monumental structures abandoned and grown over, ruins provide a favored image of a vanished past, what is beyond repair and in decay, thrown into aesthetic relief by nature's tangled growth. Such sites come easily to mind: Cambodia's Angkor Wat, the Acropolis, the Roman Colosseum, icons of romantic loss and longing that inspired the melancholic prose of generations of European poets and historians who devotedly chronicled pilgrimages to them.[18] Perhaps this is one reason why transnational institutions like UNESCO work so hard at "preservation" of such sites. But in thinking about "ruins of empire," this volume works explicitly against the melancholic gaze to reposition the present in the wider structures of vulnerability, damage, and refusal that imperial formations sustain. Nor is it the wistful gaze of imperial nostalgia to which we turn. Walter Benjamin provides the canonical text for thinking about ruins as "petrified life," as traces that mark the fragility of power and the force of destruction. But we are as taken with ruins as sites that condense alternative senses of history, and with ruination as a ongoing corrosive process that weighs on the future. Unlike Benjamin's focus, a focus on imperial debris seeks to mark the "trail of the psyche"—a venture he rejected—as much as it seeks to follow his acute alertness to the "track of things."[19]

  "To ruin," according to *The Concise Oxford Dictionary*, "is to inflict or bring great and irretrievable disaster upon, to destroy agency, to reduce to a state of poverty, to demoralize completely."[20] Attention here is on *to ruin* as an active process and a vibrantly violent verb. In this forum, we turn with intention not to the immediate violence of Iraq and recognized zones of active war, but to the enduring quality of imperial remains, what they impinge on, and their uneven distribution of impaired states. This is not a turn to ruins as memorialized monumental "leftovers" or relics—although these come into our purview as well—but rather to what people are *left with*: to what remains blocking livelihoods and health, to the aftershocks of imperial assault, to the social afterlife of structures, sensibilities, and things. Such effects reside in the corroded hollows of landscapes, in the gutted infrastructures of segregated cityscapes and in the microecologies of matter and mind. The focus, then, is not on inert remains, but on their vital refiguration. The question is pointed: how do imperial formations persist in their material debris, in ruined landscapes and through the social ruination of people's lives?[21]

Imperial effects occupy multiple historical tenses. They are at once products of the past imperfect that selectively permeate the present as they shape both the conditional subjunctive and uncertain futures. Such effects are never done with, as Derek Walcott reminds us, in the definitely closed off *passé composé*. Frantz Fanon identified the extensive mental disorders that followed French rule in Algeria as the "tinge of decay"—the indelible smack of degraded personhoods, occupied spaces, and limited possibilities—that were (and remain) hardest to erase.[22] They are also the hardest to critically locate.

Fanon worked between two poles of decay: at one pole was an evocative figurative sense that situated the breakdown of persons, their pathologies, and mental disabilities as imperial effects. Here the future of such patients was already "mortgaged" by the "malignancy" of their psychological states. Subject to what Fanon called "a generalized homicide," a whole generation of Algerians would be "the human legacy of France in Algeria."[23] Aimé Césaire in 1955 called that affliction a "gangrene . . . distilled into the veins of Europe," in the racialized rule of domestic France.[24]

Such images could be construed as mere metaphor, but the ruinous "tinge of decay" for Fanon was never figurative alone. At the other pole lay the material, tangible, and physical destruction of Algerian landscapes, drained swamps, charred homes, and gutted infrastructures of over a century of French rule and nearly a decade of colonial war. To work between these is to acknowledge both the potential and the problems in sustaining a balance between the analytic power that *to ruin* carries as an evocative metaphor and the critical purchase it offers for grounding processes of actual decomposition, recomposition, and renewed neglect. These latter processes are of our time as they build on and reactivate the traces of another. Such remainders impinge on the allocation of space and resources and on what is available for material life. The analytic challenge is to work productively, if uneasily, with and across this tension. In so doing, our project here is not to fashion a genealogy of catastrophe or redemption. Making connections where they are hard to trace is designed neither to settle scores nor, as Wendy Brown warns, to nurture undurable ressentiments and "wounded attachments."[25]

It is rather to recognize that these are unfinished histories, not of a victimized past but of *consequential histories of differential futures*.

Ruin is both the claim about the state of a thing and a process affecting it. It serves as both noun and verb. To turn to its verbal, active sense is to begin from a location that the noun too easily freezes into stasis, into inert object, passive form. Imperial projects are themselves processes of ongoing ruination, processes that "bring ruin upon," exerting material and social force in the present. By definition, *ruination* is an ambiguous term, being an act of ruining, a condition of being ruined, and a cause of it. Ruination is an *act* perpetrated, a *condition* to which one is subject, and a *cause* of loss. These three senses may overlap in effect, but they are not the same. Each has its own temporality. Each identifies different durations and moments of exposure to a range of violences and degradations that may be immediate or delayed, subcutaneous or visible, prolonged or instant, diffuse or direct.

By the dictionary again, ruination is a process that brings about "severe impairment, as of one's health, fortune, honor, or hopes." Conceptually, ruination may condense those impairments or sunder them apart. To speak of colonial ruination is to trace the fragile and durable substance of signs, the visible and visceral senses in which the effects of empire are reactivated and remain. But ruination is more than a process that sloughs off debris as a by-product. It is also a *political project* that lays waste to certain peoples, relations, and things that accumulate in specific places. To think with ruins of empire is to emphasize less the artifacts of empire as dead matter or remnants of a defunct regime than to attend to their reappropriations, neglect, and strategic and active positioning within the politics of the present.

To focus on ruins is to broach the protracted quality of decimation in people's lives, to track the production of new exposures and enduring damage.[26] Elements of this concern have been the subject of critical geography and environmental historians for some time.[27] Campaigns against what is now commonly referred to as "environmental racism" have been instrumental and effective in the public domain in documenting the grossly uneven distribution of pollution, waste disposal, and biowaste among impoverished populations in the United States and worldwide.[28] Much of this critical work targets the long-term practices of multinationals, mining conglomerates, and successive U.S. administrations and Departments of Defense, Agriculture, and more recently Homeland Security that have laid to waste and continue to destroy microecologies and the livelihoods of populations that live off and in them.[29] If critical geographers, environmental historians, and historically inclined anthropologists have taken the relationship between colonial rule and degraded environments as their subject, it is striking how little of this work has made its way back to the analytic center of postcolonial scholarship or is even considered in the archive of postcolonial situations.[30] The American studies scholar Valerie Kuletz has considered it apt to identify the abuse of the land of indigenous peoples in the United States, Micronesia, and Polynesia as "nuclear colonialism" and as acts of "social ruin," a fact which people in those places, as she notes, recognized early on, but such work still rests on the margins of the conceptual reformulations in colonial studies itself.[31]

If the multiple legacies of empire are what postcolonial scholarship has long imagined itself to arise from and account for, if not explain, one crucial task is to bring these fields of inquiry into more organic conversation. Disciplinary protocols of presentation, venues of publication, and concepts that translate poorly can impede the task. The essays gathered here traverse a heteroclite set of fields: imperialism is as much part of these accounts as imperial logics and colonial cultures. Cultural analysis is grounded in the political differentials through which the latter works. Here we envision colonial histories of the present that grapple with the psychological weight of remnants, the generative power of metaphor, and the materiality of debris to rethink the scope of damage and how people live with it.

We take it as a starting premise that what is most significantly left may not be blatantly evident, easy to document, or to see.[32] The concepts and notions conventionally used to make reference to colonial histories are symptomatic of the lack of clarity. Pervasive ones like "colonial legacy" and "colonial vestige" are deceptive terms that deflect analysis more than they clear the way. As Foucault charged, such "ready-made syntheses" are placeholders for processes that unite disparate forces under one term and gloss too easily over dispersed effects.[33] In the case of imperial formations, a "legacy" makes no distinctions between what holds and what lies dormant, between residue and recomposition, between what is a holdover and what is reinvested, between a weak and a tenacious trace. Such rubrics instill overconfidence in the knowledge that colonial histories matter—far more than they animate an analytic vocabulary for deciphering *how* they do so. Such terms do little to account for the contemporary force of imperial remains, what people themselves count as colonial effects, and, as important, what they do about what they are left with.

With this in mind, a focus on "ruins of empire" is not about a gaze, but about a critical vantage point on one. Asking how people live *with* and *in* ruins redirects the engagement elsewhere, to the politics animated, to the common sense such habitations disturb, to the critiques condensed or disallowed, and to the social relations avidly coalesced or shattered around them. What material form do ruins of empire take when we turn to shattered peoples and polluted places rather than to the leisure of evocations? Situations of disparate time and place come into renewed view. Sequestered and displaced histories do as well. Imperial ruins, as treated here, are *racialized markers on a global scale*, the Agent Orange–infested landscapes of Vietnam, the hazardous wastes in former nuclear test sites of the Bikini Atoll, the continually battered, makeshift compounds of dispossessed and exiled Palestinians—flooded with raw sewage from adjacent Israeli settlements—in which they have to dwell.[34] Imperial ruins may include the defunct sugar mills of Central Java as well as the decrepit barracks of India's railway communities, in which many Anglo-Indians still uneasily live, while others refuse to recognize that these are feasible places to inhabit.[35] These processes of ruination bear on material and social microecologies in different ways. Under what conditions are those sites left to decompose, remanded, reconsigned, or disregarded? Some remains are ignored as innocuous leftovers, others petrify, some hold and spread their toxicities and become poisonous debris. Others are stubbornly inhabited by those displaced to make a political point, or requisitioned for a newly refurbished commodity-life for tourist consumption, or occupied by those left with nowhere else to turn.

What of those sites of decomposition that fall outside historical interest and preservation, places not honored as ruins of empire proper and that go by other names? Some remains are rejected as ruins all together. Much depends, as Derek Walcott again reminds us, on who is doing the labeling. As he noted in his Nobel lecture, in 1992, the "*tristes tropiques*," which Claude Lévi-Strauss so lamented in elegy to "the already decrepit suburbs" of Lahore, may have been a pathos of empire felt more by nineteenth-century European transients—anthropologists and the like—than those who actually dwelled there. Walcott observes that "the sigh of History rises over ruins, not landscapes," but in the Antilles the only ruins were those of "sugar estates and abandoned forts" and there "the sigh of history dissolves."[36]

But the "sigh of history" can manifest in different registers. Nature rots quickly in the colonial tropics. In the Netherlands Indies, railway tracks for hauling rubber were rapidly overgrown; tobacco sheds made of plaited bamboo and wood were eaten through by termites, leaving no structural fragments of iron or stone. But more than a mere trace remains of how the land was used. What connects colonial rubber production in Sumatra to Indonesia's Reebok and Adidas factories, what land has been made available and converted for new kinds of export production, and who profits from them is easy to document, even if not recognizable in the forms that we can easily see. That colonial imprint is deep in Indonesia and elsewhere. Much depends on where we look for detritus, what we expect it to look like, and what we expect to see. That the "absence of ruins" in the Caribbean equals an absence of living history is not an assessment with which all agree. Richard Price instructs us to seek those traces elsewhere, in the "semi-parodic artworks" of the iconic Martiniquan figure of Médard, a man who in the 1950s and 1960s "made from the detritus of industrial society (cellophane from cigarette packages, silver paper from gum wrappers, bentwood from boxes of Camembert)" objects that retold stories of colonial violence as he rewrote their plots.[37]

Walcott, too, was impatient with the "consoling pity" of travelers who "carried with them the infection of their own malaise," those consumed with sadness because they "misunderstood the light and the people on whom the light falls."[38] Rejecting the pathos of ruins, he opted for a celebration of survival. But his vision was hardly romantic. It was full of rage. His descriptions of the sewers that spew into white sand beaches and "polluted marinas" call attention to ruined ecologies as the profit of some and the ruination of others. "Proceed with caution," Doris Sommer warns. Better to resist the "the rush of sentimental identification that lasts barely as long as the read" or the mournful regard.[39] Melancholy, compassion, and pity nourish imperial sensibilities of destruction and the redemptive satisfaction of chronicling loss. We are schooled to be alert to the fact that ruins hold histories, that ruins are the ground on which histories are contested and remade.[40] Still, the nominative form of a "ruin" does less work than "to ruin" as an ongoing process. Ruins can represent both something more and less than the sum of the sensibilities of people who live in them. Instead we might turn to ruins as epicenters of renewed collective claims, as history in a spirited voice, as sites that animate both despair and new possibilities, bids for entitlement, and unexpected collaborative political projects.

Some kinds of imperial ruin are easier to identify than others. Projects of cultural salvage—whether of monuments, artifacts, customs, and peoples—are available for scrutiny in the ways others are not. There are resurrected ruins, like those studied by John Collins, part of the World Bank and UNESCO cultural heritage projects designed to "harvest the economic value" and capitalize on the allure of partially restored people, things, and their ostensibly uniting essences. Yet such restorations disperse and redistribute people, making their ways of being vital to national development and productive of new inequalities.⁴¹ Then there are those ruins that stirred Jamaica Kincaid's derisive and angry view of Antigua, marked with buildings whose faded placards note "repairs pending" for decades, while damaged but "splendid old buildings from colonial times" are well maintained in carefully tended disrepair.⁴²

Some imperial ruins can be distinguished by where they are located—in metropole or colony—or on faded imperial maps. Others cannot. Strewn throughout the Caribbean, Africa, and Asia are the enticements of enjoying "ruins by day, luxury by night," as eager travelers "balance the indolence of a colonial-era luxury hotel with the more demanding task of exploring centuries-old Khmer ruins from dawn 'til dusk."⁴³ These are more than leisurely distractions for the history-minded, knowledge-seeking traveler. Edification here, like the Grand Tour of the European bourgeoisie in earlier centuries, not only distinguishes Culture from cultures. It replays the "salvage" rescue operation that European empires claimed as their expert knowledge and benevolent task. Napoleon took with him to Egypt more archaeologists and "rubble seekers" than surgeons and surveyors. Nineteenth-century colonials in the Netherlands Indies participated in Europe's obsession with visiting Hindu ruins, in pursuit of cultural capital on their days off.

Colonialisms have been predicated on guarding natural and cultural patrimonies for populations assumed to need guidance in how to value and preserve them.⁴⁴ This sort of attention to ruins chronicles a present landscape and people already found wanting. But this heartfelt gaze on the ruin, so much a part of the contemporary analysis of the ruins of modernity, a gaze that echoed Diderot's sense that he felt "freer" in the presence of ruins, is not our interest in this volume.⁴⁵ Rather than the introspective gaze of Europeans on ruins, we look to the lives of those living in them. That shift is key to trace the dried-up veins of Anaconda's copper mines that joined Butte, Montana, and Chuquicamata, Chile, and wreaked privation on the lives and bodies of their sequestered laboring populations.⁴⁶

Imperial nostalgia plays through and sells sojourns among colonial ruins in other, predictable ways. There is the "find" of worthy voyagers, the "ruins of Popokvil atop Bokor Mountain in Cambodia. . . . There, you'll find the remains of a French colonial-era town—a crumbling post office, an empty Catholic church."⁴⁷ At the Mbweni Ruins Hotel in Zanzibar guests can sleep in what was once a school for "freed slave girls," the first Anglican Christian missionary settlement in East Africa, made into a domesticated "colony." Arranged in 1871 in clusters of small neat houses and garden plots, this was precisely the bucolic vision that imperial architects harbored to domesticate their recalcitrant, racially ambiguous, and destitute populations throughout the colonial world.[48] Guests can learn the history of philanthropic imperial projects *and* can take solace in the multiple times that the buildings were abandoned and restored with the intervention of European good works, at the height of imperial expansion and after.[49] We are reminded of Renato Rosaldo's astute observation that imperialist nostalgia is not a postcolonial pleasure but a concerted colonial one, a mourning contingent and concomitant with what colonialisms destroy.[50] Such ruins might be read as vestige and remnant, but they are neither history's refuse nor unclaimed debris.[51]

Imperial ruins can also mark the contest for originary racialist claims. Zanzibar's tourists may be unknowing participants in the celebration of empire in the Mbweni Ruins Hotel, but often the political life of ruins are more explicit for all to contest and see. In Zimbabwe, it was from the sixty acres of stone ruins, "the Great Zimbabwe," that Cecil Rhodes pilfered the prized soapstone bird with which he adorned his Cape Town house in 1889, the year before he established a Royal Charter for the British South Africa Company. The stone birds and the ruins that housed them were confiscated by Rhodes, but it was successive states controlled by white settlers and later by African nationalists who each made the ruins their own. White racial supremacy and refusal of it, as Henrietta Kuklick so eloquently writes, were fought on the terrain of these ruins. "The Great Zimbabwe" was requisitioned as "proof" of racialized progenitors in the nineteenth century and reemerged at the center of heated political contest a century later.[52] Clearly, these are not all imperial "ruins" of common vintage, nor are their political entailments the same. What they might share is what the Afghanistani photographer and performance artist Lida Abdul has called sites and structures "around which stories are wrapped to hide the sounds and images that roam" through them.[53]

If imperial debris deposits in the disabled, racialized spaces of colonial histories past and present, it is gendered as well—in how it is embodied, where it is lodged, and how it is expressed. In Sharad Chari's, John Collins's, and Vyjayanthi Rao's essays, both women and men sustain these injuries, but it is women who voice the injuries to which this debris gives rise. We see it in Collins's turn to the critical repartee of Topa, a woman whose body was as marked as her bearing and her history by her precarious poverty and the assumptions of those who would claim to alleviate it.[54] It is in the demand of Jane Glover for her own "piece of oxygen," a woman to whom Chari turns to describe the atmospheric pressure in which people live close to oil refineries of post-apartheid Durban, and it is in the songs of lament that women farmers chant in their displaced fields and about their submerged village in southern India, described by Rao.[55] Over and again, it is women who seem to loudly attest. Gender may inflect how ruination is embodied and who bears the debris. Nancy Rose Hunt's essay rivets on "the sound of twisted laughter collected, convulsed, and retracted around forms of sexual violence basic to, indeed constitutive of, the reproductive ruination of Leopold's Congo."[56]

Still, none of the above seize on gender distinctions to frame their arguments (though all are keenly attuned to the gender dispositions that mark recollection, as in Chari's attention to the photographs taken by and of groups of young men on the neighborhood lanes where "recently dispossessed people made a new Coloured township their home").[57] Ariella Azoulay, who otherwise speaks so directly to how gender inequalities are "lauded and glorified" in the history of the visual fields in which she has long worked, chooses here not to do so.[58] The sleeping figures of Israeli soldiers wrapped in colorful blankets in what we quickly learn is a Palestinian home are positions staked out by male soldiers. But Azoulay does not argue that such assertions are made by them alone. On the contrary, Israeli women and men stand together on a hilltop from which "they can show their children both the symmetry that justifies Israel's devastation of Gaza, and Israel's spectacular show of force."[59] Her point is mute but explicit: it is not that imperial debris does not accumulate with different gendered effects, but this is not where she chooses to pull our attention. When she describes the applause at the sight of the smoking ruins of Palestinian homes, the exuberant shouts, "We've done it!," these are raised voices of both Israeli women and men. Hunt's treatment of the rapes committed under King Leopold's Congo is not immune to what was done to young women in particular; she is direct in arguing that cannibalism and mutilation were able to enter Roger Casement's humanitarian narrative in ways that rape could not. Still, how gendered dispositions matter to living in imperial debris is less obvious. The acoustic registers of response are shared by women and men far more than the skewed photographic archives of bodily exposures.

Imperial Debris by Other Names

Perhaps the most critical task is to address, if not answer, the question prompted by Walcott in "Ruins of a Great House": What is the rot that remains when the men are gone? What forms does rot take? What does it corrode, what interior spaces does it touch, and where is it that it remains? Walcott's language is poetic, but the dispersed ruination he looks to is not. There may be remnants that slip from immediate vision, detritus that is harder to grasp—intimate injuries that appear as only faint traces, or deep deformations and differentiations of social geography which go by other names. There are social dislocations whose etiologies are found in labels that lead away from empire and push analysis far from colonial histories, severing those connections; the terms substituted point to "urban decay," to "the perils of progress," to "environmental degradation," "industrial pollution," or "racialized unemployment"—to analyses of those places swept up by modernization and to those swept aside as the refuse of a capitalist market that has since moved on.

What work does it do to identify these as ruins of empire? What insights does it offer to recast these generic labels and processes as patterned imperial effects that produce subjects with more limited possibilities and who are hampered differently by those effects? One argument might be that such a critical move makes connections that are not otherwise readily visible. Such renaming relocates processes dislodged from their specific histories, disjointed from the connections that made some people and places susceptible to ruin or abandonment. These are not ruins of empire in any figurative sense. Sharad Chari's work with those who live on the toxic edges of oil refineries and in the remains of apartheid in Durban, South Africa, makes this clear.[60] These are zones of vulnerability which the living inhabit and to which we should attend.

Greg Grandin's riveting account of Fordlandia, Henry Ford's vision of a bucolic American settlement and way of life in the Amazonian jungle at the beginning of the twentieth century does more than remind us that Ford's success was contingent on the production of rubber in colonial possessions through Southeast Asia.[61] He underscores that "Detroit not only supplied a continual stream of symbols of America's cultural power but offered the organizational know-how necessary to run a vast industrial enterprise like a car company—or an empire."[62] Treating Detroit as an imperial nexus imbricated in and dependent on colonial labor regimes throughout the world rejects the American "exception," changes the fulcrum of Detroit's demise. By placing it in the balance of a broader sweep of imperial debris, Detroit is repositioned, not on the outer fringes of "the rust belt" but as one of the corrosive centers of one disabled form of U.S. empire.[63] The current cachet of what some critics call "ruin porn" with respect to the guided tours of Detroit's "splendid ruins" pushes those connections even further away.[64]

One impulse in addressing the admittedly broad sense of imperial ruin embraced here might be to distinguish between those processes played out in imperial centers versus those situations and sites that appear in formerly colonized regions. But there is perhaps more to gain by suspending that impulse and not making such distinctions too readily. The "interior" and "exterior" spaces of imperial formations may not correspond to the common geographical designations that imperial architects scripted themselves. Terms like *metropole* and *colony, core* and *periphery* presume to make clear what is not. We might rather think of other criteria to distinguish the contemporary zones of imperial duress that are more mutable and as mutable as imperial formations themselves: the breadth of corridors in which people can move, the virtual barriers by which they are cordoned off, the kinds of infrastructure to which they have access, the selective dumping of waste, the preemptive racialized exclusions and exemptions in which they live.

In an article for an American audience, the Israeli novelist David Grossman describes the apathy and studied indifference that ongoing political, military, and religious conflict imposes on those living in Israel, Palestine, Iraq, Afghanistan, and other war-torn places of the world. The image he conjures is of people whose moral compasses are narrowed, whose feelings are numbed, whose language is rendered shallower, thinned by the onslaught on their everyday. As he puts it, there is a *"shrinking of the 'surface area' of the soul* that comes in contact with the bloody and menacing world out there."[65] Destruction for Grossman is inside people and out—coating their micro- and material environments.[66] The resonance—and sharp contrast—with Walcott's "rot that remains" and Fanon's "tinge of decay" is striking. In the non-immediate, extended conditions of the latter, numbness can give way to critique, language can become sharpened and thickened—rather than thinned—with double entendres that mock the security measures that terrorize and destroy rather than protect.

Stories congeal around imperial debris, as do critiques. So do disqualified knowledge and subjugated histories decoupled from the processes of which they were a part. The overgrown ruins of the palace of Sans Souci in Haiti's northern mountains, which Michel-Rolph Trouillot has so powerfully described (built by its first black king after the defeat of the French in 1804), harbors a suspended, (dis)quieted history of the Haitian Revolution and the differential histories of colonial relations wedged between mortar and crumbling stone.[67] Michelle Cliff frames her novel of Jamaica, *No Telephone to Heaven*, around the Jamaican term *ruinate*, which as a noun subsumes within it the verb *to ruin*. She describes it as at once cultivated land that has been left to lapse into overgrown vegetation. *Ruinate* in its use is steeped in colonial history and marks its durability, but seems to be as mobile as the people who attempt to escape it, as they move to and return from the New York City boroughs of the Bronx and Queens. It carries both the palpable colonial history of abandoned European plantations, living waste, and as yet unreclaimed futures.[68]

Ruins, as Kuklick found in Zimbabwe, can take on a political life of their own. As Nadia Abu El-Haj writes, in Jerusalem "partly destroyed buildings were partially restored and reconstructed *as ruins* in order to memorialize more recent histories of destruction, and older stones were integrated into modern architectural forms in order to embody temporal depth."[69] Her point is now commonly shared: ruins are not just found, they are *made*. They become repositories of public knowledge and new concentrations of public declaration.

We need little more evidence that the public or state recognition of something as a ruin, as well as the claims made for it, is in itself a political act. Such recognized ruins are politicized, but the most enduring ruins in Israel are neither recognized as ruins nor as ruination wrought by colonial policies. These ruins are not acknowledged to be there at all. These are the literal ruins of Palestinian villages razed, bulldozed, and buried by the Israeli military and the state-endorsed Israeli Afforestation Project. This intensive planting campaign (for which Hebrew school children in Europe and the United States have been avidly encouraged to contribute their pennies "to plant a tree for Israel") has literally obliterated the very presence of Palestinian villages and farmsteads on Jerusalem's periphery for more than fifty years.[70] If planting is a key technology in Israeli politics, here ruination has a perverse, protracted, and violent colonial history. "Security groves" have replaced Palestinian olive orchards with cypress and pines; recreational parks dense with eucalyptus trees smooth over Palestinian cemeteries. Not least, remains of Arab villages have been effaced—as are the claims of their former inhabitants that these were never "abandoned" fields, but ones they owned, lived off, and had long cultivated.

In Bethlehem's Aida Refugee Camp such fields "abandoned" to Israeli occupation are called by other names: there, children are armed at the Lajee Children's Center with computers and cameras, and taught how to collect the stories of their grandparents whose land was seized, to locate the trees they harvested, to smell the herbs their grandparents remember, to scavenge the hilltops where their houses were destroyed to make way for Israeli settlements. Sometimes there are no ruins at all: when asked by their elders to collect thyme and sage from the fields, the children often brought back stones and soil instead.[71] Some found old olive trees among the new pines. In Beit Jibreen, twelve-year-old Suhaib photographed the ruins of an old house on the hill, imagining that it might have been his grandmother's.[72]

Ruins are made, but not just by anyone, anytime, anywhere. Large-scale ruin-making takes resources and planning that may involve forced removal of populations and new zones of uninhabitable space, reassigning inhabitable space and dictating how people are supposed to live in them. As such, these ruin-making endeavors are typically state projects, ones that are often strategic, nation building, and politically charged.[73] The fabrication of nuclear ruins, for instance, was critical in the construction of Cold War national defense policies and in shaping a U.S. public prompted to be fascinated and traumatized by the specter of nuclear war.[74] Nuclear ruins remain central to the political imaginary of the U.S. security state today. Joe Masco argues that Cold War planners saw their task to be one of molding and emotionally managing an American public. They did so with simulated bomb threats and theatrical evacuations in cities and towns across the country. Strategic public operations imagined ruins, televised ruins, and simulated ruins, all with attention to particular domestic objects, pointedly anticipating the decimation of what touched Americans most closely, the hard-won household technology and material comforts of postwar quotidian life.

Ruins draw on residual pasts to make claims on futures. But they can also create a sense of irretrievability or of futures lost. The Ochagavia Hospital in Santiago's suburbs, intended to be a "spectacular showcase" for Pinochet's vision of Chile's modernity and progressivism, in fact showcases something else: with what Jon Beasley describes as "the beached whale of a monument whose presence has been repressed and ignored," the half-built hospital recollects what could have been rather than what was.[75] How such modernist ruins differ from imperial ones would be suggested not only by the different histories they unsettle and differently call on, but also by the specific people dispossessed or otherwise laid to waste by them.

The sense of arrested rather than possible futures and the ruins they produce is one way to convey the problematic processes of development policies. As Vyjayanthi Rao shows in her essay here, the building of the Srisailam megadam in southern India—which began in 1981, displaced more than 150,000 people, and submerged over one hundred villages—makes real a failed future and the forceful presence of imperial debris in visceral ways. During the dry season every year, the submerged villages reappear to haunt those who once lived there and then disappear, as both sign and substance for those who once lived there of their precarious futures and of national development's unfulfilled promise. The village ruins contrast the archaeological salvage project of valued Hindu temples enacted in the same space. Here the critique of development is laid bare in a landscape scarred with ruined villages that have been laid to waste alongside the transplanted temple ruins, preened for historical tourism, and preserved as part of India's national heritage.[76]

Looking to imperial ruins not necessarily as monuments but as ecologies of remains opens to wider social topographies. The ruins of Native American burial sites mark only one site in a broader contested ground of new land claims and entitlements.[77] But we might also think of what I elsewhere call "the carceral archipelago of empire," which has distributed convict islands, detention centers, pauper and children's and penal colonies throughout the globe—gradated zones of containment that have mixed and matched "security" and defense with confinement, abuse, "education," and abandonment.[78] Such infrastructures of large and small scale bear what captivated Walter Benjamin, the "marks and wounds of the history of human violence."[79] It is these spatially assigned "traces of violence," more than the "deadening of affects" to which we turn.[80]

Focusing on the materiality of debris, we seek to stay in the "logic of the concrete" as Nancy Hunt urges in *A Colonial Lexicon of Birth Ritual, Medicalization, and Mobility in the Congo* when she redirects us back to Lévi-Strauss's term.[81] Ruins can be marginalized structures that continue to inform social modes of organization but that cease to function in ways they once did. What happens at the threshold of transformation when unfinished development projects are put to other use, when test sites are grown over, when Soviet military camps are abandoned and remade as in the Ukrainian-Polish borderlands?[82] What happens when island enclaves, no longer a declared nuclear zone, as in the Bikini Atoll, become repositories of vulnerabilities that are likely to last longer than the political structures that produced them? Each of these points not to ruins set off from people's lives but what it might mean to live through, with, and as bricoleurs around them.

In thinking about imperial debris and ruin one is struck by how intuitively evocative and elusive such effects are, how easy it is to slip between metaphor and material object, between infrastructure and imagery, between remnants of matter and mind. The point of critical analysis is not to look "underneath" or "beyond" that slippage but to understand the work that slippage does and the political traffic it harbors. Reading W. G. Sebald's *On the Natural History of Destruction*, a meditation on Germany during and just after the

Second World War, the numbness of living in the still-smoldering ruins, the sheer mass of debris, the (deceptive) "silence above the ruins," both contrasts and converges with the sorts of remains we write of here—in and out of focus, in and out of speakable bounds.[83]

While sites of colonial occupation are not outside our purview, our collective focus is more on what Rob Nixon calls the "slow violence" and "long dyings" that mark zones of abandonment.[84] If Giorgio Agamben developed the concept of social abandonment, it is João Biehl's extraordinary ethnography *Vita: Life in a Zone of Social Abandonment* where it is given flesh. For Biehl, that zone produces persons who become "a human ruin," "leftover" in their unexceptional, patterned subjection "to the typically uncertain and dangerous mental health treatment reserved for the urban working poor" in Brazil.[85] The social abandonments under scrutiny in these pages are ruinations of a different sort: sites of risk proportioned by imperial effects. We track the "concrete trajectory" of colonial exclusions and derailments that carve out the structures of privilege, profit, and destruction today. Naomi Klein's *The Shock Doctrine* could help lead back in that direction. There are no index entries for "empire" or "imperialism" in her scathing account of what she calls "the disaster capitalism complex," but the psychic and material connections are threaded through every chapter—from the current $200 billion "homeland security industry" back to U.S. support for military governments that eviscerated the subsistence of peoples in Argentina, Chile, Uruguay, and Brazil.[86]

This is not to suggest that complex histories of capitalism and empire should all be folded into an imperial genealogy. It is, however, to attend to the *evasive* history of empire that disappears so easily into other appellations and other, more available, contemporary terms. It is to recognize that the bio in biopolitical degradations is not haphazardly joined with histories of empire. The social terrain on which colonial processes of ruination leave their material and mental marks are patterned by the social kinds those political systems produced, by the racial ontologies they called into being, and by the cumulative historical deficiencies certain populations are seen to embody— and the ongoing threats to the body politic associated with them. Expulsion, as in the case of Palestinians, is posited as the defense of society against its internal enemies, partition and arbitrary violence the results. As David Lloyd argues for the history of British state policies in Northern Ireland, "Partition, which is the foundation of the state, is also its ruination."[87]

Zygmunt Bauman identifies the production of waste and "wasted lives" as the required, intended, and inevitable debris of the modern.[88] Bauman may be partially right, but such a frame can only account for the fact of accumulated leftovers, of superfluous, obsolete, and bypassed people and things. *It cannot, however, account for their densities and distribution.* Modernity and capitalism can account only partly for the left aside, but not for where people are left, what they are left with, and what means they have to deal with what remains. Globalization may account for the dumping of toxic waste on the Ivory Coast but not for the trajectory of its movement and the history that made West Africa a suitable and available site. Capitalism can account for the BP oil spills in the Gulf of Mexico in 2010 and for Chevron's three decades of toxic contamination and decimation of the livelihoods of rainforest inhabitants of the Amazon, but not for the worldwide coverage of, and outrage over, the former and the sparse note of the latter.[89] Again, there are ruins of empire that are called "ruins" as well as those that are not. The political economy of nuclear testing can account for the proliferation of waste dumps, but not for the campaign in 1996 to locate the Ward Valley nuclear waste dump in the heart of the Mojave Desert National Preserve and on land that Native American nations held sacred. After thirty years of uranium mining, carried out during the late 1940s through the 1960s, across Navajo lands in Arizona and New Mexico, native populations still refer to their late-onset cancers as a "legacy of tears."[90] The social and physical effects of uranium mining on aboriginal populations in Australia for the last three decades is a colonial story—of state commissions mounted and ignored, of "spillages and silences," of massively increasing cancer rates among aboriginal populations near these sites, of regard and dis-regard— of its own.[91] At issue is whether recognition produces more effective histories, what Fernando Coronil calls "relational histories," that "connect fragments to wholes" of the imperial present.[92] Rethinking imperial formations as polities of dislocation and deferral which cut through the nation-state by delimiting interior frontiers as well as exterior ones is one step in reordering our attention.[93]

Race and Imperial Debris

Might we turn back to James Agee's *Let Us Now Praise Famous Men*, not to mark the universal dignity and damages that dire poverty bestows, but as marking specific places and specific sorts of people abandoned by specific state policies and historical acts, as the embodied ruins of a racialized American empire?[94] And why does it seem so counterintuitive and forced to do so?

Kathleen Stewart makes it seem less so in her ethnography of those people who live among the detritus of West Virginia's coal-mining industry today. She excavates "the ruined and trashed" economy of the American South, whose historical veins are coursed through with U.S. Coal and Oil Company land buyouts at the turn of the century, with hills that "became a wasteland of the unemployed" during the 1930s depression, and with "over 100,000 dead in the mines since 1906."[95] She might tell that story, as she insists, in the conditional tense, but says she will not reproduce a seamless narrative. Instead, she takes the "trash that collects around people's places, like the ruins that collect in the hills" to track the composition and decomposition of people's lives, their movement between decay, melancholy, and agentive engagement.[96] As she writes, "Things do not simply fall into ruin or dissipate. . . . [They] fashion themselves into powerful effects that remember things in such a way that 'history' digs itself into the present and people cain't [sic] help but recall it."[97]

Agee's story might be rewritten in a similar vein, not as the iconic story of the dignity that emerges from the indignities of being poor whites in the rural South, nor only as a national, domestic racial story of industrializing America. One could imagine a reframing of this form of ruination as one moment in a broader history of U.S. empire, a history that would track cotton production and the creation of expert knowledge of eugenics that authorized institutionalized neglect both of newly freed blacks and "poor whites." These are not untold stories. They have been told as racialized histories, but not as racialized histories of U.S. empire.

Moving between ruins and ruination, between material objects and processes is sometimes easier said than done. Sometimes the ruins are claimed to retain ghosts in vivid form: some such phantoms haunt central Java's sugar factories, described by John Pemberton as "forces moving on their own, operating by uncertain contracts and demanding untoward sacrificial exchange."[98] But in fact, in much of the colonial tropics, one is struck by the absence of colonial ruins, as in vast tracts of Vietnam once overrun by a multinational plantation industry. In some places, as Walcott claims, there is hardly a trace of a colonial ruin at all. There are no petrified dwellings partially burned to the ground as in Dresden, no open sewers clogging the senses, no rampage of rats claiming new quarters, no zoo full of mangled animals as Sebald so horrifically described, no debris of watches that stopped ticking, no dolls with severed heads. Here we are not talking about an event of bombardment and the fast-acting decomposition that follows. The ruins of empire may have none of that sort of immediacy.

But they can be as close at hand with an immediacy of another kind. "The coolie," in Val Daniel's poem on Sri Lanka's tortured colonial history, provides a counterpoint to the master's ruinous tale.[99] As he writes in an earlier fragment of this poem,

> . . . The sole witness
> to blood shed? The land, of course, with its wounds unfurled:
> > gouged here, leveled there, with rivers dry-bedded
> run, flooding pits, filling dams, in this redeemed world[100]

Colonialism may have been "like a rash spread on the skin of the landscape for cash." But ruination can incite vibrant refusal to accept its terms and recast the story. As Nancy Rose Hunt argues, hunting down the rusted guns in the Congo is really not the point of getting at the remains of the violence of rubber extraction under King Leopold—nor is it really what is left.[101]

But sometimes, as in Vietnam today, live ammunition is the political point. These are not "ruins" per se, though of the over eight million tons of bombs dropped in Vietnam thirty years ago, there remain over 300,000 tons of unexploded ordnance that includes what the Vietnamese government estimates are 800,000 cluster bombs, M79 grenade bombs, and flechette bombs still in the soil.[102] Limbs and lives are still being lost. Agent Orange, the military colloquialism for the twenty million gallons of deadly herbicides sprayed by U.S. forces across Vietnam for ten years, between 1961 and 1971, also has potent presence still. Its purpose was described as twofold: to lay bare the jungles and the cover under which Vietcong soldiers could potentially hide, and to destroy their food supplies. It defoliated more than five million acres of land.[103] Five hundred thousand acres of crops were destroyed. Toxic residues remain in soils, riverbeds, and the food chain. But the witnesses were also bodies themselves. Ten diseases are presently linked to Agent Orange exposure at the lethal levels used in Vietnam: these include cancers, respiratory disorders, severe mental retardation, and musculoskeletal, organic, and developmental birth defects.[104]

There is nothing "over" about this form of ruination: it remains in bodies, in the poisoned soil, in water on a massive and enduring scale. In 1984 U.S. veterans of the Vietnam War filed a class-action lawsuit against Dow Chemicals, Monsanto, and five other companies. They were accorded an out-of-court settlement of $180 million. No compensation has ever been made to Vietnamese civilians.[105] Their appeals over the last decade have been repeatedly dismissed on the grounds that although dioxin is a poison, it was never intended to be used on humans and therefore constitutes neither a "chemical" weapon nor a violation of international law. This particular "imperial debris" rests in the deformed bodies of children whose grandparents were exposed. New development projects come with new risks: as new land is being cultivated, bombs buried for decades are now exploding.[106] But bed and table legs are also being made of the steel from recycled unexploded bombs. As the journalists Aaron Glantz and Ngoc Nguyen note, industrialists are not worried about their supplies running out.[107]

"Groaning among the Shadows" — Or Resentment in Them

In 1964 Derek Walcott wrote, "Decadence begins when a civilization falls in love with its ruins."[108] By Walcott's account, England is doomed, as are those transposed former colonial subjects like V. S. Naipaul who pined for the grandeur of empire (as much as, or more than, some British nostalgics themselves). Some ruins are loved more than others. One set of "nobly built but crumbling spaces" in the English "cult of ruin" enjoy particular and current favor. Ian Baucom refers to these as part of "country-house England": "This ordered and disciplinary England that at once is financed by the economics of empire and marks, in dazzling expanses of Italian marble and filigreed iron, the dominion of the metropolis over domestic and colonial countrysides — for which a current generation of English nostalgics yearn."[109] Nostalgia is often about that which one has never known or never seen. It also carries a sense that one is already always too late. As Naipaul lamented in the *Enigma of Arrival*, "I had come to England at the wrong time. . . . I had come too late to find the England, the heart of empire, which (like a provincial, from a far corner of the empire) I had created in my fantasy."[110] Lévi-Strauss shared the same sense of "missing out," of belatedness in his first ethnographic travels. Disappointed by the "already decrepit suburbia" of Lahore, annoyed by the

> huge avenues sketched out among the ruins (due, these, to the riots of the recent years) of houses five hundred years old. . . . [W]hen was the right moment to see India? At what period would the study of the Brazilian savage have yielded the purest satisfaction, the savage himself been at his peak? . . . Either I am a traveler of ancient times . . . or I am a traveler of our own day. . . . In either case I am the loser . . . for today, as I go groaning among the shadows, I miss, inevitably, the spectacle that is now taking shape. . . . What I see is an affliction to me; and what I do not see, a reproach.[111]

Lévi-Strauss cringes with self-mockery at his disdain for the now. Naipaul doesn't bother. If both are only too aware that they have been duped by an imaginary of the ruin, they still crave the Real. Naipaul wants more than the ruins of empire. Like Lévi-Strauss's, his nostalgia is for what he can never know and has never seen. For the latter, it is a primitive in his prime; for the former, the evidence that empire was in opulent and working order. Both desire a state before the fall. Ian Baucom pinpoints when "things went wrong" for Naipaul—just when his England was sullied by large-scale migration of former colonial subjects.[112] But maybe things went really wrong when those subjects more loudly refused colonialism's terms of privilege, voided the imperial contract, and had no regard for Naipaul's ruins at all.

Imperial ruins, as we locate them here, are sites less of love and lament for the bygone than of implacable resentment, disregard, and abandonment. Faisal Devji aptly refers to them as the "scene of a crime," but also as an ungraspable moment, a vanishing point that can never come into clear view.[113] As documents to damage, they can never be used to condemn the colonial alone. Nor should this be the point.[114] To call the low-income high-rises that hover on the periphery of Paris, where most of the riots took place in fall 2005, "ruins of French empire" is a metaphoric, political, and material claim. It makes pointed *material and affective* connections that public commentators have made only as a generic indictment of a colonial history that is now of the past. It reconnects the timing of their construction (beginning in 1950) with the material cement blocks that were used, with the former colonial North African people housed in them (who replaced the immigrants working for Peugeot and living in segregated shantytowns), with the political and economic barriers erected to keep them in place.[115] It connects state racism with its colonial coordinates and with the 40 percent unemployment of those who live on the outskirts of France's political and economic life and in barracks-like tenements.

The geographies of the revolts are colonial through and through.[116] More important, understanding these sites as the ruins of empire registers the claims that young people in Clichy-Sous-Bois and elsewhere in France were making when they proclaimed themselves *indigènes de la république* and demanded, as Hannah Arendt so succinctly put it, "the right to have rights." As reported in the press, Clichy-Sous-Bois has no local police station, no movie theater, no swimming pool, no unemployment office, no child welfare agency, no subway or interurban train into the city. Cordoned off and excised from the polity, young people have sought to make claims that refuse those conditions and terms. As Fanon predicted, French rule would not only wreak havoc on the futures of the colonized. Those relations would "haunt French believers in democracy."[117] And it does. It took fifty years for the French government to officially acknowledge the use of the term "Algerian War"—the same amount of time it took some French scholars to acknowledge that the French Republic was from its start a racialized colonial one.[118]

Sebald remarks that Jean Amery saw resentment as essential to a critical view of the past. As Amery put it, "Resentment nails every one of us onto the cross of this ruined past. Absurdly, it demands that the irreversible be turned around, that the event be undone."[119] I would disagree. Resentment is an active, critical force in the present. It does not demand that "the event be undone." It is about the possibility of naming injuries for what they are, a demand that the conditions of constraint and injury be reckoned with and acknowledged. The state of emergency that the French state imposed across over a quarter of its national territory in 2005 was in part a response to the riots but also in part to decades of a systematic project to disregard and destroy the agency, health, and livelihood of a very particular population. This form of ruination defines both a process and sustained political project on which imperial states did and continue to deeply depend. It does not produce passive or docile subjects but political and affective states of sustained resentment that redirect what will be in ruins and who will be living in them.

For students of colonial studies, the protracted weight of ruination should sound an alarm. The point would not be, as some French scholars have recently done, to mount a charge that every injustice of the contemporary world has imperial roots, but rather to delineate the specific ways in which peoples and places are laid to waste, where debris falls, around whose lives it accumulates, and what constitutes "the rot that remains." One task of a renewed colonial studies would be to sharpen our senses and sense of how to track the tangibilities of empire as effective histories of the present. This would not be to settle scores of the past, to dredge up what is long gone, but to focus a finer historical lens on distinctions between what is residual and tenacious, what is dominant but hard to see, and not least what is emergent in today's imperial formations and critically resurgent in responses to them. At least one challenge is not to imagine either "the postcolony" or the postcolonial imperium as replicas of earlier degradations or as the inadvertent, inactive leftovers of more violent colonial relations. It is rather to track how new de-formations and new forms of debris work on matter and mind to eat through people's resources and resiliencies as they embolden new political actors with indignant refusal, forging unanticipated, entangled, and empowered alliances.

Notes

1. Ismond, *Abandoning Dead Metaphors*, 40. As the book title implies, Ismond takes Walcott's use of metaphor to be at the center of his political, anticolonial project, with metaphor as a "major term of reference" (2–3). The relationship between metaphor in language and metamorphosis of life runs throughout commentaries on Walcott's corpus.

2. Edward Gibbon's *The History of the Decline and Fall of the Roman Empire*, written in six volumes between 1776 and 1788, was among the earliest and most well-regarded of this genre. For recent analogies, see Murphy, *Are We Rome?*; Isaacson, "The Empire in the Mirror," a scathing review of Murphy's "simplistic historical analogies" in the *New York Times Sunday Book Review*, 13 May 2007, at http://www.nytimes.com; Heather, *Empires and Barbarians*. Also see Chalmers Johnson's biting critique of contemporary U.S. foreign policy analysts who call on parallels with the Roman empire, in *The Sorrows of Empire*.

3. Among them are Rashid Khalidi, *Resurrecting Empire*; Eagleton, *Holy Terror*; Paul W. Kahn, *Sacred Violence*; Le Cour Grandmaison, *La République impériale*; Lazreg, *Twilight of Empire*; McCoy, *Policing America's Empire*; Thomas, *Empires of Intelligence*.

4. Calhoun, Cooper, and Moore, *Lessons of Empire*.

5. See, for example, Ilana Feldman, *Governing Gaza*; McGranahan, *Arrested Histories*; Stoler, *Along the Archival Grain*; David Scott, *Conscripts of Modernity*; Dubois, *A Colony of Citizens*.

6. See Mbembe, *On the Postcolony*, one effort to address how colonial logics, imaginaries, and violences are reworked and mutate in Africa's postcolonial present.

7. See Peluso and Watts, *Violent Environments*.

8. Daniel Miller, "Introduction," 5.

9. See, for example, "Historical Colonialism in Contemporary Perspective," by Arif Dirlik, who argues that "it is no longer very plausible to offer colonialism as an explanation of [the] condition" in which the "vast majority of the populations of formerly colonized society live in conditions of despair" (611).

10. Lazarus, "Postcolonial Studies after the Invasion of Iraq," 16.

11. In France, this debate has taken on a polemical and sometimes vicious tone, detracting from the possibility of a productive and generative debate. See, for example, Bruckner, *La tyrannie de la penitence*; Lefeuvre, *Pour en finir avec la repentance colonial*; Bayart, *Les études postcoloniales*, and most recently the latter's response to his critics in "Les très faché(e)s des études postcoloniales." Also see Stoler, "Colonial Aphasia."

12. See Stoler, "On Degrees of Imperial Sovereignty"; and Stoler with Bond, "Refractions Off Empire."

13. Eagleton, *After Theory*, 7.

14. Cooper, "Decolonizing Situations."

15. For a fuller discussion of this issue see Stoler, "On Degrees of Imperial Sovereignty"; and Stoler and McGranahan, "Introduction."

16. Williams, *Marxism and Literature*, 117.

17. Glissant, *Caribbean Discourse*, 20.

18. For one good example of the continuing pleasures yielded by this laconic mood, see Woodward, *In Ruins*.

19. Benjamin, *The Arcades Project*, 212.

20. *The Concise Oxford Dictionary*, fifth edition, 1095.

21. In my seminar on colonial and postcolonial disorders, Charles McDonald offered a provocative treatment of the sorts of debris that imperial formations cultivate and disavow in the "unincorporated territory" of the U.S. Virgin Islands, where he argues for understanding debris as more than what is ruined or left behind: "Debris does not materialize out of thin air; it must already be present. It is not a kind of thing, but rather a state of being into which—and less commonly—out of which things may pass" ("The Eye of the Storm," 4).

22. Fanon, *The Wretched of the Earth*, 249. The full quote, opening the chapter "Colonial War and Mental Disorder," reads: "That imperialism which today is fighting against a true liberation of mankind leaves in its wake here and there tinctures of decay which we must search out and mercilessly expel from our land and our spirits."

23. Ibid., 251–52.

24. Césaire, *Discourse on Colonialism*, 35–36.

25. Brown, *Wounded Attachments*.

26. Not all ruins located in empire are imperial ones. See, for example, Lambek, *The Weight of the Past*, for a nuanced study of Malagasy relics.

27. For foundational works that do this work on different spatial and temporal scales, see Watts, *Silent Violence*; Cosby, *Ecological Imperialism*; Grove, *Green Imperialism*; and Peluso and Watts, *Violent Environments*, which focuses pointedly on how environmental degradation has been made into a political issue, posed as a threat to national security. On state violence, nature preservation, and forced relocation in Tanzania, see Neumann, *Imposing Wilderness*.

28. See, for example, Kosek, *Understories*; Carruthers, *Environmental Justice in Latin America*; Grinde and Johansen, *Ecocide of Native America*; Brook, "Environmental Genocide"; and Hooks and Smith, "The Treadmill of Destruction," which argues that capitalism alone does not explain the distribution of toxic waste on Native American reservations. Also see McGovern, *The Capo Indian Landfill War*. On biowaste, see, in particular, Hodges, "Chennai's Biotrash Chronicles."

29. See, for example, McCaffrey, "The Struggle for Environmental Justice in Vieques, Puerto Rico"; and Simon, Bouville, Land, and Beck, "Radiation Doses and Cancer Risks in the Marshall Islands Associated with Exposure to Radioactive Fallout from Bikini and Enewetak Nuclear Weapons Tests."

30. See, for example, Showers, *Imperial Gullies*; and Beinart and Hughes, *Environment and Empire*, which seeks to "compare the impact of different commodity frontiers on colonized people" (vi). A strong tradition of such work has developed for Madagascar. See, for example, Jarosz, "Defining and Explaining Tropical Deforestation"; Kull, *Isle of Fire*; and Sodikoff, "Forced and Forest Labor in Colonial Madagascar."

31. See Kuletz, *The Tainted Desert*; and Kuletz, "Cold War Nuclear and Militarized Landscapes." Also see Vine, *Island of Shame*.

32. In this, we appreciate and share the dilemma of the ambitious volume *Postcolonial Disorders*, edited by Mary-Jo DelVecchio Good, Sandra Teresa Hyde, Sarah Pinto, and Bryon Good, whose contributors skillfully and with subtlety tack between the unspoken and the everyday, between the unspeakable and the hidden, and place both the political and the psychological at the center of what constitutes "postcolonial disorders."

33. Foucault, *The Archaeology of Knowledge*, 22.

34. Mel Frykberg, "Villages Contaminated by Settlement Sewage," *Electronic Intifada*, 29 April 2010, http://electronicintifada.net.

35. On the Indian railway communities, see Bear, "Ruins and Ghosts."

36. Walcott, "The Antilles."

37. Price, *The Convict and the Colonel*, 165.

38. Walcott, "The Antilles."

39. Sommer, *Proceed with Caution*, 15.

40. Abu El-Haj, *Facts on the Ground* lucidly makes this point as do Ginsberg, *The Aesthetics of Ruins*, and many of the contributions to Lazzara and Unruh, *Telling Ruins in Latin America*.

41. See John Collins's contribution to this volume; and Collins, *The Revolt of the Saints*.

42. Kincaid, *A Small Place*, 9.

43. Landler, "Ruins by Day, Luxury by Night," *New York Times*, 26 November 2000, 10.

44. See, for example, Beinart and Hughes's discussion of "colonial conservatism" and national parks, in *Environment and Empire*.

45. See Hell and Schönle, *Ruins of Modernity*, for a pointed critique of the "imperial ruin gazer" and the new ruins which have become part of it.

46. On the industrial ruins of U.S. empire, see Finn, *Tracing the Veins*.

47. "The Follow-Your-Bliss List," *New York Magazine*, 16 October 2005, http://nymag .com. But also see Meixner, "Cambodia."

48. On the scale and scope of this imperial vision, see Stoler, *Along the Archival Grain*, 105–39 ("Developing Historical Negatives").

49. See http://www.mbweni.com/mbweniruins.htm and numerous other sites with visitor comments. Also see Bruner, *Culture on Tour*, one of many studies that refers to African American heritage tours to the dungeons from which slaves were sent from West Africa to the Americas.

50. Rosaldo, "Imperialist Nostalgia," 68–87.

51. In *Industrial Ruins* Tom Edensor conceives of exploring a ruin as a "kind of anti-tourism" because "movement is rough, disrupted and potentially perilous, replete with sensations other than the distanced gaze" (95). But this is precisely the allure of the ruins of Detroit and the ones mentioned here, suggesting not an antitourism, but a tourist delight, orchestrated participation in the adventure of imagining another time without having to imagine what political processes displaced those who lived in them.

52. Kuklick, "Contested Monuments." Also see Fontein, *The Silence of Great Zimbabwe*. On another sort of contested colonial monument, the war memorial, see Mann, "Locating Colonial Histories."

53. This quote appears on a postcard in a photography series titled "A History of the World through Ruins, 2005–2007," by Lida Abdul (given to me by Hugh Raffles, whom I thank for them) as part of the *Memorial to the Iraq War* exhibit, Institute of Contemporary Art, London, 23 May–27 June 2007.

54. See Collins's essay in this volume.

55. See Rao's essays in this volume.

56. See Hunt's essay in this volume.

57. See Chari's essay in this volume.

58. See Azoulay, "Has Anyone Ever Seen a Photograph of a Rape?"

59. See Azoulay's essay in this volume.

60. See Chari's essay in this volume.

61. Grandin, *Fordlandia*.

62. Grandin, "Touring Empire's Ruin." See his essay in this volume.

63. This is not a focus of the current fascination with "The Fabulous Ruins of Detroit" (DetroitYES!, http://www.detroityes.com/home.htm) or with "Exploring Detroit's Beautiful Ruins" (Rybczynski, "Incredible Hulks," http://www.slate.com/articles/arts/architecture/2009/03/incredible_hulks.html).

64. See Michael Hodges, "Detroit's Ruins Bring Visitors, but Rankle Critics within the City," *Detroit News*, 1 July 2010.

65. David Grossman, "Writing in the Dark," *New York Times*, 13 May 2007, emphasis added.

66. On the relationship between people and debris and on the affective space produced by living in piles of rubbish and ruined environments, see Navaro-Yashin's analysis of Lefkosha/Lefkosa, a city divided since the Turkish invasion of Northern Cyprus in 1974, in "Abjected Spaces."

67. Trouillot, *Silencing the Past*.

68. Cliff, *No Telephone to Heaven*, 1. I thank Meredith Edwards of Furman University for alerting me to Cliff's use of *ruinate* when I delivered a version of this essay in February 2011.

69. Abu El-Haj, *Facts on the Ground*, 164.

70. See Cohen, "The Politics of Planting"; and Walid Khalidi, *All That Remains*. I thank Jennifer Lynn Kelly for the references cited here, for pointing me to the Afforestation Project, and for sharing her research with me.

71. "Dreams of Home," a brochure and photo collection created by the children of Lajee Center with Rich Wiles.

72. I thank those at the Lajee Center for sharing with me their publications, the photographs that the children took, and the stories they collected when I visited in 2008.

73. Abu El-Haj illustrates this point in detail, in *Facts on the Ground*. Joseph Masco, John Collins, and Vyjayanthi Rao each look to different features of state-managed ruins in their essays in this volume.

74. See Joseph Masco's essay in this volume.

75. Beasley-Murray, "Vilcashuamán." Also see Jaguaribe, "Modernist Ruins"; and Bissell, "Engaging Colonial Nostalgia," which looks at the critical purchase that colonial nostalgia can afford in the face of devastated landscapes and "dimming memories of modernity" (Rachel Swarms, quoted in Bissell, "Engaging Colonial Nostalgia," 217).

76. See Rao's essay in this volume.

77. On the history and contemporary battles over the theft, protection, and repatriation of American Indian remains and objects, see Fine-Dare, *Grave Injustice*.

78. Stoler, "The Carceral Archipelago of Empire."

79. Buck-Morss, *The Dialectics of Seeing*, 163.

80. Ibid., 182, 170.

81. Hunt, *A Colonial Lexicon of Birth Ritual, Medicalization, and Mobility in the Congo*.

82. See Szmagalska-Follis, "Repossession."

83. Sebald, *On the Natural History of Destruction*, 67.

84. Nixon, "Slow Violence, Gender, and the Environmentalism of the Poor"; Agamben, *Homo Sacer*, 27–28; Biehl, *Vita*.

85. Biehl, *Vita*, 18.

86. Klein, *The Shock Doctrine*.

87. Lloyd, "Ruination," 487.

88. Bauman, *Wasted Lives*.

89. On oil spills that have mattered less, see John Vidal, "Nigeria's Agony Dwarfs the Gulf Oil Spill: The US and Europe Ignore It," *Guardian*, 30 May 2010, http://www.guardian.co.uk/world/2010/may/30/oil-spills-nigeria-niger-delta-shell.

90. See Tatz, Cass, Condon, and Tippet, "Aborigines and Uranium," 3.

91. See ibid.

92. Coronil, "Editor's Column," 645.

93. See Stoler, *Haunted by Empire*. Also see de Genova, "The Stakes of an Anthropology of the United States."

94. Agee and Evans, *Let Us Now Praise Famous Men*.

95. Stewart, *A Space on the Side of the Road*, 90–112.

96. Ibid., 96.

97. Ibid., 111.

98. Pemberton, "The Ghost in the Machine," 36.

99. See Daniel's essay in this volume.

100. Daniel, "The Coolie," 267.

101. See Hunt's essay in this volume.

102. It is estimated that eighty-two million "bomblets" were dropped in Vietnam between 1961 and 1973. Duds from those continue to be found in forty-three of the sixty-five provinces in Vietnam, thirty years later. Similar cluster bombs were used by the United States in Kuwait in 1991 and in Afghanistan in 2001. See Ellen Massey, "Disarmament: Will the U.S. Finally End Cluster Bomb Imports?," Inter Press Service, Latin America, 23 July 2007, http://www.antiwar.com/ips/massey.php?articleid=11328. The

estimates of unexploded ordnance range from 300,000 tons to as much as 800,000 tons. I have taken the more conservative estimate.

103. Fox, "Chemical Politics and the Hazards of Modern Warfare." Also see Fox, "One Significant Ghost"; Weisberg, *Ecocide in Indochina*; Browning and Forman, *The Wasted Nation*; Whiteside, *The Withering Rain*; Schuck, *Agent Orange on Trial*.

104. In a recent study of dioxin use by U.S. troops in Vietnam, the epidemiologist Jeanne Stellman at Columbia University estimates, on the basis of detailed lists of over nine thousand herbicide spray missions, that far more dioxin was sprayed than any government study has ever acknowledged. See her "The Extent and Patterns of Usage of Agent Orange and Other Herbicides in Vietnam." Also see the searing photographs by the Welsh photojournalist Philip Jones Griffiths, *Agent Orange*.

105. In May 2005 a lawsuit filed by Vietnamese victims of Agent Orange against the chemical companies was dismissed. In July 2005 a program to investigate the health and environmental damage caused by the defoliant was canceled before it began. See Butler, "U.S. Abandon Health Study on Agent Orange." The case was appealed and heard by Manhattan's Second Circuit Court of Appeals in June 2007, when the court ruled again that the chemical companies were acting as contractors for the U.S. government and therefore shared its immunity. In the most recent round, in March 2009, the Supreme Court refused to reconsider the ruling of the lower court.

106. Aaron Glantz and Ngoc Nguyen, "Villagers Build Lives Out of Unexploded Bombs," Inter Press Service, 26 November 2003, http://www.ipsnews.net/2003/11/vietnam-villagers-build-lives-out-of-unexploded-bombs/.

107. Ibid.

108. Quoted in Walcott, "A Dilemma Faces WI Artists."

109. Baucom, *Out of Place*, 172.

110. Quoted in ibid., 199.

111. Lévi-Strauss, *Tristes Tropiques* (1964). I thank Trisha Gupta for pointing me to the passage on Lahore.

112. Baucom, *Out of Place*, 186–87.

113. Faisal Devji's comments at the "Scarred Landscapes/Imperial Debris" conference, October 2006.

114. See Burbank and Cooper's "Review of Marc Ferro's *Le livre noir du colonialisme*," where they make the important point that the "prosecutorial stance" and the currency of indicting the colonial in France today and equating it with totalitarianism miss "the limits of power as actually exercised, the constraints on colonial regimes' ability to transform or to exploit, . . . their frequent dependence on indigenous economic and political actors whom they could not fully control" (460–61).

115. On the history of immigrant housing in France, see Bernardot, *Loger les immigrés*.

116. The point has made been with force by Balibar, "Uprisings in the 'Banlieues,'" and by others, but with strikingly little historical analysis.

117. Fanon, *The Wretched of the Earth*.

118. Stora, *Le transfert d'une mémoire*.

119. Amery, quoted in Sebald, *On the Natural History of Destruction*, 156.

PART I   *Decompositions of Matter and Mind*

An Acoustic Register

Rape and Repetition in Congo

A 2006 documentary on sexual violence and war in the Democratic Republic of the Congo (DRC) includes words and images of raped women. Some
are bent over in pain, some speak, while others harvest new fields together.
Graphic photographs show torn body parts, vulvas mutilated by guns, Coke
bottles, and sticks. The film is set largely in eastern Congo at hospitals where
doctors have been treating many of the thousands raped in recent years.
Produced by the United Nations Population Fund (UNFPA), the film also
contains scenes in Équateur about soldiers raping women and girls. In 2003
former rebel soldiers (of Jean-Pierre Bemba's movement), at a time when
they had only recently been mixed into the national army, turned on some
two hundred girls and women in Nsongo Mboyo in a storm of angry mass
rape. In an unprecedented action three years later, Joseph Kabila's state
charged some of the soldiers, found them guilty, and sent them to jail—just
three months before presidential elections kept Kabila in power.[1]

Nsongo Mboyo is located where the notorious rubber concession company, Abir, was sited when Congo was King Leopold II's scandalous Congo
Free State (1885–1908). The 2006 documentary does not evoke this iconic
imperial violence. Its Équateur section locates history weakly, with a once
colonial geographic marker. The filmmaker was Senegalese; history was not
his purpose; and this take on a monument commemorating colonial science
is a mere placeholder. Still, it is significant that none of the humanitarian
actors making efforts to help thousands of Congolese rape victims seems to

know that this rape site, Nsongo Mboyo, was once in the Abir concession, a terrain of death, starvation, wife abduction, mutilation, and sexual violence from 1892, when the violent rush for raw rubber began.[2] (The Abir zone also became epicenter of the humanitarian campaign led by the British publicist E. D. Morel and his Congo Reform Association in the 1890s and 1900s.)[3] The absence of historicization within today's humanitarianism suggests something important about ruination and forgetting, about missed opportunities to work with "toxic imperial debris" in producing effective, urgent histories.[4]

The film does mark as "historical" the moment in 2006 when the soldiers who raped at Nsongo Mboyo were condemned to prison for life, ritually stripped of their uniforms before a crowd at the military trial. Using archival footage from the United Nations Mission to the Congo (MONUC), the editors used a long still, showing uniforms spread on the ground as detritus, symbolic evidence of guilt, but also of the firm stand of Kabila's regime. I viewed the film in Kinshasa with an educated, worldly Congolese woman, the widow of a former university professor, in 2007. As we watched this segment, she cried out that the soldiers who had raped should all be killed. Then she suddenly changed her mind: instead, she declared, "they should cut off their hands."

Boali and Visual Debris

This suggestion of a fitting punishment, unwittingly pulling a tenacious image from the past, resonates with Ann Laura Stoler's challenge, in this volume, to "think with ruins of empire" so as "to attend to their reappropriations . . . within the politics of the present." Mama Pauline's recuperation of severed hands from the psychic and visual ruins of Leopold's Congo may disturb, yet this reappropriation problematizes the key issues of this essay: duration, reproduction, and repetition in history and historical writing.

Mama Pauline and I watched the film in a context in which secure possibilities for dealing with the ubiquity of sexual violence as war seemed few. We watched knowing that Kabila's regime had since failed on its promises of impunity: ten of the eleven soldiers had escaped from Mbandaka's prison walls earlier that year. Mama Pauline Betu's suggestion of amputation implied a claim. At the same time, it recuperated images left behind from Free State times and still circulating globally: mutilation photographs have become iconic of atrocities in Leopold's Congo and all racialized violence, too.

In this essay I turn to visual detritus from Congo not as concrete "debris" that wedges open ethnographic history, nor to understand how the "phantasmagoric use of atrocity photographs" produced anti-Leopoldian humanitarian spectators in the West.[5] I take up "shock-photos" as refractory evidence whose selective circulation then and since is worthy of canny attention.[6] Some images from Leopold's Congo traveled: they were recycled, repackaged, and reframed, over and over again. Some did not. We can still find some photographic debris in recent and not-so-recent histories on "red rubber" and its ruinous violence.[7] Open Adam Hochschild's King Leopold's Ghost to its insert of archival photographs, for instance, and you will find such heavily recycled visual remains there—from the image of a father looking at the severed hand and foot of his five-year-old daughter, to a photograph of two youths with handless black stumps for arms displayed against white sheets of cloth.[8] Each image was in the standard magic-lantern show that circulated in Britain and the United States at the height of the anti-Leopoldian campaign. Most were taken by Alice Harris of the Congo Balolo Mission station of Baringa, also the site of an Abir post. As Kevin Grant has shown, Harris's photographs enabled Morel's relentless humanitarian propaganda machine to gather force and to move an ever larger British and U.S. public.[9] By 1907, the London Auxiliary of the CRA had sold ten thousand copies of a brochure called Camera and Congo Crime, which contained twenty-four photographs by Harris. The standard show of the period, marketed by Riley Brothers Ltd. as "Lantern Lecture on the Congo Atrocities," included sixty lantern slides. "A savage Abir sentry" appeared quickly, followed by a Congolese being whipped. One slide showed a group of chained women: "The treatment of women hostages." Six slides were mutilation photographs, picturing Congolese with missing hands or feet; most of those pictured were young men and boys. An advertisement listed the sixty slides in four sections that suggested a trajectory from rubber system and mutilation toward the civilizing potential of missionary work.[10]

Alice Harris's mutilation photographs were powerful, overwhelming. Ultimately their autonomous force as "shock-photos" produced an effective "public revulsion" in Britain, the United States, and Europe that changed "the course of history."[11] Cathy Caruth suggests that traumatic form combines repetitive reappearance with repression, the "insistent grammar of sight" with some kind of "effacement of the event."[12] The continued use and reuse of the Harris images reify a maimed, disfigured, individualized body. In the process, they distort and erase a complexity of forms of ruination and refusal far wider, more spatial, and more enduring.[13]

The visual nature of the evidence—what foreign observers wrote about seeing, what Congolese explained they had seen, and the photographs that circulated and shocked—has oriented humanitarian, scholarly, and popular attention toward severed hands. The mutilation shots, in particular, have directed interest away from the more hidden, tactile, and out of sight, away from another modality of violence, the sexual. And this modality of violence was intrinsically more reproductive and transgressive in its nature.

Enter Boali. She resisted the sexual advances of an Abir sentry. The armed man hired to supervise rubber collection shot her in the belly, took her body for dead, and then cut off her foot in order to run off with the brass ring of sure wealth fastened tight just above her ankle. Boali was one of Alice Harris's subjects. The photograph shows her almost naked, wearing a mere apron around the waist, holding on to a long pole to stay erect. Her belly is traced with marks of scarification, recently misshapen from the gunshot wound. That her foot is missing is just visible at the bottom edge of the frame. This image of Boali traveled far in Britain and North America as part of the standard magic lantern show, while her name became deformed as Boaji. Slide no. 34 carried the caption "Boaji, Mutilated for her constancy."[14] Appending these redemptive, evangelical words to her ambiguous image reflects an effort to turn her into a model, faithful wife.

Since then, Boali's image has tended to disappear. Morel did not include the Boali photograph in his books, although it did appear in one CRA pamphlet.[15] In contrast, the photographs of young men with missing hands—their black stumps posed in high contrast against white cloth—were cropped and reduplicated repeatedly, even brought together into an assemblage of repetition, with several photographs being cropped and shown at once within a unified frame, as in Mark Twain's *King Leopold's Soliloquy*. Often, individuals were not named in captions, and their stories disappeared. It was as if humanitarian spectators already knew the cast of figures, while the quantity and simultaneity of the images summarized all: horror.

Fields of Sound

To argue for rewriting the standard Congo atrocity narrative in relation to urgent politics of the present, I reinsert Boali back into the complexity of evidence about ruination in the Congo, then and now (since 1996). The conventional story has tended to get caught, often obsessively, on the malevolent, selfish, naughty King Leopold, who never set foot in the place, and how he should now be put on trial amid a mute row of atrocity victims with stumps for arms.[16] These histories tend to end not long after British Consul

Roger Casement's incriminating report to the British Parliament and Morel's extraordinarily energetic and effective propaganda campaign; they tend to end with the Belgian parliament being forced to intervene, requiring King Leopold to turn over his private colony to Belgian administration in 1908.[17]

I also seek to problematize and disaggregate the visual. The idea is to move beyond seeing as the primary mode of perceiving the past, by being wakeful to other senses and capacities, especially the field of hearing, producing, and muffling sound. Such attentiveness makes the following comment, from Adam Hochschild's moving yet ever redemptive and epic history about violence and humanitarianism in the Congo Free State, both stand out and smart: "One problem, of course, is that nearly all of this vast river of words is by Europeans or Americans. . . . Instead of African voices from this time there is largely silence."[18] Hochschild's words echo an idea found in his humanitarian sources. Consider these words, from a CRA pamphlet of 1904: "It is from others, mostly, that we know what there is to know of his sad story . . . of women toiling in chains . . . the severed hands. . . . But in all of this we have not heard the voice of the native himself. At most we have seen him in photographs, stretching mute, mutilated and uncomprehending."[19] Congolese voices, however mediated, may have been difficult to hear in 1904, but the historian today can still find them in a rich range of sources.[20]

Enter Boali, once again. Boali spoke, and her voice can be located in the African Archives in Brussels, alongside the mediated, translated (into French), transcribed words of the 258 Congolese persons who made depositions before King Leopold's Commission of Inquiry in 1905–6.[21] Boali was from Ekolongo in the Abir concession, and she testified at Baringa: "One day when my husband went into the forest to gather rubber, the sentry Ikelonda came, finding me in my hut where I stayed, and asked me to give myself to him. I rejected his proposition. Furious, Ikelonda fired a gun shot at me, which gave me the wound whose trace you can still see. I fell on my back; Ikelonda thought I was dead, and to get hold of the brass bracelet that I wore at the base of my right leg, he cut off my right foot."[22] Boali was one of thirteen Congolese women to speak out and make a claim before the Commission of Inquiry. Together, the depositions provide complex evidence about sexual capital and sexual abuse: some women managed to use the first to find protection, while others became reduced to objects of torture and violence.[23] It is not clear precisely when Alice Harris photographed Boali, only that the picture traveled far at the time along with the caption about marital "constancy." Boali's claim was about her wound as "a trace," her missing foot, the stolen brass anklet, her refusal to be raped. Her words were about the sentry. She knew his name. After Ikelonda's fury and gun blasted through Boali with decisive, life-altering noise, she managed to remain "quiet as death," while he used a sharp blade to separate the object of wealth from her body.[24] This capacity for lying silent and giving no "sign of life" even while a body part was "hacked off" intrigued Casement when he investigated Free State conditions in 1903.[25] But other aspects of violence during war and raiding he found "unfit for repetition."[26]

Reproductive Ruination

In my history of colonial things in the Belgian Congo, A Colonial Lexicon, "debris" was the material and concrete.[27] Debris consisted of those once colonial things—soap, baby clothes, and birth certificates—that remained as twisted objects in a postcolonial field, Mobutu's Zaire, mired but ever alive, exerting power over decisions, purchases, gifts, and secrets. The method used for tracking debris began not with words or sounds, but with observing practice and use in a postcolonial present. Debris as method cannot work for an anthropological history focused on the violence of Congo Free State's "red rubber" period and its aftermath.[28] A period in the field, trying to find remnants of concessionary posts or mutilation sites, might be evocative. But as I learned during a few trips into the region, the Albini rifles and cap guns are long gone, the hostage structures and rubber baskets, too, even if there is a "a ruined wall about a meter high" of an Arab house at the former Abir post of Mpusu.[29] Most memories of imperial violence are jumbled. More recent kinds of ruination—the structural violence of the Mobutu years, the bombardments and penury of recent war in the Basankusu area—displaced the tangible and accessible memories of 1954, when a Flemish missionary mounted an essay-writing contest to collect Congolese memories of rubber violence in the Free State period.[30]

I therefore take up the immediacy of ruination caused by the rubber system, providing a fresh reading through the senses, through fields of hearing and sound. These directions take us to fright, shame, and the unsayable, and the way anguish produced silence or, perhaps oddly, a brief eruption of laughter. The duration of duress in the Équateur region into the Belgian Congo years (1908–60) is significant to overlapping modalities of violence—structural, corporeal, symbolic, psychic, and sexual—and their reproduction and somatization over time.

The bodily effects of spectacular, transgressive, sexualized violence are of particular interest. Roger Casement found people frightened and frail in 1903, when he investigated, traveling from Lac Leopold II up the Congo, Lulonga, and Lopori Rivers into the Abir concession. He noted the visceral effects of terror and trauma: "suspicious looks," "evasive eyes," and "flutterings."[31] His investigative report included the words of Rev. J. Clark of Ikoko: "Again a lower percentage of births lessen the population. Weakened bodies is one cause of this. Another reason is that women refuse to bear children, and take means to save themselves from motherhood. They give as the reason that if 'war' should come to a woman 'big with child,' or with a baby to carry, 'she' cannot well run away and hide from the soldiers."[32] Many spoke of hunger and starvation. A missionary near Lukolela spoke of "a disappearing" and "dying people," suggesting "fear and punishment" were producing loss of appetite and amenorrhea in women.[33]

A less sensitive observer, more aligned with King Leopold, too, the British journalist Viscount Mountmorres, found much to admire in the Free State, while arguing that problems were confined to the Équateur concession areas.[34] He witnessed the violent squeeze of the Abir system when the rubber supply was almost exhausted.[35] This squeeze produced uprisings. Rubber villages were making war on food villages, while many simply fled the Abir zone. Mountmorres imagined the Mongo of this terrorized area as "indolent, timid, and sulky, desiring only to be left alone to lead a slug-like existence." He did not recognize how war, forced labor, and starvation were producing the frailty and brokenness before his eyes.

> The villages are smaller and not so well kept. . . . One scarcely sees a village worthy of the name. . . . Occasionally one or two huts . . . will still be occupied by a surly, silent, depressed people, who neither greet one nor flee before one, but accept one's presence with a dull indifference. . . . Physically the race is degenerate, being extremely small of stature and meager of build. . . . The rapidity with which these people fall ill and die is almost incredible. . . . They . . . accept death with a fatalism which goes far to encourage it.[36]

Mountmorres's idea of a degenerate Mongo race became repeated in Belgian colonial words and practice, as Équateur became neglected in decades to come, as finance capital turned to mining and its industrialization in other regions. By the 1920s–30s, when attention turned to worker shortages and the impact of labor recruitment on social reproduction, the sight of overworked, exhausted people in Équateur became frequent again. Worries about a low birth rate and infertility became commonplace. Continuing forced labor, while less murderous, remained a form of structural violence that shaped social geography and demography. Many robust Congolese simply moved away, out of the "customary" realm and its legislated, regulated work obligations (porterage, road building, agriculture) into "extra-customary" wage labor on plantations or in colonial towns. The women who stayed behind in Équateur had to carry heavy loads of requisitioned food into the 1930s; from the 1940s, they had to build roads.[37]

Colonial language about subfertility and sterility in the Mongo and Nkundo regions of Équateur spoke of degeneration, race suicide, extinction, a customary world unable to reproduce itself, and widespread childlessness. Shock became an everyday colonial word, as a string of doctors began to report on sexually transmitted diseases (STDs) and to think about infertility in a psychic lexicon from the interwar period on. The best demographic age pyramids (from Befale territory) indicate a significant reproductive downturn in 1885–90 and again in 1905–10, thus corresponding, respectively, to when Abir first arrived and again when Abir abuses reached their height, with a general regression in the birth rate between 1905–30.[38] Up to 40 percent of women were childless in the Tshuapa region of Équateur in the 1950s.[39] Much degenerationist language was figurative; but we are no longer in the realm of metaphor when we see the list of women patients' names treated by Dr. Magis in 1958 in his sterility clinic at Boende.[40]

Reproductive disruption in Équateur contradicted the Belgian colonial high-modern aesthetic of the 1950s, focused on reproductive modernity, maternity wards, and happy, helpful husbands.[41] There were few rural mothers beaming with babies in their arms in maternity beds in Équateur in the 1950s. Instead, women unable to become pregnant or give birth to live babies attended the first infertility clinic — likely in all sub-Saharan Africa — to open its doors at Befale, in 1953.[42] The contrast in birth rates and maternity services between Équateur and other parts of the colony suggests an unevenness to temporalities, modernity, and ruination within one and the same Belgian African empire.[43] Not all Congolese received welfare capitalism, maternity wards, and babies in equal measure. Ruinous resource extraction in early colonial Équateur had enduring effects — on Congolese memory, reproductive bodies, and European attitudes, and in the penury of investments made in this relatively empty region with a haunting past of widespread death and injury.

"A Callous Eye" and Acoustic Debris

Debris takes on a different meaning here, one more sensory and mnemonic in a history that contains violence, death, and mutilation, where ruination was bodily and psychic, and where war and sexual violence have resurged over the last decade. Rather than debris first sighted in a postcolonial field and tracked historically through archives, I use sensory traces parsed from a refractory colonial archive to anchor a reading of the immediacy of anguish and ruination and the sounds and images people were left with some fifty years later.[44]

Any archive may be likened to an ethnographic field, if techniques of observing, listening, wondering, and parsing are privileged. Still, we need to be careful before imagining every scrap of paper, photograph, and object in archives and museums as the debris — or ruins — of empire. Doing so would be facile, and embrace too much. Neither would it push a vocabulary of ruination to press forward questions about claims and consequences, memory and the senses, immediacy and duration, reproduction and repetition. While reading canonical, new, and underused sources, my thinking has turned to perception and "an acoustic presence": hearing, sounds, noises, hushed stillness, and silence.[45] I seek out a soundtrack and words spoken to ground a new reading of Free State ruination, the anguish and fright of the moment, forms of remembering and muteness that followed, and claims made and their potential reappropriations — repetitions — in the present.

My archive here consists of four sources. Rather than gathering inspiration from Conrad's "hallucinatory" prose, indeed avoiding the spectral frame it might reintroduce, I return to the investigative report of Casement, then British consul to the Free State.[46] Optics and acoustics operated with studied restraint in this circumspectly composed indictment of Leopold's Congo.[47] Second, I parse the daily journal of the Free State officer turned heroic veteran Baron Francis Dhanis (1904), who Abir hired to go in and investigate just as its regime spun into chaos from rubber exhaustion, increased atrocity, and scandal.[48] Baron Dhanis was neither neutral nor a humanitarian witness. Hired as special adviser, he was allied with Abir and the king. He was already a major colonial hero, in Belgian circles almost as famous as Sir Henry Morton Stanley, who helped win key battles of conquest in the so-called Arab War in Congo's Zanzibari-dominated east in the early 1890s. Dhanis was not backed into a defensive mode either, and this makes his unstudied, spontaneous, and often pained personal jottings about the visible and the heard—none intended for publication—a precious counter-point to the "studied realism" of Roger Casement.[49]

Dhanis entered into the Abir landscape of ruination in early June 1904 and left by mid-September. Embedded in his diary are notations on encounters with Congolese; most were akin to appeals for help. These suggest a range of kinds of duress, some visible, though many from the realm of the "tactile and the unseen."[50] Also present are claims, occasions when people—"natives," chiefs with names, one European agent's "boy"—came to complain, protest, or ask for intervention. These claims are an interesting counterpoint to the testimony of thirteen Congolese who testified before the King's Commission of Inquiry in 1905–6.

Congolese did not speak at the time of rubber abuses only to Dhanis, Casement, appalled missionaries, and the King's Commission, but also among themselves. And fifty years later, when the Flemish missionary Edmond Boelaert organized a Lomongo-language essay contest in a mission newspaper, 170 teachers, students, clerks, and chiefs wrote about the violence, death, cruelties, and hardships of the Free State years.[51] I use all four sources to sense violence and ruination—in their immediacy and in forms of remembering.

Stoler suggests discerning "tenacious and weak traces." As I parse this diverse archive, I attend to weaker, aural traces to complement and complicate the overpowering tenacity of the visual. Even within the visual, I distinguish among images of a basket of human hands in someone's *immediate field of vision*; of severed, counted hands in *memory's eye*; and of a mutilated young man in a *photograph that circulated* then, as it still does in histories and documentary films today, *influencing memory's eye* wherever it alights.

The idea is to push beyond the shock of the photographic, which tends to blot out all else, and seek more fragile memory pictures and acoustic traces that tell something new and more complicated about the immediacy of violence and its duration in memory. Silence and the unsayable are significant. Casement's report spoke of "the quiet of death," and, indeed, muffling sound saved lives.

Some sounds were words voiced out loud. Sometimes a girl's fear meant her "voice was very small."[52] Some sound was visceral and eruptive. A chief "broke down and wept, saying that their lives were useless to them."[53] A crowd "roared with laughter" when a sentry claimed he did not know a fifteen-year-old maimed boy whose hand the throng knew well he alone had hacked off.[54] Some sounds were technological, emitted by new objects that moved, killed, and made troops march to time: steamboats, rifles, cap guns, bugles, and military brass bands. To the young ears of the village girl Bonsondo, the sound of a bugle suggested a white officer had been present when soldiers attacked her village.

Not all objects that made sound were new. The "noise" of brass anklets put a girl on the run at risk of being sighted and caught.[55] Death produced sounds of weeping and lamentation. Fright led to the loss of voice. Bikela remembered after a massacre that "friends who were left buried the bodies and there was very much weeping."[56] When soldiers killed her mother with a gun, she "cried very much." Afterward, Bikela "was too frightened and would not answer."[57]

Elima's visuality extended to dreaming: "Bula Matadi was coming to fight them, but her mother told her she was trying to tell stories," but a little while later "she heard the firing of guns."[58] Guns, human hands, and baskets of severed hands—severed so they could be acknowledged and tallied by white agents—were among the objects that were part of this world of violence and rubber. The Congolese memories of 1954 emphasize that protective medicines were, too. These charms enabled a special visibility. Looking into the *ikakota* pot, Jean-Ambroise Yolo explained, one could see rows of troops at war.[59]

Memory smells and shudders. People recalled the stench of rotting corpses in 1954. These essays, written mostly by second-generation children of victims and survivors, are rich with sound, of the first boat that arrived "like the noise of large wind that precedes rain," of an old man with inebriated song about war confronting some and sparing others, of mocking insults hurled at white men with unkempt hair, the bang of guns as rain drizzled, and children crying from hunger.[60] Images are omnipresent: trees used for hangings, baskets, blood running like a stream or up the thighs.[61]

Casement was hyperattentive to visibility and audibility, in keeping with the charged atmosphere of accusations, investigations, and denials. When one commissioner told English-speaking missionaries their "ears [were] too long," Rev. Clark replied: "Their eyes were sharp. . . . We see and know."[62] Casement observed—and people offered him visible evidence—"broad weals across their buttocks," while "a lad of 15 or so, removing his cloth, *showed* several scars across his thighs."[63] There is no lack of toxic images of cruelty in Casement's report. Ncongo saw a basket with two hundred hands counted out.[64] Casement saw "fifteen women . . . tied together, either neck to neck or ankle to ankle, to secure them for the night."[65] When writing that people "were not happy under this system," Casement commented that "it was *apparent to a callous eye* that in this they *spoke* the strict truth."[66] He was aware that what he reported as *seen* or *observed* became fact, while reporting on things heard *"from their lips"* would double the truth effect.[67] And he made readers aware of the scopic economy at work: eyes watching and guarding all around, the filling of sacks "taking place *under the eyes* of . . . a State sentry."[68] Casement used eyes and ears to argue that there was "a very real fear of reporting" among Congolese. Even though people spoke to him, "their previous *silence* said more than their present *speech*."[69]

Seeing took precedence over hearing in the Casement report. And these were the only two senses at work. This is quite different when one turns to the 1954 memory accounts or the stories of five Ikoko mission women who had been rescued as girls around 1893; in these, sound and hearing were as important as sight. Casement took pains to collect and translate the girls' firsthand accounts. The girls had run for their lives and quickly sensed sound as risk. A misguided or inadvertent sound could cost a life, Bikela learned after running "far into the bush" with her mother. Soldiers followed and when they "came near us they were calling my mother by name, and I was going to answer, but my mother put her hand to my mouth to stop me. . . . If she had not . . . we would all have been killed."[70] The sound of gunfire produced flight. Crying was dangerous: "We heard children crying, and a soldier went quickly over to the place and killed a mother and four children."[71] This sense of danger also comes through in the memories documented in 1954. Antoine-Marcus Boyoto recalled, "When they perceived a noise or the rattling of shots, they went further into the forest. Mothers buried alive their small children because of their crying."[72] The sound of nervous laughter could produce a more violent, punitive death, as Ncongo explained: "The soldiers saw a little child and when they went to kill it, the child laughed so the soldier took the butt of the gun and struck the child with it, and then cut off its head."[73]

Sentries, Laughter, the Unsayable

People referred to the armed rubber-company men by the instruments they carried. Imome, for example, called sentries "guns."[74] And when François Bombute wrote of sentries, he penned, "The guns spoke."[75] Dhanis concentrated on Congolese sentries as the "gangrene" of the Abir system, noting theft, murder, and stolen wives. There is an arc to his observations about women, as he tried to zero in on the abduction of wives and daughters by sentries and their overseers, *capitas*. He seized on the gifting of women to sentries by chiefs, thereby seeking exemptions on the quantity of rubber to be collected. When one sentry came with a complaint, Dhanis asked him to declare how many wives he had; soon his wives gestured toward other uncounted wives with pointing fingers, turning their sentry husband into a liar. When Dhanis discussed a complex murder case, he made lists of the cast involved, naming each sentry and his servant or "boy," while working out clashes and murders among the factions.

Of twenty-five episodes of mistreatment, protest, and conversation that involved a claim made before Dhanis, ten were made by chiefs, five involved "natives," and four came from individuals. Two were by sentries: six from Besongo asked for caps for their muskets, while saying they needed Albini rifles. Only a few claims involved a soundtrack beyond the suggestion of words. Dhanis used the word *supplications* for the entreaties made by women doing basketry work in rubber-drying sites as he approached a prison. He asked a "skeleton" of an old man in the prison how long he had been there. The man's wry retort—"Judge for yourself. I no longer know."—stirred Dhanis, who sent the frail man home with an unprecedented intercession, a generous gift of cloth.

The acoustic register of Dhanis's journey also embraced the sound of laughter. A Boande "native" asked the Belgian baron how to get back his wife, who had been abducted by a sentry some time ago. Noting that the husband had never complained before, Dhanis asked him why. He entered the reply in his journal: "He laughs. The response is sufficient."[76] Dhanis also noted the sentry had been "laid off on April 1 of this year," perhaps losing access to a gun in the process.

Bakhtin on laughter is not so useful here; the husband's laugh was not a cackling, carnivalesque laughter. Nor was it a laughter that mocked. It seems closer to the nervous, agonized shaking suggested by Baudelaire's "trembling laughter."[77] Bataille's ideas about the "unknowability" and "anguish" of laughter are helpful: "That which is laughable may simply be *the unknowable . . . the unknown makes us laugh*."[78] Laughter, a "moment of release," involves "the violence of an excitement which can no longer be stopped." Bataille added: "Anguish is not the cause of the laugh . . . but anguish is in some form necessary: *when anguish arises, then laughter begins*."[79]

This husband's laughter seems to have come from the realm of the immediate and the visceral, the instant and the direct. The erupting sound suggests something important about the duration of duress. The evidence suggests a delayed laughter, coming from a delayed claim, an uncomprehending white man's question, and a prolonged and diffuse suffering.[80]

When Casement traveled in 1903, he also heard laughter. In Nganda a state soldier in his third term from the faraway Upper Bussira "spoke fully of the condition of the people." Casement asked why he had stayed so long with the work: "His own village and country were subject to much trouble in connection with the rubber tax, he could not live in his own home, and preferred, he said, laughing, 'to be with the hunters rather than with the hunted.'"[81] Perhaps the soldier's laughter revealed uneasiness, nervousness, and suppressed anguish due to relative safety and the obligation to hunt others. Bataille reminds: "The nature of laughter . . . lies in its link to a position of dominance. . . . We laugh on condition that our position of dominance not be at the mercy of laughter."[82] In *King Leopold's Ghost* Hochschild uses the word *frenzy* to comprehend what happens when killing "becomes a kind of sport, like hunting."[83] He gives examples of European "sadists," torturing Congolese with castor oil, faces rubbed in excrement, and holes shot through earlobes.[84] The complex relationships among laughter, domination, pleasure, anguish, and frenzy are worthy of further exploration, especially as they relate to fields of vision and sound in situations of sadism and torture.

Congolese memory accounts give examples of European and Congolese sadism, of transgressive, gratuitous, grotesque violence, sometimes in a repetitive, almost fanciful mode of remembering.[85]

> The one inflicted with the chicotte who defecated right afterward, they obliged eating this excrement. If you refuse to eat it, they kill you. . . . A woman is pregnant, they order: "Eviscerate her so that we see how the baby is inside." The death of the woman follows. They cut one ear from someone and left him another. They forced a woman to have sexual relations with her son. If she refuses, they kill her. . . . They had a breast cut off a woman and left her another. . . . They obliged a boy to have sex with his mother, if not they kill him.[86]

The way sadistic pleasure combined with sexual torture came through clearly in Mingo's testimony before the King's Commission in 1906. "While I was working in brick-making at Mampoko, at two different occasions in order to punish me, the sentries, N'kusu, Lomboto, et Itokwa, made me take off my cloth and put clay in my sexual parts which made me suffer a lot. The white man saw me with clay in my sexual parts. He limited himself to saying: 'If you die in my work, they can throw you in the water.' The white man Long-wango also saw the clay in my sexual parts, and he had the same attitude as Likwama."[87]

There is no way to know who dreamt up this idea of filling a woman's private parts with clay, of using the material of the work under question to threaten, humiliate, and abuse her. Vigdis Broch-Due reminds us that "violence can lead to a macabre form of creativity."[88] Mingo's words suggest that voyeurism accompanied this spectacle of punishment, torture, and looking. She spoke about suffering and visibility: "the sentry made me take off my cloth," he "made me suffer a lot," "the white man saw me." We hear about a division of labor: there were the black men who "put clay in my sexual parts" and white men who watched at a remove. This situation involved racial layers of authority and the capacity for observation: a white man could sit as if apart and look, and if he did not quite approve of what he saw, he also did not stop the situation. Another white man was also there with his eyes, looking.

The optics are clear; but the acoustics require a hermeneutic, sensory leap. It is as if through an ellipsis of sound in Mingo's deposition that we begin to hear the twisted pleasure—and tittering laughter—that accompanied the sexual torturing of a woman through hardening clay. These fragments bring near a human scale and a sensory awareness to the immediacy of ruination. The sound of twisted laughter collected, convulsed, and retracted around forms of sexual violence basic to, indeed constitutive of, the reproductive ruination of Leopold's Congo. The acts involved hunting people as animals, commandeering girls, stealing wives, and raping and sexually tormenting others. Listening for twisted sounds maintains "a technique of nearness."[89] It allows concentrating on nonnarrativity and sound, the convulsive quality of sadistic violence, and the hidden, shameful, and "unfit for repetition."

Abjection and anguish were immediate. Uncanniness and the eerie came after the fact, for some, in remembering, hearing about, and seeing again and again in a photographic image. There is not a hint of evidence that the atrocity photographs ever circulated in the colony; there were no shocking magic lantern phantasmagoria in the Congo. Perhaps this helps us understand the absence of a spectral mode of narration in the 1954 Congolese memories (quite unlike the ubiquity of this mode in the West since Morel first began miming Joseph Conrad's prose).

Some "intimate injuries . . . appear as only faint traces," notes Stoler. Dhanis jotted down a chief's swollen finger in his journal. It does important work to identify detached body fragments—hands, feet, or heads—as instant debris of empire in the Congo. A corrosive violence emerged from having access to the barrel of a gun, by which one could enlarge petty power and accumulate wealth in women in a situation of hunger, chaos, and devastation. Dhanis worried about the sentries as thieves, stealing until people had nothing left, robbing them of wives, too. Four Bongulu sentries in charge of sixty-five rubber gatherers wanted to take their women, but killed their dogs instead. "We can keep nothing" was the lament. Similarly, in the 1954 memories, François Bombute wrote: "If there were bananas in the banana patch, it is only he who cut them. If he discovered you ate these bananas, he killed you right away."[90] Even more vivid were sexual violence and transgressive excess—sentries who made mothers have sex with sons, fathers with daughters, kin with kin. Of particular note is the mention of sentries "amusing themselves while pounding the insides of women's vaginas with sticks."[91] Such a strong, graphic image suggests acute pain, writhing bodies, damaged reproductive tracts and desire, damage caused to women in an era long before there were gynecologists around to speak about psychosocial trauma or proceed with fistula repair.

Repetition and Difference

It is time to return to Nsongo Mboyo and the rape of women and girls there in 2003 by Bemba's former troops. The UNFPA film *Les âmes brisées*, by Khalil Gueye, includes the words of one Nsongo Mboyo woman raped on that December night, speaking months afterward: "I do not deserve to live any longer. Several soldiers tied my feet and legs and raped me one after the other. Then they forced my own father, threatening him with their weapons to make love with me. After that, they inserted pieces of wood and their gun barrels into my vagina. They hurt me so much morally and physically."[92] In 2007 the DVD of *Les âmes brisées* was readily available at a convention gathering together African gynecologists and obstetricians in Kinshasa. The Congolese minister of health spoke about new specialized training programs to prepare gynecologists to deal with the psychosocial and fistula repair needs of Congo's thousands of rape victims.[93] The film mentions 24,520 rapes recorded in Kindu between March 2003 and August 2005; 6,000 of these involved traumatic fistula needing surgical intervention.[94] Some tears cannot be repaired; 260 women in Bukavu in December 2007 had received surgical attention, but would live with urine-collecting pouches appended to their bodies for the rest of their days.[95]

The repetitions are multiple. At the same time, much is new. The differences between humanitarian intervention into human wreckage in the Congo Free State and again since 1996 are enormous. In each, shocking numbers and "shock-photos" produce revulsion and pity among spectators, and also produce humanitarian funds.[96] Today, however, humanitarian intervention is highly medicalized and bureaucratized. In Congo it involves all kinds of national—not just foreign—humanitarian workers, negotiating the readings of their ethnic identities at roadblocks and clinics.[97] In the case of rape, these humanitarian workers are applying, adjusting, and revising imported gynecological, trauma, and gender sciences—in ways not yet studied. Other post-1989 contexts of peacekeeping operations and rape, like Bosnia, suggest that complex assumptions about speech, shame, posttraumatic stress disorder, and psychopharmaceuticals are having material effects within this UN-administered "global reservation."[98]

The exceedingly medicalized nature of humanitarian attention to rape in the DRC includes constructing a novel gynecological category, the traumatic fistula.[99] And this injury forces a reflective return to the epidemiological theorizing of the demographic historian David Voas, who came close to wondering around twenty-five years ago if rape in "hostage houses" was not the major factor in spreading STDs and producing a low birth rate in Congo's Équateur.[100] Voas assumed a causal logic that had STDs—sterilizing gonorrhea or chlamydia, miscarriage-producing syphilis—as the mechanism linking rape and infertility. Similarly, rape in the DRC has attention focused on AIDS today. Pounding the inside of a vagina violently with sticks in an era before Coke bottles suggests tearing, blood, and infection, while unmended fistulae in the Free State years would have produced incontinence, stigmatization, and untold humiliation.

It will never be possible to quantify the number of rapes in Leopold's Congo. But the evidence on Nsongo Mboyo in May 1904 suggests that residents did not provide rubber as taxed, many women became hostages, at least eighty-three persons were killed, forms of cannibalism ensued, while in neighboring villages "guards amused themselves in forcing villagers to commit incestuous sexual acts."[101] The same kind of "grotesque excess" was present within the imaginary of memory in 1954.[102] The Nsongo Mboyo events of 1904 produced the father Nsala, who wrapped up body parts of his devoured daughter and took them to Baringa to protest before Abir agents; he ended up on Alice Harris's verandah, and one result was an iconic magic lantern photograph of this father in grief next to a small hand and foot. Cannibalism and mutilation were more sayable—and more photographable— than either rape or forced incest, which seem to have remained "unfit for repetition" among humanitarians like Roger Casement.

Afterlives

Dhanis also took refuge in his journal by trying to imagine a future, an exit from the ruination he was witnessing. He was seeking a way for the Abir company to overcome its current disaster and achieve a viable future through plantations and well-organized markets. This fantasy embraced a way to create a middle rank of industrious, partly "civilized" Congolese. It included numerical and bodily control, through counting and inscribing names in registers and identity books. Dhanis was planning a future through "civilizing" the perpetrators, the sentries, not the "savage" victims, lowly slavelike persons huddled in mere huts or prisons. Sentries' wives would be paid to clean posts and harvest fields. Rubber plantations would develop.

Dhanis's fantasy in the midst of ruination was not impossible. As memories and the archival record suggest, from about 1910 on a new kind of state, the Belgian Congo, emerged. State agents began collecting names, distributing identity books, and insisting on taxation in money and less murderous forced labor, glossed as customary and "educative." What social roles did former sentries play once Abir dissolved? Much "red rubber" violence was among familiars, and the Abir evidence suggests that whether sentries were familiars or strangers made a difference in the degree of violence and in how the sentry category was remembered. (Abir introduced outsider sentries into Nsongo Mboyo in May 1904 because harsher, more terrifying punishments were needed.)[103] The question of what became of the Free State sentries finds a parallel in the nagging question asked in the DRC these days: will military amalgamation or *brassage* (brewing) work? Can all the men and boys from various rebel armies be integrated into one national army as part of "security sector reform"?

The UNFPA film *Les âmes brisées* speaks to another afterlife, the subject positions of raped women and the difficulties of moving on and remaking lives. It contains an awkward, disturbing scene of a rape victim, whose face is blurred while her husband tries to overcome his impulse to abandon her. His smile is forced, too forced. His effort to give affection seems contrived; visibly, his gesture does not comfort his wife, who appears more strained and withdrawn as a result. The filmmaker tried; perhaps, too, did some UNFPA assistants who wished for such a scene as didactic model. However flawed, it evokes the emotional toxicity of sexualized violence within persons and relationships, within the "everyday work of repair."[104]

Compelling, too, are scenes of rape victims planting new gardens, working together in safety, and making new lives. Images of girls and women gathered in a Catholic Caritas project are disconcerting. They are learning to sew. At first, a few sewing machines suggest capital, a chance to learn an important money-making skill with a technology that costs dear. But the machines disappear quickly, and the dominant image becomes rows of girls learning to embroider with needle, thread, and circular frames. This unsettling flashback to colonial domesticity reinforces an image of the Congolese woman as homemaker, helpmeet, dependent, and needy, obedient wife.[105]

This aspect of Belgian colonial ruination should not be forgotten if we are to understand the dire state of gender relations in Congo today. A domesticizing humanitarianism came into play for girls and women across Belgian colonial terrain in the wake of the human rights disaster that was Leopold's Congo. It is still present, from sewing classes in Catholic mission stations to the fact that in 2007 only 10 of around 550 professors at the University of Kinshasa are women. Girls, even those from intellectual, middle-class families, learn quickly that their role is to be minor and obedient, to serve men (even their university fathers), to find and mind husbands, and to have children. Gender relations are reportedly changing most rapidly in the east, where women have suffered most, where the global word *genre* (gender) has appeared along with peacekeeping operations and trauma science, and where the epidemic in rape has politicized many.[106]

Consider again Boali and the magic lantern show of the 1900s. Unlike Mingo, Boali could be photographed and turned into a pat story. But this almost naked woman was nevertheless difficult to fit into missionary narratives. The lantern show sought to offer an image of the uplift that evangelical missionaries could provide, if allowed to work without the constant turmoil attendant on the rubber regime. One photograph showed mission girls at school, dressed in long, tailored dresses. Missionaries tried to underline Boali as a faithful wife, "mutilated for constancy," but turning this unclothed woman with one foot who had refused rape into a domesticated mission wife was challenging. Boali's photograph—an ambiguous, troubling image—was difficult to control and even dangerous to show repeatedly.

It is important to stay alert to the redemptive projects dreamed up for victims of sexual violence today. More domesticity training will only reinforce the minimization of women. The 2006 UNFPA film may have had multiple audiences in mind, but it remains primarily a promotional piece for Joseph Kabila and his presidency. It does not let resound the strong voices of women who came through war and rape, formed NGOs, and as activist mothers are remaking the home-based gender training of daughters and sons. Surely some are refusing embroidery for daughters and doilies for homes, as they remake lives, seek peace, and say no to rape.[107] But how to catch this, acoustically and visually, is not obvious. Linking the shame and the refusals of raped women today with the sayable and unsayable of Boali's time is one way to begin. Regardless, the point is to listen to distress and refusal as immediacy and as duration.

Conclusion

In this essay I have urged for two kinds of reflection, reading and attentiveness. One has been about remembering and sound. The other has been about duration, reproduction, and repetition.

In demonstrating a sensory, acoustic mode of reading the archive, I have insisted that the debris to be signaled and reappropriated should *not* be photographic. We should avoid repeating the tenacity of the visual and the sense of shock that it reproduces. Rather, parsing the archive means listening for images and sounds in the eye of memory. It calls for hearing a nonspectral acoustic register, the sounds of people scattering in flight, speaking in hushed voices, testifying bravely, remembering through stories marked by song, nicknames, poisonous images, and weeping. This reading has included hearing the sound of tittering, as a man pounds the inside of a woman with a stick as if she was a mortar and his instrument the pestle, crushing systematically, rhythmically.

It is no longer tenable to imagine one can write an urgent, effective history about violence in Leopold's Congo *without* tethering it to the present, to the last decades of postcolonial war, death (of at least four million persons, according to estimates), and sexual violence. Supposing that one could reach back in time and put King Leopold on trial, as the make-believe narrative structure of one historical documentary pretended to do, does little to interrogate the modalities of spectacular violence among Congolese people living then, or how they moved on and remade lives and relationships.[108]

Tethering to the present need not be about continuity or causality; one context did not necessarily produce another. Nor is the point to forge historical links between two situations of militias and sexual violence, as if each were part of a single historicist stream of history that began long ago in primitive Africa. It may be appealing to look at the history of Congo as "one single catastrophe which keeps piling wreckage upon wreckage" before us, yet the "pile of debris" still needs sorting.[109] And then it needs form. (One continuous narrative would distort much, and be impossible.)

Rather, tethering to the present should be about locating repetitions and producing history in a "mode of repetition." The first has an analytic purchase, suggesting how to read the archive, how to sort the debris. The second is about strategic—thus, for the academic historian, largely formal—reappropriations of some bits for the present producing or telling of history. Form matters: it constitutes the refining of theory and politics in historical writing and analysis. In this essay, an analytic grounded in revealing acoustics has shaped selection and form at every turn.

Boali's lost foot, stolen anklet, and verbal claim became a storied fragment, a "moment of difference from the past" used to "produce an effect of difference."[110] Repetition in a strategic mode could mean importing Boali into radio discussions and hip-hop songs about rape and war in today's Congo. Doing so might produce debate about war crimes and commissions of inquiry. That such a commission existed within the Free State remains understated, when a historian like Hochschild places too strong of a heroic spin on the pressures that Morel exerted from Britain and beyond.[111] We need to remember that this same pressure produced the king's historic Commission of Inquiry. Congolese in the hundreds spoke before it and with intimate detail about injury. Despite Leopold's success in suppressing the testimony and abridging the commissioners' report, this public forum of testifying about violence, injury, and atrocity changed the course of history. King Leopold lost his colony. He also did not manage to control or destroy all the evidence; much documentation still awaits further parsing by historians.

Seizing hold of repetitions produces questions about what has not been reproduced—about what is novel and different in today's present. A key parallel lies in complexly layered war economies, with globally sought raw products (rubber then, coltan and other minerals now) fueling violence and battles that become localized in dimension, meaning, and escalation.[112] Another parallel is spectacular, telescoped, and devastating violence. But "the signature" has shifted.[113] Images of mutilated hands have not been repeated in Congo, despite their ubiquity in media representations of other 1990s wars in Africa. The sentry may have become a child soldier, a *genocidaire*, or a Mai-Mai, but the signature of horror serving as humanitarian fuel lies in the much less photographable figure of a raped girl or woman. Three repetitions should make us pause: the armed militia (sentry) figure, the sexually transgressed girl or woman, and the partially redeemed female victim figure. Each opens issues of social roles and subject positions and their repetitions over time. It is important to keep tracking how each becomes symbolic within humanitarian phantasmagoria and within the new Congolese national imaginary still in formation.[114]

Notes

This essay is reproduced by permission of the American Anthropological Association. It originally appeared in *Cultural Anthropology* 23, no. 2 (2008): 220–53, and cannot be used for sale or further reproduction.

I am grateful to Patricia Hayes, Julie Livingston, Farina Mir, Kim Fortun, Hugh Raffles, and Gary Wilder for comments on drafts of this article, and especially to Ann Stoler for her comments, suggestions, and generous encouragement and support during the many lives and ruins of this essay.

1. Gueye, *Les âmes brisées*; Integrated Regional Information Networks, "Democratic Republic of Congo (DRC)"; Kambale, "La condamnation des soldats violeurs redonne l'espoir à d'autres femmes victimes," Inter Press Service, Kinshasa, 23 April 2007, http://www.ipsnews.net; United Nations Mission to the Congo (MONUC), "MONUC Expresses Its Satisfaction about the Verdict of the Songo Mboyo Case." The multiple wars in the DRC since 1996, which have cost around four million lives, are complex (see Coghlan et al., "Mortality in the Democratic Republic of Congo"). They date back to the Rwandan genocide of 1994, and cannot be understood without attention to the extractive economics and shadow networks involved (Jackson, "Making a Killing"; United Nations Panel of Inquiry, "Final Report of the Panel of Experts on the Illegal Exploitation of Natural Resources and Other Forms of Wealth of the Democratic Republic of the Congo").

2. Abir was founded as the Anglo-Belgian India Rubber and Exploration (ABIR) company in 1892. In 1898, at which time all British capital had been withdrawn, ABIR became Abir (Harms, "The End of Red Rubber"). In 1891–92 King Leopold issued a set of secret decrees that reversed the Free State's previous free-trade policy, made it resemble a state monopoly, and enabled the rubber regime and its brutalities. One decree gave all "vacant lands" to the Free State. At the same time, Leopold gave tens of thousands of acres to concessionary companies in which he held major investments. Thus, when Abir was founded, in 1892, the Free State gave it the exclusive right to exploit all forest products for a thirty-year period; people living in Abir territory were to collect wild rubber for the company in lieu of paying taxes to the state. Abir received rights of police and powers of bodily detention, enabling the system of company-recruited and armed militia, the notorious forest guards or sentries (see Harms, "The End of Red Rubber"). Also key to the systematicity of rubber violence was payment of bonuses or commissions to functionaries for the amount of produce collected, thus providing incentives for maximal exploitation (Síocháin and Sullivan, *The Eyes of Another Race*, 6). On humanitarian efforts, see Initiative Conjointe de Lutte contres les Violences Sexuelles Faites aux Femmes et aux Enfants en RDC, "Rapport de mis-

sion à Mbandaka, Kisangani, Kindu, Kalemie, Bukavu, Goma, Kinshasa, du 4 au 21 aout 2003"; Lussy and Matemo, "La violence sexuelle des jeunes filles à Goma"; Senga Kossy, "Kinshasa abrite le 9ème Congrès de la Société Africaine Gynécologie Obstétrique"; compare with Csete and Kippenberg, *The War within the War*.

3. Congo Reform Association, "Treatment of Women and Children in the Congo State, 1895–1904"; Morel, *King Leopold's Rule in Africa*; Hochschild, *King Leopold's Ghost*; Grant, *A Civilised Savagery*. The British consul Roger Casement mentioned at Bongandanga that 242 "men of the district named Nsungamboyo," twenty miles away, had "marched in a long file, guarded by sentries," bringing rubber to the factory grounds. According to Harms, "Sungamboyo" was an Abir post, where people rebelled in late 1905 (Harms, "The End of Red Rubber," 85–86).

4. See Stoler's essay in this volume.

5. Sliwinski, "The Childhood of Human Rights," 355. Also see Hunt, *A Colonial Lexicon of Birth Ritual, Medicalization, and Mobility in the Congo*.

6. Barthes, "Shock-Photos."

7. E. D. Morel coined the expression "red rubber" with his book of this name, suggesting that the rubber became bloody, hands were cut off, and so forth (Morel, *Red Rubber*). Historians of Africa since the 1970s have referred to this period in Congolese history (ca. 1892–1908) as the "red rubber" period.

8. Hochschild, *King Leopold's Ghost*, 116–17.

9. Grant, *A Civilised Savagery*.

10. Morel, *Red Rubber*, verso.

11. Warner, *Phantasmagoria*, 353, 202; compare with Grant, *A Civilised Savagery*; Sliwinski, "The Childhood of Human Rights"; and Sontag, *Regarding the Pain of Others*.

12. Caruth, *Unclaimed Experience*, 3.

13. The longer duration in the Abir region embraces preceding slave raiding, from at least the 1870s through the early Free State years. This aspect tends to be missed in a historiography that seeks to find a villain in King Leopold and a hero in E. D. Morel (Bate, *Congo*; Hochschild, *King Leopold's Ghost*).

14. Morel, *Red Rubber*, verso.

15. Morel, *King Leopold's Rule in Africa*; Morel, *Red Rubber*. Boali appears in Morel's pamphlet, "The Indictment against the Congo Government," E. D. Morel Papers, F13/3/2, London School of Economics Archives.

16. Hochschild, *King Leopold's Ghost*; Bate, *Congo*.

17. At the same time, the Congo Free State became the Belgian Congo.

18. Hochschild, *King Leopold's Ghost*, 5.

19. Congo Reform Association, "Treatment of Women and Children in the Congo State, 1895–1904," 22–23.

20. Hochschild works to use Congolese voices and mediations as his book progresses. His suggestion about a lack of African voices has been repeated inaccurately by a visual studies scholar who claims that "aside from Roger Casement's attempt to record the testimony of those maimed individuals he encountered directly, there are simply no accounts (oral or written) from any Congolese person during the Free

State's regime" (Sliwinski, "The Childhood of Human Rights," 357–58n2). Sliwinski misreads Casement and also misses Hochschild's argument about finding "the voices of the Congolese themselves" in "a searing collection of firsthand African testimony," the Commission of Inquiry depositions (Hochschild, *King Leopold's Ghost*, 255). The Lomongo-language essays did not become available in print in a French translation until 1995–96.

21. Few historians have used these depositions; for exceptions, see Marchal, E. D. *Morel contre Léopold II*; Delathuy, *De Geheime Documentatie van de Onderzoekcommissie in de Kongostaat*; and, in a minor way, Hochschild, *King Leopold's Ghost*.

22. Boali of Ekolongo, Deposition no. 172, 12 December 1905, testimony at Baringa, AE 528 (349), Campagne anti-congolaise, Commission d'enquête, liasse 1, African Archives, Belgian Ministry of Foreign Affairs, Brussels.

23. Hunt, *A Nervous State*.

24. Síocháin and Sullivan, *The Eyes of Another Race*, 126.

25. Ibid., 163.

26. Ibid., 140.

27. Hunt, *A Colonial Lexicon of Birth Ritual, Medicalization, and Mobility in the Congo*.

28. Numerous name and boundary changes make the term *Équateur* a shifting refer- ent over time. I use the term to refer to the southern Équateur region, thus south of the Congo, Lulonga, and Lopori Rivers, embracing the former Abir zone as well as much Crown domain and SAB territory in the Ruki, Tshuapa, and Lake Leopold II districts.

29. Chambers, "Lomako," 327.

30. Van Herp, Parqué, Rackley, and Ford, "Mortality, Violence and Lack of Access to Health-Care in the Democratic Republic of the Congo"; Boelaert, Vinck, and Lon- kama, "Arrivée des Blancs sur les bords des rivières équatoriales."

31. Síocháin and Sullivan, *The Eyes of Another Race*, 249.

32. Ibid., 144.

33. Ibid., 132.

34. Hochschild, *King Leopold's Ghost*.

35. Harms, "The End of Red Rubber."

36. Mountmorres, *The Congo Independent State*, 45–47.

37. Hunt, *A Nervous State*.

38. Van Riel and Allard, *Contribution à l'étude de la dénatalité dans l'ethnie mongo*.

39. Romaniuk, "The Demography of the Democratic Republic of Congo"; Ro- maniuk, "Infertility in Tropical Africa"; Voas, "Subfertility and Disruption in the Congo Basin"; compare with Hunt, "Colonial Medical Anthropology and the Making of the Central African Infertility Belt."

40. Magis, "Consultations de stérilité à l'hopital de Boende."

41. Hunt, *A Colonial Lexicon of Birth Ritual, Medicalization, and Mobility in the Congo*.

42. Allard, "Contribution gynécologique à l'étude de la stérilité."

43. Hunt, " 'Le bébé en brousse' "; Hunt, *A Colonial Lexicon of Birth Ritual, Medicaliza- tion, and Mobility in the Congo*; Harootunian, "Some Thoughts on Comparability and the Space-Time Problem."

44. Hunt, *A Colonial Lexicon of Birth Ritual, Medicalization, and Mobility in the Congo*.

45. Warner, *Phantasmagoria*, 273.

46. Taussig, *Shamanism, Colonialism and the Wild Man*, 10.

47. It is now available in a superbly edited edition: Síocháin and Sullivan, *The Eyes of Another Race*.

48. Harms, "The End of Red Rubber"; Baron Francis Dhanis, Large Abir Journal, 21 April–11 September 1904, Historical Section, Royal Museum of Central Africa, Tervuren, Belgium. The only historian to use Dhanis's journal is Vangroenweghe, *Du sang sur les lianes*.

49. Taussig, *Shamanism, Colonialism and the Wild Man*, 10.

50. Stoler, "Intimidations of Empire."

51. Boelaert, Vinck, and Lonkama, "Arrivée des Blancs sur les bords des rivières équatoriales."

52. Síocháin and Sullivan, *The Eyes of Another Race*, 156.

53. Ibid., 84.

54. Ibid., 170.

55. Ibid., 155–56.

56. Ibid., 149.

57. Ibid.

58. Ibid., 152.

59. Boelaert, Vinck, and Lonkama, "Arrivée des Blancs sur les bords des rivières équatoriales," 108–10.

60. Ibid., 47–49, 62–71, 165–66.

61. Ibid., 36–39.

62. Síocháin and Sullivan, *The Eyes of Another Race*, 47.

63. Ibid., 69.

64. Ibid., 158.

65. Ibid., 95.

66. Ibid., 98, emphasis added.

67. Ibid., 114, emphasis added.

68. Ibid., 75, emphasis added.

69. Ibid., 112, emphasis added.

70. Ibid., 149.

71. Ibid., 151.

72. Boelaert, Vinck, and Lonkama, "Arrivée des Blancs sur les bords des rivières équatoriales," 143–45.

73. Síocháin and Sullivan, *The Eyes of Another Race*, 158.

74. Boelaert, Vinck, and Lonkama, "Arrivée des Blancs sur les bords des rivières équatoriales," 51–52.

75. Ibid., 54–58. More research is needed within these memories on how Congolese read the ethnic identities of soldiers and sentries, and how Abir used readings to control and punish labor. How a company like Abir recruited sentries is not well documented (Vangroenweghe, *Du sang sur les lianes*).

76. Baron Francis Dhanis, Large Abir Journal, 21 April–11 September 1904, 211, Historical Section, Royal Museum of Central Africa, Tervuren, Belgium.

77. Baudelaire, "L'essence du rire et généralement du comique dans les arts plastiques."

78. Bataille, "Writings on Laughter, Sacrifice, Nietzsche, Unknowing," 90.

79. Ibid., 70.

80. My reading of laughter through Bataille may suggest that I think laughter can be read in a universal way. Rather, not unlike Mbembe in *On the Postcolony*, I find Bataille and Sony Labou Tansi useful for thinking about death, excess, and laughter in central African cultures. More ethnographic work on laughter within Africa's current zones of war and suffering would be instructive.

81. Síocháin and Sullivan, *The Eyes of Another Race*, 76.

82. Bataille, "Writings on Laughter, Sacrifice, Nietzsche, Unknowing," 97.

83. Hochschild, *King Leopold's Ghost*, 234.

84. Ibid., 166.

85. This is not to suggest that these acts of violence were fantastic, in the sense of implausible or untrue. Drawing attention to the poetic, tale-telling quality of repetition here suggests the phantastic, thus the psychic at work within this secondhand memory account fifty years removed.

86. Boelaert, Vinck, and Lonkama, "Arrivée des Blancs sur les bords des rivières équatoriales," 240–42.

87. Mingo of Ilua, Deposition no. 267, 2 January 1906, testimony at Bonginda, AE 528 (349), Campagne anti-congolaise, Commission d'enquête, liasse 1, African Archives, Belgian Ministry of Foreign Affairs, Brussels; Hochschild also uses Mingo's testimony (*King Leopold's Ghost*, 254–55).

88. Broch-Due, "Violence and Belonging," 25. I am grateful to Julie Livingston for first suggesting that I reckon with the creativity of the violence.

89. Benjamin, *The Arcades Project*.

90. Boelaert, Vinck, and Lonkama, "Arrivée des Blancs sur les bords des rivières équatoriales," 54–58.

91. Ibid., 211. See Vangroenweghe, *Du sang sur les lianes*, 134, for a similar instance near Boende. Casement never used the word *rape* (although there is a mention of removing "the organs of the mean slain by the sentries" (Síocháin and Sullivan, *The Eyes of Another Race*, 125). Nor did he use the more ambiguous word *ravish*. Historians have become less shy on a topic for which evidence is rarely explicit. "Institutionalized rape was not uncommon, and such sentries often lived en pacha," state Síocháin and Sullivan (*The Eyes of Another Race*, 321n43), speaking about rubber districts near Équateur's Irebu, but they do not say how they reached this conclusion. Hochschild speaks of "raped hostages" in passing (*King Leopold's Ghost*, 175), and quotes from a Force Publique officer's 1895 diary in Uele, far northeast of Équateur: "The women taken during the last raid at Engwettra are causing me no end of trouble. All the soldiers want one. The sentries who are supposed to watch them unchain the prettiest ones and rape

them" (*King Leopold's Ghost*, 162). Tswambe, one of Boelaert's sources, speaks—within Hochschild's book too (*King Leopold's Ghost*, 166)—of the way armed men forced people to commit transgressive sexual violence against their own kin: "Soldiers made young men kill or rape their own mothers and sisters."

92. Gueye, *Les âmes brisées.*

93. Senga Kossy, "Kinshasa abrite le 9ème congrès de la Société Africaine Gynécologie Obstétrique."

94. Gueye, *Les âmes brisées*; compare with United Nations Mission to the Congo, "South Kivu."

95. Personal communication, Madame Maria Mukaya of UNICEF, following UNICEF-Centre Culturel Américain Workshop on Gender Violence for Hip-Hop Musicians, Kinshasa, 26 November 2006.

96. Sliwinski, "The Childhood of Human Rights"; Redfield, "Doctors, Borders and Life in Crisis"; Malkki, "Speechless Emissaries."

97. Pottier, "Roadblock Ethnography."

98. Harrington, "Governing Peacekeeping"; Amitav Ghosh, "The Global Reservation." The UN Security Council set up MONUC in 1999; the council expanded its peacekeeping mandate and size in 2000.

99. Western mainstream media attention to rape in the Congo—from *Glamour* to the *New York Times*—suggests the "rape card" is effective in producing humanitarian funds; it distracts the media from asking about Laurent Nkunda's funding or the extractive economics of the ongoing war (Snow, "Three Cheers for Eve Ensler?"). Keith Harmon Snow's conspiracy-like reporting is problematic, but he points to who is benefiting from war in Congo and how, and provides information about specific persons, corporations, embassies, and organizations that rarely appear in mainstream or humanitarian media. See his website, All Things Pass, http://www.allthingspass.com. For news and articles on sexual violence in Congo, provided by Eve Ensler's Congo-related website, see http://drc.vday.org/news.

100. Voas, "Subfertility and Disruption in the Congo Basin."

101. Vangroenweghe, *Du sang sur les lianes*, 125. The village, known alternately as Nsongo Mboyo and as Wala, was located in the Nsongo Mboyo district.

102. Broch-Due, "Violence and Belonging," 25.

103. Vangroenweghe, *Du sang sur les lianes.*

104. Das, *Life and Words*, 62.

105. Hunt, *A Colonial Lexicon of Birth Ritual, Medicalization, and Mobility in the Congo*; Hunt, "Hommes et femmes, sujets du Congo colonial."

106. Harrington, "Governing Peacekeeping."

107. Puechguirbal, "Women and War in the Democratic Republic of the Congo."

108. Bate, *Congo.*

109. Benjamin, "On the Concept of History," 392.

110. Harootunian, "The Benjamin Effect," 75.

111. Hochschild, *King Leopold's Ghost.*

112. Vlassenroot and Raeymaekers, "The Politics of Rebellion and Intervention in Ituri."

113. Das, *Life and Words*.

114. Lévi-Strauss noted this, long ago, in his discussion of history in *The Savage Mind*.

The Coolie

An Unfinished Epic

The following is a selection from a forthcoming book which I have, provisionally, if immodestly, called an "epic in verse." This selection consists of nine chapters and synopses of the two opening chapters out of a complement of fifteen chapters. My debt to the great Derek Walcott should be obvious to all. I hope I am forgiven for, among other things, flattering myself by the best form of imitation that my talents allow.

For some of my readers this poem may bring to mind the call for experimental ethnography broadcast by George Marcus and Michael M. J. Fischer more than two decades ago, and they may therefore read this as a somewhat late response to that call.[1] If it happens to serve such a purpose, it is so by default, and I am willing to either apologize or accept accolades, as the case may be. The real reason for my launching this ethnohistorical poem is a much more down-to-earth and practical one, a piece of serendipity. The recent history of the island that was once upon a time known as Serendib has not itself been that serendipitous, especially for its Tamil minorities. My own work is based on one moiety of the Tamil-speaking peoples of this island, whose last name was Ceylon and which has been known as Sri Lanka since 1972.

The half that I have worked on consists of Tamils of South Indian origin, who labor on Sri Lankan plantations or "estates" as they are locally called, for periods ranging from several months to a year, at irregular intervals, over the last twenty-five years. These Tamils are distinguished from the indigenous, Sri Lankan Tamils by dialect and habitation. My father worked on one of these estates during the first twenty years of my life. Except for two periods—when I was between ages four and ten, we lived in the town of Kandy in order to be within walking distance (six miles round-trip) of a "good" school; when I was between ages fifteen and eighteen, I spent nine out of twelve months each year in boarding school in Jaffna—I grew up on a tea plantation. The first time that I did ethnographic research as such among tea plantation workers, called "coolies," who worked with their hands in the fields and factories, however, was in 1973, for three months, prior to beginning my predoctoral field research in a village in South India.[2]

Since then, my interest in the lives of estate workers has led me to two sources of information: oral history and ethnography; and written records about coffee, rubber, and tea plantations that were made available to me in far-flung private and public archives in Sri Lanka, India, and Britain and in the writings of a few pioneering historians who had researched and written on these Tamils. Apart from the latter and a handful of anthropological studies, the written record consists of very little that was about the actual lives (especially the unquantifiable aspects of the lives) of the so-called coolies.[3] In the archives was plenty of information—with dates, if not always with names—on matters that had an immediate bearing on colonial and postcolonial politics and economics. Oral history and ethnography, on the other hand, provided me with gems of information polished by tongue and time, but with very few reliable dates and names concerning the persons, places, and events that were recorded, repeated, or recalled in them. Each of these two sources was rich in one and destitute in the other, forming an irreconcilable complementarity, a challenging symmetry. After almost three decades of intermittent struggles with this duality and failed attempts at writing a documental and chronologized history, a year or so ago, in a state of pure musement,[4] as I was attempting to construct a clear sentence with "substantiatable" content, I found that the sentence took on a life of its own and settled into three tercets of iambic hexametrical, twelve-syllabic lines in terza rima (aba, bcd, cda, and so on). I was writing in verse! A bonus to this pleasant surprise came in the form of a discovery: a truth in verse that could not be conveyed in prose, a truth that was present at hand in oral history and ethnography but made distant or secondary in prose. I believe that most prose in the social sciences in particular does not merely overshadow or repress this affective truth in its secondary status but may even kill it. In the form of verse that I have chosen to narrate the ethnohistory of the Tamil coolie, the certainties of prose are neither absent nor neutralized but are given a supportive and constraining role. Whereas poiesis is responsible for the truth I speak of, prose keeps this truth honest. An analogue to the pairing of poetry and prose and prose in poetry may be found in the way ancient Tamil grammar conceptualizes vowels and consonants: one was seen as force and the other as form, as the breath and the body, as goddess and god, as female principle and male principle, as the flowing and the standing, as propelling and fixing. But even a narrative poem that could be told as a prose tale is not just another way of telling the tale. The coordinates of the aesthetic faculty employed in a poem—even in a prose poem—demand of sense and sound an economy that is so exacting that it is achieved through compression of language into an image that is neither more nor less, but just right, for conveying the essence of an event such that the desired feelings and meanings made possible by that event are made available to the reader or the listener by the singer-poet.[5] Far be it from me to claim that I have succeeded at this challenge in this poem. This is only an attempt, and for that matter, only a selection from such an attempt. Valéry once wrote what became for him a lifelong writing belief: we do not finish writing a poem, only abandon it in despair. In the case of this poem, it is too early even for that.

I have taken many liberties with the reader, some because I must, others because I may. Some names have been changed, not only because of the interpretive and composite nature of the poem, but also in deference to the expressed requests of the trustees of the letters and private journals from which I have drawn in writing this poem. I have changed the names of men and women whose lives, or excerpts thereof, figure in the poem, mostly in deference to the requests of their grandchildren, great-grandchildren, nieces, and nephews who held these letters in trust. I have tried my best to honor these requests by protecting the identities of the trustees' ancestors. A few trustees had no objections to my providing any and all details of identity of the authors. In one instance, I was told that I was free to reveal the identity of an ancestor in question without reservation, provided I secured the permission of the surviving progeny, which was too formidable a task to fulfill. In a third instance, a trustee insisted that I provide any necessary details of the authors of the journals and letters entrusted to her care. But having looked at all the permissions and requests collectively, and for the sake of uniformity, I have chosen to avoid naming anyone whose trustees placed conditions that I could not meet. Furthermore, because of my ignorance of some of these planter-patriarchs' fuller lives—lacking sufficiently comprehensive biographies on any of them—and because such details that I did gather were from (mostly) plantation workers' accounts, the accounts are likely to be partial and selective at best, decontextualized snippets of their lives and persons. Under these circumstances if I were to explicitly link event to name, I would run the risk of bringing dishonor to the dead and embarrassment to the living in their recontextualized uses. Therefore, in all but a few obvious cases, which are noted, I have taken the liberty to change and omit names. There are characters who appear in this long poem who are semblances or composites of others or of one another. Some I have, from events and facts, realized and written into being. I have also overlaid places and collapsed times in order to protect their identities.

The following individuals gave me free access to their ancestors' letters, from which I have freely drawn and adapted to the purpose at hand. These individuals, to whom I owe special thanks, are Ms. Connie Langdon, grand-niece of Mr. A. T. Sydney Smith; Mr. Robert Hatkins, grandson of Mr. John Hatkins; Ms. Myrtle Grey, grandniece of Mr. Terryl W. N. Gascoygne; Ms. Georgiana Boyd, descendant of Ms. James Taylor; Mr. Robert Hollings-worth, descendant of Mr. H. R. Trafford; and Mr. Arunachalam Somasun-deram, trustee of the letters and diaries of Byde Martin.

I have tapped a host of memories, mostly those of plantation workers. The singers, balladeers, storytellers, and raconteurs from whose talents, knowl-edge, wisdom, and recollections I draw are too many to list. I shall mention but nineteen individuals without whose help this project would not have been possible: the singers Sowpakkiam, Marimutthu, Sathasivam, Manon-mani, and Sankili; and the storytellers and raconteurs Sowpakkiam, Kutti Letchumi, Parameswari, Aravandi, Bhuma, Sellasamy, Kitnan, Dhamayan-thi, Poochiyayi, Sombu, Muruhupathy, Sokkuppulavar, Arunachalam Pillai, and Kuppusamy Thevar. In this list I must reserve a special place for the late C. V. Veluppillai, who was a rich source of the folklore of plantation Tamils, and for Mr. Murugesu Pushparajah, who has rescued me out of my ignorance on more than a few occasions. Last but mostly, I am also deeply indebted to my brother, George Daniel, who was a clerk and a field officer on a tea plan-tation for thirty years, and taught me a great deal about the workings of a tea plantation and the lives of people who worked on them.

What nineteenth-century colonialism did to more than thirty million human beings by turning them into coolies, the massive contribution of labor to colonial capitalism that was made possible by this transmogrifica-tion, and the positive role colonialism and the plantation economy played in the making of a modern nation-state amounts to but half of the story. The other half lies in the violence wreaked on the land and the people by the political economy of colonialism in general and, in particular, by the plantation economy—one of colonial capitalism's most productive enterprises of the nineteenth century and the first half of the twentieth. Unlike the urban ruins observed and written about by Walter Benjamin or W. G. Sebald, plantations are ruins that both fit more snugly and give a new twist to Georg Simmel's description of our fascination with a physical ruin as the "fascination of a ruin, that . . . a work of man appears to us entirely as a product of nature."[6] Tea estates are deceptively called "tea gardens" in tourist brochures. But looking at them as "imperial debris" gives tea gardens a whole new meaning, turning them into Benjamin's "angels of history."[7]

A peculiar feature of this poem pertains to voice. Typical of an oral epic, the poem features multiple voices telling narratives within narratives, including the author's own voice and perspective, which pops up unannounced. In the song-poems, inscapes become landscapes and landscapes inscapes. This is in keeping with a Tamil poetic tradition that goes back to the *sangam* age of early Tamil literature, even though the landscapes invoked are not neatly and necessarily the five landscapes of the classical Tamil poetry of that age (ca. 100 BC–AD 250).[8]

Three last details. The first concerns the use of French, German, and Latin in this poem. This usage is merely intended to convey, by analogy, the fact that the Tamils I worked among and whom I represent in this poem also sprinkle their speech with words and expressions drawn from two foreign languages: English and Sinhala. In fact, Tamils in general are far more "learned" in one or more languages other than their native tongue than is the average English speaker. The utterances in English or Sinhala that have been diagrammatically represented in the poem in Latin or French also indicate that they are explicitly performative, with accompanying illocutionary and perlocutionary force.

Second, occasionally in this poem, the reader will recognize a line or phrase or an echo from a renowned English poet, such as Shakespeare's "to be or not to be?" Such phrases are diagrammatic of great Tamil poets and aphorists of yore whom Tamil speakers of all classes and levels of education know by heart and take special pride in quoting.

The last detail concerns the use of quotation marks. Only the words, phrases, and sentences that are not within quotation marks are to be read as purely the author's own. Words, phrases, sentences, images, and figures of speech that are within quotation marks may not be verbatim quotes drawn from what the many friends, acquaintances, and strangers told me during my many years of research among them. However, these poetic forms are culled from the essential substance of actual interviews and archival sources.

The chunks of narrated and observed predicaments, and of expressions of emotional, sensory, and cognitive memories that have been worked on have been approached with great attention and care to cut along the grain of specific details embedded in these chunks, and thus to be faithful to the ethnographic context and archived material. Even though most of the verbal treasures I have made use of in the writing of this poem are not literal translations, all of them have been translated with a concern for faithfulness of idiom, sense, and context—and only then, for sound. Along this same vein, I have made no attempt to directly translate or transliterate, word for word, the folksongs I collected in the field; but, again, the ethnographic narratives in this poem are based on the content and meanings of these folksongs and the affect they were intended to convey by those who sang and understood them. For these reasons, the narrative herein I hold to be neither more nor less factitious than any ethnography in prose. It is just that the facts are realized in a different register, with painstaking attention for economy and accuracy of detail, especially aesthetic detail.

CHARACTERS

(In order of appearance)

Adhipathy or (Adhi for short): The name of the blacksmith and singer of tales of times past, present, and future.

Rukku or Rukkumani: The blacksmith's daughter, who doubles as the medium who receives the tales from Rāmu and whispers them into her father's ear.

Adhipathy's wife.

Rāmu: The composite ghost-spirit of many Rāmus (pl.) who lived on earth in the flesh in times past.

Gaṇapathy or Gaṇpathy (also called Gaṇesh, Vignēṣvarā, or Vināyakā, and Ekadanta, among others) is the elephant-headed deity, son of Pārvathi and Sivā.

Hanuman: The monkey-god, Lord Rama's henchman in the great Indian epic *Ramayana*.

Rāmar: A form of the name that is reserved in this poem to refer to Lord Rama.

Appu: The multiskilled servant of an Englishman named Mr. Chauncey.

Maṇkalam: Appu's "mongrel" daughter.

Kaḷḷu: Maṇkalam's husband.

Ratnam: Maṇkalam's brother and son of Appu.

Dorai: The title by which men in power, in general, are referred; and by which all white gentlemen, especially one's master, are referred.

Kaṇkāṇi: The title and form of address used for the leader of a gang of workers.

Marvel Stark: An English *dorai* who is the supervisor of a gang of workers (coolies).

Paṭṭar: A coolie who belongs to a caste of "untouchables" called Chakkili.

Thappu: Paṭṭar's sister's son. It is also the name of a drum played by Parayar.

Paṛayan (pl Paṛayar): One who belongs to a Dalit caste who were once called untouchables. Among other services provided to a village community, Parayar also served as drummers at funerals. The drums they played were generically called *parai*.

Chakkiḷian (or Chakkili): One who belongs to a Dalit caste, which was considered to be the lowest in the caste hierarchy among the Tamil-speaking community of Indian descent in Sri Lanka.

Uppu: A worker in Marvel's gang. It is also the word for "salt."

Padmini: A young woman who died in childbirth and whose ghost haunts the jungle.

Thīpori: A young female worker, daughter of Sēthupathy, a member of a higher caste. Also means "spark."

Veṇkaṭēsh: The name of a kaṇkāṇi working under Marvel.

Vāman: A kaṇkāṇi who works under Marvel's successor, a Scotsman named Jon De Witt.

John De Witt: One of Marvel's successors.

THE *KŪLI*

(A Selection)

I

Preamble

(*A synopsis*)

This chapter introduces a blacksmith named Adhipathy and his young daughter, Rukku.[9] Even though Adhipathy is by now an old and decrepit alcoholic whose memory is fast fading, he still has the most beautiful voice in a "wretched hill town" surrounded by tea estates. In a shrine on one of the plantations there has arrived an important visitor: Gaṇapathy,[10] the elephant-headed god and scribe, who once upon a time put the great Indian epic the *Mahabharata* into writing as the sage Vyasa recited it to him. A band of workers from the tea plantation arrive at Adhipathy's forge to coax him into coming with them and to sing before Lord Gaṇapathy, so that he may write down their history and heritage, the stories of their long walk and the travails of their ancestors, who began migrating from South India to Sri Lanka in the first quarter of the nineteenth century.[11] After much protesting and persuading, Adhipathy comes up with a suggestion: since his daughter knows all the songs about this disenfranchised and stateless migrant community, from having listened to him sing of them from when she was a baby, and given that she is still young and has a good memory, she could sing of the history and heritage of her people. Initially, the workers reject the idea as untenable because Gaṇapathy would not be dictated to by womankind. A bright idea dawns on one of the men. He proposes that Rukku could whisper the stories she has stored in her memory into Adhipathy's ear and that he could weave her words into the tunes he knows so well and sing them aloud in his clear-as-a-bell voice so that Gaṇapathy could write them down.

II

Supplication to Vināyakā

(*A synopsis*)

In this chapter, the workers' fear that Lord Gaṇapathy might object even to the whispering of womankind are allayed. So Adhipathy begins with a lengthy recitation of obeisance to Gaṇapathy, who, impatient with the ritual pro forma, commands him to get on with the telling of the tale. But before Adhipathy can proceed, Gaṇapathy warns the bard of one condition: "Once begun, if you should cease your telling, . . . I shall leave in the blink of an elephant's eye." Adhipathy responds with his own stipulation: "On one condition my vermillion adorned Lord and Scribe, that you write not a word more if my drift you should lose as a lutanist a quaver might. Begin anew when you find it." And the anthropologist adds, "T'is the law of hermeneutic, the detail to recover." And so, Rukku, Adhipathy's daughter, begins.

III
Generations and Time

"When I leave this island,"[12] said Rukku, "a single
witness will still remain to tell of the observed
and the absorbed of the shedders of blood mingled

"with blood shed. Mother earth here has been quite reserved,
abashed to confess that she, soaked in venal crude,
puddles her own clay to create out of this sludge,

"coolies as us, over and over again. Lewd
our senses, our ways rude, so deemed by all who judge
and miss our dialect's pulchritude. Eternal

"returnees,[13] requisite detritus. Judge not lest
you too be judged for having seen but not witnessed
harm infernal, unlike Rāmu, who has lived our every test."

"Hey, say! Must I tune my ear to a new bard's throat?
Ignore a girl's intermittent whisperer's rustle
and hearken to a man's pitched braying off note,

"I am told. I agree. Now this: a new hustle
in the mix called Rāmu. Smithy, do we need him?
Is he . . . Vishnu's avatar? The seventh, perhaps?"[14]

"Not to change the subject," said Adhipathy, whimsically, as he changed the subject, devising
distractions deliberately. "Please lend no more

"than a moment at most, the gift your father gave
you so bounteously your loss to you to restore:
those lavish ears with a most capacious head. Brave!

"For want of a stylus, a tusk to break you chose."
Ekadanta[15] winced and with new resolve returned
to press the lost subject: Rāmu. "Must I suppose,

"that spurning my question you may rest unconcerned?
Answer! Does Rāmu belong to the other sect?
Is he one or many?" "Far, far be it from me

"to show you the tiniest glint of disrespect.
Rāmu is recurrent indeed, but more easy-
peasy than Rāmar the vegetarian, who

"sent General Hanuman to this imperfect
island[16] his abducted virgin bride to rescue.
He was on his seventh birth, this Ram you suspect.

"Rāmu, our Rāmu, is non-sectarian,[17]
strictly non-vég, on his sixth—if not on this earth—
in our imagination; the custodian

"of our sensory memory of untold worth."
"Appā!"[18] interjected Rukku. "Incorrect count!
you've missed three generations, each one a life.

"Yours takes us back only to—what is tantamount
to blasphemy—1870! Girl-to-wife-
to-mother, takes thirteen." "Do watch your mouth and tone!

"Men became fathers only at twenty and four."
"'Cept his father! Was fourteen," to her grinding-stone,
his wife mumbled. He, to her indirection's score,

in indirection swore: "Gossip's cognoscenti!"
"Stop quarreling. Find the difference, and I'll be judge,"
the Lord said. "Appā knew he'd said more than plenty.

This was no time to generosity begrudge."
To halve or not to halve was no burning question.
"We shall split the difference, and dissolve the dispute.

"So, may we with no further adjudication,
in concord with language and truth resolute,
re-commence our tale, which takes us, we concluded,

"back to 1829,[19] to Rāmu of fame,
perennial witness of all lives included
since then, in the agentive line that bears his name,

"and bares the biography of an idea."
"An Idea? What ever could that be?" "Coolies
for work, work for coolies, promised panacea

"for all our ills, in this tear-drop island of trees."[20]
Ganesh declared Rāmu in with a "whatever."
A crow[21] with the wind appeared and puffed clouds bestirred

in an otherwise calm sky. Trees set aquiver
as Rāmu's *geist* upon them alit. Word on word
fell like hushed petals in Rukku's bejeweled ears.

All prattle ceased. Her whispers, transformed into song
pierced the rising mist as light would a veil of tears.
Place held time still. "Time," sang Adhi "is neither long

"nor short. Length, could not its unchanging measure be.
Some times are gaugeable, as a repast's vaunted
flavors[22] are, in x lumens of intensity."

"To tack twixt *is, will* and *might be* and the taunted
were's is to sample this, that, and the other at
a meal of cooked rice, sāmbār,[23] rasam,[24] curds, pickle,

"and — if lucky — some meat; savor the sharp, the flat,
contiguities and affinities, the trickle
of ghee; checking feeling's assent with smell and taste.

"Does the green of beans befit its crunch? Is 'just right'
a compliment? Is the sugared pāyāsam[25] chaste?"
Chronicles keep now and then apart and airtight;

they declare time long or short. In heritage,
now becomes then and then becomes now.[26] Five, eight or ten[27]
hereafters reporting to this blend, may somehow

incinder the sum, causing the now into then
to collapse and effervesce, celebrate or mourn
and thereby time's space-analog vitiate. But

never always, nor forever. Its gift to burn
makes time a tree. For in the rings of its clean-cut
wound reposes the past's presence in synchrony.

Lightning splits longitudinally its column
of history. Vignēṣvarā, blessed the journey
with raised trunk. Silence settled on all like a hum.

IV

Labor and Empire

In ancient cities turned tourist sites boys scour
the earth to disinter coins dispersed in commerce,
impressed with Arabic, Greek and Roman sour-

faced heads of men, Indian gods and beasts. These terse
co-bearers of value, the Tamils called *kāsu*.
The Sinhalese re-pitched it to "acute" *kāsi*.

"Grave"[28] *caixa* was a Portuguese amendment. To
hale — Hail Britannia! — fell the honor of re-
cashing it with a phonemic hush. Its timbre,

though, resounded the world over. Victoria
dispensed with justice, trees to fell without number
to redeem unassisted nature.[29] Gloria!

Where sandalwood, clad cinnamon and breadfruit once
flourished in equipoise of give and take with jack,
ebony and Ceylon's rosewood, there in prudence

slithered in Locke's *Law of Nature*,[30] property's lack,
to ask for, seek, find and amend. What paved the way
was *The Law of Conquest*.[31] A retinue of terms,

attendant concepts, like obliging mantissae,
marched in concert: barracks, caserns, and subalterns;
calls to muster, roll calls, check-rolls, acre and mile;

lunch-time, tea time, quitting time, overtime — all clock-
time; ounces, pounds, kilos; rupees and cents; docile
bodies, lost souls, racial types and such poppycock

as in Notes & Queries' ignorance could make one's blood so hot,
so cold. Contracts, fingerprints, promissory notes;
Companies LTD and Company Stores; lots

of debt and more interest; coolies with no votes.
A s/trapping discourse. Due process pursued with Right
and Rule, with well-tempered faith, hope and Christian

Charity. On the heathen recondite go light
unlike the Batavian or Liberian.
Honor the Trinity of Holy "C"s: Conquer,

ye called and chosen; with capital Colonize,
the burden make light; Convert with love the sinner,
by sin be Appalled. The damned corral, tame the wise

as you would the wild. Straighten the crooked—in root,
branch or man non-compliant. Horseless equites,
natives all, gave cause and moral purpose to boot

to mark trees, including some ghostly favorites
—descendants of legends, storied centurions—
for their appointed death by means pre-determined.

"In dying thus, from vagrant and Cimmerian
spirits redeemed, forest from village did exscind,
creating space to sack in from black coffee, tea

"and rubber," Rukku whispered, and Adhi sang. "Tamed
they stood, in ordered rows, in far-flung swaths made free;
owned by the likes of Smith, Gascoyne, Cameron, named

"Raven's Craig, Denmark Hill, Concordia. Prefixed
hills and dales, numbered in the thousands. Cash crops
for cash spread like a green rash on this land suffixed,

"'Estates,' for more cash crops, for more cash. Case? Dunlop's.
A gash in the trunk of an un-lyrical, grey,
seborrheic, lichen-cloaked, foreign and vulgar

"tree.[32] Its buff-flesh pearled an ooze, the color of whey,
that dripped into coconut half-shells. Lest rigor-
mortis set, a drop of pungent ammonia

"its liquidity assured, then spun to repeal
till no more than a lump in myotonia,
more rubber less latex, lay; in trays to congeal.

"These fat slabs reeked of a vinegar-butter blend;
hand-fed between steel rollers made in Manchester,
to mats compressed. Civilization to extend,

"Great Regina or Rex, upon these did confer
the approbation of their persons so Highnessed
—bless them!—in escutcheons, which Royal Right affirmed.

"When wood oven baked caramel tone sufficed,
an expert hand their elasticity confirmed.
Trained eyes pronounced them ready for the seal to fix.

"For this was sacrificed, one black fulminant night,
by the laws of imperial agronomics,
one-hundred-and-one thousand acres of daylight

"eclipsing green canopy of old growth forest.[33]
After-thought coppices of *albizia*[34] trees
were nurtured to serve, at the management's behest

"as swift-burning wood for the punctual coolies.
Colonizers and their fair consorts with much lust
and more leisure to spare, shunned its wily brilliant

"but hurried flame that would slyly lick like mistrust.
The embers dimmed their eyes even before gallant
Scots their clothes doffed. Lovers could but leer at them shrink

"to ash with a mocking hiss, as ecstasy passed.
The likes of Mark and Anne of the well-informed Inc.,
their friends, Clarisse Louder and Cudsworth Melrose Nast,

"Sir Cockshut and Lady Gwen, Nigel and Nancy
and Mark Fell's ivorine wife, had naught to forego.
They sojourned in a misnomer owned by Chauncey

"that Appu built, a villa called a 'bungalow,'
with sporting fireplaces tucked in all rooms.
Jack, rosewood, satinwood and gleam-lashed ebony."

Just because it was good to think—the question looms—
was it good to ignite this slow burning, heavy,
smoke-free hard wood? Ah! Such a Lévi-Straussian

question you say? Quite right. Once while on grubs choking
he split nature from culture, but an avian
thought from power could not tell.[35] "A bell for stoking!

"'Boy!' Ratnam, age thirty, would rush to the noblesse.
His fair half-sister, Maṇkalam, Appu's ecru-
dermal daughter—unmarried, mongrel, motherless—

"had her own story to tell. Not now," said Rukku.
"Today there burns in her a different worry;
less, of the well-lit deeds of lovemaking, Scottish-

"style, which discomposed her brother's gift at parry;
than with albizia, short-lived, yellow, corkish,
measured by the foot, rationed and booked, the steadfast

"flames of her household's hunger to douse with red rice,[36]
if lucky; mostly kurakkan-gruel,[37] ballast
to sate their abdominal languor, or else, price

"her husband's wrath. Appu watered his dorai's[38] bed
of roses with a thin golden stream. Looked further
than he saw. Spat. Shook. Too late to say the unsaid,

"too old to care, except for Maṇkalam's brother
and his three boys. The youngest on disappearance
paused; wondered if the disappeared could disappear;

"his father's sister's unruly husband perchance?
Boys will be boys, well beyond eighty and one year.
Not those boys-will-be-boys doraisānis[39] endure,

"but only what coolies can become by the rule
of race, logic of empire and indenture,
endless youth cumbering life on a squirrel's spool.

"Maṇkal[40] yearned for some time her own life to fathom.
But who'd protect Kaḷḷu[41] from himself? Palmyrah
toddy's namesake, ersatz renouncer, wastrel, bum.

2.1 Line rooms for workers; one 10′ × 10′ room was allotted per family. From S. Muthiah, *The Indo-Lankans: Their 200-Year Saga* (Colombo, Sri Lanka: Indian Heritage Foundation, 2003). Source: S. Muthiah, Indian Heritage Foundation.

"sits on the bench at the shack until dawn. 'Harah!
Hari,' he'll sing some noon. Come home to try to do
his woman, eat, filch trifles, threaten violence,

"and sell or trade his way back to the shack to construe
want. Want-annoyed one noon-day, in the men's absence
he came, kicked up curls of dust, with intent on harm

"he entered his line-room.[42] The air was motionless.
A diurnal ghoul had birthed an uncanny calm.
Maṇkal sensed the presence of inauspiciousness.

"He came, shaft-straight rod in hand, thin as a viper,
drawn from a bundle of like bamboo canes, export-
bound for English Public Schools. A moment riper

"there wasn't, he thought, to thrash his wife for high sport,
He rushed at her from behind, arm raised over head.
When she spun around, a scalding oil-filled frying

"pan in hand. Flipped it on her husband's face, then fled
west, ahead of the police chase, still un-crying
until she met the tracks of steel reposed on ties

"laid by her ancestors, with help from denizens
of local villages. Disobliged by their spies-
deposed king, these peasants re-obliged new reasons

"to bend to the new realm's coin.[43] Lest peasants at six
were to coolies become, they returned home each night,
the siege to keep over this rule of thumb and fix

"thereby Tamil-Sinhala difference as black and white.[44]
Village from sleepy village hid as Maṇkalam each bend
took through the arcade of trees, their arches of thin

"arms swayed pensively, to caress or comprehend,
or perhaps to smite. Fear as intimate as skin
embalmed her. She beseeched Amman[45] to draw nearer.

"Soothed by the early-dawn's dew-covered night cooled steel,
a far-away train's well-kept beat reached beneath her
feet when she heard the sea roar and temple bells' peal."

V
The Clearing

"The ocean, her destination, she'd never seen
but had heard Appu speak of aplenty: restless
sparkle of salty blue, at dusk a jungle green;

"the ship of fools in alimentary distress;
the white man's burden of rules that for themselves stood;
the Big kaṇkāṇi[46] in blinding white vēṭṭi[47] dressed,

"giving and taking tin tokens[48] of cooliehood.
Maṇkalam had hoped to soon reach that mountain crest
where her grandfather at sunset scanned an event:

"'A trembling cauldron of color, that distant sea
was,' he'd said. Unscrolled tales unrolled of their descent
into the grasslands and jungle-laboratory.[49]

2.2 Building the railways upcountry, ca. 1925. From S. Muthiah, *The Indo-Lankans: Their 200-Year Saga* (Colombo, Sri Lanka: Indian Heritage Foundation, 2003). Source: S. Muthiah, Indian Heritage Foundation.

"There, suspended in mid-air, stooping to espy
two rivulets of shimmering brown trickle through
a field of buttercups under a sun-reigned sky

"heading towards the forest where giant trees grew,
a surveiling kite saw two obtusely angled
streams meeting, pausing, pooling, into a circle,

"settling, uncertain as mercury bespangled
ablaze, the trick the noon-day sun in its cycle
played on their sweat-drenched brown—almost maroon—bodies.

"Circle into crescent concaved. Its horns tapered
to tips as of scorpionoid congruities,
poised equidistant from a lone prey co-pincered

"to arrest by pre-hending its ruddy victim
in its hooped claws; but alas, with no arcing tail
to sting with. The quarry, an Englishman in prim

"uniform and topee, grave in every detail,
stood with the right to come on, command and commend.
We called him Dorai the source of all injunctions,

"captain at muster, who may summon, choose and send
whomever. Rock blasters left first. Strict instructions
re: avoiding sudden death; tree-fellers—also

"men—whom chiselers and stone-crushers followed. Steadfast
diggers with strong backs left next. Weeders,[50] with bones oh
so supple or embrittled by age, were the last

"dispatched. The crescent crumbled like sand and scattered.
The sacred bird of Vishnu,[51] god most orthodox,[52]
soon lost interest in what for humans mattered,

"soared up and away, cued by booms of blasting rocks.
With each downward thrust of its white-rimmed chestnut wings,
it rose high above trees to pan the multitude

"of forest greens and blood reds, to spot rent partings
that may reveal dead flesh to that thin altitude.
Herds of elephants set in and out from under

"arboreal shades, their own lithe shadows like blue
clouds at play. A calf, just acquainted with thunder,
would soon know dynamite, gunpowder and a zoo."[53]

VI

Death in the Jungle

" 'Was that the conch or was it old Paṭṭar blowing
his nose?' A joke that had its day, a man offered
that morning to buffer the rude awakening.

"It was untimely. Paṭṭar was dead. Had suffered
they said. 'Arise! Swing your scythes,' the dorai bellows,
the collective unease was chastened and consoled.

"In this well-timed new world beset by strange billows,
surely, labor from loss, the bold future will hold,
will as love from mere labor, be partitioned of.

" 'Guards, gods, wild hogs and rabid dogs, fear! Death, accept!
Paṭṭar's end, the nest that coiled Russel's vipers wove,
dread! Now, Dorai's orders obey, Dorai respect!'

"In this speechlet, Kaṇkāṇi[54] a precept concealed:
'Acknowledge! Forget! Move!' It had served him quite well.
Our people acknowledged Paṭṭar's death as revealed

"by his still warm corpse. We could have moved on, not dwell
in place or in thought. But could we forsake custom,
bury in haste and the loss of loss then to forget?

"Of course there is caste" (a thoroughly unwholesome
subject where anthropos and hierarchy met).[55]
"Kaṇkāṇi, his kin, and few others exempted,

"most in his death-reduced gang of forty were ranked
'untouchables': Paṟayar, Pallar,[56] most shunted
Chakkiliyar.[57] From the last, all but two were yanked

"out of life at Mannar pier by a noxious
fever, which with it brought boils plumped out and charry,
on the same bright sunny day we thought propitious,

"soon after the monsoon rains in a blustery
distemper came and went. Then Paṭṭar and nephew
were the lucky two; now halved by one. Eight years old,

"the boy, dubbed Thappu.[58] Quite gifted, by all review.
He never missed, held back or sped a beat. All told,
a prodigy; could make taut funeral drums speak.

"Rāmu in the flesh said, 'His mother bedded down
with a Paṟayan.' A potion of Fenugreek,
neem,[59] limejuice, and salt, by a Vaḷḷuvan[60] renown

"made, combined with his own cryptic[61] ingredient,
was fed to drummer Thappu, which transformed him from
Chakkili into Paṟayan adolescent.

"Captain and kaṇkāṇi deployed a conundrum.
'Not soon, but *now* is when we must move,' both announced
in stern consonance. 'Now to the hills! Not later.'

"The group's hesitation to obey was pronounced.
Their response was as agile as stagnant water.
The kaṇkāṇi's eyes moved like two unstable pans

"of a balance-scale: sign of deliberation.
Dorai dipped his chin. Kaṇkāṇi seemed to gain spans
as he stood on toe-tips with no hesitation

"to whisper man to man: 'Here is the little catch.
One whose breath is still in his nostrils must abide
by the dead one, until his body we dispatch

"'with proper rite. To say otherwise I'd have lied.'
A quiet moment. Then both heads like echoes turned
and together said, 'One among you may stay!'

"Kuppu voiced a thought, which in others' bosoms burned.
'How may a good Paṟayan keep vigil? How may
he by a dead Chakkiḷiyan tarry?' A pall

"of silence eclipsed all but the sun. A pugil
of snuff which Kaṇkāṇi inhaled rent the thrall. All
turned to face Thappu. It was bell-clear who will vigil

"keep. 'The boy can stay,' said Kaṇkāṇi. In saying
so, spoke for all but one: the goatherd.[62] To propose
he stood: 'He could bury the body while waiting

"'and set his uncle's soul free.' Forthwith, to oppose,
this man's own mother her voice raised: 'Consider age,
you knave,' she said. 'Could he dig a grave or carry

"'a corpse beyond the threshold to cremate? A sage,
your father was. You? A disgrace. Your brain airy.'
'We'll go,' said conflict-averse Uppu, 'to the blue

"'hills, beyond those hills you see, Thappu. We shall slash
ten acres of Mānā[63] grass and fell twenty-two
tall trees. We shall fetch from the falls where lightnings flash

"'the water to bathe your mother's dear brother with.
Shoe-flowers, marigolds, fragrant frangipani,
three baskets filled with flowers of birth, death and myth,

"'respectively, blooms from flamboyants,[64] if any,
even rare flowers from the jungle's limits you
will see us bring just before the Sun his self hides.'

"His co-workers' impatience did not let Uppu
say more. Their concerns had shifted course like the tides.
Thappu noted, people and conflicts had limits.

"The limitless jungle had one dimension. Depth.
Its sides were all insides—wherein the kite transits—
and from whence it reappeared, and appeared its breath

"to hold when in mid-air it paused till the shriven
line of humans grew short, shorter, then like applause
crumbled and disappeared. 'Kite's a coward, even

"'for a bird,' splashing black against the sky, in caws
crows taunted, then stumbling, a sprawling lichen-flecked
bough arrogated, switched on silence uncanny

"to watch an old leopard aprowl most circumspect,
come to inaugurate the carnal ceremony.
The boy glimpsed the bird's furtive descent with affect

2.3 Montage scenery of railways construction operation, ca. 1860. Engraving.
From S. Muthiah, *The Indo-Lankans: Their 200-Year Saga* (Colombo, Sri Lanka: Indian Heritage Foundation, 2003). Source: S. Muthiah, Indian Heritage Foundation.

"infelicitous. He knew it. But with his dear
mother's brother, life-long protector and prefect,
by his side, from habit Thappu could not feel fear."

"With their throats dry as thistles and knives coarse as throats,
our weeders slashed a vast field of Occam's razors,
Mānā grass-blades sharp as two-edged swords. Clothed in coats

"caked by sweat, pollen covered faces like guisers,
the taste of blood filled our nostrils and the sweet scent
of death seeped into our souls. Thirteen days ago,

"although alone and empty-handed, Uppu went
back to Thappu, to help dig a grave, as he swore
he would, only to find a lone, accomplished kite

"keeping watch over a man's ravished rack of bones.
He looked up at a crow caw an omen in flight.
And down. The kite was gone, morphed into twilight tones.

"The thought of Thappu seized Maṉkalam's breath
until she inhaled her circumstances profound.
Dead stars blanketed the sky. Fireflies flickered death

"in Morse, casting neither shadow nor light. Just sound.
No full moon nor Venus for her grace to pronounce
as she balanced on dew-wet steel. The black woods were

"still black. The bells silent. The train her feet announced
yet to come. The sea-smell had been sheer willpower
Attention to the present can be ecstasy.

"Not tonight. She fled from the smell of brooding clouds,
gravid with shape, moisture and electricity.
Retreating to thought she saw Thappu in a shroud

"of Mānā. Thought to thought led. Mānā, in stealth came
to cattle, when they could not to Mānā go; brought
slow death, expressed through mouth and nostril, as a flame-

"colored froth with unspeakable agony fraught.
No infernal fire could kill this grass, or blade
its will subdue. When its scythe-shorn stubble malign

"you tug and pull to track and uproot, a charade
it will make of you. Its will to power, align
it will, with subterranean forces,[65] and grip

"like grapnel with doubled stubborn scorn, or transmit
your vitality to its well-spaced scalpel-tipped-
buds-bearing parallel roots, so when you draw it

"in and up, breaking open the earth's crust with ease
an endless spine to reveal. The yellow spell, its
sole threat, cast o'er Mānā's mantis-green by trees,

"sun-proof; long gone, hewn to whet capital's greed. Mitts
of rags made, these grass-blades made ribbons of. Gruesome
yet, to behold the hands that to ribbons they cut."

(What would Deleuze have made of this bloody rhizome?)[66]
"Women's palms healed to the touch of husked coconut."
(What *métaphore* might its morphology let spin?)

"Thirty eight of forty had re-entered the zone
of trees when the ventriloquy of Rāmu in
the flesh was ushered in unmolested. 'Prepone

"'your skills. Yield rock and yield tree! The king's here to loot!'
The morning star is his faithful spy. His ready
witness, the evening star. Mānā's defiant root?

"'Far out! Out of sight.' (Idioms in parody.)
Ceylon's future? Mānā. It will lead men astray,
over- and out-run them, outlive rivers that flow,

"carrying hewn timber to ships that sail away"
to dock in Britain's frigid coast, dipping below
the plimsoll line, till garlands of foam in motion

lace them. "Maṇkalam recalled what Appu had said,
'There's no need to ship wood to that livid nation
Britain is where we stand, this soil, rich, black and red.'"

VII
Marvel and the Ghost

"The mighty tamarind tree displayed an ovate
slit on one side of its trunk, tall enough from ground
to tip for a man or woman, with unbent gait,

"to step from sun or rain into its womb profound,
hollowed by nature, hallowed by echo, to curse
or bless with spells when Marvel's not around. Fruit-bat-

"licks at sundown clipping like messages in Morse,
persisting through noise to make sense of this and that
out of redundant sound. When night thickens and lends

"suspense to sound, Padmini's ghost will start her rounds
retracing her path to this cave-site of legends
wicked, night after night to this blood sullied ground

"where a Burgher, white but not quite, had unraveled
her innocence, re-wrapped her in shame and skipped town
with levity as his name. Her kin left; traveled

"lighter by one; refused their caste-name to let down.
She roamed the woods with a plan keen as embodied
pain until it was ripe to return to this altar

"of disgrace. Two lives slaughtered to live undecreed;
one unborn, one unwedded. Where oh where could her
despoiler be? His foul breath her spoor. Tamarind

"keeps her secrets. Satinwood, its boughs abrangle,
golden and glabrescent standing appressed, chagrinned,
bone-dry ebony and sandalwood, the jungle's

"sweetest scent, witnessed that grave event. Even though
those who heard the tale knew Marvel was innocent,
Marvel was quite uncertain if the ghost would know

"Burgher[67] from Englishman. His own fierce thoughts' torment
he could not bear, even though he knew that he would
not act on them, 'cos he was Presbyterian

"sworn to resist, lust's sultry rapaciousness. Should
he repent in his tent as a good Christian?
Ought he for dreaming the delights of the blitheless

"bloke for whom the ghost with child haunted habitat
camp-fruit-bat? Salubricious musings with mirthless
guilt his soul churned to a woodpecker's rat-a-tat

"on a distant tree at sundown. A teal blue-green
multitude of hanging parrots, with blue brocade
undertails, heads and bills dripping red, like pristine

"ornaments lit up the banyan tree. Their upgrade
of colors, it's said, Gran Primus' lacked. Her hatchlings
these received from a tree, a grateful coeval.

"*Ma Loriculus b the 1st*, on a dribbling
Ficus fruit divine feasted in time primeval.
Once of flesh relieved, the seeds she deposited

"in palmyrah's[68] puberulent crown. By fibers,
twigs and toddy nourished, the bliss-trapped seeds sprouted
epiphytes that sipped the dew like sly imbibers,

"slinked down, goaded by 'g' or hit ground by habit,
then grew there like giant weight-lifters' trapezii
—thick, strong—to buttress the hostess, embracing bit

"by bit, walled her in, grew tall, spread such boughs the sky
from earth split. From these, more epiphytes descended
testing the air, like aerial serpents, heads first,

"until they touched the skin Mother Earth extended,
pierced it, pausing when their tips struck the end of thirst,
an aqueduct. Their aerial past redounded

"in girth with nourishment from their roots they sucked up,
became pillars, gave the arms that spawned them needed
rest. Called the Banyan[69] tree of whose own ghostly run-up

"of tales Marvel knew not, but took its spread and shade
to be a likeness to his nation: a shelter
and veil from the burning sun. Others in the trade

"of overseers came and went. In that welter
Marvel was the sole constant. At night in his tent
he dreamt he turned blue-black like a coolie knight,

"mingled unnoticed and shared a black covenant,
to lie in weight with pitchfork and shovel, to smite
the men who came and went just because their thin skin

"was white. This dream recurrent brought him peaceful sleep
which at daybreak made him fit, his job to begin
as white overseer with a dark secret to keep."

VIII
Mastering Coolies

" 'Look down! Dig deep. Deeper! A drain, not a furrow!
double the effort, triple your strength!' Hear him bark.
'Coolie girl, Thīpori! Stop scraping and burrow!'

"She flicked her head, her eyes to fix on Marvel Stark.
Pitched, her coil of oiled hair inhaled and unraveled,
black silk. She unsnapped her waist straight up to re-coil

"her sprung hair that flashed on Marvel as unrivaled
by the crashing granite falls at sunset. To foil
her spell he kept commanding: 'Trail the root so forked.

" 'Move with gravity. Forget your tresses. Your woes
begin when I catch you upright.' Her back she arced
back, a lunar bow, breasts perked—ox heart tomatoes,

"ripe to the touch. Thus her stresses she stretched into
relief and to Marvel spite. Confused rectitude
he maintained, and did what he knew best: command. 'Do

" 'what you must. Plant that foot and press with fortitude
and with maṇveṭṭi,[70] heave the load, and cast away.'
Unlike the other whites he was a man of words,

"captain of his charges. Rāmu, his tongue his stay
against the breakers of thoughts that pierced like swords,
was the silent one. With pickaxe he shattered rock

"and broke clay. With the maṇveṭṭi she cleaved the lumps
and kept with Rāmu's rhythm, foot and rhyme. The shock
to bone they thus absorbed and dissed the bounce from stumps

"The trench around the tree to ring. 'You be worthy
of your king.' Mortal Rāmu felt the crack's impact!
'Fetch the long saw, you daughter of Sethupathy,

" 'the non-untouchable.'[71] (How to tell fact from act?)
'Draw the saw, both of you; up and down; you'll see red
rings concentric, five times five times five. A paisa[72]

" 'here, a paisa there, yet profits roll a hundred-
fold for king and country. Forgot the old geezer,
that greedy kaṇkāṇi. Coolie-pride he'll put on,

" 'and get some coins, naturally. For you, kanji,[73]
and for your coolie—ḍēy[74] coolie![75]—slave on gibbon
until you die or your passage re-paid! Scungy-

" 'man, slave on! Her Majesty's subjects, one single
tree, we all are. We, the branches spread in sunlight,
to rule you, the roots, who with the earth must mingle.

" 'Striking contrast. Earth and sky. Civil servants! White!
Paisas must capillary up to that fine class.
Blacks get some too. Proportionate disproportion.'

" 'Such uncalibrated talk. A snake in the grass
He fancies you with your flowing hair, so, caution.
He wants our labor but in labor he wants you.

" 'He's distracted showing off; *now* re-coil your hair.
Thīpoṟi, now! . . . Some day . . .' 'Pay no mind, good Rāmu.'
'Mind? My advice to him is this: Dorai take care!'

"Just bad blood twixt them. (Each thought the other evil.
In school he took his mother's name, Stark, Esquire.
His dad called him Marvel, before Captain Marvel.)

"But Rāmu's secret lover, her name was Fire.
'Hey you! Your name?' asked Marvel, sensing disrespect.
Rāmu sensed contempt. Kaṇkāṇi saw deep trouble.

"From six fathoms away, calling out, 'I inspect
him Sir. He good man. I coming on the double,'
he ran with his long, leaping shadow, to broker

"peace. In an intercepted dark revelation
Stark saw himself as torturer and strap buckler
gagging Rāmu's flesh, his epiphanic vision

"of serum seep over iron from gouged black flesh.
'Marvel's all bark,' the kaṇkāṇi assured, 'his bite
though, is light.' 'Here is one, Kaṇkāṇi Venkatesh,

" 'for you to divine. Three moons ago at midnight
I lay down to sleep, but fearing for the twinkling
stars I set my sight upon the grifting moon when

" 'in its saffron glow the shadow of a grinning
hound appeared. I held my eyes still, and still again.
The beast began to bleed and turned the moon red.' How

"to tell how much the threat of a man's eyes is worth?
Thīpoṟi forgot the field unbroken by plough;
who lived and who ended in that blood befouled earth."

IX
Disease and Death: The Price of Roads

"My people they dug trenches, my people felled trees,
named and misnamed; our bodies and our hearts bled," said
Rukku. "Some brought their women, some fled to be free.

"Steep trenches were re-filled with gravel and the dead
upon whom they built and tarred the long Kandy road,
pleasures[76] fled. In the jungle, Kaṇkāṇi was king.

"Peerless. None quite like him to cherish and to hoard.
With proceeds from ear-studs, and newcomers' gold rings,
they fired him up on a sandalwood pyre.

"When alive he was astute, watchful and skimpy.
but left plump with plenty off Marvel Stark's Shire.
So many trees he'd ordered hewn. The canopy

"undone. One tenth of the isle's green sea turned dusty
and brown. The sun beat hard on the well; the ill weaved,
coughing beads of blood, the color of black coffee.

"By heaves-propelled, they stumbled beneath fickle-leaved
wind-shaken shade that splattered sun-scattered small change
on the ground, which the dying for wages mistook.

"Rāmu's gang was cut by half, most by blood exchange
with mosquitoes: agents of choleratic puke,
blood-streaked dysentery, typhoid fever, the quaint

"ague, smallpox, chicken pox, measles, flea BB,[77]
ring, tape, thread, pin, round, all castes of bloody worms, Saint
(unholy) Vitus Dance, unromantic TB,

"despite Jay's fluid showers that killed a kiddy
at Maṇḍapam.[78] The stricken died, as expected
when monsoons lashed. As for the other moiety:

"they died from a civet cat's bite, became leopard's
lean lunch, or by a sloth bear conned, collared and mauled.
The big gun with a big gun, deemed the true hunter

2.4 Girls taking a break from wage labor (n.d.). From S. Muthiah, *The Indo-Lankans: Their 200-Year Saga* (Colombo, Sri Lanka: Indian Heritage Foundation, 2003). Source: S. Muthiah, Indian Heritage Foundation.

"and collector of heads; the brown tracker who hauled
and doubled as guide was often the confronter
with bare hands or knife, in a pinch, choice sacrifice.

"The division thorough, Euro-efficiency.
The proof in bungalows; contra line-rooms with lice,
major history versus minor *sangathi*[79]

"—forgettable tales of bare-handed kills, listless
memories of victims, and one remarkable
bull elephant which, with unhurried grace, flawless,

"impressed its measured weight, with calm unflappable,
on Kiṭnan's torso, until blood oozed from every
pore, gushed from each orifice. Close parenthesis. —

"By blood they lived, and by blood they died; from merry
cyclones and flash floods, by accident or remiss;
lay afloat, belly-up, limbs outspread, puffed up frogs.

"The loss of life was barely felt, for there was more
from whence they came, servants, saints, ruffians and rogues,
whose will to power had met becoming[80] before."

X
Mr. Spic'n Span Real Army Man

"When Marvel's successor came, he came with rumor,
tore open the earth to rummage in its bowels
for precious ores, pagan gods concealed to humor

"future Euros, until some women heard such howls
of pain that sounded English, by echo doubled,
and amplified by the silenced shocks post-thunder,

"that dumped floods over floods all night. The drubbed, troubled
low clouds, fissured by lightning that ripped asunder
dark forests and trees, had been wrung dry to nothing

"but blue skies, clearing the mountain-scape to echo
the retched and vomited howls that signaled something
amiss in the pit of Eve[81] where emeralds glow,

"where, it was rumored, she buried rubies Adam
gave her and blue sapphires gifted by the snake.
Blue he was, when the seven women found 'I am

"'that I am,' in fellowship with four kraits, his rake,
six black scorpions, a puddle of toads aghast,
all held at bay by the braying blue Englishman.

"'A strange tribe, the English,' said one prone to typecast.
'When one is naked, he's quite a phenomenon,
I swear-to-God.' 'His heart, a sour-sop sized beet,'

"claimed another. 'I saw one in a flayed-open
dorai.' 'Mookkan was hanged for that.' 'A piece of meat.'
'It pumped, as if self-copulating.' 'Yes, Watson

" 'was his name!' 'Mookkan's wife?' 'No, it was his daughter?'
To remember is to know that you can forget.
'This one here, he has his good points.' 'The Snuff-snorter!'

" 'The sun will soon make the darkness rise . . .' '. . . and regret.'
'Forsake him now; let's forgive ourselves later.' 'Flood
loves the pit, the pit the flood.' 'What if he had seen

" 'us?' 'What if he escapes?' 'If! If! If!' 'He drew blood.
Look at these stripes. The whipper, snapper.' 'An obscene
brute. Let him drown.' 'Look! Hawk in pursuit. An omen!'

" 'His omen.' 'These trees conspire to conceal us,'
said the spunky one with her calves exposed. 'Our men!
Fetch them. Let them decide.' 'Yes!' they said in chorus.

" 'He might be dead by then.' 'God is my testator.
He drew blood.' 'Come off it! We all have stripes. We all
bled.' 'So did Jesus H. Christ.' He evoked laughter.

" 'Not Christ; the Padre.' 'Good man, though white as a caul.'
'His only issue was his erectile tissue.'
'The only pit he feared was the pit of hell.' 'Pit!

" 'The pit! Think it's full?' 'The howls no longer pursue.'
'Is he dead?' 'Help me! Someone help me! I know it.
'You are there. Kooni! Kunthi! Please don't let me sink.'

" 'Kamalam! Poochi, my dear Arumpon, Paechi,
Your reward will be great. Think Ruby.' 'At the brink
he must now be.' 'Quick! If he dies,' said Kamatchi,

" 'someone will talk, someone will.' 'Not I.' 'Nor I.' 'Who?
me?' In spliced declarations they all replied, 'Aye.'
To tell, or not to tell—that is the question. 'Shoo!

" 'to camp! En route we shall decide.' A dragonfly
whisked by in fits and starts, towards the blood-red butte.
Beyond, treeless, ghosted rain taunted, southern hills,

"empurpled. Recalled images swam, of now mute
Spic'n Span, army man, the cause of many ills.
The living dead, their creaturely lives[82] to conquer

"this proud 'man of his word,' when rifled, guiltless shed
much guileless blood; termed it collateral error.
Such were their dark musings, as the sky turned to lead.

"In the thrall of fear and thrill of agroupment,
their men forgot, the last mile they walked for coolies
—for all thirty million—in silent consent.

"Blood-gift to world capital.[83] Hist'ry of follies,
foul and fair. Who shall write or scrape clean its great price?
Who will be witness to blood shed? Hear the land cry,

"its wounds unfurled: gouged here, dressed there, sealed elsewhere. Rice
paddies smothered by earth-slips, rivers running dry,
rains filling pits and breaching dams. Monks preaching fear

"and statesmen, hate, in this once green unredeemed world.
The conquerors their old wounds lick with each new year;
the freed re-bind themselves, the coolies lie recurled."

XI

Lost

(From "Upcountry")

"[H]ere's a story. It took him five miles north of camp.
Rāmu's son lost himself further among sloth bears
that ravished the lotus in the land of marsh-lamps.

"A male bear stalked him like a true believer's prayer
all night, four nights, man and beast, hider and seeker,
in deadly play unflinching, luck-dared, fearing out-

"daring luck, till the wispy mist growing meeker
exposed the reedy marsh, and soon the last white cloud
was spun away by clear sky-blue. If faith is in-

"escapable endurance, then, chameleoned
Melursus ursinus, by dawn, lost his faith in
fasting. Bored by his disingenuous prey, yawned,

"hit the woods loping in search of familiar con-
specious companionship, and for a healthy breakfast, some cinnamon tree bark to get his claws on.

"Four score and seven hours earlier, for the sake,
of a rhizome, a root, our lost man had exchanged
the fiddling faith he did possess for fathomless

"fear, a trait of his species, that keeps men estranged
from ghosts, heights, open-spaces, leopards, wasps, harmless
snakes, wild elephants, and successors of Marvel.

"Not to forget molesting bears of course. Compact
fear too shatters exhausted, with its coeval,
the vessel that bore it all night. Like a contract

"switched on at daybreak, bear and man caught up with sleep.
On the fourth morning, expectant and still, brooding
black clouds that had lain in wait all night over steep

"escarps while mountains kept watch for the colluding
spark to strike the cast-iron skies, dropped on the green
plains their charge where bacchanal winds with every tree

"consorted. Land, innocent of mill and machine
as late as yesteryear, let a river run free,
deep—not too deep—yet quiet, with such clarity

"so that every grain of sand reposed untroubled,
magnified under an undimpled, ungritty
flow. Coconut palms that drank at it were doubled

"in a flawless mirror. Daybreak! A stunning change!
The river turned black, engorged. Strange swells gained
under the current's surface. Behold, within range,

"his four nights' companion stood up as it rained:
a lotus-stem, a pink bloom on its tip, he held
between his teeth, a poster-bear's conceit; just like

"John De Witt, who'd suddenly appear among felled
trees with his brown, resin pipe, trying his best to strike
an Edwardian pose, to impress imagined

"ladies. Vāman opined, 'To find D'witt thus disposed
was to know that he was distracted as the wind.'
What Vāman supposed Rāmu's son readily chose

"and so dove head first from his arboreal bed
into the surging River Soot. He clung onto
a charred log that came his way, revealing some red

"in places underneath. It did provide a clue
and distraction too. This feller of trees divines,
while adrift, its age and species: a young, tender,

"rosewood. In the tumbling, eddying swirls, more signs
of devastation were everywhere to render
the cost of England's ruckling King's burnt sacrifice.

The reduced raft had spun him around, and mistook
him full circle, rolling him like a well-worn dice
around mountains he recognized. His grim soul shook

"like a raven in a storm. The mountains he saw
were friends betrayed, whose ancient trees his father brought
down for big Marvel, who (despite it all) in awe

"had held, their age, girth, height, grain, strength and worth. He fought
his compatriots' greed and his own need his king
to please, *ceteris paribus*; thus the young ones

"he had spared to live a hundred, when his kidlings,
all knighted colonialings, with king's big guns,
would return and harvest their birthright, from estates

"that would bear his name—no longer off alignment
with Albion's bloody elevated agnates—
pageanted, convibrant with sentiments volent,

"wanting nothing but want itself—never lacking
ever desiring—Empire's seed and secret
of greatness. Gone to black those dreams of moss-packing

"tree-toads. The velvet moss's desire most sacred,
just to be left to be, had been consumed by whumps
of fire that leapt among trees Marvel had spared

"by selective plunder. Flabby thighs and fat rumps-
of indigo-blue clouds that the flames' reach had dared
for days, at last, heeding gravity's call, had brought

"down their heavy load of despair. Liquefied soot
wrought by runnels with cat-speed, fingers of death-fraught
soup, ran downhill to transfuse every rill's offshoot,

"stream and brook, turning this river black (which seven
score years hence will run with translucent crimson blood
with majestic lethargy).[84] His young heart riven,

"eyes fixed upon the crime, Rāmu's son let the flood
take him wherever it listed. He found solace
in a solemn fact. He was no longer fleeing

"his own shadow nor a real sloth bear with malice.
His gasping lungs no longer muffled his beating
heart, which skipped with a touch of respect, for the Late

"Stark, whom his aging father took for a brother,
co-weeder in a nook of the king's vast estate.
He did well by king and country; as for lucre,

"a tad he euchred for himself. As a foreman,
he did not know the grand plan, nor what would follow
him or who. This one who came after, a Scotsman,

"was a ruddy stoker by trade. But this fellow
had no patience to pick and choose; a certified
pyrosophist, his will to power was the will

"to burn and so was his calling. With sanctified
passion-filled, and sanctioned by the king's man[85] to thrill
investors in waiting and planting pioneers,

"he poured it on virgin forests that Vāman's men
had picked, and matched it with command. The auctioneer
could sell it then, these Sterling purchased pictured glens

"for young blooters, to plant their seed. The indigene
of two thousand years would see slash and burn surpassed
by the birth of scorched earth and earth-slips never seen.

"Cryptid, Devil Bird[86] will soon scream its plaintive last,
as the boy who had cried his last harmless 'wolf.' Queer,
how its flight down-river, stitched shore to shore, to join

"where shorelines' horizons meet, and there disappear,
boding bow and arrow's end and the birth of mines,
tanks, guns, missiles and devil-birds of steel to come.

"But before then came Scots like Farmer Ferguson,
mates Sydney Smith, English Hatkins, Watkins, green-thumb
Larkins, all Wunderkinds, descending in season.

"After hours of meander, the charred rosewood
raft brought itself, its passenger and his languid
thoughts to rest. A mango tree weighted down with fruit

"by the shore stood, its arced bough sipping the torpid
drift, and then as a magic line would, with one hook
it snagged all three. His raft—its skin, a crocodile's—

"he let go to where river the sunset met; took
his thoughts with him up the steep riverbank; fragile,
and fear-drenched though they were, like sparrows, flew away

"He ate as many of the ripe fruit as he could,
in haste, and plucked how many more one could not say,
to take with him by bundling them up, as he should.

"What in? No clothes. No cloth. Not even a turban.
Black-assed and naked he was. But in what cockaigne
was he? Gone were the hills dressed in black. Once Kamban[87]

"had in verse opined that green thickens when it rains.
The green of leaves was so thick, the son of Rāmu
could hardly breathe. He longed for a vista and wind

"to clear his head, help find his coordinates. Through
brush and up a muddy slope, passing tamarind
groves, he came upon a plateau. Yet another

"hill appeared, steeper still, which he slithered up, found
himself atop a sun-blazed rain-scarp. No greener
bounty had mother earth rolled out horizon bound,

"a vista of infinite but composed green hues
lambently lit upon by feathered clouds. Les *rites
de passage* through fire and soot will soon subdue

"this too, for a dark brew that mill-minions will sweet[88]
with sugar and lighten with tinned condensed milk, fend,
hunger, between wails of fog horns, their faint spirit,

"to lift up to a new work ethic and prehend
the state of statelessness condemned to inherit.
Future past flashed off the hideous lion's sword.[89]

"Three mottled aircrafts flew up high in wide-troughed 'U's,
stooped like birds that had espied carrion ignored
by other carnivores lying under chartreuse

"jungles by the silv'ry emerald river limned;
missed, forked, flew up towards the sky trailing a discrete
misty trident. Repeat. Failed. Again repeat. Skimmed

"eight furlongs of trees—a spiteful cloud to excrete.
A murmurous wind grieved the forest. Emerald,
jade, teal, sea-green, chartreuse, in that order, the leaves,

"grew plump, then shone their last glow in pain unequaled
expressed, choked, shriveled, faded, expired. To breve
the lion,[90] the devil birds headed south aslant,

"rumpling a well-made sky, left the deformed jungle
the Scot's phosphorus spared. A baby elephant
barged in, saw a leopard cub testing a wrangle

"of singed trees, then blustered to rejoin unworded
the herd. Tattered smatters of boys with devices
of war strutted while girls tailed in silence enworded

"expectance for the command to self-sacrifice
for language, country and rebel leader; while boy
soldiers' waited to kill and be killed for the sons

"and daughters of privilege, and their precious toys
of Ferraris, Mercedes and Humvees with guns."
Each reincarnate Rāmu, will be struck by how

transience outlasts all: Queens, Kings, Imperial might,
Governors, Prime Ministers and their sacred cows,
memsahibs who can afford to be always right;

(Speech-impedimented presidents, demented
sergeants, poets with lisps, mayors of cities, towns,
plangent politicians, professors contented

with precisely adjusted anxieties; Clowns,
gen'rals, manic depressives [parenthetical].)
("Hello, rationalized Past-Futures, please, Reasoned

"Future-Pasts meet." "That's wholly hic et nuncical.
It won't last.") "Smoke blew by Rāmu's son's unseasoned
eyes from not quite dead fires that the shores limned.

"The river was reeled in by the meat-colored sun.
But even before it was done, his body dimmed.
For the light from the rain-washed stars the night had won."

Notes

Part of this essay is revised and reproduced by permission of the American Anthropological Association from Cultural Anthropology 23, no. 2 (2008): 254–78, and cannot be used for sale or further reproduction.

1. Marcus and Fischer, Anthropology as Cultural Critique.
2. The word coolie is Tamil for "wages." In Tamil, this word by itself cannot be used to refer to a person, even if she or he is a wage earner, unless a morpheme or word for "person"—commonly, the suffix āl̤ or its equivalent—is tagged onto it; hence, coolie + -āl̤ = kūliyāl̤, which literally means "coolie person." To refer to someone as "coolie" without such a complement amounts to calling someone "wage." Although ungrammatical in Tamil, it is commonplace usage in English, the language that has adopted the word into the English lexicon. The misappropriation of this word into English in the colonial context has essentially reduced the personhood of the earner to the wage he earns. See Daniel and Breman, "The Making of a Coolie."
3. Hollup, Bonded Labour.
4. Peirce defines musement as "Pure Play": "There is a certain agreeable occupation of mind which, from its having no distinctive name, I infer is not as commonly practiced as it deserves to be; for indulged in moderately—say through some five to six per cent of one's waking time, perhaps during a stroll—it is refreshing enough more than to repay the expenditure. Because it involves no purpose save that of casting aside all serious purpose, I have sometimes been half-inclined to call it reverie with some

qualification; but for a frame of mind so antipodal to vacancy and dreaminess such a designation would be too excruciating a misfit. Play, we all know, is a lively exercise of one's powers. Pure Play has no rules, except this very law of liberty. It bloweth where it listeth. It has no purpose, unless recreation. The particular occupation I mean—a *petite bouchée* with the Universes—may take either the form of aesthetic contemplation, or that of distant castle-building . . . , or that of considering some wonder in one of the Universes. . . . It is this last kind—I will call it *musement*" (CP 6.458). (The designation CP abbreviates *The Collected Papers of Charles Sanders Peirce*, and the volume and paragraph numbers with a period in between follow the standard reference form.)

5. Traditionally, poems (*kavi*) are always sung (*pāṭṭu*).

6. Simmel, "The Ruin." Also see Sebald, *The Rings of Saturn*; Benjamin, *The Arcades Project*.

7. Benjamin, *Illuminations*.

8. Ramanujan, *Poems of Love and War*, ix.

9. Rukku is a contraction of Rukkumaṇi.

10. In addition to the name Gaṇpathi, Gaṇesh, or Gaṇesha (which means Lord of a Multitude), this elephant-headed god has many other names, some of which we will encounter in this poem: Vignēshwara, Vināyakā, Gaurisudha, Ekadanta, and Nanda.

11. See Vanden Driessen, *The Long Walk*, for an excellent account of this long walk that covers the nineteenth century.

12. Soon after Ceylon's independence from the British, in 1918, the new government passed three citizenship and franchise acts that rendered most Tamil plantation workers of Indian descent stateless and voteless. The threat of repatriation to India hung over the heads of half a million of these Tamils. Many of these disenfranchised and stateless residents and one or both their parents were born in Ceylon, but spent years trying to prove themselves worthy of citizenship. Some succeeded and stayed; of the others, some were deported by force, and others, to use a more recent coinage, self-deported. In 1972 the country was named Sri Lanka. Following the anti-Tamil riots of 1983, many Tamils voluntarily left the island for India. The main speaker-singer of this poem is a young woman named Rukkkumani, who is at the brink of either being deported or voluntarily leaving following the anti-Tamil pogrom of 1983, which initiated twenty-six years of civil war in this island nation.

13. "Eternal return is the heart of Nietzsche's teaching, because it accords the highest honor to the evanescent beings of which the whole consists. Guided neither by ancestral gods nor by philosophical idols nor by some lodestar of future paradise, guided rather by its own insight into the whole of beings, and granted responsibility by this insight to maintain those beings, Nietzsche's teaching shows the way to the highest affirmation of natural beings, the new justice that shouts insatiably 'Once More!' to the whole marvelous spectacle of which the grateful celebrant is a momentary witnes" (Lampert, *Nietzsche's Teaching*, 286).

14. Rama, the hero in the epic the *Ramayana*, is said to be one of the ten avatars of Vishnu. He is also widely held to be a vegetarian, even though he is also, arguably, held to belong to the *kshtraya* (warrior) *varna*, who are by tradition nonvegetarians. Rāmu,

the perennial witness of the events in the life of the Tamil laborers, is incontestably nonvegetarian, as are most of the Indian Tamil immigrant workers.

15. *Ekadanta* means "the one-toothed."

16. In the *Ramayana*, Sita, the wife of Rama, is abducted from a forest in India by the king of Lanka, Ravana, and held captive on the island of Lanka. The Rama who appears in the several South Indian versions of the epic, especially in Kambar's Tamil *Rāmāyaṇam*, is presented in a more human and fallible form than the Rama of the Sanskrit version written by Valmiki or of the Hindi version authored by Tulsidas; and so is Rāvaṇā. See Richman, *Many Ramayanas*.

17. The allusion here is to the two major "Hindu" sects: Shaivism and Vaishnavism. Vignēṣvarā, being the son of Shiva is, naturally, a Shaivite. Ram or Rama, the mythic figure in the *Ramayana*, is an incarnation of Vishnu and is therefore seen as a Vaishnavite.

18. *Appā* means "father."

19. The earliest date on record of South Indian coolies coming to work in British colonial Ceylon is 1829.

20. In the early years laborers from South India found their own way to Sri Lanka. The methods of recruitment of labor and the recruiters themselves changed over time: from freelancing contractors—European and Indian—who recruited laborers at street junctions in the small towns and cities of the Madras Presidency to the recruitment of villagers by powerful individuals from the same or neighboring villages, who came to be known as *kaṇkāṇis*. The second method was used over a much longer period than the first. There were three factors that facilitated the recruitment of laborers. First, there was an increased frequency of famines in South India in the nineteenth century and in the first half of the twentieth under British rule, which served as the major push factor. Second, the pull factor was the enticing tales told by the recruiters of the far better life that awaited the recruits in Ceylon relative to their lot in the towns and villages of South India. The third factor was the issuance of a piece of paper, tin, or copper, called a *thuṇḍu*, which gave the recruited individual the privilege of charging for "essential" expenses against his or her future wages. These expenses ranged from advances for travel to subsequent loans for medicines, and ritual functions such as wedding and funerals. The arrangement almost always placed such individuals in a state of permanent indebtedness, a virtual state of bonded labor, first to the recruiter and subsequently to the recruiter-kaṇkāṇi. The rate of interest charged was as high as 120 percent a year. See Bandarage, *Colonialism in Sri Lanka*; Peebles, *The Plantation Tamils of Ceylon*.

21. On special occasions, it is believed, ancestors visit the living in the form of a crow.

22. In South Asian medical and culinary systems, five tastes or flavors are recognized: sweet, sour, salty, pungent, and astringent.

23. Sāmbār is a stew made of vegetables, dahl, and spices.

24. Rasam, a flavor-packed, watery soup, is prepared in several ways. The recipe

favored by Tamil plantation workers consists of tamarind, tomato, curry leaves, garlic, onion, cumin, coriander, black pepper, ginger root, and dried red chili.

25. Pāyāsam is a sweet dish with the texture of thin porridge.

26. On the differences and similarities between "heritage" and "history," see Daniel, *Charred Lullabies*, chap. 1.

27. Here we see the rule of approximations in play in this tendency to provide a range rather than a definite number. See Daniel, *Charred Lullabies*, 77–79; and Daniel, *Fluid Signs*, 134.

28. The binary distinction refers to a distinction that Jakobson creatively adopted and adapted to the study of tonality in phonetics. In technical terms, the distinction refers to the relative concentration of energy in the lower (grave) or upper (acute) frequencies of the spectrum of sounds. In the fourth lecture of his *Six Lectures on Sound and Meaning*, Jakobson writes, "The opposition between acute and grave phonemes has the capacity to suggest an image of bright and dark, of pointed and rounded, of thin and thick, of light and heavy, etc." (120).

29. Even though a rudimentary understanding of property ownership with respect to land may have existed in precolonial South Asia, it would be more correct to say that the people belonged to the land or place (Ur) in question, rather than that the land belonged to people. The insensitivity to this distinction is most starkly brought out in the European encounter with Amerindians. As James Tully puts it in his discussion on the Inuit: "Property rights and duties inhere in the clans and apply to activities and to the geographical location in which the activities take place, not, in the first instance, to the products of the activities" (*An Approach to Political Philosophy*, 154). Furthermore, we find that even in the liberal-minded Locke's view of conquest, if there was more land than the inhabitants could *possess* and *make use of*, the conqueror was at liberty to make use of "the waste," which, in Locke's yeomanesque understanding, referred to any uncultivated land (*The Second Treatise of Government and a Letter Concerning Toleration*, 85).

30. Theories of natural law are as old as the early Sanskrit, Greek, and Latin texts on the subject. However, they are not all the same. Locke's notion of natural law is based on the belief that all human beings yearn for liberty—not liberty as "freedom from" the constraints of natural desires (as it was for Hobbes, among others), but as "freedom to" perfect our nature in rational duties to god and self-preservation, extended to humanity's preservation. The rub and the danger comes with the doctrine of universal reason that Locke subscribes to, and with that reason being viewed as the foundation for what is moral and good for all human beings. In this respect, Locke anticipates Kant almost more than do any of the early moderns. Nature uncultivated is nature unowned. The natural law of self-preservation depends on the cultivation of nature. Human labor is required for cultivating nature. Labor expended in the cultivation of unowned nature transforms it into private property. Hence, the law of nature sanctions private property. So the argument goes.

31. The law of conquest originates in European antiquity. However, its wide appli-

cation, rightly or wrongly, became common in the early modern period of European colonization of other parts of the world. See Guha, *A Rule of Property for Bengal*, for the vexed history of this law as applied to Bengal in particular, but by extension to South Asia as a whole.

32. The rubber tree is native to the Amazon rainforest. It was imported from Brazil into India and Ceylon in 1875.

33. See Webb, *Tropical Pioneers*, 20–24; and Baker, "The Sinharaja Rain-Forest Ceylon."

34. The reference here is to *Albizia lebbeck* (*sirisah* in Tamil), a deciduous tree with a rounded, spreading crown and pale bark. Its flowers, which are showy and grow in clusters close to the tips of stems, produce flat and long pods that contain numerous seeds.

35. See Lévi-Strauss, *Tristes Tropiques* (1981), 160. I thank Greg Urban for this reference.

36. Unpolished rice.

37. Kurakkan is finger millet, which is resistant to insects and fungi.

38. *Dorai* is an honorific title given to a superior. In the political economy of plantations, this term of address was reserved mostly for the white man.

39. *Doraisāni* refers to the dorai's female counterpart; it is an honorific reserved for European ladies.

40. *Maṇkalam* means "auspiciousness." When one contracts her name to Maṇkal, it changes its meaning to "loss of shine," "dull," or "dim."

41. *Kallu* means "palm toddy." Kitul is a palm tree commonly found in the south of Sri Lanka. Its botanical name is *Caryota urens*, and the tree belongs to the family of Arecaceae.

42. "Lines" is the name for a barracks-style row of houses. Each living unit or "line room," as they were called, had a half-walled verandah, a 10′ × 10′ bedroom, and a 4′ × 4′ kitchen.

43. The last king of Kandy was deposed in 1815 by the British. However, the institution of *Rajakāriya* (obligatory labor to the king and state) was continued under British rule, with mixed results at best, until 1832. The Sinhala peasants were averse to the idea of working for a wage and being obligated thereby. They were even more loathe to meet their obligation to the state by paying taxes in cash or kind from their land. The Tamil coolies initially filled that lacuna in the consistency of labor and eventually took over the work on roads and railways almost completely. See de Silva, "Beginnings of Commercial Road-Passenger Transportation in Sri Lanka."

44. Sinhalese and Tamil laborers worked together in building the railways, under the supervision of British overseers and engineers. However, the Sinhalese workers in general worked on the railways only as long as their working area was within walking distance back to their villages. Indian Tamil coolies constituted the constant work force. See ibid.; and Newell, "What a Field Is Here for Missionary Exertions."

45. Mariyamman, the mother goddess widely worshiped. She is the deity to whom Tamil workers turn to when in distress.

46. A kaṇkāṇi is a labor gang leader, a supervisor, a patron, a father figure all rolled into one, and is sometimes, as well, a relative and a moneylender.

47. A vēṭṭi is the lower garment Tamil men wear.

48. These tokens served as tickets for the journey to Ceylon and back, with added value for initial expenses. Responsibility for the latter was assumed by the kaṇkāṇi when the tickets were returned to him as collateral. The "initial needs" unfailingly exceeded the "added value" of the ticket, which could then be redeemed only on the repayment of the accrued debt, a debt (with interest) which the workers could rarely repay, regardless of how long or how much they labored.

49. See Stoler, *Race and the Education of Desire*, for a discussion of the colony serving as a laboratory in which European colonizers can educate themselves to the finer points of race.

50. Children and women worked as they weeded the undergrowth.

51. Vishnu's mount or vehicle is Garuda, which is believed to be a Brahmini kite.

52. Those who hold Vishnu to be their foremost deity are called Vaishnavites, and they tend to be given to more exacting orthopraxy than the worshipers of Shiva or Shaivites.

53. The elephant population in Sri Lanka at the end of the nineteenth century was estimated at 140,000. Today the Sri Lankan elephant is endangered, its population not more than 2,500. The elephants were lost mainly to ivory poachers, especially in the nineteenth century and the first half of the twentieth.

54. See Peebles, *The Plantation Tamils of Ceylon*.

55. In textbooks in general anthropology, if India gets but one mention it most likely pertains to a discussion of the Indian caste system in the context of studying the concept of hierarchy. Also see Appadurai, "Putting Hierarchy in Its Place," 36–49.

56. *Parai* refers to a drum that is played during funerals. The drummers who play these drums are called Parayar and belong to a caste by the same name. Pallar, like the Parayar, are classified as "scheduled castes" in the Constitution of India, as they are considered to belong to an economically and socially disadvantaged part of the population. The greater part of both these castes are landless agricultural laborers, and they make up a very high percentage of those who migrated from South India to Sri Lanka for work on plantations in that country. They have also, for the greater part of their recent histories, been rivals for rank, recognition, and privileges. Once classified as untouchables, their self-chosen appellation at present is Dalits, which includes a range of castes, distributed throughout India, whose human rights are routinely violated even though such treatment is forbidden by the constitution and several other statutes of India. Dalits' struggle for equal rights continues to this day.

57. Chakkiliyar are the most disadvantaged and the most backward in all walks of life of the castes in South India. Their traditional occupation has been the removal of night soil, or human waste.

58. The name Thappu refers to a drum, specifically a tom-tom.

59. Neem's botanical name is *Azadirachta indica*. Many parts of this tree, especially its leaves, are used for its medicinal properties throughout South Asia.

60. A Valḷuvan is a priest of the Paṟayar caste and is, as a rule, a literate individual who is also a poet or singer.

61. The traditional system of medicine practiced in South India is called Siddha, the other Indian systems of medicine being Ayurveda and Unani. Siddha medical texts were written in cryptic Tamil verse inaccessible to the untrained literates.

62. A member of the goat-herding caste.

63. The botanical name for this species of grass is *Cymbopogon confertiflorus* and it belongs to family Gramineae. It grows to a height of a meter or more, and its edges have microscopic, but sharp, saw-teeth.

64. Flamboyant trees belong to the species *Delonix regia*.

65. See Nietzsche, *The Will to Power*; and Grosz, *The Nick of Time*, 125–39, for an interesting reading of Nietzsche's notion of "will to power" as force.

66. Deleuze and Guattari, *A Thousand Plateaus*.

67. In Sri Lanka "Burgher" refers to a descendant of a mixed marriage between the pre-British, Portuguese, and Dutch colonizers and Sinhala and Tamil natives. Burghers were favored over the Sinhalese and Tamils because they retained vestiges of European ways, spoke English, and were lighter skinned.

68. The palmyrah, a palm tree that grows in northern Sri Lanka and South India, is considered to be the official tree of the Tamil people.

69. "Banian- or banyan-tree, now often simply banyan: the Indian Fig Tree (*Ficus religiosa* or *indica*) a remarkable East Indian tree, the branches of which drop shoots to the ground, that take root and support their parent branches; extending in this way, one tree will often cover a large expanse of ground.

"*Banian Tree, Banians' Tree, Tree of the Banians,* was originally a local appellation given by Europeans to an individual tree of this species growing near Gombroon on the Persian Gulf, under which the *Banians*, or Hindu traders settled in that port, had built a little pagoda; thence it was extended to others, and finally taken as the English name of the species." *Oxford English Dictionary*, 2nd ed., June 2012 (Oxford University Press), edn., s.v. "Banyan."

70. A kind of hoe, used in South Asia.

71. Marvel appears to be quite adept at caste politics. He puts the girl in her place by intimating that her father's claim to belong to a higher caste is dubious; this indicates an intimate knowledge of the culture.

72. A coin of meager value, worth one sixty-fourth of a rupee.

73. Kanji is "starchy water, drained from cooked rice." *Kriyāvin Taṟkāla Tamil Akarāti: Dictionary of Contemporary Tamil* (Chennai, India: Cre-A, 1992).

74. *Dēy* is an attention-getting substitute for the second-person pronoun in slang, comparable to "Oy!"

75. "Coolie" in this instance is employed as a reference to wages, but "coolie" in the immediately prior instance refers ("ungrammatically") to the person who earns a wage, thereby reducing the person to a wage.

76. *Pleasure* was a synonym of *car* in South Asia, a contraction of *pleasure-car*.

77. Filariasis is a mosquito- or flea-borne disease that, among other things, causes

a man's testicles to swell to the size of a grapefruit or bigger and hence was called Big Balls or "BB," colloquially.

78. Maṇḍapam served as a transit camp where Tamil workers leaving India for Sri Lanka were quarantined and disinfected with chemical showers. Today it serves as a camp for refugees fleeing the civil war in Sri Lanka.

79. These are some of the connotations of the noun *sangathi*: secret, event, happening, affair, piece of news, a matter or thing (as in, "a thing about him"), gossip, enigma, mystery, Arcanum, confidence, and so on.

80. In Nietzsche's concept of "will to power," force is always described as engaged in becoming. "Instead of identity, [Nietzsche] seeks out forces or wills, instead of the dialectic, continuous self-modification, he favors the dramatic and untimely leap into futurity, instead of the becoming of being, he seeks the being of becoming, instead of identity, he seeks a model of action and activity" (Grosz, *The Nick of Time*, 466). Nietzsche, however, does not consistently distinguish force from power. Thus, by and large, Nietzsche's understanding of power in his "will to power" is of power as force. I, following Arendt (*On Violence*) and in a Peircean vein, distinguish power from force, where power is legitimized force, whereas force by definition is prelegitimized or unlegitimized. In terms of Peirce's phenomenological categories, power is a Third and Force is a Second (CP 1.322–68).

81. Many medieval travelers, Arab and European, held the belief that Ceylon was the erstwhile Garden of Eden

82. "Creaturely Life" alludes to the animal side of the human condition. See Santner, *On Creaturely Life*.

83. Thirty million is the estimated number of coolies who contributed to plantation-based world capitalism in the nineteenth and twentieth centuries.

84. The reference here is primarily to the killing of Sinhala youths belonging to the leftist Leninist party called the Janatha Vimukthi Peramuna (JVP), whose attempt to overthrow the government through random acts of violence and assassinations were met with overwhelming force by the government. Estimates of the number of Sinhala youth belonging to the JVP, associated with JVP, or accused of belonging to the JVP who were massacred by the Sri Lankan armed forces range from twenty thousand to sixty thousand. Over the two years between 1988 and 1990, several Sri Lankan rivers turned blood red from these killings, and body parts were found in the bellies of sea fish. See Gunasekara, *Sri Lanka in Crisis*; Hoole, *Sri Lanka*, 246–59.

85. The highest king's office in Ceylon was the governor general.

86. The devil bird has yet to be definitively identified by birders or ornithologists. In Sinhala, the devil bird is called *ulena* or *ulama*. It has been reported that this bird emits a cry from the depth of the jungle in the form of shrieks that are eerie and bloodcurdlingly human in sound. Older villagers in the north-central province of the country who reported hearing and described such cries to me in the late 1950s and the 1960s have more recently informed me that because of the heavy deforestation over the last few decades, resulting from the expansion of human habitation and from the use of defoliants during the civil war, they have not heard the devil bird cry in years.

87. Kamban, a medieval Tamil poet, author of the Tamil *Rāmāyaṇam* epic.

88. See Mintz, *Sweetness and Power*.

89. The lion holding a sword is the central symbol on the Sri Lankan national flag.

90. The lion represents the power of the island's Sinhala people, its majoritarian power, and its rulers, several of whom identify their prowess with that of their "totem," the lion.

Empire's Ruins

Detroit to the Amazon

In surveying the United States's last two major wars in light of this edited volume, it is apparent that the epic corruption and incompetence that has accompanied Washington's mostly privatized efforts to rebuild Iraq and Afghanistan has resulted in a landscape of half-finished, malfunctioning, or abandoned projects, including schools, roads, hospitals, power plants, and sewage treatment plants. It's as if the United States, by banking the projection of its influence predominantly on military power, contracted mercenaries, and deregulated finance, has opted to skip the "creative construction" phase of capitalism and jump to something that might be called "permanent creative destruction," where the wreckage doesn't pave the way for future accumulation but is itself, through a form of military corporatism, the main profit-generating sector, at least for the Halliburton and Blackwater wing of the U.S. economy.[1] In other words, the United States now starts with the ruins.

One doesn't have to travel to Iraq to contemplate today's relationship between capitalism and ruin. John Patrick Leary has written about the "culture boom" currently under way in Detroit, a fascination with the city's wasted industrial landscape.[2] Other places, like Youngstown, Ohio, and Bucharest, Romania, have attracted photographers documenting First World urban decline, but Detroit, Leary writes, the storied birthplace of the United States's hi-tech, labor intensive, middle-class-creating industrial capitalism, "remains the Mecca of urban ruins," its blighted baroque and modernist architecture captured in glossy coffee-table books and New York Times essays, or as backdrops for postapocalyptic Hollywood movies, like the remake, which cost a reported $75 million, of Red Dawn.[3] Leary points out the " 'pornographic' sensationalism" of much of Detroit's ruin photography, which "aestheticizes poverty without inquiring of its origins, dramatizes spaces but never seeks out the people that inhabit and transform them, and romanticizes isolated acts of resistance without acknowledging the massive political and social forces aligned against the real transformation, and not just stubborn survival, of the city."[4]

Even the best intentioned of this genre, which tries to document the particularity of Detroit, can only convey a "vague sense of historical pathos," serving as tributes of past industrial grandeur or warnings of the rusted future that awaits us all. "The past is achingly present in Detroit, and the way its citizens interact with the hulking, physical remnants of yesterday is striking," wrote Heidi Ewing and Rachel Grady in the New York Times, in an essay featuring their new documentary, Detropia. Their film focuses on scavengers—capitalism's left-behinds—who are "dismantling Detroit" and selling its scrap metal on the global market, mostly to China. The city literally disappeared before the filmmakers' eyes. After filming one salvage crew taking apart a former Cadillac repair shop, the crew returned the next day to find that the "entire building was gone." "They were," Ewing and Grady said of the scavengers, "the cleanup crew in a shaky empire."[5]

But atmospheric visuals and invocations of Detroit as a metonym for generalized decline—"We chose to focus our cameras on Detroit out of a gut feeling that this city," Ewing and Grady say, "may well be a harbinger of things to come for the rest of the country"—can't convey the fact that degeneration was always already built into the opulence. "We need no raging hurricane, we need no bolt from the blue," Bertolt Brecht wrote in his play Rise and Fall of the City of Mahagonny about boom-and-bust capitalism: "There's no havoc which they might have done that we cannot better do."[6] And so Ford, General Motors (GM), and Chrysler began to move more and more of their operations out of the downtown area to the suburbs, rural areas, and then overseas, not because, as the historian Thomas Sugrue writes, of economic competition from abroad but because they wanted to weaken union power and municipal oversight.[7] Ewing and Grady, in discussing their film, say that "Detroit lost 25 percent of its population between 2000 and 2010," relating population decline to "globalization." But the evacuation of the Motor City got under way much earlier, when U.S. corporations were able to set wage and price standards free from any pressure abroad. Even as the economy boomed in the 1950s and 1960s, fifty Detroit residents were already packing up and leaving their city every day. By the time the Berlin Wall fell, in 1989, Detroit could count tens of thousands of empty lots and more than fifteen thousand abandoned homes. Stunning Beaux Arts and modernist buildings were deserted, left to return to nature, their floors and roofs covered by switchgrass. They now serve as little more than ornate birdhouses.[8]

There have been dissections aplenty about what went wrong with the U.S. auto industry, as well as fond reminiscences about Detroit's salad days, about outsized tailfins and double-barrel carburetors. In 2008 the iconic Clint Eastwood even put the iconic white autoworker to rest in his movie *Gran Torino* (though Eastwood's sacrificial suicide, which in the film suggested a coming to terms with the rest of the world, now seems premature considering the subsequent rise of the racially aggrieved Tea Party). Few of these postmortems have conveyed, however, just how crucial Detroit was to U.S. foreign policy (although Eastwood, by linking Detroit's demise to the blowback from President Nixon's illegal war in Laos, at least came closer than most).

In mythological terms, however, Detroit remains the ancestral birthplace of storied American capitalism. And as we look back in the years to come, we may see the decline of the auto industry as a blow to American power comparable to the end of the Raj, Britain's loss of India. Detroit supplied a continual stream of symbols of America's cultural power; a marker of a world power as much as was the possession of a colony or the bomb, in the second half of the twentieth century, was the ability to make a precision V8 engine. But Detroit also offered the organizational know-how necessary to run a vast industrial enterprise like a car company—or an empire. Pundits love to quote GM President "Engine" Charlie Wilson, who once famously said that he thought that what was good for America "was good for General Motors, and vice versa." It's rarely noted, however, that Wilson made his remark at his Senate confirmation hearings to become Eisenhower's secretary of Defense. At the Pentagon, Wilson would impose GM's corporate bureaucratic model on the armed forces, modernizing them to fight the Cold War. After GM, Ford took the reins, with John F. Kennedy tapping CEO Robert McNamara and his "whiz kids" to ready American troops for a "long twilight struggle, year in and year out," as Kennedy put it in his inaugural address. McNamara used Ford's integrated "systems management" approach to wage "mechanized, dehumanizing slaughter" from the skies over Vietnam, Laos, and Cambodia, as the historian Gabriel Kolko once wrote.[9]

Among the most imposing of Detroit's relics is Henry Ford's Highland

Park factory, shuttered since the late 1950s. Dubbed the Crystal Palace for its floor-to-ceiling glass walls, it was here that Ford perfected assembly-line production, building up to nine thousand Model Ts a day—a million by 1915—and catapulting the United States ahead of industrial Europe. It was also here that Ford first paid his workers five dollars a day, creating one of the fastest-growing and most prosperous working-class neighborhoods in all of America, filled with fine arts-and-crafts-style homes. Today, Highland Park looks like a war zone, its streets covered with shattered glass and lined with burned-out houses. More than 30 percent of its population lives in poverty, with higher than 20 percent unemployment and a median yearly income of less than $20,000. There is one reminder that it wasn't always so, a small historical register plaque outside the Ford factory, which reads: "Mass production soon moved from here to all phases of American industry and set the pattern of abundance for 20th Century living."

America in the Amazon

To truly appreciate the relationship between capitalism, empire, and decay, one could tour another set of ruins far from the Midwest rustbelt; they lie, in fact, deep in, of all places, the Brazilian Amazon rainforest. There, overrun by tropical vines, sits Henry Ford's testament to the belief that the American Way of Life could easily be exported, even to one of the wildest places on the planet.

Ford owned forests in Michigan as well as mines in Kentucky and West Virginia, which gave him control over every natural resource needed to make a car—save rubber. So in 1927 he obtained an Amazonian land grant the size of a small American state. Ford could have simply set up a purchasing office there and bought rubber from local producers, leaving them to live their lives as they saw fit. That's what other rubber exporters did. Ford, however, had more ambitious ideas. He felt compelled to cultivate not only "rubber but the rubber gatherers as well."[10] He thus set out to overlay Americana on Amazonia. He tasked his managers with building Cape Cod–style shingled houses for the Brazilian workforce he hired. He urged the workers to tend flower and vegetable gardens, and to eat whole wheat bread, unpolished rice, canned Michigan peaches, and oatmeal. He named his jungle town, with suitable pride, Fordlandia.

It was the 1920s, of course, and his managers enforced, or tried to enforce, U.S. rules on alcohol, though Prohibition wasn't in effect in Brazil, as it was in the United States at the time. On weekends, the company organized square dances and recitations of the poetry of Henry Longfellow. The hospital Ford had built in the town offered free health care for workers and visitors alike; it was designed by Albert Kahn, the renowned architect who built several of Detroit's most famous buildings, including the Crystal Palace. Fordlandia had a central square, sidewalks, indoor plumbing, manicured lawns, a movie theater, shoe stores, ice cream and perfume shops, swimming pools, tennis courts, a golf course, and Model Ts rolling down its paved streets.

The clash between Henry Ford—the man who reduced industrial production to its simplest motions in order to produce an infinite series of identical products, the first indistinguishable from the millionth—and the Amazon, the world's most complex and diverse ecosystem, was Chaplinesque in its absurdity, producing a parade of mishaps straight out of a Hollywood movie. Think *Modern Times* meets *Fitzcarraldo*. Brazilian workers rebelled against Ford's puritanism, and nature rebelled against his industrial regimentation. Run by incompetent managers who knew little about rubber planting, much less about social engineering, Fordlandia in its early years was plagued by vice, knife fights, and riots. The place seemed less *Our Town* than *Deadwood*, as brothels and bars sprawled around its edges.

Ford did eventually manage to gain control over his namesake fiefdom, but because he insisted that his managers plant rubber trees in tight rows—back in his Detroit factories, Ford famously crowded machines close together to minimize movement—he actually created the conditions for the explosive growth of the bugs and blight that feed off rubber, and these eventually laid waste to the plantation. Over the course of nearly two decades, Ford sank millions upon millions of dollars into trying to make his jungle utopia work the American way, yet not one drop of Fordlandia latex ever made its way into a Ford car.

Today in the Amazon, Albert Kahn's hospital has collapsed, the jungle has reclaimed the golf course and tennis courts, and bats have taken up residence in houses where American managers once lived, covering their plaster walls with a glaze of guano. The ruins of Fordlandia, in fact, look a lot like those in Highland Park, as well as in other rustbelt towns where neighborhoods that once hummed with life centered on a factory have now returned to weed. There is an uncanny resemblance between Fordlandia's rusting water tower, broken-glassed sawmill, and empty power plant and the husks of the same structures in Iron Mountain, a depressed industrial city on Michigan's Upper Peninsula that also used to be a Ford town. These similarities are fitting, for one could read in the rise and fall of Fordlandia the history of twentieth-century industrial capitalism—or better, of Fordism, the foundation of the United States' unique empire.

Fordism in the Jungle

No commemorative plaque marks its place in history, but Fordlandia, no less than the wreck of Detroit, is a monument to the titans of American capital— none more titanic than Ford—who believed that the United States offered a universal, and universally acknowledged, model for the rest of humanity. Ford preached with a pastor's confidence his one true idea: ever-increasing productivity combined with ever-increasing pay would both relieve human drudgery and create prosperous working-class communities, with corporate profits dependent on the continual expansion of consumer demand. "High wages," as Ford put it, to create "large markets."[11] By the late 1920s, Fordism—as this idea came to be called—was synonymous with Americanism, envied the world over for having apparently humanized industrial capitalism.

The term "Fordism" has evolved since the *Washington Post*, condemning Ford for briefly shutting down his factory rather than pay high coal prices, first defined it as "Ford efforts conceived in disregard or ignorance of Ford limitations."[12] Around this time, it was often interchangeable with "Taylorism," after Fredrick Taylor, the pioneer of motion analysis, who aimed to extract ever-greater productivity out of workers through the isolation of the individual tasks needed to make a product. It also denoted standardization, efficiency, and mass production. By the late 1920s, Fordism began to take on its more comprehensive meaning, whereby it signifies a modernization of economic thought that appreciated the value of high wages as a motor of industrial growth. Sociologists and intellectuals, particularly those in industrialized European countries, started using "Fordism" in tandem with "Americanism." In 1927, for instance, an article in London's *New Statesman* identified Americanism/Fordism as an industrial system in which the pace of the factory determined productivity (as opposed to the pace being set by a wage system which rewarded output): "The worker under Fordism is speeded up, whether he likes it or not, by the pace at which the factory runs, by the endless stream of articles ceaselessly propelled toward him by the remorseless chain of machines. He must work at the factory's pace, or go; and go he will, unless he is offered a special inducement to remain."[13] But the article also acknowledged that high wages, in addition to serving as an inducement to remain on the line, actually created large markets, which allowed industrialists to increase their takings even as profit margins are reduced: "It was found, not merely that high wages were fully compatible with low costs of production, but that the offer of higher wages still might be so used to stimulate a further fall in cost. High wages therefore became, with some employers, not merely a necessity that had to be faced, but a positive policy."[14] By the 1950s, the phrase "Fordism" had worked its way into social-science terminology, as scholars began to consider the foundations and implications of the United States's unprecedented postwar economic expansion.

Fordism, it is now known, contained within itself the seeds of its own unraveling: the breaking down of the assembly process into smaller and smaller tasks, combined with rapid advances in transportation and communication, made it easier for manufacturers to break out of the dependent relationship established by Ford between high wages and large markets. Goods could be made in one place and sold somewhere else, removing the incentive employers had to pay workers enough to buy the products they made.

That unraveling is most visible in the Amazon city of Manaus, about three hundred miles west of Fordlandia. Once the gilded epitome of rubber-boom excess in the nineteenth century, Manaus in the early twentieth century became a "city of the past," as the *Washington Post* observed, with a drop in global latex process "acting more slowly but as surely as the ashes of Vesuvius in Pompeii."[15] The city revived only in the late 1960s, when Brazil's military regime decreed it a free-trade zone. (There is little "free trade" about it, however, at least in the way that term implies minimal government intervention in the market. With its remote jungle location, deep in the continent's heartland, the city as a manufacturing center could not survive without significant government subsidies, needed to offset the high costs of transportation.) Exempt from import tariffs, Manaus became Brazil's national emporium. Cargo ships arrived at its deepwater port from the United States, Europe, and Asia to unload consumer goods. In 1969 the *New York Times* reported that a "feverish prosperity" had returned, as Brazilians from Rio, São Paulo, and other points south took advantage of improved, subsidized air flight, flying into the city to purchase duty-free toys, fans, radios, air conditioners, and television sets.[16] At the same time, the military government provided subsidies and reduced export taxes to stimulate industry, turning the city into one of the world's first brand-name assembly zones — similar to the Mexican *maquilas* that were then beginning to push against the southern border of the United States. Today, Manaus's industrial parks are home to about a hundred corporate plants, including those of Honda, Yamaha, Sony, Nokia, Phillips, Kodak, Samsung, and Sanyo. In 1999 Harley-Davidson opened its first offshore factory there. Gillette has its largest South American facility in the city. When someone in Latin America buys a DVD player, cell phone, TV, bicycle, or motorcycle, there is a good chance it was assembled in the middle of the world's largest tropical forest.

With the highest population growth rate in Brazil, Manaus has gone from fewer than 200,000 people in the mid-1960s to nearly three million residents today. The city bursts out of the Amazon like a perverse Oz, steadily eating away the surrounding emerald foliage. Like many other Third World cities, Manaus is plagued by rising poverty and crime, child prostitution, grid-locked traffic, pollution, and poor health care. There is no sewage plant in the city, and its waste flows untreated into the Rio Negro. Manaus accounts for 6 percent of Brazil's total manufacturing and provides about a hundred thousand jobs. Yet no matter how dynamic its export sector, the city can't possibly give employment to all the migrants who travel from the rural Amazon and beyond, desperate for work. On flights in, visitors can see the luxury condominiums that rise high along the river's sandy banks and, pressed up against them, low-lying slums built on wobbly stilts to protect against river flooding—a dramatic landscape of inequality in one of the most unequal countries in the world. It makes the distance that separated the homes of American managers from those of Brazilians in Fordlandia negligible in comparison.

Cities like Manaus, which are based on the assembly of corporate brand-name products, are the true heirs of Ford's legacy. Their economies are made possible by a process if not started then at least perfected by Ford's factory lines, that is, by the fragmentation of industrial production into a series of reducible, routinized, and reproducible parts. Ford imagined his industrial method as leading to greater social cohesion, through paternalism. In his more utopian moments, he envisioned a world in which industry and agriculture could exist in harmony, with factories providing seasonal labor for farmers and technology making life easier for the masses. It's an easy vision to mock, especially considering the brutality and dehumanizing discipline that reigned at his Detroit and Dearborn factories.

Yet actually existing Fordism at its most vigorous albeit short-lived stage did result in a kind of holism, where the extraction and processing of raw materials, integrated assembly lines, working-class populations, and consumer markets created vibrant economies and robust middle classes—at least in the circumscribed U.S. industrial belt. Anchoring it all was a belief that decent pay would lead to increased sales. Yet even as Ford was preaching his gospel of "high wages to create large markets," Fordism as an industrial method was making the balanced, whole world that Ford longed for impossible to achieve.

Today, the link between production and consumption, and between good pay and big markets, has been broken, invalidated by the global extension of the logic of the assembly line. Harley-Davidson, for instance, does not make motorcycles from start to finish in Manaus, but rather assembles bikes from parts manufactured elsewhere, which it then sells in the Brazilian market. Sony likewise uses free-trade zones—not just Manaus, but Colón in Panama, Ushuaia in southern Argentina, and Iquique in northern Chile—as low-tax entrepôts into national markets. The final convection of the product in these cities is a formality, done to exempt the product from import tax.

In other words, there is no relationship between the wages Harley-Davidson pays to make its product and the profits it receives from selling them. Instead of Ford's virtuous circuit of high wages and decent benefits generating expanding markets, a vicious one now rules: profits are derived not from well-paid workers affluent enough to buy what they have made, but from driving prices as low as they can go; this in turn renders good pay and humane benefits not only unnecessary for sustaining the economy, but impossible to maintain, since the best, and at times the only, place to cut production costs is labor. The result is a race to the bottom, a system of perpetual deindustrialization whereby corporations—including, most dramatically, the Ford Motor Company—bow before a global economy that they once mastered, moving manufacturing abroad in order to reduce labor costs just to survive.

In the lower Amazon, then, along about a three-hundred-mile axis, runs the history of modern capitalism. On one end is Fordlandia, a monument to the promise that was early-twentieth-century industrialization. "Ford built us a hospital; he paid his workers well and gave them good houses," a Fordlandia resident told a *Los Angeles Times* reporter in 1993, and I often heard, during my visits to the town, the following sentiment: "It would be nice if the company would come back."[17] On the other is Manaus, a city plagued by the kind of urban problems Ford thought he could transcend, but whose very existence owes much to the system he pioneered. Trying to reproduce America in the Amazon has yielded to outsourcing America to the Amazon.

Neoliberalism in the Americas, however, did not emerge simply from the economic and technological logic of Fordism. Much like the deliberate and self-aware efforts of Detroit's Big Three to lessen municipal oversight and union strength by moving operations out of the city—well before international competition justified such a move as unavoidable—U.S. corporations, among them the Ford Motor Company, organized themselves to confront increasing labor power and demands for reform in Latin America. In the mid-1960s, executives from over thirty U.S. firms founded the Business Group for Latin America, which included participation by Ford, U.S. Steel, DuPont, Standard Oil, Anaconda Copper, ITT, United Fruit, Chase, and other blue-chip industrial and financial companies. David Rockefeller, whose family had extensive holdings in Latin America, served as its liaison with the White House. The idea was both to influence Washington's hemispheric policy and to apply direct pressure at the source, funding the campaigns of friendly politicians, helping allies hold down prices, and providing financial guidance to cooperative regimes. When lobbying proved insufficient, members of the group, either individually or in concert, worked with the CIA to foment coups, as they did in Brazil in 1964 and Chile in 1973.[18]

Some went further: a number of multinational corporations, including Ford, Coca-Cola, Del Monte, Chrysler, Mercedes Benz, Firestone, Volkswagen, and others, have been accused in recent years of working closely with Latin American death squads—responsible for hundreds of thousands of killings throughout the hemisphere from the 1960s through the 1980s. In Brazil the daily O Globo reports that Volkswagen, Phillips, Firestone, and Chrysler organized a "working group" to coordinate with the military regime to identify militant workers.[19] Where in the 1960s, the former Ford CEO McNamara applied industrial "systems management" to reorganize the Pentagon to wage large-scale bombing missions in Southeast Asia, a subsidiary of the Ford Motor Company in Argentina worked on a smaller scale. As the historian Karen Robert has documented, with the help of Buenos Aires unionists, Ford provided Argentine death squads key support during the late 1970s and early 1980s. The company, for instance, established a detention center on the premises of its manufacturing plant outside Buenos Aires, where union activists were held. Ford also provided the death squads with a fleet of greenish gray Falcons.[20] The locally built Falcon had served as a symbol of Argentine modernity, a true badge of the promise of Fordism: the factory workers who built it were some of the highest paid in Latin America, making enough to purchase the product themselves. Now it became an emblem of terror, used to kidnap many of those same workers, many of whom were tortured, some disappeared. "Ford's exclusive contracts with the Argentine security forces throughout the dictatorship eventually made the Falcon the single most recognizable icon of repression," Robert writes, one that clearly still resonates today. She quotes Eduardo Pavlovsky, a well-known argentine psychologist and playwright: "Whenever a Falcon drove by or slowed down, we all knew that there would be kidnappings, disappearances, torture or murder. . . . It was the symbolic expression of terror. A death-mobile."[21]

Robert notes that the Argentine auto industry had exploded in the late 1960s, with strong unions winning high wages and even challenging "management's control of the factories." After a U.S.-backed 1976 coup, however, "Ford managers anxious to regain control over their factory found natural allies in the military faction that planned the coup. The wave of disappearances from Ford began the day of the coup and wrapped up within a few weeks. And they worked. All union activity ceased at Ford" until the early 1980s.[22] By placing this assault in an inter-American context, we can escape the allure of "ruin porn," as Leary writes, and chart the linkages connecting deindustrialization in Detroit and neoliberalism in Latin America; it was a precursor, in extreme form, of the assault on unionism that began in the United States under Ronald Reagan, itself part of the larger project of shifting the United States's economic center of gravity from the industrial Northeast and Midwest to the sunbelt South and Southwest, and hastening the transition to financial capitalism.

Errand into the Wilderness

It would be easy to read the story of Fordlandia as a parable of arrogance. With a surety of purpose and incuriosity about the world that seem all too familiar, Ford deliberately rejected expert advice and set out to turn the Amazon into the Midwest of his imagination. The more the project failed on its own terms—that is, to grow rubber—the more Ford company officials defended it as a civilizational mission; think of it as a kind of distant preview of the ever-expanding set of justifications for why the United States invaded Iraq in 2003. Yet Fordlandia cuts deeper into the marrow of the American experience than that.

Over fifty years ago, the Harvard historian Perry Miller gave a famous lecture which he titled "Errand into the Wilderness." In it, he tried to explain why English Puritans lit out for the New World to begin with, as opposed to, say, going to Holland. They went, Miller suggested, not just to escape the corruptions of the Church of England but to complete the Protestant reformation of Christendom that had stalled in Europe.

The Puritans did not flee to the New World, Miller said, but rather sought to give the faithful back in England a "working model" of a purer community.[23] Put another way, central from the beginning to American expansion was "deep disquietude," a feeling that "something had gone wrong" at home.[24] With the Massachusetts Bay Colony just a few decades old, a dissatisfied Cotton Mather began to learn Spanish, thinking that a better "New Jerusalem" could be raised in Mexico.

The founding of Fordlandia was driven by a similar restlessness, a chafing sense, even in the good times, that "something had gone wrong" in America. When Ford embarked on his Amazon adventure, he had already spent the greater part of two decades, and a large part of his enormous fortune, trying to reform American society. His frustrations and discontents with domestic politics and culture were legion. War, unions, Wall Street, energy monopolies, Jews, modern dance, cow's milk, both Theodore and Franklin Roosevelt, cigarettes, and alcohol were among his many targets and complaints. Yet churning beneath all these imagined annoyances was the fact that the force of industrial capitalism he had helped unleash was undermining the world he hoped to restore.

In Rome, the ruins came after the empire fell. In the United States, the destruction of Detroit happened even as the country was rising to new heights as a superpower.

Ford sensed this unraveling early on and responded to it, trying at least to slow it, in ever more eccentric ways. He established throughout Michigan a series of decentralized "village-industries" designed to balance farm and factory work and rescue small-town America. Yet his pastoral communes were no match for the raw power of the changes he had played such a large part in engendering. So he turned to the Amazon to raise his City on a Hill, or in this case a city in a tropical river valley, pulling together all the many strains of his utopianism in one last, desperate bid for success.

Ironies abound: in the Amazon, soybeans, which Ford promoted as a wonder crop that could sustain farming communities by creating an industrial market for agricultural products (soy plastic, soy oil, soy food), are today the most socially violent agent of deforestation, far surpassing the havoc caused by logging and ranching. Large-scale, low-labor, highly mechanized—that is, Fordist—soy plantations are pushing deeper into the jungle with new soy hybrids able to sustain more and more humidity—hybridization is in effect the logic of Fordism pushed into the cellular structure—displacing whole communities, generating urban sprawl in Amazon cities like Manaus and elsewhere, and disrupting local food markets. In fact, one major area where

Ford planted rubber is now given over completely to soybeans. And while no Fordlandia rubber ever made it into a Ford car, today plastic made from Amazon soy can be found in some Ford models. In Detroit, Ford's pastoral of worker-farmers never took hold. But today local community activists, with help from desperate municipal officials, are promoting urban gardening, hoping to return large, abandoned areas of the city to seed as a solution to its food crisis.

Nearly a century ago, the journalist Walter Lippmann remarked that Henry Ford's drive to make the world anew represented a common strain of "primitive Americanism," reinforced by a confidence born of unparalleled achievement. He then followed with a question meant to be sarcastic but which was, in fact, all too prophetic: "Why shouldn't success in Detroit assure success in front of Baghdad?"[25] We know the ruination that befell Detroit. Whither Baghdad? Whither America?

Notes

1. The term "creative destruction" comes from Shumpeter, *Capitalism, Socialism, and Democracy*, 83.

2. Leary, "Detroitism."

3. See, for example, Marchand and Meffre, *The Ruins of Detroit*. As to *Red Dawn*, John Patrick Leary writes in "Detroitism" that a "long-abandoned modernist skyscraper coincidentally undergoing demolition served as a backdrop for battle scenes between American guerrillas and the Communist occupiers, now Chinese. For weeks, Chinese propaganda posters fluttered in the foreground of the half-destroyed office building, whose jagged entrails were visible through the holes opened by the wrecking ball. A pedestrian routinely bumped into Asian-American extras with Michigan accents and fake Kalashnikovs, while a parking garage played the role of a Communist police station. It was an uncanny spectacle: the very real rubble of the Motor City's industrial economy serving as the movie backdrop for post-industrial America's paranoid fantasies of national victimization. What made it even weirder was the fact that the film's producers just left the posters hanging when they packed up. A red-and-yellow poster on that same parking garage assured us for weeks afterward that our new rulers were 'here to help.'" After the film was shot, the producers decided to make North Korea the main occupying country, so as not to offend the Chinese. The Chinese invasion is coming in another form: the *New York Times* reported that in 2011, "Chinese-made cars have quietly arrived in North America for the first time" (Nick Bunkley and Ian Austen, "In Canada, a Car Built in China," *New York Times*, 20 December 2011).

4. Leary, "Detroitism."

5. Heidi Ewing and Rachel Grady, "Dismantling Detroit," *New York Times*, 18 January 2012, http://www.nytimes.com/2012/01/19/opinion/dismantling-detroit.html.

6. Willett and Manheim, *The Rise and Fall of the City of Mahagonny*, 27.

7. Sugrue, *The Origins of the Urban Crisis*.

8. In the summer of 2010, about twenty thousand grassroots activists arrived in Detroit to hold a Social Forum, affiliated with the World Social Forum, highlighting that it is in the U.S. neglected urban wastelands where some of the most creative efforts to build a humane, sustainable life in the midst of what for many is a permanent crisis are being worked out. For a more detailed discussion of Detroit's devastation, particularly as it relates to the distribution of food, along with efforts by local community organizers to turn the city into a showcase for social movements, see Ben Ehrenreich, "Detroit's Social Forum: Hope in a Crisis," *Nation*, 24 June 2010. See also Solnit, *A Paradise Built in Hell*; and Klein, *The Shock Doctrine*.

9. Falk, Kolko, and Lifton, *Crimes of War*, 15.

10. "Fordlandia, Brazil," *Washington Post*, 12 August 1931.

11. Nevins and Hill, *Ford*, 604.

12. "The Ford Shutdown," *Washington Post*, 18 September 1922.

13. Reprinted in the *Living Age*, 15 May 1927.

14. Ibid.

15. "Brazil's Famous City of Folly," *Washington Post*, 15 February 1914.

16. "Boom, Bust, and Now Boom Again in Amazon Town," *New York Times*, 1 July 1969.

17. "Ford's Dream Lies in Decay," *Los Angeles Times*, 9 March 1993.

18. Langguth, *Hidden Terrors*, 104, 123. See the discussion in Grandin, *Empire's Workshop*, 14–15.

19. José Casado, "Como as empresas ajudaram a ditadura no Brasil," *O Globo*, 15 May 2005.

20. Robert, "The Falcon Remembered"; Robert, "The Case against Ford." See also Basualdo, "Complicidad patronal-militar en la última dictadura argentina."

21. Robert, "The Falcon Remembered," 12.

22. Robert, "The Case against Ford," 4.

23. Perry Miller, *Errand into the Wilderness*, 11.

24. Ibid., 2.

25. Quoted in Brinkley, *Wheels for the World*, 232.

PART II   *Living in Ruins: Degradations and Regenerations*

Detritus in Durban

Polluted Environs and the Biopolitics of Refusal

I'm not worried about the environment. All I want is my piece of oxygen!
—JANE GLOVER, interview by Sharad Chari, Durban, South Africa, 23 August 2003

Every epoch not only dreams the next, but while dreaming impels it towards wake-
fulness. It bears its end within itself, and reveals it—as Hegel already recognized—by
a ruse. With the upheaval of the market economy, we begin to realize the monuments of the bourgeoisie as ruins even before they have crumbled.
—WALTER BENJAMIN, "Paris"

Jane Glover and I sat at the doorstep of the flat she had recently occupied in
the section of the Woodville Road Flats that she calls "the ghetto within the
ghetto." From our vantage, we could not see the oil refinery at the center of
the former Coloured township of Wentworth in Durban, South Africa.[1] I had
been coming to Wentworth and neighboring Merebank to research changing forms of state racism and struggle in these areas, which are cheek-by-
jowl with oil refineries (Engen, owned by Malaysian Petronas, and SAPREF,
a joint venture of Shell South Africa and British Petroleum South Africa),
a pulp and paper mill (Mondi Paper, formerly of the Anglo-American con-
glomerate), a former airport, and the industrial areas of Jacobs and Mo-
beni.[2] Located in a valley that traps pollution, South Durban has witnessed
the rise of one of Southern Africa's most important community-based and
internationally networked environmental justice movements. Residents in
these areas have been engaged in struggles over housing, services, contract

labor, and health care, as they refuse to be forgotten in the toxic valley of South Durban.

Jane and I sat facing engineering workshops as she spoke of insecure work and familial violence, homeless children living like a band of Artful Dodgers in an abandoned warehouse, rampant theft and resale of stolen objects which makes suspects of friends and lovers, drug and sex trades, and "gangsters" in and out of prison. Against this freighted narrative backdrop, Jane Glover praised God for her survival and looked out wistfully at the neighborhood she calls home. When I suggested a shift of registers to the effects of living next to oil refineries, the focus of media coverage on Wentworth, she laughed and exclaimed, "I'm not worried about the environment. All I want is my piece of oxygen!"

Jane had recently been part of a group of women who occupied flats left vacant by the Provincial Housing Department. This group had challenged the authority of the main community organization, the Wentworth Development Forum (WDF), which they saw as dragging its feet in negotiations over construction tenders, which would not have been much benefit to them. When they could wait no longer, the women held hands and prayed to the Holy Spirit for the strength to act. By the next morning, they had taken over the flats and could not be dislodged. The WDF called a meeting with prominent Durban activists at the Austerville Community Centre, above the public library, and the women of Woodville Road were publicly censured for defying their purported leaders. In an impromptu response, Jane invoked feelings of stigma and frustration widespread in Wentworth: "I woke up one morning and I said to myself, 'What is it that depresses me so much about living here?' And when I looked around, I looked at the flat and I said, 'My god! It looks like the walls are closing in on me!' So, if we failed somewhere along the way, we are so sorry. You know, when we needed some men around, there were no men available. So we took it upon ourselves to get in there and take on the task." Through well-worn themes like the difficulties of sexual intimacy in overcrowded flats that had become claustrophobic, Jane performed the betrayal of a proper sexuality.[3] Her appeals to God, population pressure, and family values may have been strategic, but they provided an opportunity for a sharp lambaste against the political inactivity of the men around her, as well as against the idioms of struggle through which politics had been conventionally construed. Ideas of purity and pollution pervade her comments, despite a lack of reference to oil refineries. Pentecostalism, pervasive in Wentworth's backyard churches, adds emotional intensity to her fight for the fruit of this world.

I have revisited this vignette before; it continues to challenge the research I have been engaged in through multiple revisits since 2002.[4] As I replay her public speech, I imagine Jane Glover amassing all forms of ruination, heaping them in a pile in middle of the Austerville Community Centre. I have puzzled over her rejection of an environmental idiom that would seem to explain the most obvious and politically expedient form of degradation next to an oil refinery. While thinking through popular refusal to become detritus, or political evidence forged in relation to changing forms of racialization, or the remains of a long and discontinuous history of state racism and opposition, I have experimented with concepts that in different ways attend to how people refuse to be ruined, while surrounded by processes of ruination.[5] I have come to see Jane's demand for "a piece of oxygen" as a ruse in Walter Benjamin's sense, in that it does not just refuse environmentalism, but also points in its tone and texture to simmering, emergent critique in the imaginations of people living with chronic exposure to toxic pollution.

I went to Wentworth in 2002 to understand how people living in a place saturated by industrial pollution contend with and refuse a variety of forms of detritus, remains, and waste foisted on their corner of South Africa's turbulent present. I soon found that my key concept, detritus, ran the risk of conflating quite different processes.[6] I was not the only one who ran this risk. In the face of corporate and governmental dissimulation about the health effects of air pollution, the most obvious kind of detritus in South Durban, Wentworth's residents reflect on other markers of degraded life and landscape, as in the range of horror stories about sex, drugs, and crime that Jane Glover and several other residents have regaled me with. When the former president Thabo Mbeki visited Wentworth before the elections of 2005, he was met with a similar litany of tales of moral and social decay. Debates circulate in Wentworth about whether environmental critique ought to be primary vis-à-vis multiple forms of suffering and deprivation, and whether to accept "social responsibility" funds from industry or whether this was pollution of another kind.

In contrast to this differentiated and fragmented contagion talk, South Durban had gained a certain kind of visibility on the Left after a highly visible strike in Wentworth opened the possibility of a conjoining of labor and environmental militancy. A primer on post-apartheid activism uses this event to argue for a brewing movement linking struggles across South Africa's townships.[7] However, this work only begins to ask how, between peaks of protest, people actively engage problems and revise their conception of politics.[8] I sought to intervene in these debates by turning precisely to what they evade: how people live with and refuse the detritus of industrial capital and state-sanctioned racism through critical sensitivities that are contradictory, uncertain, and "not (yet) counter-partisan."[9] Ann Laura Stoler frames the problem as "what people are *left with* . . . in the gutted infrastructures of segregated cityscapes and in the microecologies of matter and mind."[10]

In unpacking multiple senses of detritus, remain, ruin, ruination, and debris, I draw on several areas of scholarship. The first concerns the transition from apartheid, whether conceived through the lens of capital, livelihoods and social transformation, changing forms of activism, or changing modes of racism.[11] The materiality of racial infrastructure is relatively neglected in this scholarship, despite pioneering work on geographies of segregation, instabilities of labor control, and emergent forms of urban life during and after apartheid.[12]

In asking what does not transform, what is striking is that the industries that surround Wentworth and Merebank have retained the state-sanctioned right to pollute. Seemingly incontrovertible evidence of the effects of atmospheric pollution on children's health has been flouted by an alliance of local government and corporate power. Moreover, the technocratic approach of city management, which claims to incorporate civic interests as "stakeholders," denigrates popular determination of urban form and process, or what Henri Lefebvre called "the right to the city."[13] This demand, I argue, was one aspect of anti-apartheid critique from the recent past of the 1970s and 1980s which has returned with a vengeance in post-apartheid times.

To think of built environments, state–capital alliances, and limits to popular struggle in relation to the material infrastructure of racism extends a line of thinking from Walter Benjamin's classic essay, "Theses on the Philosophy of History." In his oft-cited parable of the Angel of History, faced backward against the gale of progress, Benjamin writes, "Where we see a chain of events, he sees one single catastrophe which keeps piling wreckage upon wreckage and hurls it in front of his feet."[14] Scholars have followed this cue to interrogate the modernity of ruins, from the collection of things in the lives of the Appalachian poor, to the ruins of Fordist industry in the U.S. Midwest, to the ruins of colonialism in Namibia, to legendary ships stranded by a shifting river in Argentina's Gran Chaco.[15] Stoler's intervention in this body of work has been to insist on the differential and active nature of imperial debris in people's lives, and the varied forms of refusal immanent in situations of ruination.[16]

Photography and film have been potent in attempts at arresting narratives of progress, in documenting debris and refusal.[17] Postindustrial dereliction is such a widely accepted form of debris that, as George Steinmetz wryly observes, the city of Detroit "markets its ruination to Hollywood as a backdrop for dystopian science fiction fantasies and gritty crime films."[18] What remains less explored is Benjamin's call to see the monuments of capitalist production and consumption *also* as piles of waste, productive of profit and of suffering. In this light, the thriving industrial geography of South Durban is also a festering site of pollution and injustice.

If focus on ruination tells us how people live with ruins in dialectical geographies of destructive creation, this lens also points to the evidentiary means through which people critically interrogate their ruination. This takes me to a second key area of debate in South Africa, concerning archives, memory, and testimony after apartheid. Several scholars have approached the profusion of memoir, oral history, museum studies, and forms of narrative that question the awkward temporality of "post-apartheid"; the truth-telling imperative unleashed by the Truth and Reconciliation Commission; and memoir writing that variously confronts the intimate erasures of anti-apartheid narration.[19]

When popular testimony is invoked as counterpoint to statist or nationalist narratives, however, it often reproduces elite fantasies of subaltern autonomy and representation that Gayatri Spivak famously cautioned against.[20] To think with ruins and remains provides a different view of popular critique than that expressed by subalternity as the aporetic moment in representation. Indeed, if subalternity is conceived of in relation to imperial crisis and ruination, the problem of the subaltern is not a choice between redeeming a repressed authentic past or fashioning a different present.[21] To think of subalternity relationally in this way shifts focus from the problem of the subaltern as agentive subject to the differentially ordered material terrain in which past and present are unequally lived.[22] If subalternity and material ruination are seen relationally, the latter is less about restoring the truth about the past or present, than about tracking discontinuities between critique that is recognized and that which is disqualified or deemed inappropriate.[23]

In this light, Jane's statements can be seen as an argument in ruin in two senses: as speaking from a space saturated by despoliation, and as a compromised articulation that mocks the power to transform reality. Unlike the subaltern presumed by much of postcolonial studies as a site of withholding of otherness, Jane and others in Wentworth speak precisely in the ruinous terms of elite discourse in ways that Stoler argues of subalterns in the Deli plantation belt of Sumatra, who "tapped into the uncertainties, fears, and fantasies of European hidden scripts by playing them back to planters and officials for their own political purposes."[24]

While Jane appears contemptuous of environmentalism as a way to resolve the many forms of inequality and suffering she has experienced and witnessed, she also affirms a god-given right to the natural means of life. With the simple demand for "a piece of oxygen," Jane pulls the emergency break on the notion of inevitable democratization in post-apartheid South Africa, where not even clean air can be assumed to be an inalienable right. Her demand is absolute and visceral, a call to consign inequalities to an actual past.[25]

From exploring the evidentiary means with which residents like Jane formulate critiques of the racialized present, my research began to shift back to the discontinuous and struggled history of racial infrastructure and opposition, to layers of authorized and disqualified critique.[26] Following a materialist interpretation of biopolitics in an imperial frame, I suggest that this momentary mobilization of poor women as an instance of what Jean Comaroff reservedly calls a reimagining of "(bio)politics" in contemporary South Africa, most vividly through the politics of HIV/AIDS.[27] Widespread protests over housing, services, land, health care, and the means of livability and livelihood, deepening under the presidencies of Thabo Mbeki and Jacob Zuma, attest to something deeper than the critique of neoliberal economic policy and of the technocratic language of "service delivery"; rather, they express a critiques of politics itself.[28] "(Bio)politics" is a rhetorically apt term, as South African realities push Foucault's concept beyond its Euro-American comfort zones, specifically in the tendency to think in epochal and Manichean ways about the fate of biopolitical tools, for instance in the notion of the proliferation of "the camp."[29]

Drawing on Foucault's insight that biopolitical techniques have been contingently instrumental to varied forms of state racism, some scholars turn to the ways in which biopolitical tools have been deployed in struggles over unequal means of life, in producing what Didier Fassin calls "bio-inequalities," and in calling them into question.[30] Fassin argues that concrete attention to the lived experience of inequalities in the means of life elaborates Foucault's commitments. The same could be said for historical and ethnographic research on struggles over biopolitical expertise in contexts ranging from the compromised "biological citizenship" of Chernobyl survivors, to the suppression of health risks associated with asbestos mining in apartheid South Africa, to various strategies employed in breast cancer activism in the United States.[31] Rather than the proliferation of a genocidal imperative assumed by some readings of Agamben, these studies prompt questions about how degraded or dishonored subjects seek to critique expert knowledge in the ruins of biopolitical sovereignty. In the latent space of knowledge that is disqualified but never destroyed, and in the face of censure from community activist leadership, Jane questions the efficacy of environmentalism as a liberatory discourse, marking in angry words the bio-inequalities that she refuses.

The following section turns to the broader forces that shape specific forms of detritus and refusal in what Nancy Peluso and Michael Watts call "violent environments."[32] My argument is that South Durban has been shaped into a kind of biopolitical space that has prepared its Indian and Coloured residents for political engagement, within limits set by capital and the racial state. When the lines have become sharp, the obstacles to change have been sharpened and expert knowledge about pollution and degradation more tightly circumscribed. In the face of official dissimulation, I then turn to critical sentiments fostered in this space, particularly through photography and film. These have been powerful media for drawing sentiment into the realm of critique, to question dominant as well as emergent critical imaginations as they literally occupy space.[33] Photography and film also provide an opportunity to think about how expert and disqualified knowledge are presented alongside each other as spatially subjacent, conserving the means of argument in ruins.

What follows is an exploration of the conditions for refusal of the life-degrading presence of the infrastructure of state racism. The immediate paradox that people living in conditions of multifaceted and protracted degradation face is the evasive character of admissible evidence of their plight. Nothing seems proof enough; not even, in South Durban, incontrovertible scientific evidence of air pollution. When I told an interlocutor in Wentworth who I call Frank that my broader research project is called "Apartheid Remains," he responded, "True!" My point was not that all that was solid in apartheid South Africa lives on, but Frank's response is that many remnants continue to frustrate change today. I conclude with this figure, as he cautiously treads the borders between expert and disqualified knowledge each day as a self-taught community health care professional.

Racial Remains in Violent Environments

Wentworth is not, two decades after the repeal of the Group Areas Act of 1991, a designated "Coloured township." Yet the effects of racial identification stick to people and their neighborhood despite their best intentions.

When residents speak of their "race" trouble, they follow well-worn tracks, whether in repeating stories about parents unable to help children complete assignments on "Coloured culture" or in statements like "We weren't white enough then, we're not black enough now." Talk about "race trouble" circulates with such facility that it ought to be understood as indexing a more general philosophical problem faced by Indians and Coloureds in the new South Africa.[34]

Unlike Indians in neighboring Merebank, who can resignify racial artifacts as markers of "culture" to engage in moral debate about "cultural loss," as Thomas Blom Hansen notes on the township of Chatsworth, Wentworth's Coloureds constantly face the charge, and challenge, of racial inauthenticity.[35] As Grant Farred puts it, Coloureds "have no a priori or pre-lapsarian moment; [nor can they] retreat into a mythic precolonial 'innocence.' Coloured difference is . . . insufficiently different for them to conceive of themselves as anything but South African."[36] Indeed, if South Africans as a coherent people do not yet exist, as Ivor Chipkin provocatively argues, Colouredness presents a yearning for a postracial nation.[37] In this popular turmoil about "race" and "nation," what evades consciousness but permeates practice is the visceral materiality of "race" as linguistic and bodily performance and as "infrahumanity" engineered into bodies, hearts, and lived environs, or rather necropolitical landscapes.[38]

Wentworth's juxtaposition of racialized, polluted life abutting corporate power represents in microcosm what scholars argue about geographies of accumulation and disaccumulation across the continent. James Ferguson perceptively argues that the coexistence of securitized, enclaved, extractive accumulation alongside humanitarian hinterlands that contain l'Afrique inutile or "the unusable Africa" revives a colonial spatial imaginary of extractive territoriality alongside structured neglect.[39] Modern South Africa, fundamentally shaped by imperial extractive capital and racialized dispossession, incorporates this dual dynamic in varied ways.[40]

To call the material effects of these processes "imperial formations" is to think beyond functional articulations of racial capital and despoliation, a key objective in radical anti-apartheid writing on relations between capitalism and apartheid.[41] With time, both theory and its political scaffolding have shifted. Protracted imperial effects continue to shape a fissured landscape of securitized territoriality and structured neglect in examples that are legion, from gated communities shielded from shack settlements, to faux-public shopping malls that exclude informal traders.[42]

Specific histories of space matters considerably, if we are to understand how South Durban's residents have been not entirely excluded but enabled to participate in what Partha Chatterjee calls a "politics of the governed."[43] South Durban was forged as a particular kind of biopolitical space through a set of processes of dispossession, spatial transformation, population movement, and differential investment in the means of life. In the late nineteenth century and early twentieth, while discourses of contagion were drawn into new projects of exclusion and segregation across white supremacies, South Durban was something of a frontier zone. Here, a sprawling "black belt" of informal peasant-workers, fishermen, and migrant workers settled the urban perimeter, making it habitable, cultivable, and open to new uses.

White residents within the Borough of Durban mobilized the city, particularly through discourses of public health, to incorporate the southern periphery and transform its character.[44] Importantly, and decades before apartheid, the local and provincial state effected mass forced removals of people by "race group" in South Durban in the 1930s and 1940s, for industrial or infrastructural spatial uses.[45] Durban's undulating hills, rivers, and ridges provided useful physical barriers for zoning. The relatively flat topography of South Durban was highly sought after for industrial expansion, and South Durban Basin took its specifically pernicious spatial form by the 1940s, providing residence for intermediate groups of Indians and Coloureds in a deadly toxic sink.

Forced removals of Indian and Coloured populations to segregated housing schemes between the 1940s and the early 1970s paralleled the construction of South Durban's two oil refineries and the Mondi Paper Mill. In 1989, just as the Mobil refinery was being divested under pressure from the Global Anti-Apartheid Movement, the refinery began taking more seriously the authority of environmental discourse. In 1990 the Merebank Ratepayers Association (MRA), the main civic organization in the Indian area neighboring Wentworth, tried to use the moment of the unbanning of the African National Congress (ANC) to conduct a survey of residents' experience of atmospheric air pollution and respiratory ill-health; the results were striking and the MRA proclaimed a "pollution crisis," but the survey was quickly disqualified by the Health Department and the refineries for its lack of scientific evidence.[46] The refinery attributed problems of ill-health to a generic industrialization and urbanization, in which it had disappeared as a culpable agent. If pollution is a thing that knows no color, the corporations were arguing that it knows no owner either.

Industry signaled the possibility, not the actuality, of industrial jobs for its residential neighbors. While Wentworth surrounds the Engen refinery, it has never been a company town reliant on local labor, despite the recognized skills of Wentworth men as exemplary industrial artisans who built refineries across the country. By the 1980s, the most fortunate of these artisans in Wentworth had risen from being semiskilled pipe fitters and boilermakers to being "independent" contractors of artisanal labor. In contrast, most of Wentworth's residents have watched the refineries turn to contracting out and limiting local employment, particularly after the formation of a militant independent labor union, the Chemical, Engineering and Industrial Workers Union (CEIWU). Wentworth's artisans face a final insult when they return from limited-duration migrant contracts to witness jobless growth in the transformation of South Durban into a chemical-industries hub in which their skills have not been considered significant.

An opportune moment for public action emerged in 1995, when the newly elected President Nelson Mandela stopped en route to the Engen refinery to listen to the concerns of protesters.[47] This chance encounter initiated a course of events leading to the formation of South Durban Community Environmental Alliance (SDCEA) in 1997, linking civic organizations from across South Durban's racial divides with the mandate of the icon who embodied democratic transition and racial reconciliation. SDCEA is tied through organizers and campaigns to the neighborhood-based Wentworth Development Forum (WDF), and to the environmental justice organization groundWork. Formed in 1999 to focus on oil and air pollution from chemical industries, health care waste and incineration, and hazardous waste groundWork subsequently became a chapter of the international NGO Friends of the Earth. This alliance of organizations links activism across spatial scales, from "fenceline communities" that live cheek-by-jowl with industry, to city, provincial, national, and international advocacy.

There are resonances here with the multiscalar Global Anti-Apartheid Movement, but with a new premium on transparency and publicity not always possible in the era of apartheid. Indeed, this activism challenges the valorization of hierarchy and secrecy inherited by the ruling alliance of the ANC and the South African Communist Party (SACP) from the exiled and underground liberation movement of the past. The multiscalar alliance of WDF, SDCEA, and groundWork has effectively pressured all scales of government, juggling research, campaigning, legal activism, street demonstration, and local pollution monitoring.[48]

Legal struggles highlight concretely how objects from the past persist past their legitimate expiry date in a democratic era. For years, the key legislation regulating air pollution was the Atmospheric Pollution Prevention Act

(APPA) of 1965, which was largely unenforced with respect to black communities.[49] An important means to challenge this legislation came from the environmental clause enshrined in the Constitutional Bill of Rights, which enshrines the right "to an environment that is not harmful to . . . health or well-being; and . . . to have the environment protected, for the benefit of present and future generations."[50] In fighting for a new air pollution act, groundWork used this environmental clause and other constitutional and legal rights to information, protection for whistle-blowers, and representation by parties acting in the public interest.[51]

As a result of the long history of civic engagement, Durban was chosen as the site for the piloting of an air-quality management system under the auspices of the Multi-Point Plan, and the new Air Quality Act of 2004 was signed into law in late 2005, replacing the 1965 act. What this struggle shows is that elements of imperial power can be consigned to the past through the courts, but groundWork has remained vigilant of loopholes and backdoors through which corporate power can continue to hold onto its historic subsidies. In this spirit, groundWork argues for a broader list of hazardous chemicals, ongoing ground-based monitoring, strict enforcement of pollution standards, and popular participation in monitoring of enforcement. The struggle against environmental violence is ongoing.

Local debates in 2004 highlight the importance of naming industrial waste and attending to its disposal. The key issue was the proposed expansion of the Mondi paper mill through what industry called a combustor, but which SDCEA and groundWork insisted was an incinerator. Mondi first made the proposal in 1998 to install a "fluidised boiler," following thwarted attempts to extend their ash landfill sites in Merebank as well as in the nearby former African township of Umlazi. SDCEA mobilized quickly to prevent both extensions, and effectively closed down the Umlazi toxic dump in February 1997, a high point in the making of an interracial environmental movement in South Durban. Faced with rising transport costs for landfills farther afield, Mondi shifted to re-burn wastes in a boiler on plant. This, SDCEA argued, is what an incinerator does.

The ensuing struggle brought several points into view. First, definitions were key: Was this a combustor to produce steam and power, or an incinerator to burn waste? Second, legal activists who caught Mondi out on a technicality in their exemption from an environmental impact assessment report illuminated the close level of informal ties between local government and capital. Finally, tensions between legal counsel and environmental activists over the possibility of negotiating a settlement brought to the fore the importance for SDCEA and groundWork in maintaining a strong stance against incineration. Anti-incineration, they found, works as a strong emotive tool for local mobilization, as well as for linking with international anti-incineration activism.

A second legal struggle fought by civic and labor organizations in Wentworth, as across South Africa, concerned the renewal in 2007 of the National Key Points Act of 1980, apartheid legislation to protect places of strategic national interest from sabotage. Oil refineries and other key industries and infrastructure were zoned as strategic sites under this legislation. The Wentworth refinery was in fact subject to a failed attack with rocket-propelled grenades by members of Umkhonto we Sizwe (MK), the armed wing of the ANC, in May 1984; all the militants were killed in a shoot-out with the police.[52] Had the rockets made their mark, the fireball would have decimated the neighborhood. In contrast to this suicidal impulse to turn the refinery and its neighbors into ash are ongoing efforts to show concrete evidence of unemployed workers, infirm bodies, and unlivable environs on the corporation's doorsteps. For both labor and environmental activists, the space around the refinery has been invaluable for collecting evidence of pollution and for staging confrontation.

After 1994, protest, confrontation, and civic monitoring on the rise around Engen for both environmental and labor concerns could be deemed illegal under the National Key Points Act. This is a clear contradiction of citizens' democratic rights to gatherings, demonstrations, and information. Unlike the Air Quality Act, which replaced its predecessor with a potentially more democratic legal form, the draft National Key Points Act and Strategic Installations Bill of 2007 sought to renew this remnant of apartheid's security apparatus for neoliberal times, criminalizing labor and civic groups employing constitutional rights, while protecting corporate power under the guise of security.[53]

Labor and civic organizations came out strongly against the new bill. In 2002, after a militant strike led by the independent Chemical, Engineering and Industrial Workers Union (CEIWU), supported by a large section of the neighborhood, the Ministry of Defence arbitrarily extended the National Key Point around Engen Refinery to encroach on a local mosque and people's private homes. A subsequent CEIWU workers' strike was pushed out to the grounds next to the swimming pool, and the collection of air samples by SDCEA was disrupted. This seizure of public space around the oil refinery was secured through the language of security in the time of the

United States' War on Terror. Contemporary imperialism breathes new life into corporate power, in a violent environment that further insulates the oil refineries as occupying powers in South Durban.

Scientific evidence of ill-health continues to be dismissed by the city and industry as "unscientific," clarifying the latent class politics of biopolitical sovereignty. In a highly visible series of newspaper articles, the journalist Tony Carnie called South Durban a "cancer alley"—a term used to fight environmental racism in Louisiana, in the U.S. South—with leukemia rates 24 percent higher than the national average.[54] The corporations ignored altogether a more rigorous joint study conducted by researchers from the University of KwaZulu-Natal Medical School with public health scholars from the University of Michigan. That study found 53.3 percent of students at the Settlers Primary School between the Engen and SAPREF refineries suffering from asthma and other respiratory problems. These results were calculated from a dynamic model, which took into consideration air flows and multiple industries in attributing responsibility for pollution. Neither city government nor industry found this data worthy of significant response. The refineries question the scientific certainty of medical surveys that use statistical probabilities to argue for causal connections between pollution and ill-health. groundWork argues that "the struggle is really against official silence and the wilful ignorance that serves to frustrate . . . demands that industry must clean up and compensate those it has harmed."[55]

SDCEA and WDF continue to use technical language and scientific evidence to attempt to rearticulate biopolitical expertise to "community," whether in community-led air sampling, or in documenting the long-term damage from exposure to toxic pollutants. Participants in these efforts note in asides that a long history of embodied suffering is rarely accorded the status of fact, but the alternative of resignation to biopolitical sovereignty is actually an investment in premature death. groundWork notes the broader problem as one in which the state has devolved regulatory responsibility to civil society, a standard in neoliberal times, with few resources for effective, ongoing regulation. The result is widespread dissimulation about pollution knowledge, countered to some extent in South Durban through monitoring by SDCEA.[56]

Routine ailment and acceptable ill-health in South Africa involve a profound process of official dissimulation. The Health Department does not collect statistics to demonstrate long-term exposure. Scientific evidence is routinely flouted. Population politics in Wentworth is ongoing. SDCEA-

WDF-groundWork continues working on multiple fronts, to fight ruination in fenceline communities as well as in the apparatus of metropolitan spatial planning and national infrastructure policy.[57]

When the municipality has suggested that people relocate, activists and residents have been vocal at public meetings that they do not want to relive the forced removals of the past. The refinery and its quasi-public boundary space continue to be things out of time, cloaked in the security blanket of the apartheid-era National Key Points Act, remade for today's imperial War on Terror. One of the effects of environmental justice discourse has been to powerfully link the violence of the present with the staying power of apartheid's corporate subsidies. In their own admission, environmental groups have not been successful in mass organizing or in popularizing the collection of evidence of pollution-related ill-health. Without an effective counterforce, official dissimulation continues to blunt critique, normalizing South Durban's violent environment, preventing it being apprehended as an imperial formation of another kind.

Since its formation in the early twentieth century as a particular kind of biopolitical space that trapped intermediate racial populations in a polluted industrial valley, South Durban has kept active the politics in biopolitics. While those entitled to biopolitical expertise were initially white, Indian and Coloured residents in South Durban sought to use public health, planning, and environmental knowledge at various points to limit the powerful alliance of capital and racial government. Rather than a Hegelian renovation of biopolitical tools in the service of decolonization, however, the lessons of the latter half of the twentieth century have been that the obstacles to change have been more rigid than many had imagined. After apartheid, environmental groups have sought at various moments to make the lineaments of this violent environment apparent, only to find new forms of official dissimulation frustrating their attempts. Alongside attempt to wrest control of expert knowledge, more prosaic forms of knowledge have continued to critique degraded life and environs in other ways.

Critical Sentiments

For much of its apartheid history, Wentworth was seen as a conservative area buffering African and white zones of the apartheid city. By the 1970s, the state's security apparatus and mainstream press portrayed Wentworth as preoccupied with gangs, drugs, and violence to such an extent that it was unlikely to house anti-apartheid activists of any significance. The idea was

4.1 "Playing Soccer at Highbury Sports Ground, Wentworth, 1995." Source: Cedric Nunn file. Courtesy of the Local History Museums' Collection, Durban.

called into question only after the arrests of members of two anti-apartheid sabotage units operating from Wentworth in the 1980s, as well as the explosion of mass urban revolt across the city of Durban in the 1980s. For various reasons, Wentworth continues to be thought of from without and within as a subaltern Coloured area insulated and confined by specific forms of poverty and suffering. The iconic character of life next to an oil refinery in a particular kind of carceral space, captured perfectly in Cedric Nunn's photograph from the mid-1990s, draws outsiders to think and feel very quickly that they understand what life here is like (fig. 4.1). This visual ideology is also a ruse that has drawn experts in poverty, development, and social welfare to Wentworth like moths to a flame. They come, they propose, they leave quickly, and residents comment on nothing much changing, despite an inflow of projects and heated debates about tainted money.

When Wentworth's residents speak of suffering hidden behind the seemingly decent walls of formal housing, they recirculate dominant stereotypes of stigma and depravity that permeate poverty talk. Rather than the content of this circulation, it is the anxious pace with which it circulates that is important. As I replay multiple conversations over periodic revisits between

2002 and 2008, I continue to be struck by the structures of feeling through which people conserve critical sentiments in the wake of official dissimulation. These sentiments provide a different window into the ways in which people contend with the degradation of life in Wentworth as they attempt to articulate critiques of the present. Photography and film have been particularly potent means, for both residents and passing interlocutors, for conserving a kind of critical melancholy, a blues tradition specific to Wentworth.

The interplay of dominant stereotypes and Wentworth blues came to light in an exhibition at the Local History Museum in Durban in 2002 called *The Cycle of Violence*, curated by a resident of Wentworth.[58] The focus was on the rise and decline of gangs in Wentworth, scripted through four movements: building Wentworth as an "unplanned mistake," migrant labor and social conditions in the apartheid township, "a search for the identity?" through gangs, and "the community takes charge" with the church in the lead. The script followed a well-worn formula, as it portrayed forced removals of people to Wentworth in the apartheid era in turn forcing young men into a dystopian world of gangs, later to meet their redemption through an alliance of church, police, and "community." The curator's intentions were to shift focus from dystopian stereotypes about Wentworth, so that when an outspoken Wentworth resident asked why it was necessary to have another presentation of "gangsterism" in Wentworth, the curator responded, "We want to show people how people in Wentworth came out of it, how people survived it."[59]

While constructing his intervention in this progressive-redemptive mode, a wholeheartedly affirmative dialectics, the curator also displayed private photographs of young men in an area called SANF, for the former homes of the South African Naval Force (figs. 4.2–4.3). In this set of images, quite a different set of relations are set in motion. The micro-neighborhood of SANF is remembered in Wentworth with a particular reverie, as people recall life in semidetached homes separated by little lanes running down a hillside. The lanes are a crucial part of the idyll in these recollections, and they recur in narratives of gangs ducking from each other, of people avoiding danger at night, and of anti-apartheid militants escaping the police. These private photographs taken in the 1970s, largely though not entirely of young men, provides a particular record of being in the lanes.

What is apparent in these and other images in this sequence are a set of gendered poses, displays of style and fashion, and an evident pleasure in being in the lanes. The broader set includes images of girlfriends and families, but the images appear primarily to be of and perhaps for young men.

4.2–4.3 Life in the lanes of SANF, ca. 1970s. Private photographs on display at the *Cycle of Violence* exhibit, KwaMuhle Museum. Courtesy of Local History Museums Collections, Durban.

There are no obvious references to gang turf. The most important visual convention across the images is that people share the photographic frame with the lane, to give the lanes their due. All the photographs either frame people within the lanes or split the frame between people and the lanes. Several men and women recall the lanes while describing an early period of settlement in Wentworth, when recently dispossessed people made a new Coloured township their home. In these narratives, the lanes mark a new common space after the violence of forced removals and before the arrival of drug lords and the departure of jobs. They mark exasperation with the interior, with parental authority, and with the heat of Durban's summer in a neighborhood next to an oil refinery.

What *The Cycle of Violence* exhibition did not say was that one of the mechanisms used in the eradication of gangs was the privatization of the lanes. The lanes are now gone, enclosed by private walls, with narrow gaps to mark a lost geography. The lanes do not appear in anti-apartheid archives. To many, they would appear illegitimate, insular, and possibly dangerous gang turf. This is not to say that the photographs do not provide evidence of territorial gangs. They may provide precisely that which is missing in generic accounts of gangs as an inevitable consequence of forced removals, showing that young men forged what Clive Glaser calls "overlapping personal and territorial familiarity."[60]

What is certain is that these were intimate spaces of masculine affirmation and stigma, injury and pride worth photographing and keeping. The lanes may have provided some young men precisely what Jane Glover demands, release from the claustrophobia of everyday life that Lefebvre calls "lived space": emergent, sensual, and practical space appropriated for as long as is possible, but not codified for easy translation.[61] The photographs demonstrate what Kathleen Stewart calls "the strange agency of fashioning aesthetic effects out of things that are always falling apart or already fallen into decay."[62] In contrast to the mass of objects through which people "remember" in the ruins of Appalachia in Stewart's work, this space of memory in Wentworth has been lost. What remains are photographs from personal albums, now also catalogued at the Local History Museum. People in SANF recollect the lanes through fragmented comments on masculine style, low-level violence, and attachment to neighborhood. While people rarely look at these photographs in their albums, they recall the lanes with a specific nostalgia.

This structure of feeling is more broadly felt in contemporary South Africa in forms of nostalgia that hark back to pre-township residence in informal and multiracial settlements in early-twentieth-century cities. This is nostalgia that is specifically geared toward a sense of collective loss of a pre-apartheid social context.[63] The dominant tendency within this nostalgia is a desire for a late-twentieth-century South Africa that could have taken a different turn. There are privileged sites of memory where such nostalgia is reassured, as in the District Six Museum in Cape Town and in various commemorations of life in Sofiatown in Johannesburg's Soweto. What is not adequately accounted for in such representations is that there were no Halcyon Days of simple happiness in the poverty of informal settlements. Far less do such memory practices attend to the vibrancy of certain places created as a product of forced removals, like Wentworth.

Walter Benjamin comments on Eugène Atget's photographs of deserted Parisian streets: "He photographed them like scenes of a crime . . . for the purpose of establishing evidence."[64] How might we think about these photographs of young men in Wentworth, which are anything but deserted? In what sense might they be crime scenes other than as evidence of youth descending into gangsterism? In a subsequent essay, Benjamin returns to Atget's photographs to ask: "But is not every square inch of our cities the scene of a crime? Every passer-by a culprit? Is not the task of the photographer—descendant of the augurs and haruspices—to reveal guilt and to point out the guilty in his pictures?"[65]

If, as Faisal Devji provocatively suggests, post-apartheid is something like the scene of a crime, naming this landscape an imperial formation is the beginning rather than the end of the forensic process that must follow.[66] One forensic exercise through film was undertaken by a photojournalist, Peter McKenzie, who lived in this part of Wentworth and knew its street scene intimately as a young boy in the early 1970s. McKenzie returned when he became a politicized black photographer documenting township inequalities in the turbulent 1980s. As he puts it, he returned all the way back to his street corner at Pascal Place, to spend time in the space he had to leave as a young man tired of its insularity and lack of critique of the broader, crumbling apartheid order. His film and photography are about capturing the traces of the past, and of the melancholic afterlife of youth affiliation in the lanes and gulleys of SANF. In the interim, several of his friends served time in prison, they say for wrongful arrest. There are multiple layers of ruination in these memories of lost times in lost places, and of remembered frustrations in a differently frustrated present.

Over the few times I have interviewed him, McKenzie has always turned back to his corner or gulley in Wentworth. His memory practice, and the way he commits it to film, are useful to think with in relation to the possibility of a critical melancholy in Wentworth that is quite different from the nostalgia for pre-apartheid settlements.[67]

> There was a corner you could go to, always people you could talk to. There was help if you needed, to go and fuck someone up on the other side of town. You learnt about sex on the corner. . . . Everybody walks up and down 'cause it's too hot to stay inside. You got this continuous mobility of people going "Ey, howzit?" The life of those gulleys was also about being in Durban, and the heat of summer. You could not stay in your house. It was too crowded. It was too hot. So life was to be lived on the streets outside.[68]

McKenzie contrasts the openness of the gulleys to the claustrophobia of parental authority, to evoke the visceral quality of young male appropriation of public space. The photographs of the lanes at the Local History Museum could not quite represent this feeling of compression, though they share a similar desire to make an apartheid township their home. McKenzie's work and the narrative he provides about his life are shaped by a profound unease. Frustrated by the insularity of township life, McKenzie left Wentworth, returning years later after embarking on a career as an activist photographer. When given the choice, he says he picked up a camera rather than an AK-47 machine gun. While he has returned periodically to Wentworth, he maintains a dual sense of being an insider-outsider in his "kasie," or township: "I am from Wentworth but not of Wentworth. . . . Ambivalent feelings of frustration, both mine and those of the community, coupled with the apathy of its peoples within a political system they feel has once again marginalized them, portray these Coloured folk as waiting, waiting . . ."[69]

Here, McKenzie echoes Vincent Crapanzano's insightful ethnography of whiteness in a Cape village in the turbulent 1980s as a particular structure of feeling with respect to time and various others, particularly Coloureds. In what would be the last decade of apartheid, whites appeared to sense a narrowing future with no clear object of desire, leaving them "waiting for something, anything to happen."[70] Crapanzano suggests that this banalized fear was shaped by disengagement from "those others with whom they cannot vitally engage."[71] Less convincingly, with some of the presumptions of anti-apartheid politics, Crapanzano suggests that whites wait in fear, while blacks wait in hope, reassured that time will be on the side of justice, and that Indians and Coloureds wait in some combination.[72] *Waiting* was important for focusing on the pathos of domination from one vantage in uncertain times. However, rather than expecting racially distinct modes of waiting today, we might rather follow Crapanzano's cue in thinking relationally about the ways in which critics like Peter McKenzie attempt to spark "vital engagement" by widening their representational focus.

While the amateur photographs of "the lanes" can be read as hopeful and utopian in embracing a local commons in the wake of dispossession and apartheid, McKenzie's work is structured by a profound disenchantment with both past and present. This is not waiting with a ticking time-bomb of revolutionary expectation, nor is it nostalgia for lost possibilities about the past. Rather, McKenzie's lens focuses on fraught attempts at spatial introversion and renewed racialization after apartheid. What is at stake here is a recent sense of suffering, in the 1970s and 1980s, and an ambivalent stance with respect to anti-apartheid politics then, and democratic politics now. This is not the kind of nostalgia that the images of the lanes might provoke, but rather a more ambivalent and charged form of melancholy that disavows the past while demonstrating its active presence.[73]

McKenzie turns to these themes in his documentary film of 2007 with Sylvie Peyre, which links disenchantment with the present with a diffuse sense of waiting for justice that may never come. The film *What Kind?* (a greeting like "What's up?") turns to the theme of waiting for justice through the lives of five of Peter's childhood friends, erstwhile members of the K-1 Trucks gang. In 1983 these five received exemplary sentences for the alleged murder of a young man from the rival Vultures gang territory. To this day, they claim innocence. Peter "Piet" Usher repeats ruefully, his hat covering his eyes, "We paid the time; they did the crime." After having served nine to thirteen years in prison, they began coming out after 1994, and McKenzie uses the coincidence with the first elections to question their perceptions of freedom in the new South Africa. The resulting film is powerful and multilayered.

One thread is handheld video footage from a moving car, a passerby's montage of daily life, with industrial pipes, smokestacks, and barbed wire as backdrop. Interspersed are black-and-white photographs taken by McKenzie since 1994, the most striking of which are portraits for his project "Vying Posie" (Going Home). Another set of interjections are from recognizable community leaders or experts, two of whom are the key environmental activists from the area, and another who is the author of a published memoir.[74] These experts and McKenzie speak in general terms, with occasional

Coloured township slang, recounting various aspects of Group Areas forced removals, the emergence of gangs, and the frustrations of youth, not unlike the narrative in *The Cycle of Violence*.

What is striking in the visual and documentary evidence is the contrast between these key personalities, including that of the narrator-filmmaker, who speak for the situation in the neighborhood, and McKenzie's often diffident friends. The experts speak in measured tones and standard English, looking directly at the camera, while the former gangsters speak in fragmented slang. The filmmakers approach these men carefully, at their *shebeen* (informal bar). The camera follows Terrence "Terrible T's" Fynn as he laughs, playfully showing the camera the tattoos all over his body, and his language is strikingly different. He jokes, "When I *vyied* in [went to prison] I was a young *laaitie* [youngster], *check* I'm like a drawing board!" There is a pause in the narrative as music and the shebeen make room, and set a context that is not meant to be a staged interview. The men do not have the onus of having to explain anything. They just have to present to the camera that they are haunted by their past and that they live in a state of despair.

When they recount details from 1983, of the scene of the crime and of their unheard alibis, they often speak in generalities about the times. "Wentworth was bad, my *bru*. . . . They didn't even have doctors and nurses to stitch the holes up. They had to bring soldiers in to stitch the people up that time, for about two–three years, they had to bring the army-*ous* [army men] to stitch them up, that's how *blind* it was, it was bad!" (Terrence Fynn). "Piet" Usher insists that in this context young men didn't have a choice but to associate with gangs. He speaks softly about his innocence, as someone who "*made like* [pretended to be] a gangster" and was wrongfully arrested: "Wherever you went, they included you. They said you come from that area, you're part of that place, so you're a gangster from that area. . . . There wasn't people that were gangsters; they just *made like* gangsters, by the opposition. . . . I didn't even see the guy who died on that particular day, but I was put in this case because of the enemy; the enemy. . . . I don't know if they feared me or what but they just put me in this case, in fact all of us."

What is profoundly unclear, and perhaps necessarily so given the layers of the accusation he lays, is who exactly "the enemy" is. The gangsters of Wentworth did not become activists, as, for instance, did Soweto's *tsotsis*.[75] The lack of a recognizable anti-apartheid idiom brings an anticlimactic character to the way in which these men respond to the film's brief, to reflect on their release in the time of transition. Terrence Fynn says nothing has changed, repeating the stock racialized statements that circulate in Wentworth. "All that time in jail, nothing's changed. . . . Ey, but even like now, it was still like the same, *nevermind* things is changing and *whatwhat*, it's like the same, my bru. Like me I don't even vote, because the *witous* [white men] were doing things that time, the *darkie-ous* [black men, or Africans] are doing the same thing. I'll tell you *waaruit* [straight out], it's *darkie* for *darkie*, *witou* for *witou*, *charou* [Indian] for *charou*, my bru." What he does not say is *bruinou* [brown men, or Coloureds] for *bruinou*. Despite repeating the same racial common sense as the experts in the film, none of these young men reference Coloured or community figures as their representatives in any way. Neither do they make any attempt at reclamation of the terms of their ruination, as for instance attempted by the curator of *The Cycle of Violence*.

While Fynn speaks about racialization in society at large, Usher, the most discerning figure in the film, expresses the collective feelings of the five men. His words are measured, but heavy with remorse: "We tried to put our past behind us . . . but you can see what's happening to us, the people is bring our past forward. We're marked with our past, for things what we never even do." The film does not adjudicate on the guilt or innocence of the five men. In this sense, it leaves a forensic exercise aside. However, it does give them the space to present themselves as living with the effects of their sentence and with the injustice of not being able to prove their innocence. They never actually name the "enemy," but they do indict apartheid's police and juridical apparatus as much as the rival gang across the street and the forces that drove them be perceived as dangerous gangsters. They display their despair, showing off their prison tattoos, as well as their emotional scars. The shebeen they inhabit is saturated with what Frantz Fanon calls a "tincture of decay," protracted suffering that is difficult to identify but that is intensely felt.[76]

There are some things that remain unquestioned in McKenzie's social documentary. The refinery and other industry pokes through the narrative as a backdrop that is always there but not always recognized. Only the experts, who speak with clarity in standard English about Wentworth as a whole, connect gangs, poverty, apartheid, post-apartheid racism, and life next to refineries. The former "gangsters" are left to display their burdens on their persons. Theirs is a visceral, sentimental critique, a subjacent display of knowledge that has been disqualified but which retains its critical presence through McKenzie's powerful film. The order of things in the film *What Kind?* captures a key aspect of life and struggle in Wentworth: the differential production of "community workers" and those who embody ruination, and their divergent modes of critique. These adjacent modes of representation on film have much to say about the remains of biopolitical struggle in necropolitical times.

Conclusion: Refusal in the Ruins of Biopolitical Sovereignty

The iconic character of life next to an oil refinery, as well as proximity to the city, has made Wentworth a hub of interest in various kinds of private investments in development and social welfare. This and the mobilization around environmental and labor concerns have led the city and corporations to try to engage community representatives through the technocratic language of stakeholder management. Finance for social projects through the corporate social responsibility sections of the refineries and other major industry has been the topic of fierce debate in community meetings. The environmentalists of SDCEA refuse what they see as tainted money, while other groups and individuals have taken a more pragmatic perspective on making every crumb from corporations count for something meaningful to the lives of residents.

These debates aside, a significant part of Wentworth's population participates in a range of community organizations concerned with social welfare, labor, health, youth, women, domestic violence, and the environment. Some groups are aligned to churches. Most, though not all, are not formally employed. Elsewhere, I suggest that this "political work" is about refusing participation in the sex and drug economies that erode personal and community resources.[77] I argue that this political work mimics the bureaucratic practices of the development industry more generally.[78] What is certainly important in these organizations is the production of an associational life forged through rituals of meetings, committees, site visits, consultations, and, not least, prayer groups. In the wake of multiple forms of degradation, this "connective tissue" is a site of uncertainty and frustration in the wake of corporate occupation.[79]

"Community work," as it is locally called, requires agents and recipients of betterment. While some experts have become known figures, with ties to sources of recognition, funding, and support, the lines between expert and those in need of expertise are often quite blurred. The late "Skido" Joseph was one such figure. With complicated and somewhat murky "struggle credentials," Joseph was never, in his view, properly recognized for his antiapartheid activism. He bemoaned the trajectories of his former comrades who managed transitions from the struggle to lucrative careers in government or the private sector. As we drove around the neighborhood in his beat-up car, he blared "struggle music" to display his claim to a past that was never acknowledged.

Joseph repeated the same racialized complaints about the post-apartheid order that circulate locally, and resolutely supported community work. He would circuit between organizations and homes, lending an ear, having a cup of tea, and providing emotional support, particularly to women. It helped that he was a gifted charmer. Joseph's thoughts were saturated with what I call "Wentworth blues," the particular kind of melancholy that also permeates the work of Peter McKenzie. People knew that Joseph also suffered from alcoholism and depression, which ultimately took his life. What I witnessed in Joseph was an uncanny ability to play the expert and also to make it known that his commitments lay beyond a demonstration of respectability.

Another figure, J.D., heads a prominent community organization and is an articulate man who spent many years in the trade-union movement and in the private sector before returning to Wentworth to engage with widespread domestic violence.[80] J.D. questions the primacy of environmentalism and the refusal of social-responsibility funds from the corporations, on the grounds that if neither industry nor people move from this landscape, there will have to be a permissible level of pollution. Once this level is reached, residents will not have recourse to exacting resources from the corporation. He also expressed to me a view that social welfare and development can only feasibly reach some people in Wentworth, and that a layer of people at the bottom will have to be written off. This is the view of someone who is no longer at risk of falling into this expendable class.

A third figure, whom I call Frank, came out of the same milieu of youth gangs and drugs as the men in Peter McKenzie's film. A chronic asthmatic, this wiry and engaging man embodies the challenges of fighting for life in this violent environment. He has worked in various organizations, on environmental issues, public health, domestic violence, and children's rights, but has steadily built an expertise in sexuality and HIV/AIDS. Frank has had no formal training, but has attended workshops and seminars from the city, and he has a base of clients whom he sees and advises confidentially, in their homes, across the township. He has had to carefully maneuver around the churches in Wentworth as their main response to the spread of HIV/AIDS has been abstinence. Like Skido Joseph, Frank treads the fine line between experts and the poor, but he also manages to do what Joseph could not.

In acquiring the medical knowledge necessary to work as an HIV/AIDS counselor and caregiver, and as a kind of community nurse, Frank indexes the shifting terrain of politics in the 1970s and early 1980s. Efforts such as the Black Community Programs of the Black Consciousness Movement began to widen the focus of anti-apartheid activism to the biopolitics of racial infrastructure. Experts in public health and medicine, social work, urban planning, and geography subsequently offered their services in clandestine and open ways to activist networks. In Durban, the effect was to root the internal struggle, putatively led by a banned, exiled, and jailed leadership, in the lived fabric of the city. This effervescence of biopolitical struggle, moreover, called into question the long history of articulation between biopolitical expertise and racism, through which South Africa's segregated geographies had been forcibly remade since the early twentieth century.[81]

If imperial biopolitics in the areas of public health, urban planning, the circulation of labor, and the regulation of sexuality remain fraught and subject to constant breakdown, the more important question might be to ask how biopolitical tools are used for a variety of ends.[82] Such an approach departs from abstract and ahistorical conceptions of biopolitical sovereignty, or the use of biopolitical tools in defense of power, as leading inevitably to the gulag.[83] The renewed urban struggles in South Africa in the 1970s and 1980s point to a different possibility. The confluence of mobilizations that came together under the United Democratic Front of the 1980s were *also* drawing on biopolitical expertise, subjectivity, and intervention. They were doing so, I suggest, to dismantle rather than to construct racial infrastructure.

In the ruins of this recent past, debates about community work in Wentworth take on a different light. Individuals like Frank stand out as artisans who fashion political tools out of the remains of expert knowledge from a variety of sources and sites. These are ruins of a different sort: fragments of anticolonialism and antiracism that are still potent instruments of refusal of the necropolitical present. In his daily practice as a community HIV/AIDS counselor, Frank engages resolutely in a Brechtian refunctioning of decaying remains of biopolitical struggle.

Notes

This chapter emerged from the workshop on "Scarred Landscapes, Imperial Debris," Anthropology Department, New School, New York, October 2006, for which I am grateful to Ann Stoler, as well as to comments from Faisal Devji, Nancy Hunt, Hugh Raffles, Genese Sodikoff, and Gary Wilder. Elements of "Critical Sentiments" draw from my "Post-Apartheid Livelihood Struggles," for which thanks to the Human Science Research Council of South Africa, and the concluding section draws from part of my "Photographing Dispossession, Forgetting Struggle," for which thanks to *Transactions of the Institute of British Geographers*. For insight at various points, I remain grateful to Gill Hart, Vishnu Padayachee, Richard Pithouse, Kerry Chance, John and Jean Comaroff, Catherine Alexander, George Steinmetz, and Grant Farred. Last, but not least, I am grateful to many residents of Merebank and Wentworth in South Africa whose thoughts have guided my work.

All names of people interviewed have been changed unless they are figures in the public domain or they have requested that their real names be used. Ethnographic and historical research for this project was conducted over multiple visits between 2002 and 2008, with support from the London School of Economics and the School of Development Studies at the University of KwaZulu-Natal, South Africa.

1. "Coloured" is a complex and changing category in South Africa's changing racial formation: in the early twentieth century it marked anxieties about "mixed bloods" and "race mixture"; it was used to distinguish "Africans" divisible into tribes from "nonwhites" who weren't, with implications for residence, work, and possible franchise; it became a "race group" under the Population Registration Act of 1950, subsequently subdivided in 1959 to include Cape Coloured, Cape Malay, Griqua, Indian, Chinese, Other Asiatic, and Other Coloured populations, all subject to "race determination" at various stages and through the workings of a racial "common sense." See Reddy, "The Politics of Naming"; and Posel, "What's in a Name?" In Natal, Coloured became an affirmative category for some in the 1940s, after "mixed-race" tenants were expropriated and located in residentially segregated areas like Wentworth. On the ways in which the stigma of "race mixture" and inauthenticity haunts people with this classificatory baggage, see Erasmus, "Introduction," 16. I capitalize Coloured as a proper noun, like Indian or African, while I leave black and white uncapitalized, realizing that all these are complex racial categories.

2. According to the 2001 census, Wentworth and Merebank areas have roughly similar populations of twenty-seven thousand and twenty-one thousand, respectively. Merebank is one small part of Indian Durban, while Wentworth concentrates Durban's working-class Coloureds. Comparison with African townships and with former white areas places these areas in the middle of the income spectrum. See Statistics South Africa 2001.

3. Austerville Community Centre, Wentworth, undated recording from early 2003. Recording in the possession of Jane Glover, Wentworth, Durban, South Africa.

4. Chari, "Post-apartheid Livelihood Struggles in Wentworth, South Durban," 437–38. Many thanks to Ann Stoler for insisting that I think more carefully about what is at work in this simple statement, and also for Stoler's introductory statement on ruination at the workshop on "Scarred Landscapes, Imperial Debris," Anthropology Department, New School, New York, October 2006. See Stoler, "Imperial Debris," and her introductory essay to this volume.

5. Chari, "Post-apartheid Livelihood Struggles in Wentworth, South Durban";

Chari, "How Do Activists Act?"; Chari, "Silencing the Present"; and Chari, "State Racism and Biopolitical Struggle." For provoking me to rethink the question of "detritus" in relation to ruins and ruination, I am grateful to Ann Stoler and the participants at the workshop on "Scarred Landscapes, Imperial Debris," Anthropology Department, New School, New York, October 2006.

6. Thanks to Hugh Raffles on this point, which he noted at the workshop on "Scarred Landscapes, Imperial Debris," Anthropology Department, New School, New York, October 2006.

7. Desai, *We Are the Poors*.

8. Pithouse, "Solidarity, Co-optation and Assimilation"; Comaroff, "Beyond Bare Life"; Chance, "Living Politics"; and Figlan, Mavuso, Ngema, Nsibande, Sibisi, and Zikode, *Living Learning*.

9. Farred, "The Not-Yet Counterpartisan," 589–94.

10. See Stoler's essay in this volume.

11. On the political economy of transition, see Fine and Rustomjee, *The Political Economy of South Africa*; Freund and Padayachee, *(D)urban Vortex*; Hart, *Disabling Globalization*; Marais, *South Africa*; and Padayachee, "Development Discourses." On activism, see Barchiesi, "Classes, Multitudes and the Politics of Community Movements in Post-apartheid South Africa"; Desai, *We Are the Poors*; Gibson, *Challenging Hegemony*; and Pithouse, "Solidarity, Co-optation and Assimilation." On changing racisms, see Comaroff and Comaroff, "Occult Economies and the Violence of Abstraction"; Farred, "Where Does the Rainbow Nation End?"; Mangcu, "Liberating Race from Apartheid"; and Posel, "What's in a Name?"

12. Key works on the geography of segregation include Swanson, "The Sanitation Syndrome"; Robinson, *The Power of Apartheid*; and Parnell, "Creating Racial Privilege." Insightful work on the instabilities of labor control include Breckenridge, "Verwoerd's Bureau of Proof"; and Macdonald, "Durban-Bound." On innovations in urbanism, see Nuttall and Mbembe, *Johannesburg*; Hansen, "Sounds of Freedom"; and Robinson "(Im)mobilising Space."

13. Lefebvre, *Writing on Cities*.

14. Benjamin, "Theses on the Philosophy of History," 259.

15. Stewart, *A Space on the Side of the Road*; Veitch, "Colossus in Ruins"; Steinmetz, "Harrowed Landscapes"; Steinmetz, "Colonial Melancholy and Fordist Nostalgia"; and Gordillo, "Ships Stranded in the Forest."

16. Stoler, "Imperial Debris," and her essay in this volume.

17. See Bernd and Becher, *Typologies of Industrial Buildings*; images of South Asia's ship breaking yards, in Salgado, *Workers*; the degradation of the Niger Delta, in Watts, *The Curse of Black Gold*; and a critique of "ruingazers" in Namibia and Detroit, in Steinmetz, "Harrowed Landscapes."

18. Steinmetz, "Detroit," 762.

19. For a thoughtful take on the temporality of post-apartheid, see Farred, "The Not-Yet Counterpartisan." Among several important works on testimony, archives, and memory in South Africa, see Nuttall and Coetzee, *Negotiating the Past*; Hamilton,

Harris, Taylor, Pickover, Reid, and Saleh, *Refiguring the Archive*; and Saunders, *Ambiguities of Witnessing*. There is a much larger genre of post-apartheid memoirs, of which one important feminist critique situated in Durban is Govender, *Love and Courage*.

20. Morris, *Can the Subaltern Speak?*

21. Stoler, *Carnal Knowledge and Imperial Power*, 169; Chari, "Subalternities That Matter in Times of Crisis."

22. Stoler, *Carnal Knowledge and Imperial Power*; Trouillot, *Silencing the Past*.

23. Stoler, *Along the Archival Grain*, 20.

24. Ibid., 186.

25. Rancière, *Disagreement*; Steedman, *Landscape for a Good Woman*; Williams, *The Country and the City*.

26. Stoler, "Racial Histories and Their Regimes of Truth"; Stoler, *Along the Archival Grain*; Chari, "The Antinomies of Political Evidence in Post-apartheid Durban, South Africa."

27. Foucault, *The History of Sexuality*; Foucault, "*Society Must Be Defended*"; Foucault, *The Birth of Biopolitics*; Stoler, *Race and the Education of Desire*; Breckenridge, "The Biometric Obsession"; Chari, "State Racism and Biopolitical Struggle"; Comaroff, "Beyond Bare Life"; Robins, "From 'Rights' to 'Ritual'"; and Fassin, *When Bodies Remember*.

28. Pithouse, "Solidarity, Co-optation and Assimilation"; Pithouse, "Burning Message to the State in the Fire of Poor's Rebellion"; Hart, "The Provocations of Neoliberalism"; Comaroff and Comaroff, "Millennial Capitalism"; and Gibson, "What Happened to the 'Promised Land'?"

29. Chari, "Silencing the Present"; Li, "To Make Live or Let Die." Key to my understanding of biopolitical techniques as part of the broader, spatially differentiated dialectics of state racism and opposition is the distinction Stephen Collier makes between Foucault's early statements on biopower, which are rather epochal and binary, and his unfinished later thoughts. See Collier, "Topologies of Power."

30. Foucault, "*Society Must Be Defended*"; Fassin, *When Bodies Remember*, 49.

31. Petryna, *Life Exposed*; McCulloch, *Asbestos Blues*; and Klawiter, *Biopolitics of Breast Cancer*, respectively.

32. Peluso and Watts, *Violent Environments*.

33. Williams, *Marxism and Literature*.

34. Adhikari, *Not White Enough, Not Black Enough*; Hansen, "Melancholia of Freedom," 297.

35. Hansen, "Melancholia of Freedom"; Hansen, "Sounds of Freedom."

36. Farred, "Where Does the Rainbow Nation End?," 186.

37. Chipkin, *Do South Africans Exist?*

38. Saldanha, "Re-ontologising Race"; Gilroy, *Against Race*; Mbembe, "Necropolitics."

39. Ferguson, "Seeing Like an Oil Company," 377–82.

40. Legassick, "South Africa"; Hart, *Disabling Globalization*; Breckenridge, "The Biometric Obsession."

41. Stoler, McGranahan, and Perdue, *Imperial Formations*. The classic radical works

include Wolpe, "Capitalism and Cheap Labour-Power in South Africa"; and Hall, "Race, Articulation and Society Structured in Dominance."

42. Ballard and Jones, "Natural Neighbours."

43. Chatterjee, *The Politics of the Governed*.

44. Sparks, "Playing at Public Health"; Dianne Scott, "Communal Space Construction."

45. Dianne Scott, "Communal Space Construction," 118.

46. Sparks, "Civic Culture, 'Environmentalism' and Pollution in South Durban," 12.

47. This section draws from Chari, "Post-apartheid Livelihood Struggles in Wentworth, South Durban."

48. Peek, "Doublespeak in Durban."

49. Butler and Hallowes, *The groundWork Report 2002*, 10.

50. Government of South Africa, *Constitution of the Republic of South Africa*.

51. Butler and Hallowes, *The groundWork Report 2002*, 13.

52. Truth and Reconciliation Commission, AC/2001/128, Amnesty Committee, Application from Special Operations Unit (SOU) of uMkhonto weSizwe (MK), Durban, 2001, http://www.doj.gov.za/trc/decisions/2001/ac21128.htm.

53. What is more, the new bill used elements from the Labour Relations Act of 1995 — limits to strikes and lock-outs in *essential services* — to allow National Key Points to be declared where provision of *essential services* are in question. See "No. 66 of 1995: Labour Relations Act of 1995," Office of the President, National Employment Center, 13 December 1995, http://www.yourcv.co.za/Documents/Labour_Relations_Act.htm.

54. Wright, "Living and Dying in Louisiana's 'Cancer Alley.'"

55. Hallowes and Munnik, *The groundWork Report 2006*, 149.

56. Butler and Hallowes, *The groundWork Report 2002*, 63.

57. Ibid., 67; Butler and Hallowes, *The groundWork Report 2003*, 168.

58. This section draws from Chari, "Photographing Dispossession, Forgetting Solidarity."

59. Curator of *The Cycle of Violence*, interview by Sharad Chari, Durban, South Africa, 15 August 2007.

60. Glaser, "Swines, Hazels and the Dirty Dozen," 726.

61. Lefebvre, *Writings on Cities*.

62. Stewart, *A Space on the Side of the Road*, 44.

63. Steinmetz, "Colonial Melancholy and Fordist Nostalgia," 299.

64. Benjamin, *Illuminations*, 228.

65. Benjamin, *One-Way Street and Other Writings*, 256.

66. Faisal Devji's response to my paper at the workshop on "Scarred Landscapes, Imperial Debris," Anthropology Department, New School, New York, October 2006.

67. I am grateful to Ann Stoler for her provocations about whether a critical nostalgia is possible.

68. Peter McKenzie, interview by Sharad Chari, Cape Town, South Africa, 31 July 2008.

69. McKenzie, "Vying Posie."

70. Crapanzano, Waiting, 41.

71. Ibid., 21.

72. Ibid., xxii.

73. George Steinmetz's analysis of nostalgia and melancholy in counterpoint is particularly insightful on this point. See Steinmetz, "Colonial Melancholy and Fordist Nostalgia," 299.

74. Lottering, Winnifred and Agnes.

75. Glaser, "Swines, Hazels and the Dirty Dozen."

76. Fanon, The Wretched of the Earth; see Stoler's essay in this volume.

77. Chari, "Post-apartheid Livelihood Struggles in Wentworth, South Durban."

78. Chari, "The Antinomies of Political Evidence in Post-apartheid Durban, South Africa."

79. Comaroff, "Beyond Bare Life," 212; see Stoler's essay in this volume.

80. J.D., interview by Sharad Chari, Durab, South Africa, 20 March 2005.

81. Chari, "State Racism and Biopolitical Struggle."

82. Breckenridge, "Verwoerd's Bureau of Proof"; MacDonald, "Durban-Bound."

83. Comaroff, "Beyond Bare Life."

Ruins, Redemption, and Brazil's Imperial Exception

In 1999 I was privy to what I can only recall as a remarkable event, one that unfolded amidst the $100 million transformation of Brazil's first capital into a restored UNESCO World Heritage site. While interviewing squatters in an eighteenth-century building located on the twisting Ladeira da Misericórdia (Hillside of Mercy) in the city of Salvador, Bahia, I heard the squeal of spinning tires. All present rushed to the door since vehicles rarely traversed the Ladeira da Misericórdia (hereafter "Misericórdia") due to its steepness, its pitted roadbed, its location far from modern shopping centers favored by the bourgeoisie, and its residents' reputation as violent and diseased threats to the social body.

The van climbing the hillside belonged to CETAD, or the Center for Studies and Therapy of Drug Abuse. It carried health professionals performing outreach with residents of the Coaty, a poured-concrete nightclub built in the 1980s into the shell of a ruined Portuguese structure. After middle-class Bahians refused to descend this fraught hillside, the bar was shuttered and then squatted in the mid-1990s by three families. The new occupants cooked in its central area, a space from which *jiboia* vines and a shiny-leafed mango tree protruded onto a roof from which they could survey the docks of Salvador's lower city, the Americas' most important arrival point of African slaves.

In spite of the rarity of vehicles on the Misericórdia, the event around which I drape the present chapter is not CETAD's arrival. It involves instead the remarkable response one resident of the Coaty performed *within* the public-health script dispensed by the hygienist team, which invited all present to learn about health, sanitation, and ourselves. This woman's self-insertion into a pedagogical discourse directed to a purportedly problematic population spurred an insightful and historically embedded dialogue—or what I will refer to as a "gutsy insurrection" for reasons that will become obvious—about health, quotidian practices, and citizenship. My representation of the exchange, enabled by a coincidence that placed the ethnographer temporarily within an audience composed of marginalized Bahians interpellated as in need of symbolic cleansing, is intended to reveal some of the ways populations configured as requiring civilizational improvement perceive and live alongside, or even within, such potentially ruinous forms of attention. And I argue that this perspective suggests novel means of making out the contours of empire today.

The extent to which a seemingly beneficial series of initiatives directed at the preservation of Afro-Brazilian culture as national patrimony in Salvador turn on state-directed attempts to reform Afro-Bahian lifeways and foment a "will to improve" suggests something of the ways imperial violence may spill beyond, and thus gird, those institutions, laws, and histories most easily identifiable as imperial today.[1] I am thus interested in how people situate themselves on the Misericórdia, and in relation to an array of state institutions and NGOs, so as to recognize and even contest those symptoms of empire too often compartmentalized within concerns over race, class, and gender-based exclusions. Nonetheless, my approach to specifying the imperial is not some denial of the salience of such categories. It seeks instead to link them more effectively via an appreciation of a woman's performative historicization that resituates the sliding scales of exclusion central to ongoing and arguably colonial forms of exploitation.[2] This chapter is thus at base an excursion into perception, or the ways engagements with historically sedimented presents might be honed so as to focus more forcefully on empire's troubling appearances and apparent reappearances that take form today as more than historical remainders of some long-gone colonialism.

In seeking to sharpen an ethnographic focus on empires, I lean on Richard Parmentier's conceptualization of "signs in," as opposed to "signs of," history.[3] In analyzing how some Pelourinho residents situate information gathered about them within a type of history conceived of as an ongoing flow in which they participate in a commentary on the past, but not necessarily an evidence-based, truthful discourse that bears an affinity to stable objects or events, I thus follow as one person makes clear how her interactions with the Bahian state and associated NGOs are essential to the production of shared stories about what has taken place. Such a move that engages history as an indexical or deictic exercise which emphasizes the contiguities, if not quite the continuities, between contemporary social processes and representations of the past is more than a deconstruction: it encourages perspectives that may make public how much we are all parts of an imperial world which gains form, and power, through ongoing claims about communities' and populations' apparent deviance from posited norms in ways that permit, or even encourage, a series of missed connections. I therefore struggle to situate exceptions and temporalities as part and parcel of that which they supposedly set off. My goal is to come closer to making visible colonialism's surprising modes of durability or, at very least, the extent to which claims about novelty as well as about unbroken continuity may obscure the extent to which empire both emerges from and structures our understandings of the past.

I begin with a discussion of exceptions while offering a snapshot of Salvador and its UNESCO historical center, the Pelourinho, within which the Ladeira da Misericórdia lies. This highlights how people and buildings' consecration as cultural heritage, or objects presented as special in their supposed evocation of or proximity to a society's defining essences, may be reread in ways that specify overlaps between cultural heritage and associated genres' universalizing gestures, the exclusions on which they rest, and the histories they naturalize. But these insights are not my own: they stem from a decades-long conversation with a remarkable woman, now deceased, who does not seem to have benefited from her dialogues with health authorities or with the author of this chapter. Even as this is not something I can resolve here, it is not something I can ignore. And this is but one reason an effort to understand the difference between signs in, and signs of, history seems so important to carving out a position for making out empire today.

On the Importance of Exceptions

Social scientists have directed substantial attention to the ways communities and those histories imagined as belonging to them distinguish nation-states around specific contents, or a supposedly discrete national culture. Around the world, such assumptions are basic to the "preservation" of national heritage as a good, or thing in itself.[4] Yet in the decade following the destruction of New York's World Trade Center and the U.S. invasions of Iraq and Afghanistan it seems increasingly clear that perceptions of empire, and not just the nation, have taken form around an even wider range of exceptional events and qualities. These include catastrophes, disasters, and assertions of negligence.[5] Here it may even appear that the emergency has become the rule.[6] But more important than some epochal argument about empire's contemporary resurgence and thus a fetishization, or even a defetishization, of exceptions is the observation that claims about informal or indirect colonialism and the insecure boundaries between trusteeship and domination have long helped except, and thus insulate, the United States from comparisons to European empires.[7] Hence exceptions, and the identification of contents or communities' particular "natures" that motivate assertions about special statuses, figure not simply in defining imperial actors, but also in shutting down accurate assessments of empires' continued effects.

Yet Partha Chatterjee argues that today, with empire immanent in the nation-state, the "imperial prerogative . . . is the power to declare the colonial exception."[8] From this perspective, attention to pedagogical or ameliorative projects directed by international bodies legitimated through their ostensible ability to resolve emergencies or recuperate deviant populations may permit social scientists to identify imperial actors more clearly.[9] Might the ethnographer who attends to assumptions of global responsibility thus pinpoint the imperial entanglements of apparently distinct institutions like the United States Agency for International Development (USAID), the World Bank, the Inter-American Development Bank (IDB), and UNESCO without arguing that they fit seamlessly into one dominant, enduring, colonial web?[10]

My road into "imperial formations" associated with claims to exception passes through Salvador, Bahia's Pelourinho Historical Center, a UNESCO World Heritage Site reconstructed in the 1990s as a symbol of Brazil's pasts and a motor for tourist-based development.[11] This "restoration" draws on IDB expertise in marketing residents' quotidian practices as Afro-Bahian culture. Such initiatives are resonant sites for making out empire not because development organizations or the United Nations constitute a neat grid of exploitive actors, but because heritage management purports to make aspects of the everyday special in the name of collective memory. As such, Bahian cultural heritage's elevation of colonial edifices and citizens' everyday practices to the level of shared and enduring properties supposedly delivered from a unifying past shines a spotlight on the power of the exceptional, or sacred, in modern life.

A specific conception of the sacred, and its role in the formation of the political and of definitions of sovereignty, has been influential in anthropological considerations of a modern politicization of life itself, philanthropy, and Brazilian citizenship in evidence in CETAD's programs.[12] In Giorgio Agamben's extension of Michel Foucault's conception of biopower, legality takes form around a political rationality dependent on the excluded figures of the sovereign and *homo sacer*, or a living dead which might be killed but does not rise to the level of the sacrificial victim.[13] Such an assertion might describe inhabitants of the Misericórdia, where police often murdered to applause from a bourgeoisie frightened by residents' criminalized practices and association with disease. In fact, the populace's purported immorality provided a powerful rationale and a public health–oriented methodology for ridding the Historical Center of people during the 1990s.[14]

Working-class people first began to occupy the Pelourinho's colonial buildings as the religious orders and the slave-owning families who dominated Bahia, the world's richest tropical plantation region from the sixteenth century through the mid-eighteenth, moved to seaside suburbs at the beginning of the twentieth century. In disseminating their cultural expressions, developing social movements instrumental to civil rights struggles, and becoming famous for iconoclastic lifeways after taking possession of this Pelourinho neighborhood construed in nationalist thought as Brazil's "cradle" and "brown mother," the new inhabitants of Lusitania's ruined mansion gained fame as producers of an Afro-Bahian culture that differentiates their nation. Central to this modern Brazilian exceptionalism are claims about racial hybridity, tropical joie de vivre, and sexuality. While I cannot do justice here to recent contestations of this so-called racial democracy, a configuration predicated on alleged intimacy between nonwhite women and male slave-owners and their descendants that "pulses at the center of Brazil and its unique history," the recent Pelourinho restoration was conceived in part as propping up this threatened formation.[15]

The Bahian state's primary means of entifying Pelourinho residents' habits as cultural heritage, a form of property often called a "secular sacred" because of its ability to set off almost anything as a possession of the nation or humankind, has involved the surveying of Afro-Brazilian lifeways by the institution in charge of the Pelourinho reconstruction.[16] This is the Bahian Institute for Artistic and Cultural Patrimony (IPAC), founded in 1967 and a locus of a governmentality enacted through the documentation of domestic habits in reams of archived information about residents. This data is often employed to grant content to the stories of national character spun today in the Pelourinho, a depopulated shell from which some five thousand working-class inhabitants were removed during the 1990s. Additionally, documentation of what become coded as cultural expressions which define Brazilianness even as their authors have been exiled to distant slums has generated a ghostlike cast of historical actors, essential to the national imaginary. One might thus argue that Pelourinho residents like the interlocutors described below are in a sense victims of a progress predicated on the resuscitation of the past through cultural heritage's methods of registry. As such, they might appear, like Agamben's *homo sacer*, as exceptional figures which gird the political through their suspension in a patrimonialization linked to a social death. Yet I offer a different interpretation of this liminal state, one I hope will improve understandings of the salience of the sorts of colonial projects still very much a part of the Pelourinho's "recuperation" today. But before exploring how a local, objectifying idiom associated with cultural heritage was redeployed in ways that promise to make clearer global patrimony's logics and effects due to residents' particular takes on how they are imbricated in histories produced in Salvador's Historical Center, I highlight the stakes and techniques at play in the restoration of colonial Portugal's most important South Atlantic entrepôt.

Brazil's Cradle

The Pelourinho, or Pillory, Brazil's first capital, the Portuguese South Atlantic's commercial center, and Salvador's red-light zone from 1940 until 1992, has long been central to claims about the inheritances that individuate Brazil. This is perhaps unsurprising given the neighborhood's salience in early-twentieth-century accounts of Brazilian specificity and the importance of its Iberian baroque ruins to contemporary attempts to restage colonial origins. In fact, Pelourinho edifices are one manifestation of the preeminence of Salvador, founded in 1549, in the Atlantic triangle trade. Yet this importance waned by the mid-eighteenth century, as the Caribbean replaced Brazil as the world's main source of sugar. In 1763 the capital was transferred to Rio, and by the end of the nineteenth century, workers and immigrants had begun to occupy and divide downtown mansions built for Bahia's elites.

Police reports from the 1920s indicate growing arrests for public indecency, and by the end of the decade the Pelourinho's still-stunning buildings began to be celebrated, alongside their occupants, in travelogues important to forging modern Brazil.[17] By 1940 authorities had declared the city center an official red-light zone, or a type of intimate public sphere where powerful men communed in the bars, brothels, and dance halls that employed mainly Afro-Bahian women like Topa, this chapter's protagonist. Yet by the 1970s, as Bahia underwent a sexual revolution, the red-light district declined. An illegal drug trade grew as the community became more impoverished and buildings increasingly unstable (see fig. 5.1). Crime increased even as the Pelourinho became a hotbed for the black politics sweeping Salvador during Brazil's return from two decades of military rule. This contributed to a contradictory focus on Salvador's downtown as a site of cultural production, black mobilization, immoral or diseased people, and threatened colonial monuments. Thus the federal government landmarked the neighborhood in 1984, and in 1992 the Bahian state began a $100 million reform based on what it referred to frequently as a "restoration" of people and buildings.

Since 1992 IPAC has divided residents into those permitted to stay, because they produced a sanctioned version of Bahian culture, and those marked for removal through indemnifications calculated by IPAC on the basis of length of residence, use of space, and a variety of subjective and even nefarious evaluations.[18] This culling based on ethnographic appraisal means that those who remain have been made aware of social science's roles in defining cultural attributes, in controlling territory, and thus in moralizing and representing. Many people point out that across the 1990s they faced a key irony: as their state claimed to care for popular memories, it removed their subjects. Thus Afro-Bahians have been preempted by representations of their lifeways archived by a state that draws visitors to a shrine authorized by social science. This is critical to understanding how histories, and historicity, have come to be approached by people subject to transformation into patrimony.

By the early 1990s, IPAC's ethnographers, together with public health researchers such as the leaders of the CETAD discussed below, had become virtually the only members of the local bourgeoisie who exercised a presence downtown. Interactions between researchers and a community configured as composed of informants produced reports, planning documents, questionnaires, and blueprints for reforms that codified people's habits as culture. Hence a "tradition of the oppressed" became reconfigured as a possession of the nation and, following UNESCO's 1985 acceptance of the neighborhood onto its World Heritage List, of all humanity.[19]

As they faced quantification and indemnifications calculated in relation to IPAC's evidence, residents created fictitious personas or *fantasmas*; invited people into their households so as to glean a commission from these allies' indemnifications; took up multiple residences so they could profit as IPAC moved through the neighborhood; and blackmailed IPAC employees into including them in payments. One result of this co-production of everyday

5.1 Pelourinho residents extracting possessions from a ruined building, 1998.
Photo by author.

life as a thing measured in anticipation of cash rewards was a fetishization of interior essences and identities understood as concrete entities made real by social-scientific enquiry. Here the production of evidence about residents of a neighborhood configured as a remnant of colonial pasts and African inheritances helped generate a specific consciousness as to peoples' importance to the nation as a historical phenomenon.

Tombamento as Redemption

In April 2000, as carnival morphed into Holy Week commemorations of Christian resurrection, I found myself near Salvador's São Joaquim market. Soaked by showers, I sat in a Volkswagen alongside Indio, a twenty-six-year-old former "street child." This normally stoic friend, confidant, and former resident of the Misericórdia who, before he died in 2004, asked that I someday represent him "as he was," quivered with emotion. His head lay on Rita, his wife whose thrust of a paring knife in repayment for his philandering had left him quadriplegic. The two shed tears as three friends from Rita's birthplace, the peripheral neighborhood of Sussuarana, slouched in the back seat and suffered alongside us.

The day had begun as I parked above the polymer-roofed house on the embankment in Sussuarana to which Indio had moved after indemnification in return for his living space in the Pelourinho. He had thus returned to the sort of neighborhood he fled as a child. Yet even as Indio's state sought to banish him from its once ruined, and now valuable, symbolic birthplace, he had managed to document his HIV+ status and claim a disability pension. As his health deteriorated, Indio gained a place in CAASAH, an NGO dedicated to the treatment of HIV infection.[20] Yet by the time we found ourselves in front of the market trying to convince Rita to leave her new boyfriend, Indio had abandoned CAASAH for the distant home he and Rita purchased with IPAC funds. Nonetheless, Rita experienced her removal from the Pelourinho differently: she refused to enter the car, moaning, "I just can't! I can't go back to that place [Sussuarana]. There's nothing there for me. Just tedium. And death. . . . I love you, Indio, but I can't go!" Indio, allowing Rita to smooth his hair, asked me to drive to his brother Gaguinho's home in another neighborhood, Fazenda Grande do Retiro.

As we pulled up, Gaguinho bounded to the car. Like Rita and Indio, he was HIV+. Also like his brother, Gaguinho had been evaluated by IPAC and removed from the Pelourinho, receiving $1,100 for the home he had shared with his common-law wife, Topa, on the Ladeira da Misericórdia. After this cash ran out, Gaguinho could not maintain contact with former neighbors because of fragile health and a lack of money.

Gaguinho was thus overjoyed. As greetings melded into reminiscences, he introduced a woman whose features recalled another, deceased, Misericórdia resident. "This is my mother-in-law," Gaguinho announced as the woman sobbed, "Topa was so beautiful, so smart . . . too smart for the [Fazenda Grande do Retiro] neighborhood." Rivaled only by her brother-in-law, Indio, Topa had been the Misericórdia's most respected inhabitant. Her kindness permitted me to conduct fieldwork among Misericórdia residents, a group reviled by respectable Bahians, feared by neighbors, and wary of outsiders due to attacks by death squads hired by business owners. And now Topa's mother explained how her daughter had run away to the red-light district. During one excursion home, Topa met the younger Gaguinho and convinced him to join her, arguing, like Rita when denying Indio's pleadings years later, that the Pelourinho offered alternatives to her natal neighborhood. This highlights its role as an apparent zone of moral exception that animates representations of unruly, Afro-descendant Bahianness in national imaginaries while also naturalizing calls for "improvement" of buildings and people. Yet it points also to the extent to which the supposedly degraded exception may be, even prior to authorities' attempts at sanitization, a rather iconoclastic means of redemption.

As we rolled up to the general store in Fazenda Grande, relatives greeted Indio. Beer circulated and Gaguinho introduced me to Topa's mother as Indio announced, "Yeah, people. Here I am, patrimonialized in this passenger seat. Looking good, ain't I? That's why the *gringo* takes such good care of me."[21] Read in English, Indio's words indicate that as patrimony he was able to attract a foreign chauffeur. Yet "patrimonialized," or the Portuguese adjective *tombado*, has a number of meanings relevant to the discussions of difference and its reification with which Indio enmeshed himself that day and throughout his life in the Pelourinho.

Linked to the Latin *tumulum*, or storehouse, the verb *tombar* is traceable to Portugal's national archive, the Torre do Tombo. *Tombar* means to crystallize, to fix the form of something, to fall, to knock down, or to drop dead. In the Pelourinho, IPAC employees and residents employ the word to describe registry in archives. Indio, Gaguinho, and Rita joked frequently about what it meant to tombar, or patrimonialize, people, habits, places, and dwellings. The claim "Está tombado," or "He/she/it is patrimonialized," often served as a way of explaining a building's poor condition because in anticipation of eminent domain owners had halted maintenance. Likewise, residents, exasperated by IPAC, would exclaim, "Espero que eles tombem meu predio antes de eu tombar morto," or "I hope they patrimonialize [tombar] my building before I fall down [tombar] dead." And people often argued that their identities, or inner essences, constituted properties of the nation and were thus tombado.

This rendering static highlights possessive logics critical to the construal of difference as economic resource. For residents who faced ethnography and then, via indemnification, the placing of a price on habits, to be patrimonialized is to be in a sense dead or immobile. But this is also a preservation and evidence about the value of one's being. Hence tombamento is an entombing that empowers as it exploits: Indio, weakened by AIDS and unable to walk, sat in a car and recuperated himself by arguing that he was a bit of patrimony that, despite its frozen state, had value. This drew on residents' interpretation of patrimonialization as a gathering of essences. But they resignified IPAC's designation of the neighborhood's population as in need of recuperation, or as exceptional, by arguing that their subjection to such pedagogies was simply the state's method of recognizing their intrinsic specialness.

A language of recuperation around cultural essence is apparent in newspapers, speeches, government public relations, and IPAC planning since the 1990s. Yet as illustrated by Indio's strategies, claims about reconfiguring formerly stigmatized or no longer useful origins—ruins, if you will—are polyvalent. The downtown to which people fled to reinvent themselves has been set off as exceptional through purification, rather than denigration. In an example of this process's diffusion, I overheard Indio say about me as I walked toward Topa's mother's house, "Eh, and that guy's from antiquity [antiguidade] too. I've known him since I was a [street] kid."[22]

As part of UNESCO's "Living Human Treasures" program which seeks to valorize producers of cultural knowledge, and which gave rise in 2003 to the augmentation of existing natural and cultural patrimony by a new category of "intangible" heritage, people may be construed as possessions of humankind.[23] Overseen by UNESCO, which separates out natural, cultural, and intangible registers, each with distinct archival registries and preservation protocols, heritage thus links places, phenomena, and life-forms through property regimes. It mediates different scales and sites within, and for, the invention of tradition. Indio's statement suggests that he comprehends the power of this technology. He thus points to the power of heritage, a technique employed to lift objects out of impoverished contexts and burnish them in the name of some shared, if factitious, basis for belonging. And what makes heritage special is, tautologically speaking, its exceptionality.

In the 1990s residents became increasingly aware of the ebb and flow of exception and exceptionalism. This emanated from more than their familiarity with social scientists and, until the 1980s, with the elite men who maintained second families downtown and thus sometimes fathered (but rarely recognized) some of the people whose stories contribute to this account. It arose also from people's transit between a relatively secure downtown where "money flows" (corre dinheiro) and the poverty of Salvador's periphery. Residents who fancied themselves malandros, or rogues, skilled with fists, knives, and capoeira kicks, found themselves in far-off neighborhoods facing shotguns and neighbors who broke down front doors with crowbars. Unlike in the pre-restoration Pelourinho, they could not turn for help to roving police patrols. Pickpockets who argued that they could filch a billfold and return it empty to a drunk's pockets complained about having to live with gente bruta or rude (brutal, rude people). Such accounts indicate how a population configured as a bit of patrimony, and hence as sacrosanct even as it faced the symbolic death of removal, represented life on the periphery as indeed much starker, if not barer. They understood just how special, and easy, life in the supposedly denigrated downtown really was, at least in comparison to the rural districts and slums many had fled as "street children." And many struggled, even as few succeeded, to convince IPAC to allow them to remain in or reenter the city center following the indemnification process of the 1990s.

As it became apparent how Salvador's spatial apartheid hurt their life chances, it also became clearer to residents how much life was forged around continually shifting, nuanced gradations of privilege and privation. Claims about tombamento, the status of former denizens of the red-light zone, and arguments about knowledge and intercourse with politicians became not spaces for carving out subjectivities in a context of poverty, but rather relations within larger webs of favor and exclusion that constitute Brazil. There was, then, no zone of exception: it became clear that Pelourinho residents were not people who, degraded or exalted, stood askance, outside of the polity like sacred signs. Rather, all moved both inside and outside in a continual struggle to survive. The exception could never suspend or authorize the norm because the exception was not a space, but a relation woven in and out of the social fabric. Hence there was no norm counterposed in a fixed manner to the emergency or figure in need of tutelage. Instead, much like the baroque recesses of people's former abodes celebrated by some as untouchable signs of antiquity and employed by others as toilets and kitchens, sacrosanct status was an effect of positioning, or a question of multiple, shifting plays of shadow and illumination. In this sense people's experiences mimicked the development of the Brazilian nation that did so much to temper their outlooks. And I turn now to this historical engagement with entwined exception and redemption, both in terms of the nation and the Pelourinho's populace, as forged in a historical space predicated on the treatment of the biological life of a historicized populace.

At the Margins of History

After I left the gaggle surrounding Indio, I sat with Topa's mother and mourned. Gaguinho then dropped a paperback into my lap, saying, "When Topa died she was reading this. She wanted you to have it." Perhaps he was being kind, inventing a story and a gift. But at the time, touched, I did not entertain this possibility. I was curious: "What was this gift I could never return?" And, moving beyond the logic of the gift, "What was Topa reading?"

The book, by Euclides da Cunha, one of Brazil's pre-eminent nationalist thinkers, astounded in part because it was unknown to me. In a retrospection made possible by that gift, I have realized that da Cunha's representation of the late-nineteenth-century and early-twentieth-century making of a Brazilian people configured in tension with landscapes painted as brutal and degenerative has inflected powerfully my own understanding of the Pelourinho's restoration: sanitation and redemption mean something special in a Brazil where urban renewal purifies a Pelourinho from which the nation emerges symbolically today. But here I get ahead of myself.

When I received Topa's gift, its title, À Margem da História (At the Margin of History), struck me as significant. "At the margin of history," I thought, "Topa and the margins, or edges, of history. Topa, a woman called a marginal throughout her life and then exiled from the Pelourinho." I wanted, in that ostensibly inclusionary move so basic to modernist anthropology, to prove that Topa was more than marginal, and thus make her part of universal history. But as I thought about the contradictions at the heart of the recuperative operations, I became dispirited. I cradled À Margem da História and remained silent as this token, sent by a friend now in her grave, lay weightily on my rain-soaked shorts, which had begun to dry in the midday heat.

The book's objectness faded as conversation resumed. I struggled to make sense of this addition to my knowledge. Topa, who neighbors used to tell me had once been renowned as a beautiful prostitute and had then become adept at *suadeiro*, or the robbing of colleagues' clients via hidden doors or duplicate keys, had come to survive through scams and donations from AIDS-prevention organizations. She would also search through trash, a practice that led her to share with me castoff texts, including printouts of indemnification data she extracted ahead of street vendors who wanted to use them to package their wares. Such uses of writings demonstrate the particularity of my desire to know À *Margem da História* by interpreting its contents, rather than by wrapping peanuts. But Topa and I had discussed and read together many books. And Gaguinho had just made a point of telling me Topa was reading da Cunha when she passed away.

Here was a text by the engineer and journalist who, in 1902, published the better-known *Os Sertões*. Translated as *Rebellion in the Backlands*, *Os Sertões* describes da Cunha's travels to hinterlands with troops sent to quell a rebellion by former slaves and peasants in the Bahian village of Canudos, a space inscribed in the nation's consciousness as a sign of barbarity and resistance ever since. Da Cunha's ethnography of *sertanejos*, or backlanders, slaughtered by an army in which the author was embedded, stands as one of the clearest expressions of the nineteenth-century dialectic of "civilization and barbarism." Such civilization and barbarism is usually portrayed as an attempt to describe relations between cities and countrysides depicted as antithetical to civilization. Fears of oscillation between the two, or of a degeneracy associated with Latin American nature, thus gird Lamarckian theories of redemption like Brazilian racial democracy.[24] In this understanding, by the 1920s cosmopolitan denunciations of ostensible infection by nonwhite peoples and degenerative landscapes spurred a countermovement in which Brazilian thinkers celebrated deviance from European norms as a cleansing vision of progress, or alternate modernity.

À *Margem da História*, like *Rebellion in the Backlands*, examines an ostensibly barbarous corner of Brazil, in this case Amazonian borderlands. Again like its antecedent, the description is ambivalent and strategic: da Cunha worries about Peru's "wastrel adventurers . . . opening up with rifle balls and machete strokes new paths . . . where they would leave behind . . . in the [form of] fallen-in buildings or the pitiful figure of the sacrificed Indian, the only fruits of their . . . *role as builders of ruins*."[25] But then he celebrates the colonization of Brazil's Amazonian territories by sertanejos, the same people whose apparent backwardness fascinates him in *Rebellion in the Backlands*. And even while lamenting the destruction of indigenous life-ways, da Cunha draws on models gleaned from the Union Pacific, from comparisons of the Punjab to the Amazon, and from the British projects in India he took as indicative of state-of-the-art engineering. However, in working to authorize Brazilian control of territory by appropriating ideas from European imperial ventures, he celebrates the sertanejos' "practical knowledge," rather than Europeans' calculations.[26] But, again, these sertanejos are the putative barbarians who captured his fancy as they were wiped out by the troops with whom he traveled to Bahia in the 1890s.

Da Cunha's account of Amazonian settlement, as opposed to the fanaticism he attributed to sertanejos in Bahia, reveals an ambivalently postcolonial Brazil whose emergence runs contrary to the imaginings of community in its Hispanophone neighbors. Brazil spent 1808 to 1888 as an American regency and empire: in a maneuver catalyzed by Napoleon's invasion of the Iberian Peninsula in 1807, the British Navy transported Portugal's court, mint, and archives to Brazil. There, Emperor Dom João VI oversaw possessions stretching from the Amazon to Angola and on to Macao and India until his return to Lisbon in 1822. Thus, Rio de Janeiro served as a metropole, and an independent monarchy, at a moment when British troops sacked Washington and Latin America's creole republics waged wars of independence. And by the time João's son, Dom Pedro I, took over his father's American throne in 1831, Brazil had surpassed Portugal in geopolitical importance.[27]

Nonetheless, even as João's grandson, Pedro II, would assume power in 1841 as an emperor born and raised in Rio, the Brazilian empire does not gain exceptional status through a story of monarchical succession. Nor do I touch on Luso-American history to prove Brazil imperialist. It is true that the tropical monarchy threatened its neighbors and appropriated territory. And the extent to which histories of internal dissent, interclass and interracial struggle and love, anti-Portuguese sentiment, and national consolidation around racial ideologies silence accounts of this expansionism is astounding. Yet an attempt to forge a perspective for contesting a much broader range of imperial mufflings, and relationships between such occlusions and Topa's life and UNESCO's cultural heritage, are what most interest me here.

I began this chapter with observations about exceptions and populations subject to patrimonialization, treating these as nodes that make aspects of the everyday special while reflecting a society's techniques for narrating social bonds into existence. At the same time, these techniques are potentially discriminatory ways of managing the overlaps between different aspects of political life. I then illustrated how heritage may be reworked by its subjects, who have become invested in the production of ethnographic data that establish heritage objects as icons of shared pasts and collective futures.

At each nexus I have struggled to show how that which is exceptional is part and parcel of mutable forms of inclusion and exclusion selectively available to differentially situated actors. The argument revolves around civilization and barbarism as a trope reanimated, reimplanted, and at times denied at distinct points in the construction of the Brazilian nation.[28] And this civilization and barbarism was imperfectly resolved within Brazilian history through an array of purificatory emphases on racial hybridity brought together under the umbrella of so-called racial democracy.[29]

Meanwhile, heritage has come to the fore today at a moment when racial democracy is under attack, and thus offers an increasingly weak yet accepted way of including, and excluding, citizens. Nonetheless, an analysis based on heritage as exception covers up its real links to the sustaining paradoxes of Brazilian life and histories, a process integral to empire's veilings. And for this reason the exchange between Bahian public health professionals and Topa, a woman who lived much of her adult life in the midst of sustained state- and NGO-based attempts to transform her everyday into patrimony and to sanitize her in the process, presents one way to reconstitute the history of the Pelourinho while suggesting how this production of what might be called "properly historical subjects" may help a variety of people understand empire more clearly.

Delineating Self, Other, and Bahianness on the Hill of Mercy

The Misericórdia, where I came to know Topa, Gaguinho, Indio, and Rita, connects Salvador's waterfront to the Pelourinho. In keeping with its location behind the Hospital of the Santa Casa da Misericórdia (Holy House of Mercy), the Americas' oldest philanthropy, the street appears notably in eighteenth-century concerns with public health.[30] A center of houses of prostitution by the 1930s, it plays a prominent role in landscape painting, newspaper reports, and bohemian histories. For example, Godofredo Filho, the director of the Bahian office of Brazil's federal heritage bureaucracy (IPHAN) for much of the postwar period, published "Ladeira da Misericórdia" in 1948. According to Filho, the Misericórdia is

> the hill without an origin
> or in its very origins, it is without an end . . .
> the hill of Bahia . . .
> That in the greatest irony
> Claims that it arises from mercy . . .

the hill of negressess,
Of syphilitic mulattas,
Of soldiers and drunks
The street of miserable whores . . .
It is I who kisses your stones
I, who, in an agentive lamentation
Find myself thickening, becoming densely real, through your mystery;
Who lashes myself to those, your lips . . .
And who translates it in the light of the pre-dawn
Of impossible redemption[31]

Yet Filho's memories of carousing and bohemian desires to know others and selves had been replaced by ethnography and the activities of NGOs like CETAD by the time I conducted my research in the 1990s. Composed of medical doctors and outreach workers, CETAD has long worked in Salvador's Historical Center and, especially, on the Misericórdia, which, although no longer a location for wide-scale prostitution, was home to many prostitutes and an open drug trade.

On the day we crossed paths on the Misericórdia, CETAD personnel handed out folders, pads, pens, and AIDS education literature designed to encourage participation in a theatrical exercise. They listed Topa, a resident of the Coaty, as an event organizer and handed out a sheet titled "Awareness: Preventive Information about STDs/AIDS, Drug Abuse, and Quality of Life."[32] Asked to define "health" and to draw a body, we scribbled while listening to lectures about taking responsibility for our bodies.

As people sketched while mumbling that it was strange that the bourgeoisie should speak about bodies, Topa drifted in and out. She admitted later that she was upset that her space had been penetrated by experts who judged her habits, and hence *pessoa* (person). Agitated, she pulled out a paper, wrote something, and dropped the sheet in my lap. It read, "For those who know, $2 + 2 = 4$." Farther down she had written, alongside the number 4, "I am José. No, I am nena, neno," as her pen trailed off in a squiggle.[33]

Soon a nurse from the Pelourinho's medical post asked residents to act out "private" activities like bathing, cooking, and washing dishes. My notes, taken on CETAD's donated paper, indicate that she emphasized, "Each person is the owner of her body" and "You have value."[34] In response to a question about parasites, the nurse encouraged proper disposal of feces and toilet paper because "uncivilized" habits might infect water supplies.[35] Topa huffed and puffed as friends silenced her, embarrassed by their "problematic" neighbor ("Pare de ser pobremática [*sic*] e deixe de bulir!") who frightened "Ministry of Health" doctors.[36]

As the nurse finished, Topa remarked, "*Doutora*, . . . I have just one doubt that needs to be cleared up about this issue of feces. Doctor, you say that we should not throw our shit-laden—sorry, I mean soiled—paper on the ground. This is an important issue. I just want to understand it a little better."

The nurse responded, "Yes, I'm glad you're asking about this. I think we really need to talk about hygiene."

Topa went on, "So as I understand it. Well, let me ask it this way. If I am walking on a Saturday afternoon, out looking for useful items in the trash in your neighborhood . . . and I need to defecate, I should look for a bathroom. There's no way I should crap—I mean defecate—in the street. Right?"

"Right!" answered the nurse.

"Well, OK, so let's say that I walk up to your house on a Sunday and knock on the door because I really need to defecate. Or rather, if I am in danger of soiling my pants [*pause*] No! What I really mean is, what I'm really going to do is to make poop. If I am going to make [*pause*] No! Not poop! If I am going to shit all over myself and the street, and instead I walk up to the door and knock, and you answer the door [*pause*] No, sorry, not you, but your maid, answers the door."

"Eh, eh, eh, eh," sputtered the nurse as Topa continued: "And I say 'Excuse me, I need to use your bathroom so that I don't shit all over the sidewalk and soil the street and endanger public health,' what do you think your maid is going to tell me? Is she going to let me in to use your bathroom that she's been scrubbing all morning? Or when she calls back and you answer, 'Who is it?,' are you going to tell her to let me into your house to use your clean toilet so I don't get shit and toilet paper on the sidewalk? What if I should need to defecate in *your* neighborhood, madame?!?"

The educator stood speechless until a social worker asked, "Well, what would *you* do in that case, Topa?"

Topa hissed, "Don't butt in! I'm doing the asking!"[37]

The nurse, a kind professional I came to know later through my son's checkups at the Pelourinho health post, responded, "Ah ah ah ah ah, well, I would hope that anyone who answered the door in my house would let you in."

"But would *you* tell your maid to let me in?" insisted Topa.

"This is truly a difficult question," responded the nurse, honestly. A silence settled over CETAD and the residents of Salvador among the most prone to new HIV infection. Friends hushed Topa as Gaguinho pulled her from the room. She began crying, refusing to rejoin the end of the lesson. At that moment, another woman blurted, "I just want to know when the doctors are going to come see us. I've had enough with this education stuff. When are the doctors coming?" At this, the CETAD team announced that the meeting and street theater were over. Promising to stop by again, they departed "the hill without an origin / or [that] in its very origins . . . is without an end."[38]

A Marginal at the Epicenter

There is much to say about acting up in the midst of a public health drama designed to convince Topa she "had value" at a time when IPAC construed her habits as patrimony. On one level, it permits the anthropologist to present himself as occupying an "outside" more real than the circuits of knowledge activated by CETAD or IPAC. But if such a position were possible, it would configure Topa and her neighbors as authentic exemplars of a popular consciousness, a claim I struggle to contest. Nevertheless, as should be apparent, I enjoyed, and find inspiration in, Topa's creativity. But backtalk did not prevent her from losing her home or from serving as fodder for IPAC and accounts such as the one my reader digests here.

Topa underscores the importance, and the contradictions, of the space between the two of us and between institutions like CETAD and IPAC and the Pelourinho's population. It seems that CETAD has taken on something of the role of the IPAC of 1970s. Even as it did not involve itself in heritage, it offered holistic care as doctors ministered to the sick and outreach workers passed out condoms. Meanwhile, IPAC had helped residents obtain medical care in the 1970s, but subsequently sought to configure people as problems. In fact, when I first visited IPAC offices as a new researcher in 1994, the director of public relations offered a story from a newspaper, controlled by the then governor of Bahia, that warned of AIDS infection among Pelourinho transvestites. He told me, "Look how the press treats these people. For the press, the people of the Pelourinho are a problem. They are marginals, a scourge, diseased. But here at IPAC we understand the social nature of these problems and we work to find them homes, to valorize them, and to get them into treatment centers." Regardless, or perhaps as a result, IPAC forced a number of HIV+ people out of the Pelourinho around the time of my visit. But in spite of attempts to employ a language of care to paint residents as a scourge to be removed, it is not obvious that the contact zone between CETAD and IPAC is expressive of, or directed at, anything resembling empire. Yet issues of obvious resemblance, or how connections come to seem evident but unavailable in other contexts, are what I work to connect to the segmentations of knowledge effected by empire around exceptions and sentiments. And they are why, in addition to its brilliance, an interaction between a subject population and the institutions that claim to represent and mold that group is my focus.

In speaking to CETAD in the Coaty, Topa mimics hygienists, drawing professionals out of their pedagogical roles and transforming them into actors within, and hence of, their own theater. This rupture of the naturalized position of actor and pedagogue is significant in itself. But Topa then draws in her teachers by voicing "just one doubt that needs to be cleared up about this issue of feces" before moving through a glossary of slang terms for excrement. She does so while narrating her approach to the nurse's home. Here Topa, who once worked as a servant, raises the possibility of the wrong type of woman's entrance into the bourgeois home, precisely the scene of the narrative of national purification and hybridity so important to modern Brazilianness. A maid who guards this space then checks whether or not to admit the woman from the Pelourinho. Yet Topa, a former prostitute and hence the doorkeeper's immoral doppelgänger, paralyzes the *patroa* (nurse) by performing an imagined interaction on the threshold of house and street. Thus this solicitation of a toilet enables Topa to interpellate the hygienist who arrived on the Misericórdia so as to educate, or to render palatable to the public that would soon flock to the historical center some of Salvador's most marginalized and diseased quasi citizens.

From residents' perspectives, CETAD and IPAC are both state institutions. Topa's "gutsy insurrection" may thus be read as an analysis of a state's appropriation of her quotidian through surveillance of hygiene, sexuality, and domestic habits. The inversions permit Topa to situate her own objectification within a history of IPAC cleansing. More than a Rabelaisian overturning or even an anthropological fetishization of abjection, Topa's challenge recalls Begoña Aretxaga's description of political prisoners' "dirty protest." There, IRA partisans' complaints forged around feces, urine, and menstrual blood reconstituted colonial representations of Irish filth "as a materialization of the buried 'shit' of British colonization, a de-metaphorization of the 'savage, dirty Irish.'"[39] In something akin to Topa's upending of IPAC constructions of belonging through the materialization of racial democracy around her own habits, Irish prisoners' manifestations of excreta made public relations to the state, colonial history, and contemporary society. Yet Topa never manipulates feces in the face of CETAD surveillance. Instead, she employs witty speech to uncover how her role in the production of origins is hidden. In other words, Topa reveals not the content of biopolitics, or the histories written around biopolitical surveillance of everyday habits in the Pelourinho, but the mutual imbrication of socially distinct interlocutors in a broader, imperial framework. What appears key here is how Topa makes visible the normalizations and fragmentations of critical-perceptual landscapes that pave the way for "accumulation by dispossession."[40]

IPAC relies, as do historical centers in general, on monumentalized "signs of history" that "instantiate general patterns of meaningful order" typical of states' attempts to widen nationalisms' iconic or indexical attachments into a more fully symbolic, or habitual, register.[41] Such symbols call up their objects in manners that construe their significance as turning on an ability to materialize traces as preserved phenomena, rather than as ongoing aspects of a still-unfinished history. For example, when, in interactions with a post-1990 IPAC, a resident answers a questionnaire designed to fix her as a problem, she may become a manipulatable datum whose form is constituted within the play of the questionnaire and the archive. When that questionnaire remains in the archive as a hidden yet authoritative source of representations in the present, its preserved status pulls it, in a sense, out of history: the document becomes a sign of history in that its symbolizing activity rests on its storage in an archive of materials that gain power as materials that were "there" at the moment of field research. As such, they permit claims about a past moment which, abstracted or distilled from them, requires their preservation, but not necessarily their ongoing activation. They no longer serve as active signs in ongoing history, but rather as testaments to what supposedly has taken place. And this is one reason that heritage has been described as a secular sacred set off from the everyday. In such a linkage of sign vehicle and referent, or of Pelourinho practices committed to paper and the historical degeneracy IPAC employs them to represent, both monuments and documents require preservation so as to maintain an aura of having once participated in what they connote. Nonetheless, such signs *of* history may, under certain circumstances, become deployed in social action in such a way that they stand mimetically *within* or closer to actions in ways that continue to comment on what has supposedly already passed. In the process they may evince a "token-level contiguity with [the] ongoing social processes" that they constitute and, thus, become signs *in* history.[42]

There is a great difference between standing in monumentalized relation to history like a bit of patrimony that calls up an event and standing, iteratively deployed, within that history in a manner that nods at its uneven flows.

And this divergence is key to my attempt to make out empire's workings in light of Topa's interventions.[43] Put simply, a sign of history represents what happened. But a sign in history touches or points at, and thus makes clearer how, that which is said to have happened represents by serving as a type of "present evidence of a significant past" that does not so much specify history's contents as gesture at its valences.[44] In other words, Topa as a sign in history illustrates her role in producing the narratives that exclude her. She does so by highlighting diverse actors' ongoing imbrications in a force field forged in the public health scripts co-produced by CETAD and Misericórdia residents: rather than demonstrating relations between a context and an event, Topa shows how relations are delineated as events or spaces in ways that point to the ongoing production of history and the extension of processes, like colonialism, that might be relegated to the past so as to obscure their ongoing valences. And if those temporal segmentations produced by, and definitive of more standard definitions of, empires engaged in the production of mini-events called crises, emergencies, and exceptions are raised to the level of consciousness, there exists the possibility that all involved, whether CETAD pedagogue, anthropological analyst, or ethnographic subject, may make out not simply what is arbitrarily available, but rather a spectrum of social processes in which all participate. But how does one inhabit this slot, one that I refer to as "proper historicity"?

When Topa inhabited IPAC and CETAD discourses she revealed performatively how Pelourinho institutions identify people and events as problems as well as monuments productive of identity and history. By bringing to the forefront the hubris of middle-class benefactors who would regulate her domestic space, Topa makes clear the distinct bases of her own and the researchers' and educators' participation in a project configured as shared, pedagogical, restorative, and productive of both pasts and futures. Yet she did so in a manner that moved beyond any argument about authority, or even about who was indeed immoral, unhygienic, or correct. She demonstrated instead a series of connections dependent not on direct contiguity or a mimetic affinity with the object itself—as is the case in cultural heritage management where the "restoration" of buildings mimics colonial origins or where the surveillance of Afro-Bahians' lifeways configures living people with idealized, folkloric models of black Brazilianness mobilized in nationalist imagery—but on a shared participation in a heritage-based invention of tradition basic to development projects and liberal democratic participation in the world today.

Here the pressing issue is no longer one of making out what Bahian origins really are. Nor does it involve demonstrating cultural heritage's constructedness. Instead, as the Pelourinho nurse and I discussed subsequently, Topa forced all present to recognize how erudite knowledge and popular practice become entwined in producing a version of Bahian origins around the Pelourinho as exception. Topa thus helps make apparent the sedimentation of IPAC representations, and the temporal and geographical valences of knowledges that gird them, that establish a ground from which she must speak and from which her state configures her as a source of information. Such an ability to demonstrate heritage's and thus public history's formulation of a shared yet contested space in real time and alongside its production of materiality around human figures, and to do so by forcing the exception to point to the rule, may appear a small contribution by one woman. This is especially true when viewed in light of the weight of some undifferentiated, or even quite specifically defined, thing called empire. But it is an important aspect of understanding, and perhaps even altering, empire in light of contemporary claims about its unbridled novelty, on one hand, or enduring legacies, on the other.

Conclusion

Topa did much in life. How capably she could open up perspectives became apparent a year after her insurrection. As the nurse examined my son during a routine checkup, we talked of the Misericórdia and she exclaimed, "These people are quite difficult. They're really needy. One never knows what they put in their bodies and how those substances are going to make them react." I had felt a kinship with the nurse because her facial expression suggested a recognition of the pain Topa felt when CETAD sought to teach her hygiene and value. However, this attachment dissipated as the nurse focused on "these people" and their neediness. Perhaps Topa was needy. But anthropologists and health professionals who make a career traveling to the Misericórdia are, in their own ways, needy as well.

The nurse's explanation of Topa's practices through claims about uncontrolled emotions contrasts with Topa's actions: in the Coaty Topa did not claim in a categorical sense a difference from the nurse who interpellated her. Instead, she illustrated, through metaphor, how she imagined that the nurse would, and has, construed her in the past, present, and future as an exception in light of public morality, precisely the sentiment at the core of Brazil's racial democracy and the Pelourinho restoration. She did so by inviting the nurse to specify how she would receive or wall herself off from Topa, in her own home. She thus asked the nurse to reflect on how her configuring of Topa would permit her in turn to appear civilized, or not, in contradistinction to the figure from the Misericórdia her profession suggested she could sanitize or perfect.

Thus on the terrain of the elite home and its servants, precisely that from which Brazil's racial democracy was materialized and then generalized as a public formation supposedly emanating from the truths of the intimate sphere, Topa, a denizen of the red-light district, began a history of her ties to other citizens.[45] And impossible ties to other citizens are what I have argued racial democracy and cultural heritage function, at different moments, to resolve or cover up. In other words, Topa's challenge to CETAD is a history. Yet it is not a dispute over facts and interpretations. It is a working out of a positioning in the world, or a "deictics of historical remembering" which, beyond "any referential representation of the past . . . legitimates action in the present through the alignment of remembering agents within a spatio-temporal field."[46]

Deictics, or indexical, means of historical recollection through the alignment of remembering agents in a given field—a basic feature of cultural heritage centers' experiential "histories of the present"—are a significant area of dispute, cooptation, and even new forms of commodification in Latin America today.[47] The Pelourinho is one such landscape in which commemorations constructed around patrimony produce links to the past with little, if any, referential content.[48] In fact, IPAC's expulsion of residents unable to claim an Afro-Bahianness amenable to state-sanctioned representations underscores how constricted versions of cultural inclusion may work as dissimulatory signs of broader attention to rights and justice.[49] In a Bahia in which the Pelourinho supposedly represents a new type of inclusiveness inspired by UNESCO's humanistic guidelines, citizenship often becomes configured as an indexical, presentist relationship to specific forms of belonging to ethnic and racial groups associated in Latin American nationalism with prior states. Here, under "neoliberal multiculturalism," the Bahian state arbitrates "correct" markers of ethnic identity and national history that qualify bearers for political rights, while residents who exhibit incorrect behaviors face exile on Salvador's periphery.[50] This describes also a situation in Bahia more generally where peasants who argue that they are part of quilombola (maroon) communities gain land titles, whereas neighboring communities do not.[51] Yet, as should now be apparent, such exceptions are not limited to neoliberalism: similar gradations of "sovereignty and sliding scales of differentiation are hallmark features of imperial formations."[52] Thus what is important is not to claim a neoliberal novelty to indexical, deictic claims to histories and identities. Nor is to show that they are but factitious links or arguments without a content proper to "real" history. Rather, it is to begin to reveal the historical reasons that such claims make sense, and continue to make both novel and timeworn sense in a shared field, at a moment when empire seems both eminently deniable and palpably present.

I have sought to explore sliding scales, and their manipulation, by thinking empire alongside Topa, Indio, and their families and neighbors in and around a Misericórdia of the 1990s tamed through hygienic projects that continue a Brazilian engagement with civilization and barbarism and prepare the Pelourinho's landscape as a site for the production of value around cultural difference. This helps "make the human and material face and frailties of imperialism more visible, and . . . make challenges to it more likely" while revealing how scaled differentiations "framed as unique cases . . . are 'exceptions' in a context in which such exceptions are a norm."[53] And the overlaps between the apparent ubiquitousness of exceptions, an interest in approaches to empire that would go beyond macro perspectives, and the blurred boundaries between everyday life and cultural products suggest in turn the importance of an ethnographic engagement with empire today.

Instead of focusing broadly on the ways excluded or stigmatized figures gird the production of a norm portrayed as an essence of the nation or the true subject of history, the approach begun above turns on the details of how that norm is negotiated in different series of incomplete exclusions. What this promises is twofold. First, it follows influential works in colonial studies that provide a picture of subjectivities developed within the constitution of the social body through exclusions or negations.[54] Yet it does so not in relation to nineteenth-century European initiatives that are by now widely accepted as constituting the colonial. Instead, it examines models of personhood and belonging that emerge as mutating perches actively co-produced in state-citizen and NGO-client interactions in a late-twentieth-century Brazil. And this extension of empire's temporal and geographic horizons through a focus on state-directed research projects makes clear something else, namely, the extent to which the continuing salience of imperial formations helps structure and fill the evidentiary bases of future histories. This is especially salient when such histories and their contestations are construed as rule-bound, symbolic relationships and sources of truth rather than as more indexical or even contiguous relations between people and objects in which what counts most is not one's contiguity to the source, or to restored monuments and authentic Afro-Brazilians, but rather an understanding of one's ongoing insertion into this force field. In other words, empire is reproduced today to no small degree through interactions that produce sanctioned forms of knowledge which, as mobilized within the discourse of cultural heritage, individuate the nation and its subjects and objects in ways that extract them from history while claiming to restore that which lies in the past. And for this reason the novel approach to retrospective, or historical, interpretation put together by a woman named Topa is so important for specifying how empire is reproduced, and might be contested, in a world where some would claim it is no longer salient. This approach involves an ability to tie oneself not to history's ostensible content, but to its valences as a space of contestation.

Following Topa, I have thus linked crises or abnormalities and attempts at their amelioration or resolution. But I have struggled to make out this space of ongoing emergency through microarguments about practices that link broad claims to ongoing contestations. Topa looks, from within her own house invaded by sanitarists, across space and time at multiple exceptions by means of questions put to a wealthier woman who would teach her correct behavior. She pushes for an analysis that is so dispersed that it leads the nurse to explain away Topa's unruliness in terms of neediness and the influence of illegal substances. Yet Topa does not respond to the AIDS crisis, or the threat of feces, as a specific problem of her own, delimited context on the Misericórdia. Instead, she pushes into new contexts and new refusals of the walling off of the nurse's house, gender boundaries, and history as simply the past or an elite space from which she is barred as a diseased prostitute. And I have sought to do justice to the brilliant openings she provides by following her genealogically, via an exploration that examines the formation of exceptions and the production of Pelourinho histories as linked solutions to enduring problems, rather than through a consideration of individual exceptions and their discrete contexts.

In an imagined dialogue with a now deceased Topa, and drawing on the gift of a text that she may or may not have willed to me, I have thus extended our shared yet still disparate analyses into the Bahia sertão of the 1890s, the Iberian Peninsula of the first decade of the nineteenth century, and late-twentieth-century NGO politics. And this rethinking of context both in terms of people and spaces that supposedly have nothing to do with empire, and components of histories that indicate a shared situation rather than what really happened, recalls Bruno Latour's advice that when speaking of system or structure the researcher's "first . . . reflex should be to ask 'In which building? In which bureau? Through which corridor?'"[55] Here I

5.2 Topa kisses her neighbor JoJo, 1997. Photo by author.

recall that Topa did not denounce the CETAD nurse. She did not slot her interlocutor into a category of personhood. Nor did she explain that she, as opposed to nonpopular actors like CETAD's professionals, knew all about something called "public health." Rather, she asked the nurse if she would allow her to cross the bourgeois home's threshold if she needed a bathroom. This is a narrow query. But it is also one that might be followed through a variety of corridors and across a number of spaces and moments. And it is a fitting question from a woman who knows well that "for those who know, $2 + 2 = 4$." Perhaps someday we may all begin to realize how $2 + 2 = 4$, and thus how it is that someone like Topa really does know how, who, and what to count. A critical component of the next stages of this project is to begin to understand on what basis, and to what effect, we have begun to recognize and analyze the truth of such an apparently simple statement.

Notes

Research for this chapter was made possible by grants from the Institute of International Education Fulbright, the Wenner-Gren Foundation for Anthropological Research, the U.S. National Science Foundation, the Brazilian Programa Institucional de Bolsas de Iniciação Científica (Institutional Program of Scientific Initiation Fellowship), and the Professional Staff Congress at the City University of New York. Its current form is indebted to discussions organized by Donald Scott at the Queens College Faculty Workshop, as well as to the New School for Social Research's "Scarred Landscapes / Imperial Debris" conference put together by Ann Laura Stoler. I thank these organizers, and in particular Ann Stoler, together with Kim Fortun, Mike Fortun, and two anonymous reviewers from Duke University Press, for pushing my arguments as they developed. My discussion draws also on suggestions by Núbia Rodrigues, Roca Alencar, Val Daniel, Silvia de Zordo, Roger Sansi, and Cam McDonald, who helped me develop my analysis in relation to insights offered by Topa, Indio, Gaguinho, Bebel, and their families and neighbors, especially the Família Gomes de Jesus. I am indebted also to Tarcísio Matos de Andrade and the health professionals of CETAD.

1. Li, The Will to Improve.

2. Stoler, "On Degrees of Imperial Sovereignty," 137.

3. Parmentier, The Sacred Remains.

4. Handler and Gable, The New History in an Old Museum.

5. Abélès, The Politics of Survival; Agamben, State of Exception.

6. Benjamin, "Theses on the Philosophy of History."

7. Kramer, The Blood of Government; Neil Smith, American Empire; Stoler, "Introduction"; Stoler, "On Degrees of Imperial Sovereignty."

8. Chatterjee, "Empire and Nation Revisited," 495.

9. Even as Chatterjee offers an important response to the issue of the identification

of apparently imperial relations in a world without "classical" nineteenth-century, northern European empires, his suggestion that indirect control is new obscures the extent to which empire has long depended "not on stable populations so much as on highly moveable ones" (Stoler, "On Degrees of Imperial Sovereignty," 137).

10. Anthropologists attentive to exceptions have done much recently to explore politics under neoliberalism. Charles Hale ("Does Multiculturalism Menace?"; *Más que un Indio / More Than an Indian*) suggests that under a "neoliberal multiculturalism" states withdraw from the provision of basic services to their citizenries by offering instead, on a selective basis in relation to minority subjects' ability to articulate resonant claims to difference, rights based on difference itself. João Biehl, working also in Salvador with Pelourinho residents, has argued that under neoliberalism the poor are left with little more than networks of relatively isolated spaces where they might partially transform a "diseased biology, marginal and excluded, into a selective means of inclusion" (Biehl, *Will to Live*, 326). And Aihwa Ong (*Neoliberalism as Exception*) has performed for neoliberalism something akin to what Chatterjee suggests may be revelatory of empire: she examines oftentimes contradictory, global, spaces of exception to argue that neoliberalism depends on the construction of multiple exceptions.

11. Stoler and McGranahan, "Introduction."

12. Biehl, *Will to Live*; Caton, "Coetzee, Agamben, and the Passion of Abu Ghraib"; Caton and Zacka, "Abu Ghraib, the Security Apparatus, and the Performativity of Power"; Fassin and Vasquez, "Humanitarian Exception as the Rule"; Redfield, "Doctors, Borders and Life in Crisis."

13. Agamben, *Homo Sacer*; Agamben, *Remnants of Auschwitz*.

14. Collins, "Patrimony, Public Health, and National Culture."

15. Sheriff, *Dreaming Equality*, 220. Also see Collins, *The Revolt of the Saints*; Collins, " 'But What If I Should Need to Defecate in Your Neighborhood, Madame?' "

16. MacCannell, *The Tourist*.

17. Collins, " 'X Marks the Future of Brazil.' "

18. Collins, *The Revolt of the Saints*.

19. Benjamin, "Theses on the Philosophy of History."

20. The Casa de Apoio e Assistência aos Portadores do Vírus HIV/AIDS (House for the Support and Assistance of HIV/AIDS Carriers), or CAASAH, is the subject of Biehl's ethnography of pharmaceutical governance and people's ability to cobble together lives in Brazilian zones of exception (Biehl, *Will to Live*). For histories of AIDS treatment and pastoral institutions in Salvador, see Biehl, "Pharmaceutical Governance"; Biehl, "Will to Live"; and Biehl, *Will to Live*. See also the institution's website at http://www.caasah.com.br/.

21. "Sim, pessoal. Aqui estou, tombado na garupa. Estou bonito, não e não? É por isso que o gringo cuida bem de mim."

22. "Esse aí é da antiguedade. Eu conheco ele desde pivete."

23. Collins, "Culture, Content, and the Enclosure of Human Being."

24. As Nancy Stepan outlines (*The Hour of Eugenics*), Brazilian racial thought turns on Lamarckian theories of ongoing mutability rather than on Darwinian natural selec-

tion. Thus the manipulation of milieu during a subject's or a population's lifetime is understood to produce moral and physical redemption in manners that may seem quite strange in contexts in which more gene-based, and hence biologically genealogical, conceptions of racial belonging operate.

25. Da Cunha, *The Amazon*, 55, emphasis added.

26. Ibid., 82.

27. I write "degenerately metropolitan" because Portugal, since at least the beginning of the eighteenth century, had been understood as an incompetent and backward colonial power quite unlike British, French, and Dutch empires.

28. Caldeira and Holston, "State and Urban Space in Brazil"; Holston, *The Modernist City*.

29. Readers unfamiliar with Brazil may find it difficult to believe that hybridity purifies. Nonetheless, within racial democracy, mixture is configured as leading away from originary infections and toward a modern, forward-facing, and hence cleansed, nationalist "brownness" unique to Brazil (Freyre, *The Masters and the Slaves*). This is also called "whitening" in its more extreme manifestations. For an overview by a U.S. historian, see Skidmore, *Black into White*.

30. It was also a place denounced by virtuous citizens who opposed the "dumping of animal carcasses and performance of libidinous acts at night." See, for example, the 23 May 1742 petition from the Santa Casa da Misericórdia bureaucrat Francisco de Oliveira Telles to Salvador's municipal council requesting that a gate be erected at the upper entrance of the Misericórdia Hill (Arquivo da Santa Casa da Misericórdia, Book 14, 3d register, 1742), so as to attend to citizens', and the Santa Casa's, concerns over the "immoral" acts perpetrated on the Ladeira da Misericórdia.

31. Published in Filho, *Irmã poesia*.

32. "Sensibilização: Informações Preventivas Sobre DSTs/AIDS, Abuso de Drogas e Qualidade de Vida."

33. The words *nena* and *neno* are a feminization and masculinization of the Bahian term for baby, or *nené*. I understand her use of these words as referring to her own gender identity as well as her infantilization by the CETAD social workers.

34. "Cada pessoa é dono do seu proprio corpo" and "Você tem seu valor."

35. Feces left on hillsides may indeed infect water supplies. Nonetheless, as Briggs (*Stories in the Time of Cholera*) points out in relation to Venezuela's 1992–93 cholera epidemic, most important to protecting water are major infrastructural projects and not issues of personal sanitation. These are a red herring when directed at the individual level.

36. Founded in 1985, CETAD by the late 1990s was codirected by Antônio Nery Alves Filho, a graduate of the Federal University of Bahia's medical school who received his psychiatry degree and doctorate in sociology in France, and by Tarcísio Matos de Andrade, a medical doctor and graduate of the Federal University of Bahia, who Misericórdia residents respected greatly and always called "Dr. Tarcísio." In fact, before I met him on that day we crossed paths on the Misericórdia, I had been told by people throughout the Pelourinho that he was not only an excellent doctor, but

someone with whom "people can talk easily" (*a gente conversa legal*). According to the UN Office on Drugs and Crime (UNODC), CETAD negotiated with police and in 1995 opened Bahia's first needle exchange in the Pelourinho and a number of working-class neighborhoods. After 1997, as crack replaced intravenous injection, CETAD branched out. Today it maintains a harm-reduction program, mobile prevention educational service, a community program in outlying neighborhoods, and an initiative designed to reduce the spread of AIDS in Salvador's penitentiary. In 2002, at which point CETAD had a staff of slightly more than thirty professionals and provided almost fifty thousand occasions of service annually, UNAIDS declared CETAD a "model program." It has received funding from a number of institutions and private donors, including the Bahian Ministry of Health, USAID, and a number of "social marketing" corporations such as DKT International, a Washington-based charitable organization associated with UNAIDS and UNICEF that employs market-driven mechanisms to deliver AIDS-prevention materials, including female condoms, in eleven nations.

37. "Não se meta! Estou perguntando!"

38. Filho, *Irmã poesia*, 287.

39. Aretxaga, "Dirty Protest," 135; see also Allen Feldman, *Formations of Violence*.

40. Harvey, *The New Imperialism*.

41. Parmentier, *The Sacred Remains*, 308.

42. Ibid.

43. In other words I am, in a sense, repeating salient aspects of IPAC and CETAD research techniques as I seek to gain insight into an "other" world via Topa as a symbol deployed in the present text. I do not have a solution to this conundrum at this point. But to ignore it would be to commit even more violence against Topa and my memories of her. Furthermore, to take the position that I cannot learn from and alongside Topa, despite the extent to which the geopolitics in which all social scientists are involved in different ways does indeed configure her as a datum for the appreciation of the outsider, would be to shut down one avenue into the possibility of challenging such an unequal system.

44. Parmentier, *The Sacred Remains*, 308.

45. Freyre, *The Masters and the Slaves*.

46. Orta, "Burying the Past," 488.

47. Foucault, *The Archaeology of Knowledge and the Discourse on Language*; Foucault, *Discipline and Punish*; see also Handler and Gable, *The New History in an Old Museum*.

48. See also Price, *The Convict and the Colonel*.

49. Bahia's population is usually estimated to be approximately 80 percent Afro-descendant, while, in light of Brazil's specific racial ideologies, the percentage of the national population that calls itself black is, according to the 2000 federal census, only about 6 percent.

50. Hale, "Does Multiculturalism Menace?"

51. French, "Buried Alive."

52. Stoler and McGranahan, "Introduction," 9.

53. Respectively, Lutz, "Empire Is in the Details," 594; Stoler, "On Degrees of Imperial Sovereignty," 139.

54. Stoler, "Sexual Affronts and Racial Frontiers"; Stoler, *Race and the Education of Desire.*

55. Latour, *Reassembling the Social,* 183.

When a Demolished House Becomes a Public Square

Where Are the House Owners?

Colorful blankets, each different from the others, wrap those sleeping on the floor, crowded against one another. Without the khaki sleeve that catches the eye, one can recognize the room as a Palestinian one. A ray of light crossing the frame from the right leads to the sleeve. Then one more easily notices a pair of army boots peeking out from under another blanket, a flexed knee in uniform, and an upside-down helmet. These are Israeli soldiers. They are sleeping in a Palestinian home in Gaza. There is no trace of the inhabitants. These must have "fled" once more as refugees.

This photograph (fig. 6.1) showed up along with twenty other photographs in my e-mail inbox on 10 January 2009, a few days after the onslaught of the Israeli attack on Gaza. The accompanying letter iterated: "*We* should all be proud of the IDF [Israeli Defense Force]. . . . These brave kids defend our country." Following this was a recommendation—clearly an authorization—to distribute the images.[1] The photographs were disseminated as photos of "our" soldiers, for whom we have to care, whom we have to thank, and with whom we have to identify. This appeal can be disturbed only once one realizes that the colorful blankets under which the soldiers are curled up are not their own, and that the people for whom that place had been home before the soldiers arrived have now been made homeless.

Once we reconstruct the scene shown in the photo for what it is—a Palestinian house that has been violated by Israeli soldiers who have evicted its owners and are now sleeping there peacefully—it becomes clear that what

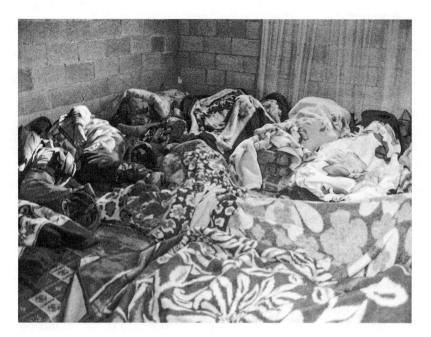

6.1 Israeli soldiers sleeping in a Palestinian house, Gaza, 2009. Photograph by an Israeli soldier.

we are facing is actually what Ann Stoler calls "imperial debris." Although this is not a common ruin—or a photograph of a ruin—what can be seen in it is the ruination of the Palestinian house as a private space, as a space that should remain outside of the reach of naked political power, designating its limit. Out of this photo we can reconstruct the "uneven temporal sedimentations in which imperial formations leave their marks," as well as the ways "empire's ruins carve through the psychic and material space in which people live, what people are left with, and what compounded layers of imperial debris do to them."[2]

The Observation Point

Let me dwell briefly on the conditions that prevent such images—the violation of a Palestinian house—from becoming news items. In the past few years the Israeli authorities have kept the press away from Gaza. The media have had a meager supply of images of the ongoing horror there. This was all the more true during the attack on Gaza in January 2009. During that time, Israel allowed press photographers to set themselves up on a hill adjacent to the Gaza Strip and shoot—from long distance—the smoke billow-

6.2 The Journalist Hill, 7 January 2009. Photograph courtesy of Merav Maroody.

ing over the horizon, thus screening the inferno within (fig. 6.2).[3] The hill from which Gaza can be observed is open to visitors. For their convenience, benches, trashcans, and information about the surrounding landscape have been placed here. During that assault of Gaza, people came there with binoculars and cameras, and while holding conversations in situ, acquired or enhanced their military savvy of missiles, range, precision hits, and impact.[4] From their observation point, what they see is exactly the picture that Israel wishes to show: a war fought on equal footing by two sides. Missiles launched in Gaza hit Israel, and Israel retaliates. The violation and destruction of more than fifteen thousand Palestinian houses is the order of things, nothing special to report about.

The people who bring their children to this hill to show them Gaza under bombardment do so in fascinated wonder at Israel's might. From this hill, they can show their children both the symmetry that justifies Israel's devastation of Gaza, and Israel's spectacular show of force. Their gazes follow the trajectories of missiles and fighter helicopters; they try to guess the nature of their hits, and applaud at the sight of smoke billowing (fig. 6.3). "Yes!" We've done it! We've hit them! "Yes!" We've destroyed them! "Yes!" We've shown them. In elated patriotic camaraderie, individuals, couples, and families can go back home, fully certain of their righteousness—their government's, their army's, their own.

The combined preparatory work done by the Israeli government, army, and media concerning the terror of missiles launched at Sderot and making Gaza inaccessible to the world was systematic and effective to such an extent as to remove all doubt: there could be nothing more just and more right than to destroy fifteen thousand houses in Gaza. The political and military leadership that counted on its soldiers to carry out this mission—and on

6.3 Israelis gathered on a hill near Gaza to see the "show" during one of the last days of bombing by the Israeli Air Force, January 2009. Photograph courtesy of Miki Kratsman / Chelouche Gallery, Tel Aviv.

such citizens who would show up right there to applaud and to misrecognize the continuous exposure of the Palestinian house to ruination—could also count on the previous mobilization of its citizens to devastate Gaza. Nothing new under the sun—except the magnitude of destruction that can be effected in a short period of time, which steadily increases. The ritual pattern stands at the ready, both in political lingo ("Gaza first") and in military jargon ("terrorist infrastructure"). The people who came to that hill do not need pictures from Gaza. What they see from "the Journalists' Hill" suffices. Thirteen hundred dead? From this vantage point, it seems justified.

The person who proudly forwarded the photograph of the sleeping troops did not see in it that which the soldiers of the NGO Breaking the Silence or a civil gaze sees in such images. The soldiers in the picture, or the person who took it, all of whom had invaded the home of others and removed its inhabitants in order to sleep there, were received by the state's citizens with open gratitude. After all, their act is an "act of state."[5] However, this is not a simple act of house demolition; rather, it is a "colonial debris." It consists in the ruination of the civil capacity to recognize that such a project is a regime-made disaster that mobilizes citizens and turns them into its executioners.

Let's look again at this photograph of sleeping troops, which is not, on its surface, a particularly harsh image. One of the soldiers, wakened by a first ray of morning light before his pals, is taking pictures—for himself, for them, for their families—a souvenir, an image of a night's sleep in Gaza.

But, after all, this is Gaza. How can Israeli soldiers who have participated in the destruction of Gaza; the devastation of entire neighborhoods and public buildings; the total ruin of vital infrastructure; the wounding of thousands; the bombing of hospitals, civilian shelters, and schools; the killing of more than a thousand human beings—how can these soldiers, who are, to say the least, not exactly welcome guests, how can they possibly afford to sleep so peacefully in the midst of the inferno they have produced without fearing for their own lives? The answer lies in one of the occupation's most common practices: the creation of a "sterile zone." A sterile zone is an area emptied completely of Arabs so that the Israeli military can carry out its missions. In the image of the sleeping soldiers we are most likely witnessing the heart of the sterile zone. We have no knowledge of the exact size of the sterile zone, its perimeters. But for these soldiers to sleep so serenely, so safely, not only would the dwellers of this house have to have been removed from the sterile zone, but the residents of the entire area would have to be gone as well. For the Israeli soldier, a Palestinian home is a violable space, a violability that was not born in the most recent Gaza campaign.

Gaza as the Moral of a Story

The residents of the Arab towns of Al-Ramle, Bir Al-Saba, Al-Majdal, and Isdud, occupied by Israeli forces in the 1948 war, either escaped or were forcibly expelled. Most of them were removed to Gaza, which tripled in population with the influx. At the end of the war, the Egyptians controlled Gaza and instated their own military administration. Israel had not been able to manage that last "military victory"—the conquest of Gaza—before signing ceasefire agreements with Egypt in 1949, thus giving birth to the narrow, troublesome "strip" at the edge of the nascent State of Israel, dooming its houses.

A "strip" is a military-political term that designates a region that must be dealt with as undetermined, a situation to be solved. The "Gaza Strip" was born as a problem. Since this birth, Israel has never ceased proposing "solutions to the problem." In 1949 Israel proposed a political solution, which was to annex the Strip, along with some of the refugees it harbored. But this "solution," with its military scent, was rejected by the parties involved. In the

Sinai operation in 1956, the Strip was occupied along with the entire peninsula, and Israel imposed a military administration. This did not last long, as under American-Russian pressure Israel was forced to retreat from the territory it had conquered.

In 1967 Israel managed to reconquer the Strip and take control of the refugees of 1948 yet again. Since then, for over forty years, Israel has controlled the Palestinian population in Gaza. At least since the general closure Israel imposed on the Gaza Strip in 1991 during the first Gulf War, such control has entailed cutting off the Strip from the West Bank, as well as strict control over entry into and exit from it. By means of administering the crossings, Israel regulates life in Gaza. Since the Second Intifada, and ever more tightly since its "disengagement," Israel has been managing a measured, chronic disaster, ever watchful not to cross the fine line into "humanitarian catastrophe," enabling or preventing the flow of goods, people, and means. Following its latest assault, which destroyed fifteen thousand houses in Gaza, Israel has prohibited the import of building materials, thereby preventing the Gazans whose homes have been destroyed from rebuilding them.

The House Walls

The house in the photograph from Jayyus (fig. 6.4) stood in the right place to serve as a military outpost. The house's height and location near the separation wall have turned it into a strategic point for snipers, who could hit anyone in the crowd that took part in the weekly demonstrations against this wall. The photograph was taken a few minutes after the soldiers had entered the house and a few minutes before they clashed with its residents and ruined their living space. One can see in the photograph how Palestinians, together with Israelis and international activists, reacted to the soldiers' invasion into what used to be a private space. They endowed this no-longer-private space with a public meaning of gathering together and resisting power in the place and moment in which they had encountered it.

My house walls, sturdy and protective—as I experience them—isolate me from the exterior. So far they, or my presence within them, have managed to keep at bay the madness of political leaders whose malice is steadily on the rise. The house walls keep out winter storms, "occasional" showers, the memory of a pathetic figure that threatened to sneak in like a Trojan mare, the hum of airplanes dropping bombs, and the rumble of bulldozers constantly grating their colossal teeth on building materials just a few dozen

6.4 Israeli soldiers face resistance as they prepare to take possession of a Palestinian house, Jayyus, February 2009. Photo courtesy of Keren Manor, Activestills.

kilometers from here. Our house walls enable us to forget the outside even when it is being experienced as unbearable. Although I have spent many long days carefully studying the images of house demolitions, as I leaf through the newspaper that publicizes photographs of the arenas of destruction, and although I come in from the street and lock the door behind me, sharing the common space of home with my family, I do not worry that my walls will tremble in a moment without my understanding what has happened, that my lungs will be filled with dust, that I will find myself brushing off pieces of plaster still patchy with flowery wallpaper, or that my picture could be taken as I stand next to a pile of objects that once were my home.

The moment I finish writing this description, I feel a rush to delete it, not leaving a trace, to rewrite it as an explicit confession of its factual refutability and some of the half-knowledge-half-prediction that goes through my head from time to time—under circumstances whereby today those are "their" homes, but tomorrow they will be "our" homes. But something urges me not to give up the description I began, to leave it there and take it seriously, insist on the reality it depicts and from it outline a psychopolitical reality that is not private but rather shared by Israeli citizens of Jewish descent. The regime to which I am subject has demolished close to 300,000 houses since it was founded in 1948. And yet something in this reality has caused me—for most of my life, except for those moments when I made myself think about the possibility that my home, too, could be demolished—not to sense any real threat to my home.

What is this confidence that the bulldozer—never resting for a moment—would not reach my neighborhood? It is easy to write off this confidence as marginal to the phenomenon of house demolitions and to regard thinking about demolitions in that way as a luxury of those who are not the direct victims of them. But any analysis of house demolitions that leaves this thought unaccounted for actually perpetuates the banality of destruction as it takes place in democratic regimes. It is banal to the extent that Israeli citizens of Jewish origin do not wonder why only "their" houses are demolished and why those who partake in the whole chain of destruction—from intent to finish—are not incriminated and prosecuted. The "differential demolition" as well as the inability to perceive continuous destruction as a crime organized by the regime are forcibly remnants of imperial time.

The destruction of 250,000–300,000 houses since the founding of the State of Israel, destruction carried out by the state or bodies acting on its behalf, is a phenomenon that can only be understood in the context of the regime and as a part of the way in which the regime regulates the mode of existing-together of all those governed by it. After the mass expulsion carried out in a relatively short period of time—about 700,000 Palestinians in the years 1947–49—the demolition of houses has been, and continues to be, the most extensive and consistent disaster carried out by the regime that came into power here.[6] Since it was founded in the late 1940s, this regime has turned the home into the arena where the boundaries of the body politic are demarcated. These boundaries separate those whose homes are protected—and worthy of protection—from those whose house walls are exposed, penetrable, given to violation and demolition. The protected, confidence-inspiring home space enjoyed by citizens of Jewish descent is a decisive contribution to the way in which, in spite of the regime's consistent actions, those citizens continue to imagine the regime under which they live as a worthy one. They can imagine it this way because they experience it as a regime in which separation is maintained between the private and the public domains. They can imagine it as such—just as this separation is imagined as reality—because they imagine the regime only in relation to the body politic of which they are members (which admittedly does not include those whose homes may be violated). Destruction is an arena which exposes the lack of agreement between a certain governed population—those not considered or counted in a regime's discourse—and the ruling power, a lack of agreement about the separation between the private and the public domain. I wish to conceptualize this lack of agreement and contain it in the description of the regime.

Hannah Arendt turned the actual distinction of the private and public domains into a political question, thereby reshaping the boundaries of political philosophy. Inspired by her, I return to this distinction, which both separates and binds the private and the public domains, in order to discuss the conditions in which the demolition of people's homes has become a foundation of a democratic regime, as well as a banal event in it.[7] However, I shall not make do with the manner in which Arendt distinguished between the two domains; instead, I propose a renewed conceptualization of their relationship that will enable me not only to describe the world and criticize the way it is run, but also to designate some new possibilities it contains. I do so through a civil discourse, the principles of which I shall present toward the end of the present discussion.

"No doubt, wherever public life and its law of equality is completely victorious," Arendt wrote in 1949, "wherever a civilization succeeds in eliminating or reducing to minimum the dark background of difference, it will end in complete petrification and be punished, so to speak, for having forgotten that man is only the master, but not the creator of the world."[8] From among the various characteristics that differentiate the two domains, I shall emphasize one that arises from Arendt's own words: the public domain is characterized by *equality* and the necessity to protect it, while the private domain is characterized by *difference* and the necessity to protect that. Vis-à-vis the threat of the reasoning of one domain overtaking that of the other, Arendt rose as a prophet of doom to warn against impending catastrophe. The separation of the two domains and the protection of their unique characteristics was essential, she claimed, not only to preserve the distinction, but also to protect humans from man's distorted conception of himself as creator of the world, instead of understanding himself as one who shares the world with others, limiting them and being limited by them. The horror clearly emerging from Arendt's description results from the fact that instead of looking for equality in the political realm—equality of all those governed—the desire for equality is aroused distortedly in persecuting its objects in the private domain and acts to remove anyone designated by it as a carrier of difference. This desire aspires to create racial, ethnic, or religious uniformity in the private domain and, in the image of this purified space, to mark the boundaries of the body politic and the "egalitarian" political space that would accommodate it. This accommodation is impossible by definition, even though the powerful—in the modern age, the civil-privileged are among them—imagine the body politic to which they belong as clear of any difference as all belong to the same race, ethnicity, or religion. But the differences among individuals can never be erased by political equality, and they remain constant by the mere singular existence of each and every individual. Instead of focusing on panic at the sight of "the different," Arendt identifies panic at the sight of "the same," those who instead of taking part in the world with others who share its design, act as though they were its creators and act to establish it in their own image.

Ethnic cleansing is an ultimate solution for the creation of such a world because it strives toward a complete removal of difference and the eradication of that which is left. However, in most cases efforts at complete ethnic cleansing end in failure, manifested in a political language that invents such categories as displaced, dispossessed, and refugees. These categories, describing vast populations the world over (their number in the modern age is constantly on the rise), are part of a political language that enables political regimes to turn humans into "that which is left" and therefore can be thrown into those particular internal-external zones shaped especially for them. At times, these categories prove beneficial by generating struggle for recognition and restitution; but in most cases they mask the political status of those to whom they are attributed. Their political status, in the space where they live, is first and foremost that of *governed*, while that of refugees expelled from their land is *nongoverned*, with regard to that same regime that has excluded them from the governed generality. My use of the category "governed" (and "nongoverned") enables me to emphasize or renew the link between those contained within it and the regime responsible for it. Furthermore, the use of this category enables me to suspend the differentiation that the governing power creates between those governed, whom it recognizes as its own, and the others, whom it governs without recognizing its responsibility for them and thus designates as refugees, stateless, or displaced persons.

Three Relation Forms between the Private and the Public

Although the distinction between the private and the public domains has ignited stormy debate in the past three decades revolving around the nature of each of these domains and their interrelatedness, apparently none of the parties in the debate denies the actual existence of some distinction between the two. I propose to name this basic relation between the private and the public which everyone assumes an *empty and necessary* relation. Empty because its mere existence is not affected by the various forms it takes, and necessary because we do not know of any forms of human coexistence not based on distinctions and differentiations that enable humans to congregate and separate by various criteria of limiting and enabling entry, exit, and accessibility. In other words, this basic form describes the separating and binding relation of various realms of activity that are characterized anew in different contexts, times, and cultures.

The second form of relation is a specific historical one, and its basic model is familiar in its various appearances throughout history, at least since ancient Greece. The condition for partaking in "worldly matters," the prerequisite for entering the public domain, wrote Arendt in her discussion of the Greek world, is home ownership, the possession of a private place in the world.[9] This form of relation I propose to call *the protective condition*. This form establishes a relation of conditioning between the two domains—a place in the one domain as a precondition for placement and protection in the other—and thus the direction of this conditioning, from the private to the public. Modern citizenship formed by the French Revolution continued at first to identify the private place with possession of property and regarded it as a condition for political participation. However, shortly thereafter, it was established that human males as such—even non-owners of property—could partake of political life. It sufficed to be male and placed within the territorial boundaries of France to become a citizen. Placement of one's own—whether as property owner or not—became institutionalized for centuries as a condition for moving between the two domains. The form of protective condition presupposes the differentiation between the two domains as well as the necessity to keep them separate in order to administer and regulate the possibilities of passage from one to the other. As long as this form is preserved, the private domain of those allowed to take part in the public domain is supposed to be protected—or at least negotiable—from activities taking place in the public domain, and all the more so from governmental power intervention. This link between this precondition of access to the public domain and the protection of the private domain (consequence of the separating and binding relation between the domains) should be seen as part of the regime and the hypothetical agreement between the governed and governmental power over the boundaries of governance. A test of the stability of this form of relation and the scope and nature of its implementation on all its governed, as well as the possibilities open to them to demand its enforcement, can attest to the nature of a regime more than do its constitution, laws, or common representations.

In discussing a phenomenon such as the massive demolition of houses, when the governmental power handles the private domain of its governed as if it were its own theater of operations and destroys their possibilities of partaking in the public domain, one might claim critically—or perhaps hastily—that the first form of relation no longer exists as the private domain had already lost its main private features (fig. 6.5). However, if one accepts the ontological claim that an empty or formal relation between the private and the public domains is necessary and perpetual, one must explore another way of thinking how the reality in which such a relation seems not to take place can be accounted for. Nor can one rule out the second form of relation, arguing that it has an ideological role because it creates a false impression of a stable interrelation while rendering accountable only the movement of citizens between the two domains and ignoring that of all other governed. However, if one wishes to understand the relation between the domains as a part of the regime, one must take into account the ideological role played by this form of relation in representing the regime as proper.

Assuming, of course, that this second form of relation does not illuminate the way in which relation between the domains is maintained toward governed noncitizens, the consistent and massive practice of house demolitions continues to appear as an exception and not as a constitutive part of the regime.

A third form of relation is therefore necessary to account for the way in which ongoing massive destruction shapes the relation between the private and the public. However, if such a form will account only for the condition of the dispossessed, then it too would contribute to the description of a split reality such as governmental power wishes to present—a reality involving citizens and a proper regime versus a reality involving the noncitizens who are governed only temporarily and as there is no alternative, until circumstances free them of the world of the former. In order to turn massive house demolition into a part of the discussion of regime, I wish to show that the third form of relation cannot replace the first two, but rather joins them in a way that will provide a complex account for reality that encompasses both the regime's mode of action and the way in which it is experienced and represented by citizens and all governed alike. I propose to name this third form of relation, which is the reversal of the protective condition, *the condition of unprotected exposure to power*. One can identify and characterize it by observing the state of the dispossessed, internally displaced, and refugees against whom it is directed. Their presence in one political territory or another does not serve as a condition for their entry into public space, nor does it entitle

6.5 The private domain stripped of privacy, Gaza, Beit Lahiya, 15 August 2010.
Photo courtesy of Anne Pacq, Activestills.

them to a place within the body politic. Moreover—and that is the meaning of the reversal of the protective condition—the absence of this place/ment constitutes a condition for injuring and exposing them to violence within the private space of their residence. The inhabited house does not pose a physical or symbolic obstacle in the way of rampantly violent governmental force. It is perceived as a spatial disruption of the movement of the governmental force that does not regard itself as limited by those whom it does not recognize as its governed. Unlike the protective condition, I claim, the third form is neither universal nor unanimously acceptable, and it is usually not formulated as an explicit political project, but rather finds its own winding ways to expand. The displaced and dispossessed are not perceived as a part of the body politic, and therefore what the regime does to them is not perceived as a part of the regime. The erasing of their governed-ness from the representations of the body politic fixes the boundaries of the citizens' political imagination. These boundaries do not enable civil intention—unmediated by some loyalty or other to the differential relation of governmental power to its governed—to find and shape a place for itself. Those governed designated as displaced, dispossessed, or refugees are not invited to take part in this act of the imagination, and so this distorted political imagination, without an iota of civil intention, can proliferate undisturbed. When the protective condition is reversed, it is not merely the change in direction of movement, as though the private and the public have remained two stable domains, but rather disruption of the individual's ability to possess his or her own place/ment in the common space as a universal condition for participating in public space.

These three formations of relations between the private and the public domains do not have the same status as categories describing reality, nor any less as categories through which thought shapes reality. I propose to regard the first form of relation—empty and necessary—as a tool of civil imagination that enables one to retrieve and present as necessary the distinction between the domains: the public, characterized as aspiring to equality with all others governed, and the private, characterized as containing difference of all others governed. In other words, the ontological claim of the necessity of distinction serves as a basis for civil discourse. The demand that is the very heart of such civil discourse—to rehabilitate the distinction between the spaces in a way that is universally applied to all governed—is a demand to limit the governmental power and a call for a regime change.

This discourse is based on the assumption that although citizens benefit from this form of relation between the domains, it is faulty when the noncitizens governed alongside them are denied the same benefits. A civil discourse assumes that the only way to limit the governmental power is to speak from the point of view of all governed. Thus, in a reality of massive destruction of a certain governed population, it cannot assume that the second form of relation—the protective condition—is maintained. However, instead of faulting this form of relation, which citizens are right to defend and keep for themselves, I propose to place it as a favorable form of relation between the two domains. And as a consequence of this, I propose to regard the third form of relations describing, as it were, only the state of the displaced and dispossessed as the general form of relation, a description of the state of things relating not only to this particular population, but a description through which one must think the nature of distinguishing the two domains in relation to all governed. After all, when house demolitions become a state project, whose perpetrators are the citizens who benefit from the second form of relation—the form of protective condition—they cannot continue to be described as relevant merely to the population whose houses are being demolished. It must be discussed as a phenomenon that shapes the form of coexistence of all governed, those who commit house demolition and those who suffer from it.

What Is House Demolition?

Since 1948, the local landscape of Palestine—which became Israel—has been sown with tens of thousands of house ruins (forming statistics that are sorted by years and regions), photographs of ruins and rubble have been produced and distributed, and various linguistic patterns have been shaped to report the destruction ("in time of warfare," "terrorist nests," "illegal construction," "razing," "military needs," etc.). These are naturally assembled into the matter-of-fact category of "house demolitions," as if it were some routine phenomenon existing somewhere in the private domain of the relevant homeowners, with no interest whatsoever to the general public in whose name and for whose sake it is carried out.

What hides behind the category "house demolitions" that gives a name to so many horrors? What is counted as such? What exactly does it mean? What is "house demolitions" when referred to in the plural sense? Is that which it refers to even countable? Justifiable? Can the number of houses that the State of Israel demolished between 1948 and 1949, estimated at about 100,000, possibly justify any end whatsoever? What does the number 100,000 refer to, reflecting as it were the number of houses that Israel has demolished since 1967 to the present?[10] This datum must refer to the individual countable units that have been totally demolished. And what about the collateral damage, the neighbors' houses that were not slated for demolition but whose windows and doors were torn out when another house was demolished? And the house whose walls were "only" perforated while the army chased its "wanted men"? And the house where a huge hole was blown open in the children's room because it bordered on the house destined for a targeted killing? How about the one where "only" its former peace and quiet were destroyed? Or the one whose walls, thick as they were, could not shelter its inhabitants from the horrific noise of the demolition of the neighbors' house? And the houses scattered in between and around them, a part of their built-up landscape where the owners of the demolished home and their neighbors whose houses still stand continue to live their lives? Those houses not totally demolished are not included in the tally, but their numbers are legion, and the question begs to be asked—what is the point in counting them?[11]

By acts of destruction, the sovereign shapes the nature of space and changes it irrevocably. Under such conditions, most of the activity carried out in space, both by the sovereign and by the subjects, is not the fruit of regulated negotiations with the governed or of agreement. Such negotiation supposedly held by democratic regimes cannot take place here as long as the sovereign does not recognize the governed as citizens and the governed do not recognize the regime as their sovereign. By means of the architecture of destruction, the sovereign strives to finalize the lack of structural agreement between it and the governed and the negotiation that has not taken place.[12] The justification that accompanies house demolitions, in each individual case, presents the policy of destruction as an accumulation of particular cases that are handled in a matter-of-fact, focused, and legal manner, and characterize the victims, the homeowners and their families, as felons who forced the law to act as it did. For many years, these justification mechanisms—and, in a way, the negotiation over concrete justifications as well—did not enable one to think of the destruction as a complete, independent project, as a form of relation between public and private space—that which I have described as the condition of unprotected exposure to power—which the regime intends for Palestinians only.

A comprehensive picture of house demolitions is still inexistent, and can be only partially assembled from several existing databases. The postulated solidity of the category "house demolition"—it seems one can state this with certainty today—is generated a posteriori, from the ongoing, daily destruction, which is justified by the regime and outrageous to only a few, to the original, constituent destruction that took place in the late 1940s. The governmental effort to stabilize the category of destruction and limit its discussion to one of ways, means, and justifications preserves house demolitions as a marginal phenomenon existing within a proper political space where the "protective condition" is the dominant, characteristic relation between the private and public domains.

The current destruction, carried out mainly in the West Bank and Gaza, but also, on a more modest scale, within the Green Line, uproots house by house, individually, having established for each a special file and enriched it with warning notices and decrees, evidence and justifications extracted from both local and international law. That destruction—the one that constituted the Israeli regime in 1948—introduced an outline for a nationwide destruction plan whose justification has constituted the law, which, in turn, has furnished it with inspiration and license—a plan as abstract and general as the aforesaid contours.

The Israeli regime has demolished hundreds of thousands of houses since 1947. The creation of a continuity between these different practices of destruction (in the 1940s and today), as well as the difficulty in seeing through or beyond this continuity, are part of the system responsible for the transformation of destruction into *a means*, a part of the constituent violence of the regime. This continuity is preserved by Israeli citizens of Jewish origin in their denial that the destruction is part of the regime to which they are subject. The continuity between the current destruction and the constitutive destruction lies primarily in the fact that destruction was shaped as a vehicle—one in a repertoire of available means whose significance is determined only according to the end to which they are subordinated. There are those whose home gives them access to public space and is immune to demolition, and there are those whose own home does not give them a place in public space, and therefore their home loses its sanctity as a human dwelling and is designated for demolition or invasion.

Thus, while the end is dissociated from the means and determines its meaning from the outside, the demolition of houses becomes an available means whose use is self-explanatory. When destruction becomes an automatic means in the hands of the regime, the authorities and their servants become authorized to generate destruction and to generate knowledge that enables and justifies the use of destruction to obtain goals defined as external to it. The Palestinian house has thus lost its sanctity as a home, and can therefore be violated.

The Condition of Unprotected Exposure to Power

The history of this violability goes back more than sixty years. It can be told from the destruction of Palestinian houses, but it should be told also from the silencing of Jewish voices opposing the uprooting of Palestinians from their houses. These voices were hushed that very moment by the nationalist voice that overtook the military and political leadership of the Jewish public, making expulsion a given. This leading voice stammered in its official declarations but was nonetheless determined in its concrete practices and managed to expel 750,000 Arabs from the areas of British Mandate Palestine. Beginning in 1948, over the course of a year, Jewish soldiers went from village to village and, when called on, from home to home, tearing Arabs away from their dwellings and lands. At times the soldiers used indirect means—rumors about the destiny of Arabs who chose not to leave their homes, truck convoys to help them leave—and at others, direct physical threat and violence. Expulsion aimed first and foremost to remove Palestinians from their place in public space in order not to disrupt the creation of a Jewish majority with governing institutions in its image.

The exclusively Jewish public space cleansed the Palestinian home of the sanctity with which individuals imbue their private space and which is supposed to make it inaccessible to others unless they admit them. Since that time, the Palestinian home has not ceased to be threatened by the very logic and operating patterns that present that home to the Israeli public (as well as to world public opinion) as an existential menace to the intactness of the public space and to the possibility of preserving the protective relation between the private and public space solely for Jews.

The Palestinian home has never been perceived as a private domicile whose four walls shelter its dwellers from invaders and strangers. The Israelis do not regard the Palestinians as homeowners in the usual sense of the term, and do not conceive of themselves as invaders or strangers. Palestinian homes are vulnerable to nightly incursions, bulldozer activity, bombs dropping from the skies, missile barrages, and shootings that make them uninhabitable. They are appropriated to create army outposts, positions, and headquarters, depending on changing circumstances and increased "security necessities." The explanation given for these actions is that they are necessary in order to "flush out the terrorists from their nests," "suppress resistance," or "destroy insurgent infrastructure." Thus the Palestinian home is presented as a military outpost of the enemy, calling for military intervention. The Palestinian home constitutes a problem; military intervention is its solution—or at least a means to "solving the problem." More precisely, the home becomes penetrable and violable because it has been perceived by some local Israeli commander as a "security problem" or as providing a means toward a solution.

The Enterprise of Destruction

The United Nations Partition Plan of 29 November 1947 was a formative moment in the process of ruination of Palestine-Eretz Israel.[13] It gave international validity to the efforts of Jewish leadership to determine, by themselves, the future of a place with an Arab majority, into which Jewish immigrants had blended over several decades. The establishment of a Jewish state was the professed, explicit goal, the realization of which entailed mobilizing the majority of the Jewish population in the land for a whole range of activities. The nation-building (binyan ha'aretz) ethos infused everything that happened in Palestine in the late 1940s with sense and direction. Under the guise of construction activities, or concurrent with them, hundreds of thousands of destructive acts were also carried out. This duality was part of the British imperial legacy.[14] The destructive acts were shaped as a means to obtain an aforesaid explicit goal. The destruction was built into the discourse as subordinated to a higher cause, whereby it was systematically dwarfed, and for several decades never emerged in its exposed form—as literal destruction. It was a large-scale destruction enterprise in which thought, resources, and talents were invested, whose implications went far beyond the instrumental nature ascribed to it by its architects.

The history of the destruction enterprise—which has shaped, and continues to shape, the economic, cultural, political, moral, and civil world of the residents of this place—has yet to be written; on occasion, however, a fault line may be identified which has begun to mark the destruction as the object of research independent of the justification story conceived by those responsible for it. The fault line enables us to start regarding the destruction as an enterprise in and of itself, to gauge its scope, to reflect on its depth, and to analyze it not only in the national context.[15] Such dissociation is necessary, yet it calls for great caution, lest destruction emerge as one-dimensional—as a delimited activity executed and completed within the boundaries determined by its perpetrators, an activity affecting only the lives of those whose homes were destroyed—and the assumption emerge that all that remains is to put it in writing, to record it as a chapter of the past.

Transforming destruction into a means expresses the sovereign power, its strength not only to render destruction a matter of course, but also to conceal information pertaining to it, thereby striving to stabilize its meaning alone, to compel its derivation from the target and from the intentions of those implementing it. Tracing the meanings of destruction independent of the subordinated means–goal relations, one realizes not only that it is not a means, but that it is also not entirely in the hands of the perpetrator, as if there were only one party that could ruin construction and hide the traces of that ruination. The destruction occurs between those who destroy and those who suffer destruction, and sometimes also between many, as they were before splitting into two parties—those destroying and those suffering destruction. When one begins to regard destruction in this manner, it turns out that the act of destruction destroys not only that which its architects declare that they are destroying, but also the very configuration of life which is devoid of destruction, destroyer, and the victim of destruction. The ruination and its concealment are akin to betrayal of the pact, the partnership, and the promise which formed the basis for being-together.

The destruction enterprise initiated by the leaders of the Jews in the late 1940s was applied, as aforesaid, to isolated houses only rarely: focused rescue of an ancient synagogue, of a Crusader fortress, or of "ordinary" buildings which, left isolated and intact, were no longer perceived as a temptation and a catalyst for the return of the deportees. New construction which soon surrounded these isolated buildings lent them an "antiquated look" devoid of a concrete history. The destruction began with momentum and was aimed at entire residential environments, whose destroyers—who became the masters of the land—no longer wanted their existence. Today it is hard to isolate a single cause and determine whether it was due to national, political, economic, demographic, spatial, or cultural reasons—or all of these together. The implementation of the demolition plan was made possible through the collaboration of the new Jewish citizens of the land. Many of them were thrilled by the plan to establish a state for the Jewish people, and were thus harnessed for an act of construction which also included destruction. The destruction included in the plan was built in as a means to overcome threats and obstacles on the way to its realization: paving safe roads, creating territorial continuity, or absorbing the persecuted Jews of the world. The general goal which could have been obtained in different ways—establishment of a state for the Jewish people—was translated by the Jewish leadership (and, subsequently, of the state) into a destructive goal whose means were equally destructive: establishment of a state for the Jewish people on the ruins of the society that had lived here in the late 1940s. In many ways, that society was already the outcome of Jewish-Arab blending that spawned different forms of being-together.[16] Being-together is not an ideal characterization, but rather a term intended to describe the way in which people lead their lives among and together with other people. Against the backdrop of the forms of life that existed here, the destruction, which was structured and presented as a means in the service of something other than destruction, became in fact an end in itself—*destruction of the mixed society that had developed here, and the removal of anything that might enable its resurrection.*

A Single (Flawed) Public Space

Through practices of destruction, the Jewish military and political leadership managed to tighten its grip of space, and to administer the movement of the local population in that space—differentially. Immediately following the United Nations resolution to partition the land, public space was conquered with the military reasoning that enabled the mobilization of Jewish citizens around the idea of a total national war—with the Arab residents in the role of the enemy to be vanquished—and around the necessity of creating a public Arab-free living space. Expelling the Arabs from their homes and the demolition of those homes in order to prevent return was then constructed as a mean to that end. That end would not have been attainable without mobilizing Jewish citizens to take part in the destruction project as civilians and as soldiers.[17] Thus, the destruction practice expresses not only power relations between sovereign and governed, but also between the governed of one ethnicity and those of another, relations which, in the State of Israel, have been polarized and conflictive.

In the years 1947–49 local space was irrevocably changed: entire Palestinian villages were destroyed; Palestinian construction became sparse in certain crowded urban areas of the larger cities; Jewish immigrants were housed in homes of Palestinians who had been expelled; and new construction and forestation enterprises emerged, vigorously covering up much of the destruction's scarring. Of the various characteristics of the new space that emerged, I point only to the appearance of boundaries and spatial delineations that objectivized the new ethnic division of the space. The Palestinian inhabitants who were expelled were crowded over the border, turning into refugees, or what I call nongoverned by the new regime that was instated here. The Palestinians who remained in the land and became a minority were concentrated in ghettos and subjected to military rule. The Jews, now a majority, were busy building for themselves a national Jewish home. This violent differentiation of populations and the radically different possibilities that opened up to one population and closed for the other, invite us to describe the Palestinians as denied public space or as denied the right to take part in it, and the Jews as permitted to move "freely" in public space. But this description misses the point because it presupposes that public space can be measured regarding one population, while distinguishing it from another population that is governed alongside it. Moreover, this description itself bears witness to the public space, flawed as it is, captured in its logic of replacing generality with differentiality as its organizing principle. In other words, since 1947 until the present, public space has lost its most important principle—being open for participation to anyone who owns his or her own place/ment in that space. The 1967 Occupation and the horrific destruction it entailed has settled within this model and was conducted as a part of that destruction enterprise that has not ceased to this very day.

Destruction as a Regime Feature

Israeli citizens of Jewish descent are permanently living their lives in destruction arenas originating in 1947–48, but they do not see them as such because in most cases these places have been naturalized through categories— such as "ruins," "Ottoman architecture," "oriental construction," "sheikh's tomb," "Forest of the Righteous," and so on—that conceal the violence of "'ruination' as an active, ongoing process."[18] Israelis are also constantly exposed to arenas of destruction that are still produced in the occupied territories. Nor do these appear to them as arenas of destruction, which is due to the massive justification and intimidation mechanisms of the "security" kind. Destruction that does not appear as such. It does not then expose itself as the naked truth—an expression of disagreement between governed and government as to the nature of the shared space.

The figure of the sovereign—founding cities, appointing architects and engineers, even commissioning professionals from faraway lands to help him make his mark on the space without asking permission of the governed—is familiar to us since antiquity. Evidence of this dimension of sovereign power abounds in the modern era as well and is manifested in the sovereign's right to erect monuments that change built-up space without official tender or civil agreement. In modern France, for example, this right— reserved for the president of the republic—has an architectural context par excellence and an explicit royalist connotation: fait du prince. In democratic regimes the sovereign is entitled to this privilege as long as he makes measured, controlled use of it. The monument is supposed to glorify the president through the pleasure and benefit he bestows on all citizens.

In its more than sixty years in the Gaza Strip, sovereign power has made extensive use of this privilege reserved for the sovereign in special cases although its governance is not agreed on and although at least its nongoverned in the refugees camps and its subjects in the occupied territories do not recognize its authority. It has extensively interfered in space without sharing such space with its governed, the Palestinians. This massive intervention exceeds the authorities and right of the sovereign, and has been enabled chiefly through the "divide and rule" policy applied to citizens and noncitizens. The "agreement" of the governed and "their participation" in decision-making processes about their habitat have solidified in the past decade into important categories of public discourse, promoted by Jews and for Jews, tolerant of the fact that they have been systematically denied the Palestinians, who are still naturally perceived as noncitizens and as "stateless," and who are therefore denied the rights to which citizens are entitled.

The Oslo Accords divided the occupied territories into differentiated areas of Israeli and Palestinian control. But even after the accords, the occupation regime—using its massive military might—did not refrain from functioning as the ultimate ruler with regard to all matters concerning the administration and organization of space, even in areas assigned to the Palestinian Authority. The Israeli government acts as one who wishes to show publicly and unequivocally that no walls pose an obstacle and no domicile is a sanctuary. Homes of those suspected of resisting the occupation serve as a favorite site for the Israeli government's demonstrations of force— "watch and beware." Often the inhabitants of demolished houses are not themselves the suspects, but the families of suspects.

However, resistance to his force is not the only pretext used by the sovereign when he comes to demolish houses. Thousands of homes, vegetable gardens, fruit groves, and orchards are destroyed because their situation is in the way of some combat operation or prevents some colony from developing and expanding. In the areas left under its full control, the occupation rule sanctions the demolition of houses through legalities. The process is relatively simple and is based on a systematic rejection of applications for building permits, a diabolical ploy assigning structures an illegal status and thus fating them to be demolished.

These interventions in space, a sign of frequent exercise of the sovereign's privilege, hurt Palestinians and cause them immediate damages.[19] Such damages, naturally, exceed the simple multiple sum of the damages of "home demolition" or "checkpoint" to their direct victims. Such damages, taking place in shared space, affect the ways space is used by the population at large, not only those whose body, property, mind, or private time have been assaulted. These interventions are present in public space in several main forms.

1. Spectacle, usually limited in time, of the momentary occurrence of destruction.
2. Ongoing presence of the results of the damage in the form of various textures of destruction.
3. Architectural "phrases" whose syntax is made up of modular units created for military needs of administering population.

These three forms are imposed on the Palestinians, hurt them, and perpetuate subjugation in the power relations between them and the Jewish citizens. The status of Palestinians as noncitizens does not suffice to exclude them from shaping their living space. To keep them in the status of passive subjects necessitates subjugation mechanisms that operate everywhere, all the time. The sovereign, unrecognized by them and not recognizing them, appears in their living space and disappears from it while pulling the strings of the disaster it causes them. The disaster and the urgencies it produces, like the architectural language it dictates, serve to rivet the subjects even after it retreats from the ground, to administer and monitor their movement, to diminish their activity to the bare minimum of needs, and to paralyze their ability to act. These interventions hurt the essence of shared public space: being open to movement without exercising violence, and being shared by all subjected to agreed and accepted regulations and standards. The Palestinians are prevented from moving freely; their limited movement is managed through violent means (spatial or others); spatial interventions aspire to isolate them from others and deny them the ability to maintain ties, hold public assemblies, and—in general—lead a reasonable civil life.

Regime-Made Disaster and Civil Discourse

Much has been written about the fragmentation of Palestinian space (beyond the "green line") in the early 2000s, and about the exposure of Palestinian homes to military intervention at all times.[20] From different reports, photographs, and descriptions, a horrifying picture arises of Israel's systematic effort to seriously hurt the Palestinians' ability to take part in public space and be protected within their homes. As a rule, these descriptions dutifully present the horror of life on the verge of disaster to which the Palestinians are fated. Usually, they allow no more place for the categories "private" and "public" and the distinction between them. Giving up this distinction is an indirect contribution to the delineation of the injustice wrought on Palestinians by the Israeli regime and the construction of such acts of governance as eternal.

Reviving these categories and distinguishing them in a discussion of Israel's destruction enterprise is therefore necessary to avoid the impasse of discussing destruction as an accumulation of private instances and to turn civil discourse into a discussion of destruction as regime-made disaster. Civil discourse does not wish to create something out of nothing. Civil discourse seeks to observe reality in a complex manner without accepting a priori the exclusion of certain governed populations from the categories by which reality is described. Such discourse is characterized by seven precepts, which are based on the discussion of the forms of relation between the private and the public which I have here presented.

1. Civil discourse suspends the ruling power's point of view and the national characteristics that serve it to divide the governed population and set one part of it against the other, and enables citizens and noncitizens to join the discourse as partners in the world which they share as governed.

2. In civil discourse, room is made for the form of human being-together that is committed to all governed as abstract beings. Civil discourse is used to resist the outlines of regimes that presuppose the differentiation between the governed as both problem and solution.

3. Civil discourse assumes the necessity of distinguishing between the private and the public as an expression of a being-together of individuals, and not as a product of the governing power. Civil discourse activates civil imagination wherever governing power's logic threatens to take over the form of human being-together and wherever the common categories help make this reality appear as the real state of things. Civil imagination is the means of protection that the governed have from the governing power which holds mighty means to shape reality so that it would appear as the natural state of things. Civil imagination is not science fiction, but rather an effort to locate potentials in reality and activate them wherever sovereign power threatens to destroy them.

4. Civil discourse insists on a single form of relation shared by all governed toward the private and the public domains, a form that includes protection of public space equally open to all governed, and protection of private space containing differences—national ones as well.
5. Civil discourse insists on a reconceptualization of the categories it uses and a denser, more heterogeneous description of reality.
6. Civil discourse refuses to identify disaster with the population implied by it and demands the reconstruction of conditions that enable one to regard any disaster as *disaster* and not just *disaster from their point of view*, "they" being those subject to it.
7. Civil discourse insists on seeing disaster striking a certain governed population as a regime disaster for which the regime is responsible.

In Public

A house demolition, the locus par excellence of private space, always takes place in public. Invading the boundaries of the Palestinian home and its intimacy, the sovereign also breaches the boundary between the private and the public. The interior, to which only close friends and family members have been invited, is exposed to the view of all and sundry, and the home's most cherished objects fly up in the air and are shattered amid the ruins, abandoned to any hand. However, the distinction between private and public, as much as the sovereign abhors it and expresses this in acts of destruction, is never a result of a sovereign plan. The sovereign can hurt this distinction, or strive to regulate or monitor it, but in fact it is maintained by the governed in a way not entirely subjugated to the sovereign's intentions and plans.

A look at dozens of arenas of destruction delineates a picture that challenges the existing categories for discussing private and public space. Especially in the arenas of home demolition, where its rule without the governed's consent and recognition can be seen clearly, we can identify the efforts of the governed population to reestablish this distinction.

The sovereign power, wishing to display force, turns the arena of destruction into a permitted place of public congregation, while prohibiting it in other contexts. Thus, the assembly of noncitizens at the arena of destruction *becomes the permitted and most common mode of public gathering* (fig. 6.6). *Such mass gathering is usually seen both at the time of the disaster and around the textures of destruction which remain in the space after the disaster and begin to function as public squares.* The sovereign wreaking destruction does not bear responsibility

6.6 Brazil camp, Gaza Strip, 2007. Spectators standing together around a crater where a house once stood is one of the few forms of public gathering in a public space that the occupation regime not merely tolerates, but even initiates and supplies with ample spectacle. Photograph courtesy of Miki Kratsman.

for the ruin that it sows, nor does the sovereign handle the consequences of ruin. The disasters it perpetrates are justified such that the sovereign is able to shirk its responsibility toward its victims, who become dispossessed and displaced overnight. It presupposes, in its stupidity—characteristic of governing power that disregards the agreement of its governed—that it has the power to determine how the spectators will view the horror spectacle it perpetrates, and to determine what morals and lessons will be drawn and resonate at what has now been turned by the governed from arena of destruction into a public square. It is likewise convinced that it has the power to "brand these lessons into their consciousness": "We have delivered an unequivocal message to the population—namely, that anyone engaged in terrorism, as well as his close family, will pay a steep price."[21]

But the sovereign's efforts to rule the meanings and uses of space cannot change the ontology of the political as something that emerges "among human beings" and is instituted as relations among them. Even when these spatial interventions are a severe blow to the individuals' ability to act and to their shared horizon, their joint coping with their disaster and with the restrictions imposed on their movement creates areas in joint space that are not entirely controlled by the sovereign's intentions, his objectives and plans. In shirking responsibility for rubble removal, reconstruction, and restitution, he leaves sustainable scars in space and forces the Palestinians — but also gives them room — to cope with the consequences and through this to rehabilitate a space of assembly. During an act of destruction, the Palestinians are distanced from the site, to prevent violent resistance. When they are permitted to return, they discover that the damage is irrevocable and that vertical, three-dimensional structures have become horizontal textures in one fell bulldozer swoop. Movement in the streets has been stopped, and its renewed flow is reshaped along the new surface, which is but the texture of destruction, piles of rubble serving as a kind of public square. The Palestinian Authority and various aid agencies, such as the International Red Cross or the United Nations Relief and Works Agency, who care for veteran refugees as well as new types of refugees that Israel produces at present, and for the residents themselves, all try to cope with the goings-on under the harsh limitations which the army imposes on their freedom of action and movement on the ground.

Thus, from the place of disaster which the sovereign has deserted and abandoned emerges the acting-together of residents which is prohibited on other occasions. A view of sites of destruction shows that congregating around them is not harnessed entirely and merely to address urgent survival needs and provide caregiving for the wounded. Every focus of disaster becomes a public square in which Palestinians assemble around a common object of their gaze, and they establish its boundaries during this assembly. Their stance on the edge of rubble and craters which the sovereign power has sown in their landscape contains more than a glance of wonder at the scope of destruction. In their gaze, and most likely in the discussion they hold while standing there, they link the place of disaster to the rest of the city. Their faces are sealed and distant, and at times seem to bear contempt or hatred toward those who have imposed on them to act within a public space formed by disaster. With endless patience, those who acknowledge the limited intervention of the ruling power and know that it will never be able to completely destroy public space and deny them their common existence view the sights of disaster and dismiss its perpetrators' pretension to reduce the disaster to an unequivocal lesson. At times it is difficult to tell whether they wonder at the might of human destructiveness or at the stupidity of the sovereign's behavior. The efforts and resources the sovereign invests in practices of blocking and separation — meant, among other things, to limit disaster to only one side of the space and thus to disengage from it and defend itself from it — show how difficult this separation is, and how scant the chances are to achieve it. The Palestinians' viewing of the acts of destruction transcend the urgency wrought by disaster and open a wider perspective through which one can see disaster as a form of ongoing rule and not as just an event at a certain point in time. The more sovereign power destroys space and etches it with disasters, blockages, and separations, the deeper its grip and the more difficult it becomes to pry loose. The gaze is layered and mutual, and the noncitizens, destined to view their disaster, look through it at the citizens who view them from afar and deny the active role they themselves play in its production and the way in which this disaster is theirs as well—the disaster of being the perpetrators of disaster.

Notes

1. This e-mail was signed by the CEO of the Israeli branch of a large European firm. His full personal data were prominently noted at the bottom of the letter. This is the most abstract photograph of a very harsh series, the last two of which come with a warning: "These are not to be viewed by children." The rest, according to the sender, may apparently be shared with kids, as a part of this war's booty.

2. See Stoler's essay in this volume.

3. In order to counter the images coming from this "zoom out" site, from which ruination can't be seen, one may look at the project "The Destruction of Destruction." The photographs shown there are drawn from an archive titled Verification of Building-Destruction Resulting from Attacks by the Israeli Occupation, which has been compiled by Ibrahim Radwan and Mohammed al-Ostaz of the Palestinian Ministry of Public Works and Housing in the Gaza Strip, with photographs by Kai Wiedenhoefer and Antonio Zazueta Olmos, also of the Ministry of Public Works and Housing. The photos were collected and edited by Eyal Weizman, with Yazan Khalili and Tony Chakar. This project is based on the idea of a "zoom in" into the destruction. This collection appeared in the Anti-photojournalism exhibition, curated by Carles Guerra and Thomas Keenan, held in Barcelona in July 2010.

4. Many of these people, or those close to them, have been in the army and privy to its codes, and this was their chance to show off their know-how.

5. For more on "acts of state," see Azoulay, Atto di stato.

6. An exemplary expression of this is the official position of Israeli political and military leadership, beginning in the late 1940s, wherein they strive to reduce the injury to civilians while focusing the damage on their homes. Thus, for instance, in the assault on Gaza in December 2008, Israel demolished 15,000 houses (with nearly 100,000 inhabitants) and killed "only" 1,300 persons.

7. Much criticism has been directed at Arendt's distinction between the private and the public domains. It focused mostly on two matters: the identification she drew between the public and the political, and her designation of the home as nonpolitical. Returning to this distinction within Arendt's comprehensive ideas, these claims ap-

pear inexact. In Azoulay, *Civil Imagination*, I point at another failing in Arendt's thinking about the political (which I shall not elaborate here) — turning the political into an object of the taste judgment "it is (not) political" in a way that abandons her ontological claim about the political. In her book *The Human Condition*, Arendt indeed identifies political action with the public sphere and designates the home as a space outside the political, but I claim, contrary to the criticism she has received, that she articulates the relation between the two domains, making the distinction itself unstable and necessary only as an empty form (on which I shall elaborate shortly), enabling one to keep the two domains separate. She thus turns the question of boundaries between the public and the private into a political one, in other words, a question that cannot be finally resolved and remains open to a permanent participation of humans in its shaping, just as the very conceptualization Arendt herself proposes actually does. Her participation is in fact the problematization and historicization to which she subjects the division and bond between the two domains.

8. See Arendt, "The Rights of Man — What Are They?," 33.

9. See Arendt, *The Human Condition*.

10. See the website of the Israeli Committee against House Demolition, http://www.icahd.org/eng/projects.asp?menu=3&submenu=12. The committee, jointly with Palestinian residents and international volunteers, acts to rebuild some of the demolished houses. On the history of house demolitions, see Badil, "A History of Destruction," Electronic Intifada, 18 May 2004, http://electronicintifada.net/v2/article2700 .shtml. Badil's report explicitly states that these data do not include the demolition of housing units in the refugee camps, among them about ten thousand units demolished in the early 1970s.

11. I do not doubt the necessity of documenting the acts of destruction and insisting on tallying them for specific needs such as preparation for the eventuality of negotiation over reparations. Such tallying, though, is hardly sufficient on its own, and does not make superfluous the need to problematize the categories that serve it.

12. I elaborated on the "architecture of destruction" in the exhibition that was held under this title at Zochrot's Gallery in Tel Aviv in 2009, in Azoulay, *From Palestine to Israel*.

13. For a further visual documentation of the beginning of the project of destruction, see Azoulay, *From Palestine to Israel*.

14. In 1936, allegedly in response to the "Arab uprising," the British authorities in Palestine destroyed the urban heart of Jaffa (a total of 236 houses were demolished) during the "anchor" operation. More generally, control over the land and its inhabitants was achieved either by ruination, as in the anchor operation, or through construction, as in the vast architectonic project of installing infrastructure all over the land. For more on the projects run by the British Mandate, see Rotbard, *White City, Black City*.

15. In recent years, Israeli and Palestinian scholars have been gathering data about the scope of the demolition, but its full history as an enterprise of destruction has yet to be told. See Khalidi, *All that Remains*; Weizman, *Hollow Land*. See also the databases

of the Israeli Committee Against House Demolitions, http://www.icahd.org; the continuous work by the NGO Zochrot; the exhibitions *Constituent Violence* (2009) and *Architecture of Destruction* (2008) presented at Zochrot Gallery, Tel Aviv; and Eyal Weizman on house demolition in Gaza during the last Israeli attack, in "Lawfare in Gaza."

16. The fact that no systematic study examines the scope and nature of these relationships, and that trying to explore this is considered an unprecedented move in the historical research is an effect of intentional measures to erase the memory not only of the Palestinian Nakba but also of the destruction of the civil mixed society of Jews and Arabs. For further reading, see Zachary Lockman's *Comrades and Enemies*, which describes relations between Jews and Arabs working in Haifa in the period prior to the deterioration of relations that began shortly after the Partition Plan was announced. See also "Local Jewish Resistance to the Palestinian Nakba," an unpublished lecture by Eitan Bronstein that discusses statements and actions by Jews who explicitly opposed the obligatory division between Arabs and Jews imposed by the state's institutions, or who did so by not accepting their particular political ideology (Zochrot, 2006, http://www.nakbainhebrew.org/index.php?id=629; Yahav, *Paths of Co-existence and the Joint Arab-Jewish Economic and Social Struggle*). See also photographic references to the issue in Kabha and Raz, *Remembering a Place*; Sela, *Photography in Palestine / Eretz Yisrael in the 1930s and 1940s*. And recently, Lev-Tov, "Cultural Relations between Jews and Arabs in Palestine during the Late Ottoman Period."

17. On the participation of civilians in the occupation through commercial firms, see Weizman, *Hollow Land*, as well as the Who Profits website, http://www.whoprofits.org, which offers an initial mapping of those commercial enterprises profiting from the occupation.

18. See Stoler's essay in this volume.

19. Numerous testimonies of people whose homes were demolished, and whom delays at the checkpoints have physically and psychologically damaged, and whose lives the Separation Wall has ruined may be found in reports by B'tselem, Badil, Physicians for Human Rights, and others.

20. Handel, "Chronology of the Occupation Regime"; Azoulay and Ophir, *This Regime Which Is Not One*.

21. Quoted in Avichai Beker, "Enlightened Destruction," *Ha'ar etz*, 27 December 2002.

PART III

Anticipating the Imperial Future

The Void

Invisible Ruins on the Edges of Empire

In 1585 Spanish troops founded the town of Concepción del Bermejo several hundred miles west of Asunción del Paraguay in a remote region, the Gran Chaco, which until then had been in full control of local populations. The Spanish turned Concepción into a large, profitable slave center, but a few decades later, in 1632, they had to abandon the town, fleeing a generalized insurrection. Subsequent attempts to reassert imperial power in that area failed, and armed resistance intensified all across the region.[1] The Gran Chaco remained a space beyond and hostile to state control for close to three more centuries. This restlessness created a political vortex stretching between the foot of the Andes and the Paraguay and Paraná Rivers in the heart of lowland South America: a dense maze of forests, savannas, and marshes that allowed highly mobile groups to repel and undermine recurring attempts at domination. The politically dissolving force of this space led generations of officials to believe that the ruins of Concepción del Bermejo had vanished, swallowed up by forests and the emptiness of savagery, and the Gran Chaco became in their eyes an opaque, feared, uncontrollable void.

No space of the globe is currently beyond the reach of capitalism and imperial military operations. There is no outside, as Michael Hardt and Antonio Negri put it, of global formations of sovereignty.[2] But the Spanish and subsequently Argentinean siege of the Gran Chaco reminds us that prior to the late 1800s, imperial expansion into vast geographies of the world encountered political limits that acquired a spatial form. To this day, the people who descend from the original inhabitants of the Chaco articulate a strong memory of having lived without the state in a space beyond its direct political reach. But this beyondness was not a pristine outside, the product of closure, separation, or impermeability. The opposite is the case: this was a *political* and relational folding of imperial space, the product of anti-imperial insurgencies, mobile patterns of confrontation, flows of people, goods, and cattle crisscrossing vast regions, and regular imperial forays into the Chaco. Yet in these fluid spatial formations, the state encountered a threshold at which its power was negated, a space in which state settlements were destroyed and turned into ruins that subsequently seemed to vanish. These positive expressions of power dissolved on the imperial edge of the void: the unsettling space of friction that is internal and external to the geography of global imperial formations.

Based on their personal correspondence, Alain Badiou wrote that Gilles Deleuze saw the expression "on the edge of the void" as the intersection between the territory and the process of deterritorialization, the "overflowing of the territory by the event."[3] And, Badiou tells us, Deleuze argued that "this is the point at which what occurs can no longer be assigned to either the territory (the site) or the non-territory, to either the inside or the outside. And it is true that the void has neither an interior nor an exterior."[4] The Chaco was for centuries a space of intersection in which the territory of empire was overflowed by the event of deterritorialization by anti-imperial insurgencies, in a political process in which notions of inside and outside of the state melted away.

Theodor Adorno argued that the dominant common sense under capitalism emphasizes the positivity of things as they *are*, making us forget what these things have negated and destroyed in order to acquire their positive form.[5] And this positivity celebrates manageable spaces bearing noticeable, positive markers of state sovereignty. The Chaco was a node of negativity that folded and eroded not only the positive form of imperial space but also the positive presence of its ruins. And this negativity unsettled state imaginings because it created spaces constituted by absences. W. G. Sebald noticed what the void created by absences feels like when he visited the place on the English coast where the medieval town of Dunbwich used to be, whose vestiges have been dissolved by the North Sea: "If you look out from the cliff-top across the sea towards where the town must once have been, you can sense the immense power of emptiness."[6] The void of the Chaco, likewise, was the immense power of emptiness that state agents experienced when they were confronted with a space that negated the state and made imperial ruins elusive, hard to find, invisible.

In this essay, I examine how state anxieties about the invisible ruins of the Chaco are revealing of the type of space generated on the edges of empire, but also of the selective patterns of visibility that state agents projected onto this void. While resisting state encroachment, this allegedly empty space and the people living there were often ravaged by what Ann Stoler calls imperial ruination, the ongoing, degrading domination that "lays waste to certain peoples, relations, and things."[7] And this ruination increased after the void of the Chaco was destroyed by state violence. Yet the officials preoccupied with the invisible ruins of the Spanish empire made these other ruins invisible. I will examine the history of the Spanish and Argentinean conquest of the Gran Chaco through the lens of these different patterns of ruins, those generated by anti-imperial resistance and those created by imperial ruination. I draw from documents by officials, missionaries, explorers, military officers, and from my own fieldwork in different parts of the region in the past two decades. The ruination of the Chaco produced by conquest and made invisible by the state, I aim to show, surfaces in the experience of people living in rural areas and currently haunted by its latent presence on the landscape.

The Vanishing of Imperial Spaces

In 1733 the Jesuit historian Pedro Lozano wrote that the destruction of Concepción del Bermejo a century earlier "closed all roads to the light of the Gospels" in the Chaco and meant that local people were condemned to die "in the darkness of their stubborn infidelity."[8] A shroud of darkness had fallen upon the ruins of Concepción primarily because a century later Spanish officials had still been unable to reach them and were unsure as to where they were.[9] Concepción became *una ciudad perdida*, a lost city whose ruins seemed to have been wiped off the face of the earth. In the 1600s three additional towns founded by the Spanish Crown near the western edge of the Chaco had been abandoned largely due to the resistance posed by local groups: the two towns of Esteco on the Salado River and Santiago del Guadalcázar in the Zenta Valley. These places also came to be known as lost cities, in most cases with the location of their ruins also relatively unknown. The exception was the second (and legendary) town of Esteco, devastated by an attack launched from the Chaco and subsequently by an earthquake, whose ruins were at the foot of the Andes near a well-traveled road.

While tales about lost cities hidden in remote geographies have been integral to imperial imaginaries, they tend to refer to places created by local actors, such as the mythical El Dorado in the Amazon or Machu Picchu in Peru. The lost cities of the Gran Chaco, on the contrary, were created by the defeat of European schemes in the face of revolts. And their disappearance revealed the spatial limits of the project of conquest. This was a spatial voiding created through recurring violence that undermined frontier settlements but also devastated local populations in the interior of the Chaco. In the 1600s on numerous occasions troops left Esteco or descended from the highlands of the Andes to capture serfs. And in 1710 the governor of the Tucumán Province organized the largest military campaign ever conducted by the Spanish in the Chaco, instructing his troops to unleash terror and execute all armed males on the spot, for they were "unworthy of Christian mercy." Shortly thereafter, the western Chaco was littered with the debris of villages destroyed by Spanish forces or abandoned by people fleeing their advance.[10] The impact of this violence reverberated for several decades, and in 1749 another large military campaign consolidated the frontier on the Salado River with a chain of forts and Jesuit stations.

Yet this violence did not substantially alter the view that the Chaco was a terrifying space made up of forests and swamps "almost impenetrable for the Spaniard," a space able to withstand wave after wave of state terror, as if these civilizing efforts, as a missionary put it, "were ocean waves that crash against a granitic rock."[11] This allegedly solid impenetrability kept at bay state power but not the many individuals of European and mestizo background who, as many explorers noted, entered the Chaco fleeing persecution by the state and lived fully integrated among local people—and as hostile and weary of officials as anybody else. For those human constellations, the Chaco was certainly not a void but, on the contrary, a space of collective affirmation they controlled and defended by negating imperial power. It was because of this negativity that the Chaco became for the state an impenetrable object whose spatial viscosity had swallowed up Concepción del Bermejo and other Spanish cities. And these lost ruins were a recurring source of unease.

State functionaries and Jesuit missionaries tried to counter the void of the Chaco through the production of maps that, in addition to delineating rivers and the distribution of various *naciones* (nations), marked the approximate location of the lost cities with an "X" that highlighted their vanquished status. On the most famous colonial map of the Chaco—by Father Joaquín Camaño and published in José Solís's *Essay on the Natural History of the Chaco*

7.1 Detail of map of the Gran Chaco by Joaquín Camaño, 1789. From José Solís, *Ensayo sobre la historia natural del Gran Chaco* (Resistencia: Universidad Nacional del Nordeste, 1972 [1789]).

(1789)—four different Xs mark the approximate location of the lost cities mentioned above (fig. 7.1). The caption informs the reader that "X" stands for "destroyed city," in other words, for a civilizing space negated by the Chaco.[12]

Those "destroyed" places on the maps made it clear that something violent had happened there, powerful enough to force the Spanish forces to withdraw to the edges of the Chaco for several centuries. These maps sought to counter the void of the region by historicizing its space and revealing the past presence of former bastions of Christianity and civilization. Yet in trying to conjure away this void, these Xs irrevocably brought it to light by evoking these towns' negativity as ghosts, accentuating the perception that the void emptied out conquest of its positive spatial forms: that is, that this terrain was a black hole of sorts because everything that had been built there by the Spanish Crown had been turned to dust. The Xs revealed a geography permeated by absences, for the very idea of a lost city necessitated a surrounding space of emptiness (fig. 7.2).

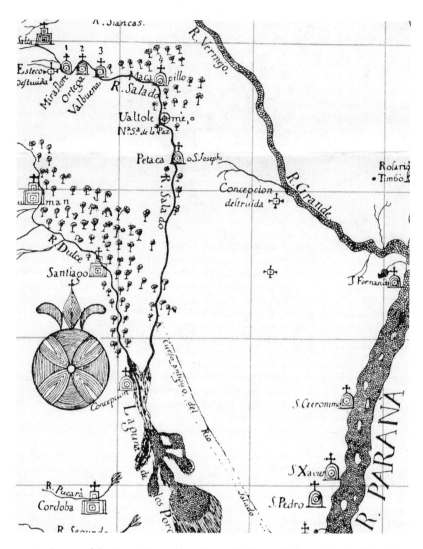

7.2 Jesuit map of the Gran Chaco, 1772. From Guillermo Furlong, *Cartografía jesuítica del Río de la Plata* (Buenos Aires: Jacobo Peuser, 1936).

Many of the officials who looked out to the Chaco from the Andes were overwhelmed by the view. In 1883 Daniel Campos, a Bolivian army officer, wrote about how he felt when he was about to descend from the mountains down into the void: "At our feet, immense, mysterious and overwhelming, like a terrible ocean . . . stands out the incommensurable Gran Chaco. There was the Chaco, overwhelming us with its immensity, stirring up our soul like the sea, pulling us like the abyss."[13]

Entering the Void

The Jesuit missionary Martin Dobrizhoffer wrote that the Chaco is a space that Spanish soldiers dreaded entering, for it was for them "a theatre of misery."[14] In 1759 a large expedition made up of close to a thousand soldiers led by the Tucumán governor, Espinoza y Dávalos, marched from the Andes into the Chaco aiming to cut through to its eastern frontier. At one point the troops were "intimidated by the desert" and "refused to go farther."[15] Facing a mutiny, the governor decided to turn around and ordered that a cross be carved on the trunk of a large tree together with a written message that read: "Year of 1759. Don Joaquín Espinosa y Dávalos reached up to here [hasta aquí llegó] with 300 cows, 4,000 horses, and 900 men and they performed well [y fueron destacados]."[16]

The production of markings such as this became common in Spanish expeditions in the Chaco, and could be seen as what Patricia Seed called "ceremonies of possession": the ritualized assertion of colonial power over new territories.[17] Yet in the Chaco, these performative gestures took place in a hostile space the Spanish did not control. And in the case of the 1749 expedition, the text was an admission of defeat in their attempt to cut through the region, which required trying to save face by praising the troops that felt intimidated by that space. The text also marks a spatial limit ("reached up to here"), a threshold that imperial forces were unable and unwilling to cross. And in trying to turn a tree, part of the physical form of the terrain of the Chaco, into a more manageable and readable space, these officials also revealed that they found the landscape illegible, disorienting. The engravings testify to the fear that on their leaving the Chaco, space would fold and wipe out all traces of their presence.

In the 1760s Jesuit missionaries made deep sojourns in the Chaco hinterland and along the Bermejo River in search of converts, and many of them were also keen to leave traces of their presence, as if trying to counter the emptiness of the landscape. The positive object they left most regularly was the Christian cross, planting large wooden crosses in remote locations to which they did not plan to return.[18] These solitary crosses were attempts to create positive nodes that would radiate the presence of Christianity around them. And like the text carved out on a tree by the Tucumán governor, they were also messages for future explorers to reassure them that fellow civilized men had already been there. And they were also messages to those living there, political gestures of defiance that claimed control over uncontrollable geographies.

Local people understood the political message carved out on that tree by the Tucumán governor without needing to read the text. In 1774 an expedition led by Governor Matorras reached that area and found feeble traces of the text. The tree was semi-burnt, and the message was barely legible "because the sign has been axed by the Indians."[19] That local people had defaced the engravings suggests they seemed committed to negating even the smallest traces of an imperial presence and that they intuitively knew of the political salience of spatial markings.

Yet what made Governor Matorras's 1774 expedition historically important was that it represented a new strategy by the Spanish Crown in the Chaco. Since indiscriminate military force had failed to control the region, Matorras set out on a diplomatic mission.[20] His forces crossed the spatial threshold marked by that text and pressed on, reaching a site called Lacangayé in the geographic center of the Chaco on the Bermejo River. His aim was to secure a peace treaty with Paikín, a Mocoví leader who exerted considerable influence in a wide region. After the governor distributed vast amounts of gifts, Paikín agreed to become a subject of the king of Spain and to allow for the future foundation of two mission stations but on condition that his people retain control of their lands and not be subject to servitude. The treaty was signed following formal royal protocol, and in order to commemorate the event, Matorras ordered that numerous texts and signs of the cross be engraved on trees. On one trunk, one of these texts read: "Year of 1774. Peace between Señor D. Gerónimo Matorras, Governor of Tucumán, and Paikín." Matorras also sent men with the directive of finding the ruins of Concepción del Bermejo, "ruined by these barbarian nations," but the search proved futile. Yet the expedition had managed to reach a remote area of the Chaco where, according to the official report, there was "no memory" of Spanish troops ever having been there.[21]

The signing of the treaty led to the first major attempt since the demise of Concepción del Bermejo to create a civilizing, positive spatial form in the heart of the Chaco. In 1780 Francisco Arias led an expedition to Lacangayé to implement the foundation of the two missions stipulated in the treaty. On arriving in the area, Arias noted that the texts engraved on trees by Matorras six years earlier had held their ground and were still there, as if he had not been sure that would be the case.[22] Arias proceeded to found two stations forty miles apart from each other, Santiago de Lacangayé and San Bernardo de Vértiz, to be run by Franciscan missionaries, despite noting in his diary that local people were weary of their presence.

The erection of positive nodes of Christianity in the heart of the Chaco demanded that the ruins of Concepción del Bermejo be found and wrested from that opaque terrain, in order to conjure away their status as a ghost. Arias sent a party south with the aim "of discovering the site of the old Concepción destroyed" and locating it on a map. On returning, his men brought back a bell and reported they had found la ciudad and its irrigation canals thirty Spanish leagues (eighty miles) from Lacangayé. This is the first recorded visit to these ruins in a century and a half. But these men also warned that the ruins were amid "impenetrable forests."[23]

Arias ordered that the bell brought from the ruins be used in the chapel of Santiago de Lacangayé, in a clear indication that debris from the lost city affirmed the continuity of the imperial project initiated in Concepción del Bermejo. Yet the discovery of the ruins of Concepción proved as short-lived as the attempt to create new centers of imperial socialization in the region. The two missions were far from the frontier, and their supply lines were weak and intermittent at best. They lingered in a sorry state for about a decade and were abandoned in the early 1790s.[24] The brief visit to the overgrown ruins of Concepción, for its part, did not generate a map.[25] Those vestiges were in hostile territory, and shortly thereafter references to "Concepción destroyed" acquired once again a ghostly aura. The same voiding was to engulf the ruins of the Lacangayé and San Bernardo mission stations, which were to engross the list of places that seemed to have been dissolved by the Chaco.

The wars of independence of the 1810s and early 1820s, the collapse of the Spanish empire in South America, and the civil wars that followed independence meant that attempts to conquer and explore the Chaco were put on hold for several decades. But when a unified Argentinean nation-state finally consolidated its power in the 1870s, the elites in Buenos Aires began focusing their gaze on this old bastion of barbarism, now seen as an obstacle to the territorial expansion of capitalism and a new national project.

The Assault on the Desert

In the late 1800s the Argentinean elites began conceptualizing the voiding of space by savagery as *el desierto*, the desert, a term that was used to define all geographies beyond the reach of the state and that therefore included not just the Chaco but also the pampas and Patagonia in the center and south of the country, also under the control of armed nonstate actors. What defined these geographies as "deserts" was not the barrenness or dryness of their physical terrain, which ranged from cold steppes in Patagonia and temperate savannas in the pampas to tropical forests in the Chaco. The desert was defined by the absence of civilization, state power, and capitalist modernity. As the noted historian Tulio Halperín Donghi put it, the Buenos Aires elites sought to create "a nation for the Argentinean desert" (*una nación para el desierto argentino*)—that is, filling up that emptiness with the positive form of the nation.[26] And the Gran Chaco was the most overwhelming of the deserts that prevented that positivity from materializing.[27]

The first sign that the conquest of the Chaco would not be a smooth process was the collapse of the attempt to create a trade route by steamships on the Bermejo River in the 1870s, which aimed "to light the shining torch of progress in spaces ruled by barbarism for eternal centuries."[28] By the early 1880s, the wrecks of stranded and sunken steamships testified to the obstacles posed by a shallow and meandering river.[29] Yet for a few years, during their slow progress upstream, crewmembers speculated about their relative distance from the ruins of Concepción del Bermejo and the Franciscan missions. Suspecting they were somewhere out there, the ruins became imaginary orientation devices amid unknown territory.[30]

The same preoccupation with these invisible ruins guided the final assault on the region. In October 1884 the Argentinean army launched the largest military campaign ever conducted in the Chaco, and several cavalry regiments entered the region from the west, the south, and the east. Local groups put up a fierce resistance, but the times had changed and they were no match for well-organized troops armed with Remington rifles. After numerous clashes, most of the regiments converged on Lacangayé (now called La Cangayé), the area that the Spanish Crown had been unable to secure through nonviolent means a century earlier. And teams of technicians, engineers, and scientists accompanied the army with the mandate to survey and map an unreadable space and gather data on its geography, flora, fauna, and on the habits of local populations. These men were given the directive to engrave topographic information as well as their names on large trees, drawing on an old Spanish practice that was now used to make the terrain readable and manageable once and for all.[31]

These men immediately noted, and many were troubled by, how hard it was to find not just ruins but any trace of the state. An engineer named Gerónimo de la Serna noted with disappointment there was nothing on the landscape around La Cangayé that signaled this place's historical importance as the site where the Spanish Crown had briefly secured a foothold in the late 1700s. Like other officers, he tried to locate the ruins of the mission of Santiago de Lacangayé and the famous engravings written on trees in 1774. But, he wrote, "no vestige was found."[32]

General Benjamín Victorica, the head of the campaign, shared this concern and sent several telegrams to President Julio Roca from the Chaco informing him of the failure to locate those legendary ruins. One of them read: "We have been unable to find the ruins of Concepción shown by the maps. Its vestiges must have disappeared; old Indians born in these places do not know them."[33] Officers operating south of the Bermejo were also disturbed by their inability to find traces of Concepción: "The Indians who are coming with us do not give us the slightest indication of the place where these ruins exist."[34] The disappearance of the ruins was even more perplexing because not even local people seemed to know them, as if the void of the Chaco had dissolved those vestiges to such an extent that their presence had escaped even those long assumed to master that space.

The men who participated in the 1884 military campaign articulated a more openly modernist preoccupation with progress and decay, and their concerns about the voiding of space were particularly marked. This was often articulated as the terrifying experience of being immersed in a space of sheer absences, totally devoid of positivity. Leopoldo Arnaud, the head of the main scientific team, wrote shortly after entering the Chaco: "The trek across the desert is imposing, it triggers true terror."[35] A few days later, Arnaud got lost in thick forests while on a hunting trip and experienced this spatial voiding as particularly overwhelming: "The Indians, the beasts, the deadly reptiles, that was the picture I was facing. Nobody can fully understand . . . the sensation you go through when stepping onto a totally virgin terrain, on a land on which there is not even the slightest trace of civilized man."[36] This emptiness emanated from the terrain and from all its living forms: humans, animals, and suffocating masses of vegetation had joined forces to wipe out all traces of civilization and dissolve the very distinction between human and natural forces.[37] And the absence of positive traces of "civilized man" made the voiding of space all the more unsettling. It is probably not surprising that Arnaud and his colleagues, replicating the practices of their predecessors, engraved their names on trees.[38]

Yet the members of the expedition eventually did come across traces and ruins of those who had preceded them. Because the absence of traces of civilization had long augmented the power of savagery, even the faintest of vestiges were seen as positive, enthralling presences that seemed to pierce, at last, through the void.

Pulsating Ruins

While following the old course of the Bermejo River (which had recently shifted its main course to the north), the troops with which Gerónimo de la Serna was traveling encountered the stumps of numerous axed trees. De la Serna was deeply moved by the sight, which revealed that "civilized people" had been there, most probably the crews of the steamships that had navigated the Bermejo the previous decade and disembarked regularly to obtain firewood. He added that "it was gratifying for us, amid those deep solitudes, to evoke the memory of other travelers who had preceded us and who, like us, had experienced the unforgettable emotion of that immense forested desert [*desierto boscoso*], with the ambition of incorporating those remote regions into commerce and industry."[39] Despite their ruptured form, those stumps were in de la Serna's eyes sheer positivity: the affirmation of a civilizing quest and the source of an affective connection with those men with whom he shared the same "unforgettable" fragility created by "that immense forested desert." Whereas the absence of positive traces created anxieties about the voiding of space, the discovery of the weakest of traces seemed to fill up that void with the prospect of progress.

Shortly thereafter, a cavalry regiment that had entered the Chaco from the west stumbled on an even larger trace of civilization: the overgrown remains of San Bernardo, one of the two stations founded on the Bermejo in 1780.[40] The news soon reached the army headquarters at La Cangayé. General Victorica was thrilled and wanted to visit the ruins in person, but since his health was weak he ordered Arnaud's team and a group of engineers to survey them.[41] Thirty Wichí men who had surrendered were ordered to clear and excavate the site. The dig revealed the foundations of a building that contained a chapel and several rooms. In order to commemorate the importance of the discovery and name those mounds as positive space, as "ruins," a message was carved out on the trunk of a large tree: "Ruins of the Reducción San

Bernardo, founded in 1774 [sic] by the most renowned Don Francisco Gavino Arias. Victorica Expedition, year of 1884."[42]

De la Serna joined the group and was profoundly moved by his encounter with those "weak vestiges of civilization," which, he emphasized, all explorers search for "with zeal" amid that "absolute solitude." He noted that the ruins were orderly, "allocated in geometrical lines on the terrain." More important, those ruins "show the traveler, with imposing eloquence, amid the solitude of the desert . . . how much can be accomplished by perseverance and divine faith when they are put at the service of a noble, generous ideal."[43] The seeming weakness of those ruins, comprising a few overgrown mounds, in fact revealed their positivity and power. Those were orderly, geometrical, and ultimately imposing and eloquent ruins, sources of a moral light whose positive force emanated from their location in the void, "the solitude of the desert."

The army officers and the members of the scientific team were so impressed by their discovery of these ruins that they organized a celebration in honor of "the ancient explorers of the Chaco." On 10 December 1884, the soldiers of the Tenth Cavalry Regiment stood in formation next to the ruins crowned by the Argentinean flag. Angel Carranza, the war attorney of the campaign, read the main speech.

> Fellow members of the expeditionary column to the southern Chaco: we have just wrested the mystery of the ruins that we are contemplating. They belong to a foundation that reveals the bravery of our elders, who with their faith as their sole weapon, conducted dangerous tasks, setting off to live among barbarians, with the aim of taking them to the light of Christianity . . . across these deserts that still today fill up the soul with terror [pavor]. How many changes in only a hundred years! Of San Bernardo, like Babylon, only piles of dust remain. . . . But the generations of the future that he [Francisco Arias] probably invoked, overwhelmed by a difficult situation, do justice to his merits in the presence of this rubble that does not speak, but pulsates [palpita].[44]

Carranza could not have been clearer. The light emanating from those vestiges reduced, like Babylon, to piles of dust was particularly moving because it emerged from an emptiness that was terrifying: the desert. But this was light that they had to *wrest away* from the viscosity of the terrain. These ruins were silent but not dead, still resonating at the beat of Christianity and blending the legacy of missionaries from the 1700s with the experience of officers and scientists who, like them, had gone there to put an end to barbarism. After the speech, Arnaud read aloud their report on the excavation. Three copies were made. One of them was put inside a bottle and buried in the ruins, "marking our presence there."[45] The officer in charge of the regiment shouted, "¡Viva la Patria!" (Long live the Motherland!), and all men mimicked him in unison.[46]

In their encounters with these ruins, these men were haunted not only by the past, but also by the future of the project of conquest. Carranza speculated that back in 1780 Arias had invoked, in that mission station now in ruins, "the generations of the future." Likewise, Carranza finished his speech emphasizing that the Tenth Regiment of Cavalry was being "applauded by our contemporaries" and would be doubly applauded "by those to come."[47] The engraving on a tree and the burial of their report reveal that they were aware that those ruins would be soon taken over by the forests surrounding them. De la Serna suspected that those documents and markings would indeed vanish and feared that those ruins, which he had briefly seen as imposing, would be overgrown and forgotten shortly after their departure. "How long will this inscription [on the tree] be preserved? Will the ruins ever be found again?"[48]

The remains of the San Bernardo mission were the only ruins found by members of the Victorica Campaign. Confirming de la Serna's fears, the site was covered again with forests, and public references about these ruins faded away, as if the void of the Chaco was as dissolving as ever. Yet the geography that was overgrowing these vestiges was not the same as that which had long overwhelmed and intimidated officials, missionaries, and explorers. The firepower of those cavalry regiments that crisscrossed the Chaco from all sides had indeed caused widespread havoc among the human constellations that had created the negativity of the void in the first place.

The Destruction of the Void

In December 1884, General Victorica sent out a dispatch to celebrate "the most complete success" of the military campaign. He began by proudly pointing out that in the heart of the Chaco the troops raised an Argentinean flag wrapped up "on the blood-drenched spear of the last Toba chief who paid with his life the affront of having assaulted one of our soldiers." And as in the ceremony conducted at the ruins of San Bernardo, he drew a direct genealogy between this civilizing violence and that initiated by the Spanish empire. He emphasized that the army accomplished "in a permanent manner" what the Spanish, "our elders," had unsuccessfully tried before.[49] This genealogy reached closure with the planting of the flag soaked in the blood of those who had prevented the territorial expansion of state power for so long.

The vortex of the Chaco could only be destroyed with indiscriminate violence. While sporadic forms of armed resistance continued in some regions for a few decades, particularly along the border with Paraguay and Bolivia on the Pilcomayo River, this former spatial emptiness was now being rapidly eroded by, and folded upon, state sovereignty. And the Chaco was now riddled with ruins that state agents could simply not conceptualize as such. The same officers and observers preoccupied with finding Spanish ruins in the Chaco noted in their diaries, but only in passing, that as they advanced on the region they encountered a persistent sight: a widespread detritus of tolderías (villages) abandoned by people fleeing the army. Shortly after noting that he was unable to find any trace of the mission of Santiago de Lacangayé, de la Serna wrote: "Numerous abandoned tolderías lay all over the place, on both sides of the river or scattered on the edge of the forest."[50] He also wrote that the men and women surrendering to the army looked worn out and defeated. "The look of these prisoners was sad. In general, they were weaklings without strength to flee."[51]

Yet while the Chaco was no longer a vortex that unsettled state agents, for decades many areas remained opaque, heavily forested spaces devoid of roads or railroads. And the memory of those invisible imperial ruins continued informing state commemorations. In December 1943 the Argentinean government decreed that the ruins of Concepción del Bermejo and of the missions of Santiago de Lacangayé and San Bernardo were historic sites and patrimony of the nation. Yet the actual location of the ruins was still to be determined (or, in the case of San Bernardo, publicly disseminated).[52] The decree was a performative commemorative gesture that, like the old Jesuit maps from the 1700s, claimed mastery over spectral places whose location was unknown, but that affirmed that the imperial legacy embodied in those ruins was now part of the nation.

The transformation of the regional geography via the construction of new roads was nonetheless by then accelerating. In fact, right before the publication of the decree mentioned above, and as if anticipating their sanctification by the state, in September 1943 a local businessman found vestiges of an ancient city on a recently cleared dirt road, fifty miles north of Saenz Peña in the territory of Chaco. Subsequent historical and archaeological research confirmed that those were the ruins of the elusive Concepción del

Bermejo.[53] The man who found them was in fact an avid ruin-hunter, and in 1945 he also found the vestiges of Santiago de Lacangayé.[54] Fifty years later, in 1996, officials announced the discovery of the remains of San Bernardo, which had already been found in 1884. On the Salado River, for decades several people searched unsuccessfully for the remains of the first city of Esteco.[55] It was not until the very end of the century that academics located the site. In 1999 archaeologists from the University of La Plata identified, amid extensive media coverage, the vestiges of the lost city near the village of El Vencido in the province of Salta.[56]

By then it was apparent that the ruins of the Spanish empire in the Chaco had never fully vanished and had, in fact, been there all along. That these ruins were so intractable for so long primarily expressed that they were in a densely striated space that state actors neither controlled nor knew. The thick foliage shrouding these vestiges certainly contributed to their relative invisibility well into the 1900s. Yet despite the media announcements made at the time about the "discovery" of "lost ruins," these sites had long been known by local people and had been excavated by generations of treasure hunters.[57] But the experience of these subaltern local actors was usually silenced in the media for the sake of cultivating the image of these ruins as self-enclosed relics, fetishized objects disengaged from their surrounding living spaces.

Similar invisibilizations have guided official commemorations of these ruins. In 1946 the Catholic Church and functionaries from the territory of Chaco organized a ceremony at the recently discovered ruins of Santiago de Lacangayé. José Alumni, a priest who participated in the dig, wrote that the aim was to celebrate this "bastion of progress and civilization in these remote regions" and "the heroes of our past."[58] The ceremony focused on the remains of a missionary buried at the chapel in 1780 and identified by medical doctors as "the human remains of a man of white race." His bones were transported in a solemn ceremony to the town of Castelli, where they were reburied underneath the church altar.[59] These were not the only human remains found on the site, however. The ruins of Lacangayé were in fact littered with the bones of at least forty-five men, women, and children, scattered inside and around the chapel and with clear signs of having suffered a violent death. Alumni speculated that they were Mocoví converts slaughtered by an Abipón group that attacked the mission.[60] Yet whereas he devoted several pages to celebrate and victimize the missionary (of white race) whose remains were found in the ruins, he wrote about those dozens of human skeletons only in a footnote.[61] This footnote reveals, and also partly hides on the margins of the central text, that "the ruins of Santiago de Lacan-gayé" were actually a mass grave. And Alumni never said what happened to those bones, the most bodily of all ruins, and often the most invisible.

The Invisible Ruins of the Chaco

State agents envisioned the conquest of the Chaco as an affirmative nega-tion of barbarism that in destroying the vast emptiness of the desert would create something positive: a land of enormous prosperity and wealth, or as de la Serna put it, "a promising land" destined to become "one of the most productive regions of the Republic."[62] The capitalist looting of the Chaco began as soon as Victorica's 1884 campaign came to an end, and while posi-tive spaces of state and capitalist power were gradually created in the region, the ruins of this new devastation blended with the older debris created by state violence. The ruination of the Chaco, therefore, did not finish with mili-tary conquest but has been an ongoing force ever since: a destructive process that, as Stoler would put it, "brings ruin upon" and has degraded not just spaces or buildings but primarily lives.[63] The Gran Chaco is today the poor-est, most marginalized region in Argentina and most of the descendants of those who were defeated by the Argentinean army face recurring poverty, ex-ploitation, and discrimination.[64] This experience has generated perceptions and imaginings that reveal a damaged collective body, as I have analyzed in the case of Toba villages where people's subjectivity is haunted by memories of alienation.[65] But the ruins of the geographies that resisted the state also involves debris of the type noticed by the army officers advancing on the region in 1884: abandoned and destroyed hamlets that testified to a wide-spread defeat. In the Toba villages, people evoked the debris of old settle-ments as well as the rumored sites of mass graves as ghostly presences that had been washed away by flooding of the Pilcomayo River and the formation of marshlands in the 1970s. And they also talked about the bones of their own people buried in the sugarcane fields at the foot of the Andes, where they worked for decades and died by the score, decimated by previously un-known diseases.[66] But elsewhere in the Chaco people know of the ruins that testify, in their surrounding spaces, to the destruction of the void.

The area of Esquina Grande in the province of Salta, on the old course of the Bermejo River, was in 1863 the site of one of the largest massacres in the history of the Chaco. Amid an insurrection triggered by the arrival of settlers keen to take advantage of the navigation of the Bermejo, probably two to three thousand Wichí men, women, and children were murdered over several months.[67] In 2006 two Wichí men took me to Esquina Grande, now an outlying area accessible only by trails, to see the feeble traces of a village that probably dated from the 1850s, for it was once linked to a short-lived and small Franciscan station abandoned in 1860.[68] Tiny fragments of ceramic, glass, and a few nails covered a relatively wide area of hardened, dry soil. I would not have noticed that debris if my companions had not pointed it out to me. As they were showing me around and we were picking up those small traces here and there, they could not stop evoking memories of bloodshed. Gabriel, in his late sixties, told me that his father-in-law (who, he said, was a hundred years old when he passed away) witnessed the massacres as a young boy and told him about them. "They cut their throats like animals," he said several times. "It was a sad life."

Gabriel added that in his youth he once found a hueserío, a field of bones and skulls in the forest. "Such a huge amount of bones [semejante hueserío]. Just like this place. Years later, I tried to find it again, but I couldn't." He said he wanted to find the place to prove that what had happened was true. Juan, who was with us, added, pointing to the traces on the ground, "These are the vestiges that we always come to see." They were drawn to that debris because it was one of the last feeble traces of the ruination of their ancestors. This was a node of negativity, a reminder of the now elusive detritus of human remains generated by state violence.

Farther west, at the foot of the Andes, the former frontier is dotted with debris of the forts, towns, and mission stations once built by the Spanish Crown on the edge of the void. Few indigenous people currently live in this region. Those who inhabit the area see themselves as criollos, people of mestizo background who work as gauchos (cowboys) on cattle farms. Most of them are well aware that in addition to those more noticeable ruins left behind by the Spanish empire, another type of debris testifies to other types of ruination.

In 2004 I visited the small criollo village of Balbuena, which bears the name of a Spanish fort once located a mile away. A tall, bright, energetic man in his seventies named Carlos took me to see "the fort," which is on his midsize farm and consists of an overgrown quadrangle surrounded by cornfields. The place looks like an ordinary patch of forest, but the four corners reveal steep mounds, fifteen to twenty feet high. While we were exploring the mounds, Carlos told me that a group of men came to his house forty years earlier and asked him for permission to dig the mounds. They were treasure hunters who suspected that the mounds hid some of the legendary riches allegedly buried in the region by the Jesuits. He agreed to their request, and they all began digging. Yet instead of riches they found human bones. Plenty of them, "all piled up." "It was a mass grave," Carlos told me. "I think that when they killed large numbers of indios [Indians], the Indians rebelled. And the army of the Spaniards liquidated them and they buried them here. There're four mounds here, and we only opened one. But I think all four of them are the same and have bones." On discovering the bones, they covered them up again. On my subsequent visits to Balbuena, other people confirmed Carlos's account about the mass grave.

Over several centuries, state agents imagined the imperial ruins swallowed up by the Chaco as nodes of positivity that countered this region's emptiness. By contrast, ordinary people in rural areas (indigenous and criollos alike) currently tend to see those ruins, like the ruins of fort Balbuena, in conjunction with other forms of debris and view these spaces as fractured nodes that evoke collective patterns of destruction. For Carlos, the mounds at Fort Balbuena are just huge piles of bones. The site is the sedimentation of corpses that, he assumed, could not but be those of indios. And the treasure hunters that in looking for riches found instead human remains probably learned that behind the forms of an overgrown imperial fortification lies the hardened, invisible debris of the ruination of the Chaco.

Human remains, as Robert Ginsberg put it, are the most intimate of all ruins.[69] The Baroque poets from the 1600s who fascinated Walter Benjamin had long identified bones as the epitome of human ruin.[70] And the myriad fields of bones remembered, imagined, or found in actual spaces in the Chaco confirm that the destruction of the void demanded indiscriminate levels of violence. These are the invisible ruins of the Chaco, made invisible by the state and the hierarchy of the Catholic Church. Myriad books and documents, after all, have sanctified the remains of Concepción del Bermejo as transcendent ruins. And the latter are currently not only open to the public but also marked on most maps of the province of Chaco, fixing in space and making visible what the Jesuit maps evoked as ghosts.

A growing number of people, however, have been searching for the debris of the ruination of the Chaco made invisible by the state. The same way that in the 1940s the triumph of conquest was symbolized by the state celebration of the formerly lost ruins of the Spanish empire, in the 2000s the activists and ordinary people seeking to undo this imperial legacy are making public and in some cases locating the debris of bones created by state violence. This is best exemplified by the recent court cases and exhumation of mass graves involving the 1947 massacre of Rincón Bomba (province of Formosa) and the 1924 massacre of Napalpí (province of Chaco), which have attracted the interest of the media and have been opposed by the center-left federal government.[71] These are patterns of debris that activists and local leaders try to make visible amid the often overwhelming capitalist and state voiding of the Chaco.

Ruins and Ruination on the Edges of Empire

As part of the journey this volume is part of, a journey away from ruins as dead objects and toward ruination as an active process of degradation, it is now time to see ruins with new eyes. The relative visibility of certain ruins over others is inseparable from the way they are read politically, based on their positive or negative connotations. As I argue elsewhere, ruins can be seen as nodes of negativity congealed in positive spatial forms.[72] By the mere fact of existing and not having fully disappeared, ruins have indeed a positive presence on the landscape, as Robert Ginsberg and Jon Beasley-Murray have emphasized; yet they are also spaces that evoke ruptures and absences: what has been negated and is no longer whole.[73] And while no ruin escapes this unresolved tension between positive and negative elements, social actors tend to gravitate toward highlighting one over the other.

Imperialism and capitalism have long been founded on the celebration of existing, positive spatial forms. Likewise, those who view ruins as fetishized objects with transcendental historic value, such as the Colosseum in Rome or Chichen Itza in Mexico, tend to highlight their positivity, presence, and resilience—like the men who in the Chaco commemorated the ruins of San Bernardo in 1884 or the ruins of Santiago de Lacangayé in 1946 as timeless emblems of civilization. This affirmative view of ruins was exemplified by Albert Speer, who famously persuaded Hitler to remake Berlin using stone instead of concrete so that in a distant future the ruins of Nazi Germany, like those of Rome, would look grand and imposing.[74] The Left has not been immune from this fetishization, as in its nostalgic idealization of the ruins of Machu Picchu or Tiahuanacu as epitomizing the ancient grandeur of indigenous Latin America. Except that no ruin is positivity alone. In the vestiges of Santiago de Lacangayé, the presence of myriad solidified corpses negated the sanitized view of those ruins endorsed by the state and the Catholic Church. And in Machu Picchu, an indigenous man visiting from Colombia cited by Michael Taussig could only see in the ruins a monument to the whip used by "the rich" to make slaves work to build that place.[75] This is the type of negativity that subaltern actors in rural areas of the Chaco tend to highlight when referring to the bodily debris that conquest left on space.

These patterns of destruction reveal not only the political spatiality of ruins, but also the political nature of space. The view of ruins as affirmative spatial forms is often inseparable from that of space as an entity free of ruptures. The commonsense view of progress, after all, cannot but see ruination "as the enemy of human beings," as something disturbing that should be kept at a distance.[76] A scene in Terry Gilliam's movie Brazil (1985) embodies this hegemonic attitude toward ruined landscapes: roads walled off with endless lines of billboards that hide from view, with sunny advertisings, the scorched and lifeless terrain that dominates the horizon on the other side. What is feared, and what must be kept invisible, is the voiding of the positivity of space and the political illumination that this may generate—the same illumination that drew Benjamin to study the petrified debris of bourgeois Paris.[77]

But this essay has also explored how ruins and ruination are affected by a particular type of space: those spaces generated on the edges of empires by collective refusals to abide by state power. These may not be the "non-state spaces" that James Scott writes about in the case of Southeast Asia, but they are spaces in which the state form is negated, dragged down, slowed down, and often halted.[78] Even if today "there is no spatial beyond the state," in a not-too-distant past the edges of empire encountered voids that confounded the very distinction between inside and outside.[79] These voids were not trascendental abstractions; they were tangible, immanent negations that affected countless bodies and the production of political boundaries over several centuries. In The Persistence of the Negative, Benjamin Noys wrote that negativity is "an immanent voiding of existent positivities."[80] This is what the Chaco was: a tangible node of negativity that voided imperial territorialization.

Tim Hetherington's documentary Restrepo shows that in today's globalized geography without an outside, anti-imperial insurgencies still have the power to void the positivity of imperial space, creating a vortex that overwhelms imperial ground forces.[81] Hetherington's gripping images reveal one of the voids of the twenty-first century: the Korengal Valley in Afghanistan, a feared, uncontrollable space subjected for this reason to imperial violence and a permanent state of exception. The void in the Korengal Valley, however, is different from that of the Chaco, and is certainly much less opaque. Imperial forces have now full command of airspace and a vertical field of vision that enables them to scrutinize and visualize all spaces of the world from above, and bomb the most entrenched corners of the void from the distance with unmanned drones. On the imperial frontiers of yesteryear, by contrast, the field of vision and mobility of state power was constrained by the horizontal flatness and dense striations of the terrain. And in the forests and savannas of the Gran Chaco, those who fought off the state for centuries were able to do to its ruins what state actors do with the ruination they create, to make them invisible—pulling them toward the void in which the solidity of the state melted into air.

Notes

The research for this chapter was funded by a grant from the Social Sciences and Humanities Research Council of Canada. I am particularly grateful to Shaylih Muehlmann, Ann L. Stoler, and an anonymous reviewer for Duke University Press for their critical insights on earlier drafts.

1. On Concepción del Bermejo, see Torre Revelo, *Esteco y Concepción del Bermejo, dos ciudades desaparecidas*; Zapata Gollan, *El Chaco Gualamba y la ciudad de Concepción del Bermejo*.

2. Hardt and Negri, *Empire*.

3. Badiou, *Deleuze*, 84.

4. Ibid.

5. Adorno, *Negative Dialectics*.

6. Sebald, *The Rings of Saturn*, 159.

7. Stoler, "Imperial Debris," 196.

8. Lozano, *Descripción corográfica del Gran Chaco Gualamba*, 121. My translation. Hereafter, all translations of original quotes in Spanish are mine.

9. No map of Concepción was produced prior to its destruction, and the scant documents about it alluded to imprecise references to its distance from the Paraguay and Bermejo Rivers. See Alumni, *El Chaco*, 36; Torre Revelo, *Esteco y Concepción del Bermejo, dos ciudades desaparecidas*, 135 and n1; Zapata Gollan, *El Chaco Gualamba y la ciudad de Concepción del Bermejo*, 20, 61–65.

10. Lozano, *Descripción corográfica del Gran Chaco Gualamba*, 349; also 319, 326–27, 348.

11. Ibid., 205; Tommasini, *La civilización cristiana del Chaco*, ii, respectively.

12. On other eighteenth-century maps, the "X" stands next to "Concepción destroyed" or "Esteco destroyed" (Furlong, *Cartografía jesuítica del Río de la Plata*, map 18; see also map 23).

13. Campos and Quijarro, *De Tarija a la Asunción*, 45–46.

14. Dobrizhoffer, *An Account of the Abipones, an Equestrian People of Paraguay*, 124.

15. Rodriguez, *Campañas del desierto*, 22.

16. De Brizuela, "Diario de Matorras," 141.

17. Seed, *Ceremonies of Possession in Europe's Conquest of the New World*.

18. Furlong, *Entre los Vilelas de Salta*, 120, 124.

19. De Brizuela, "Diario de Matorras," 141.

20. See Gullón Abao, *La frontera del Chaco en la gobernación del Tucumán*.

21. De Brizuela, "Diario de Matorras," 145–53.

22. Tomas de Matorras, "Diario de Arias," 396.

23. Ibid., 404–5.

24. See Fernández Cornejo, "Diario de la expedición de Cornejo al Chaco."

25. See Tomas de Matorras, "Diario de Arias," 404–5; Zapata Gollan, El Chaco Gualamba y la ciudad de Concepción del Bermejo, 49, 59; and Alumni, El Chaco, 41.

26. Halperín Donghi, Una nación para el desierto argentino.

27. See Wright, "El desierto del Chaco."

28. Tommasini, La Civilización Cristiana del Chaco, 211.

29. I analyze the contemporary social salience of the debris of ships in the region, in Gordillo, "Ships Stranded in the Forest."

30. See Aráoz, Río Bermejo, 53, 68, 75; Aráoz, Navegación del Río Bermejo y viajes al Gran Chaco, 121–22, 125–26; and Castro Boedo, Estudios sobre la navegación del Bermejo y la colonización del Chaco, 47, 107–8.

31. Olascoaga, "Instrucciones que Deben Cumplir los Ingenieros, Jefes y Ayudantes de las Comisiones Organizadas para el Estudio y Levantamiento Topográfico de la Región del Gran Chaco," 34.

32. De la Serna, 1,500 kilómetros a lomo de mula, 78, also 81, 91.

33. Victorica, "Correspondencia telegráfica del General en Jefe con el Presidente de la República," 200.

34. Garmendia, "Diario del Coronel Garmendia," 101.

35. Arnaud, Del Timbó al Tartagal, 38.

36. Ibid., 76–77.

37. See also Muehlmann, Where the River Ends; Taussig, Shamanism, Colonialism and the Wild Man.

38. Arnaud, Del Timbó al Tartagal, 162.

39. De la Serna, 1,500 kilómetros a lomo de mula, 129–30.

40. These ruins had been briefly explored in 1878 by men who had previously abandoned a stranded steamship downstream (Pelleschi, Eight Months on the Gran Chaco of the Argentine Republic, 56).

41. Host, "Informe del Comandante Host," 661; Arnaud, Del Timbó al Tartagal, 116, 140; de la Serna, 1,500 kilómetros a lomo de mula, 88.

42. Arnaud, Del Timbó al Tartagal, 128.

43. De la Serna, 1,500 kilómetros a lomo de mula, 7–8.

44. Cited by Arnaud, Del Timbó al Tartagal, 136–37; see also de la Serna, 1,500 kilómetros a lomo de mula, 108.

45. Arnaud, Del Timbó al Tartagal, 140.

46. See the detailed accounts by Arnaud (Del Timbó al Tartagal, 140–41) and de la Serna (1,500 kilómetros a lomo de mula, 108, 112).

47. Arnaud, Del Timbó al Tartagal, 139.

48. De la Serna, 1,500 kilómetros a lomo de mula, 102.

49. Victorica, "Proclama del General en Jefe en la ceremonia de la inauguración del Puerto Presidencia Roca," 73–74.

50. De la Serna, *1,500 kilómetros a lomo de mula*, 75, also 84. See also Carranza, *Expedición al Gran Chaco Austral*, 54, 58, 63, 81; and Garmendia, "Diario del Coronel Garmendia," 103, 107, 108.

51. De la Serna, *1,500 kilómetros a lomo de mula*, 81.

52. The information produced in 1884 about the vestiges of the San Bernardo mission remained in the army archives and was mentioned only in obscure publications.

53. Morresi, *Las ruinas del km. 75 y Concepción del Bermejo*; Zapata Gollan, *El Chaco Gualamba y la ciudad de Concepción del Bermejo*. Previously, the ruins of two villages subordinated to Concepción, Matará and Guacara, were also partly excavated (Alumni, *Nuestra Sra. de los Dolores y Santiago de la Cangayé*, 45n42; Zapata Gollan, *El Chaco Gualamba y la ciudad de Concepción del Bermejo*, 57–58).

54. Alumni, *Nuestra Sra. de los Dolores y Santiago de la Cangayé*, 55.

55. See Gorostiaga, *El misterio de Esteco*; Reyes Gajardo, *La ciudad de Esteco y su leyenda*.

56. Tomasini and Alonso, *Esteco, el Viejo*.

57. The vestiges of Santiago del Guadalcázar (a town that lasted for less than a decade and was abandoned in 1632) are the only ones that have not been located, but scholars agree that the town was north of Orán, province of Salta, in a region whose landscape has been thoroughly transformed by sugarcane cultivation.

58. Alumni, *Nuestra Sra. de los Dolores y Santiago de la Cangayé*, 64–65.

59. Ibid., 62, 65.

60. This is a plausible explanation, for at the time Mocoví and Abipón groups were at war with each other (see Dobrizhoffer, *An Account of the Abipones, an Equestrian People of Paraguay*).

61. Alumni, *Nuestra Sra. de los Dolores y Santiago de la Cangayé*, 44n41.

62. De la Serna, *1,500 kilómetros a lomo de mula*, 156.

63. Stoler, "Imperial Debris," 195.

64. The provinces within the region—Formosa, Chaco, Santiago del Estero, and the Chaco salteño—consistently rank at the bottom of national indicators of quality of life, life expectancy, nutrition, and levels of basic infrastructure. Capitalist expansion and state investments have certainly created zones of prosperity, exemplified recently by the agribusiness expansion that is transforming the western and southern Chaco. Yet like the capitalist expansions of the late 1800s and early 1900s, these patterns of growth have shipped most of their profits elsewhere and left behind social and spatial dislocation, embodied in the displacement of local populations and the destruction of vast forested landscapes by the expansion of soybean fields.

65. Gordillo, *Landscapes of Devils*.

66. Ibid.

67. Fontana, *El Gran Chaco*, 105–7.

68. Teruel, *Misiones, economía y sociedad*, 86–87.

69. Ginsberg, *The Aesthetics of Ruins*, 407.

70. Benjamin, *The Origin of the German Tragic Drama*.

71. Marco Díaz Muñoz, "Masacres de Napalpí y Rincón Bomba 'El Gobierno se ha

opuesto a que se sigan excavando las tumbas,'" Copenoa, 18 September 2006, http://www.copenoa.com.ar/Masacres-de-Napalpi-y-Rincon-Bomba.html.

72. Gordillo, *The Afterlife of Places*.

73. Ginsberg, *The Aesthetics of Ruins*; Beasley-Murray, Comments to "Ships Stranded in the Forest: Debris of Progress on a Phantom River."

74. See Woodward, *In Ruins*.

75. Taussig, *The Nervous System*, 39–40.

76. Ginsberg, *The Aesthetics of Ruins*, 287.

77. Benjamin, *The Arcades Project*.

78. James Scott, *The Art of Not Being Governed*.

79. Li, "Beyond 'the State' and Failed Schemes," 384.

80. Noys, *The Persistence of the Negative*, 101.

81. See my review-essay on *Restrepo*, "On the Imperial Edge of the Void," Space and Politics (blog), 27 April 2011, http://spaceandpolitics.blogspot.com/2011/04/on-imperial-edge-of-void.html.

Engineering the Future as Nuclear Ruin

Has any nation-state invested as profoundly in ruins as Cold War America? While many societies have experienced moments of self-doubt about the future, perhaps even contemplating the ruins that might be left behind as testament to their existence, it took American ingenuity to transform ruination into a form of nation-building. In this regard, the invention of the atomic bomb proved to be utterly transformative for American society: it not only provided the inspiration for a new U.S. geopolitical strategy—one that ultimately enveloped the earth in advanced military technology and colonized everyday life with the minute-to-minute possibility of nuclear war—but also provided officials with a new means of engaging and disciplining citizens in everyday life. For U.S. policy makers, the Cold War arms race transformed the apocalypse into a technoscientific project and a geopolitical paradigm, but also a powerful new domestic political resource.

Put differently, a new kind of social contract was formed in the first decade of the nuclear age in the United States, one based not on the protection and improvement of everyday life, but rather on the national contemplation of ruins. Known initially as "civil defense," the project of building the bomb and communicating its power to the world turned engineering ruins into a form of (inter)national theater. Nuclear explosions matched with large-scale emergency response exercises became a means of developing the bomb as well as of imagining nuclear warfare.[1] This "test program" would ultimately transform the United States into the most nuclear-bombed country on earth, distributing its environmental, economic, and health effects in different ways to each and every U.S. citizen.[2] By the mid-1950s it was no longer a perverse exercise to imagine one's own home and city devastated, on fire, and in ruins; it was a formidable public ritual—a core act of governance, technoscientific practice, and democratic participation. Indeed, in early Cold War America it became a civic obligation to collectively imagine, and at times theatrically enact through "civil defense," the physical destruction of the nation-state.[3]

It is this specific nationalization of death that I wish to explore in this essay, assessing not only the first collective formulations of nuclear fear in the United States, but also the residues and legacies of that project for contemporary American society. For today we live in a world populated with newly charred landscapes and a production of ruins that speaks directly to this foundational moment in American national culture.[4] The notions of preemption and emergency response that inform the United States' "war on terror" derive meaning from the promises and institutions built by the Cold War security state. Indeed, the logics of nuclear fear informing that multigenerational state and nation-building enterprise exist now as a largely inchoate, but deeply embedded, set of assumptions about power and threat. How Americans have come to understand mass death at home and abroad has much to do with the legacies of the Cold War nuclear project and with the peculiar psychosocial consequences of attempting to build the nation through the contemplation of nuclear ruins.

What follows is largely a study of visual culture, and specifically, the domestic deployment of images of a ruined United States for ideological effect. I argue that key aspects of U.S. security culture have been formed in relation to images of nuclear devastation; the constitution of the modern security state in the aftermath of the Second World War mobilized the atomic bomb as the basis for American geopolitical power, but it also created a new citizen-state relationship mediated by nuclear fear. This essay considers the lasting effects of nation-building through nuclear fear by tracking the production and ongoing circulation of nuclear ruins from the Cold War's "balance of terror" through our current "war on terror." It is not an exercise in viewer response, but rather charts the development and circulation of a specific set of ideas and images about nuclear war. I begin with a discussion of the early Cold War project known as "civil defense," then track how the specific images created for domestic consumption as part of that campaign continued to circulate as afterimages in the popular films of the 1980s and 1990s.[5] I show that the early Cold War state sought explicitly to militarize

U.S. citizens through contemplating the end of the nation-state, creating in the process a specific set of ideas and images of collective danger that continue to inform American society in powerful and increasingly complex ways. In the aftermath of the terrorist attacks on New York and Washington in 2001, the affective coordinates of the Cold War arms race provided specific ideological resources to the state, which once again mobilized the image of a United States in nuclear ruins to enable war. Ultimately, this essay follows Walter Benjamin's call to interrogate the aestheticized politics that enable increasing militarization and that allow citizens to experience their own destruction as an "aesthetic pleasure of the first order."[6]

Be Afraid but Don't Panic!

> The disaster ruins everything, all the while leaving everything intact. . . . To think the disaster (if this is possible, and it is not possible inasmuch as we suspect that the disaster is thought) is to have no longer any future in which to think it.
>
> —MAURICE BLANCHOT, *The Writing of the Disaster*

Nuclear ruins are never the end of the story in the United States, but rather always offer a new beginning. In the early Cold War period, ruins become the markers of a new kind of social intimacy grounded in highly detailed renderings of theatrically rehearsed mass violence. The intent of these public spectacles — nuclear detonations, city evacuations, duck-and-cover drills — was not defense in the classic sense of avoiding violence or destruction, but rather a psychological reprogramming of the American public for life in a nuclear age. The central project of the early nuclear state was to link U.S. institutions — military, industrial, legislative, academic — for the production of the bomb, while calibrating public perceptions of the nuclear danger to enable that project.[7] As Blanchot suggests, this effort to think through the disaster colonized everyday life as well as the future, while fundamentally missing the actual disaster. The scripting of disaster in the imagination has profound social effects: it defines the conditions of insecurity, renders other threats invisible, and articulates the terms of both value and loss. In the United States, civil defense was always a willful act of fabulation, an official fantasy designed to promote an image of nuclear war that would be, above all things, politically useful. It also installed an idea of an American community under total and unending threat, creating the terms for a new kind of nation-building which demanded an unprecedented level of militarism in everyday life as the minimum basis for "security."

After the Soviet's first nuclear detonation in 1949, U.S. policy makers committed to a new geopolitical strategy that would ultimately dominate American foreign policy for the remainder of the twentieth century. The policy of "containment," as formalized in 1950 in NSC 68: A Report from the National Security Council, proposed, in response to the Soviet bomb, a total mobilization of American society based on the experience of the First World War.[8] NSC 68 articulates the terms of a permanent wartime posture funded by an ever-expanding domestic economy, transforming consumerism into the engine of a new kind of militarized geopolitics. NSC 68 identifies internal dissent as perhaps the greatest threat to the project of "Cold War" and calls for a new campaign to discipline citizens for life under the constant shadow of nuclear war. Thus, in Washington, nuclear fear was immediately understood to be not only the basis of American military power, but also a means of installing a new normative reality in the United States, one that could consolidate political power at the federal level. The nuclear danger became a complex new political ideology, both mobilizing the global project of Cold War (fought increasingly on covert terms) and installing a powerful means of controlling domestic political debates over the terms of security. By focusing Americans on an imminent end of the nation-state, federal authorities mobilized the bomb to create the "Cold War consensus" of anticommunism, capitalism, and military expansion.

Defense intellectuals within the Truman and Eisenhower administrations, however, worried that nuclear terror could become so profound under the terms of an escalating nuclear arms race that the American public would be unwilling to support the military and geopolitical agenda of the Cold War.[9] The immediate challenge, as U.S. nuclear strategists saw it, was to avoid an apathetic public (which might just give up when faced with the destructive power of the Soviet nuclear arsenal) on the one hand or a terrorized public (unable to function cognitively) on the other.[10] For example, an influential civil defense study from 1952, Project East River, argued that civilian response to a nuclear attack would be all-out panic and mob behavior: American society, it concluded, would be not only at war with the Soviets but also at war with itself as society violently broke down along race and class lines.[11] A long "Cold War" consequently required not only a new geopolitics powered by nuclear weapons, but also new forms of psychological discipline at home. One of the earliest and most profound projects of the Cold War state was thus to deploy the bomb as a mechanism for accessing and controlling the emotions of citizens.

As Guy Oakes has documented, the civil defense programs of the early

Cold War were designed to "emotionally manage" U.S. citizens through nuclear fear.[12] The formal goal of this state program was to transform "nuclear terror," which was interpreted by U.S. officials as a paralyzing emotion, into "nuclear fear," an affective state that would allow citizens to function in a time of crisis.[13] By militarizing everyday life through nuclear fear, the Cold War state sought to both normalize and politically deploy an image of catastrophic risk. Rather than offering citizens an image of safety or of a war that could end in victory, the early Cold War state sought instead to calibrate everyday American life to the minute-to-minute possibility of nuclear warfare. In addition to turning the domestic space of the home into the front line of the Cold War, Civil Defense argued that citizens should be prepared every second of the day to deal with a potential nuclear attack. In doing so, the Civil Defense program shifted responsibility for nuclear war from the state to its citizens by making public panic the enemy, not nuclear war itself. It was, in other words, up to citizens to take responsibility for their own survival in the nuclear age. As Val Peterson, the first head of the U.S. Civil Defense Administration, argued,

> Ninety per cent of all emergency measures after an atomic blast will depend on the prevention of panic among the survivors in the first 90 seconds. Like the A-bomb, panic is fissionable. It can produce a chain reaction more deeply destructive than any explosive known. If there is an ultimate weapon, it may well be mass panic — not the A-bomb.[14]

Panic is fissionable. The idea that emotional self-regulation was the single most important issue during a nuclear attack (not to mention the ninety-second window on success or failure) sought quite formally to turn all Americans into docile bodies that would automatically support the goals of the security state. Civil Defense planners sought ultimately to saturate the public space with a specific idea about nuclear war, one that would nationalize mass death and transform postnuclear ruins into a new American frontier, simply another arena for citizens to assert their civic spirit and ingenuity. At the heart of the project was an effort to install psychological defenses against the exploding bomb, as well as a belief in the possibility of national unity in a postnuclear environment—all via the contemplation of nuclear ruins.

Indeed, as the Eisenhower administration promoted the idea of "Atoms for Peace" around the world to emphasize the benefits of nuclear energy and provide a positive face to atomic science, it pursued the opposite emotional-management strategy within the United States.[15] The domestic solution to the Soviet nuclear arsenal was a new kind of social-engineering project, pursued with help from the advertising industry, to teach citizens a specific kind of nuclear fear while normalizing the nuclear crisis. The goal, as one top-secret study put it in 1956, was an "emotional adaptation" of the citizenry to nuclear crisis, a program of "psychological defense" aimed at "feelings" that would unify the nation in the face of apocalyptic everyday threat.[16] This took the form of the largest domestic propaganda campaign to date in American history.[17] Designed to mobilize all Americans for a long Cold War, the Civil Defense effort involved town meetings and education programs in every public school; it also sought to take full advantage of mass media—television, radio, and particularly film. By the mid-1950s, the Federal Civil Defense Agency (FCDA) had saturated newspapers and magazines with nuclear war planning advertisements, and could claim that its radio broadcasts reached an estimated audience of 175 million Americans per year.

As the campaign evolved, the FCDA turned increasingly to film, creating a library of short subjects on nuclear destruction and civil defense that was shown across the country in schools, churches, community halls, and movie theaters. The FCDA concluded in 1955, "Each picture will be seen by a minimum of 20,000,000 persons, giving an anticipated aggregate audience of more than half a billion for the civil defense film program of 1955."[18] A key to winning the Cold War was to produce the bomb not only for military use but also in cinematic form for the American public. It is important to recognize that the circulation of these images relied on a simultaneous censorship of images from the atomic bombings of Hiroshima and Nagasaki in 1945. U.S. authorities made available images of destroyed buildings from Japan, but withheld the detailed effects of the atomic bomb on the human body, as well as some firsthand accounts of the aftermath.[19] An immediate project of the nuclear state was thus to calibrate the image of atomic warfare for the American public through the mass circulation of certain images of the bomb and the censorship of all others. In this way, officials sought to mobilize the power of mass media to transform nuclear attack from an unthinkable apocalypse into an opportunity for psychological self-management, civic responsibility, and, ultimately, governance. Civil Defense ultimately sought to produce an "atomic bomb proof" society in which nuclear conflict was normalized alongside all other threats, making public support for the Cold War sustainable.

Civil Defense theorists argued that citizens could achieve this contradictory state of productive fear (simultaneously mobilized and normalized) only by gaining intimacy with nuclear warfare itself, by becoming familiar with language of nuclear effects from blast, heat, and fire to radioactive fallout. As the RAND analyst Irving L. Janis put it, the goal of civil defense was ultimately an "emotional inoculation" of the American public.[20] This inoculation, he cautioned, needed to be finely calibrated: the simulated nuclear destruction in civil defense exercises, as well as the atomic test film footage released to the public, had to be formidable enough to mobilize citizens, but not so terrifying as to invalidate the concept of defense altogether (a distinct challenge in an age of increasingly powerful thermonuclear weapons, which offered no hope of survival to most urban residents). A central project of Civil Defense was thus to produce fear but not terror, anxiety but not panic, to inform about nuclear science but not to fully educate about nuclear war. The microregulation of a national community at the emotional level was the goal. Put differently, alongside the invention of a new security state grounded in nuclear weapons came a new public culture of insecurity in the United States; figuring the United States as global nuclear superpower was coterminous with a domestic campaign to reveal the United States as completely vulnerable, creating a citizen-state relationship increasingly mediated by forms of inchoate but ever present nuclear fear.

Indeed, one of the first U.S. civil defense projects of the Cold War was to make every U.S. city a target and every U.S. citizen a potential victim of nuclear attack. The FCDA circulated increasingly detailed maps of the likely targets of a Soviet nuclear attack through the 1950s, listing the cities in order of population and ranking them as potential targets. In one 1955 FCDA map, the top seventy Soviet targets include major population centers as well as military bases in the United States, revealing not only the vulnerability of large cities to the bomb, but also the increasingly wide distribution of military-industrial sites across the continental United States (fig. 8.1). As the size of U.S. and Soviet bombs, and the means of delivery, grew (from bombers to intercontinental missiles), so too did the highly publicized target lists. Thomas J. Martin and Donald C. Latham's 1963 civil defense textbook, Strategy for Survival, for example, presented a case for 303 ground zeros in the United States in case of nuclear war. Designating 303 U.S. cities and towns that would be likely targets of nuclear attack, they concluded,

> No one can predict that any one or combination of these cities would be attacked in any future war. Thus, it might appear that we are trying to know the unknowable, to predict the unpredictable, to impose a logical rationale upon war which is, itself, illogical and irrational. But such an

8.1 Map of presumed Soviet nuclear targets, Federal Civil Defense Administration, 1955.

inference is incorrect. It was shown in Chapter 5 that there are good reasons to believe that a large fraction of these cities would be attacked in a future war—but what specific cities would be included in this fraction? Because there is no precise answer to this question, civil defense planning must assume that all could be potential targets. Any other approach is thermonuclear Russian Roulette played with 100 million American lives.[21]

Thermonuclear Russian roulette. Marking every population center with more than fifty thousand people a likely target, Martin and Latham saw no "safe" area in the United States. From New York to Topeka, from Los Angeles to Waco, from Albuquerque to Anchorage—each community could increasingly argue that it was a "first strike" target of Soviet attack. Indeed, citizens were informed from multiple media sources that their community—indeed, their very living room—was the literal front line of the Cold War, with Soviet thermonuclear warheads poised to attack.[22]

From 1953 to 1961, the yearly centerpiece of the Civil Defense program was a simulated nuclear attack on the United States directed by federal authorities.[23] Cities were designated as victims of nuclear warfare, allowing

ATTACK PATTERN OPERATION ALERT –1955

FALLOUT PATTERNS FROM GROUND BURSTS OF MEGATON BOMBS

OTHER TARGETS BOMBED

8.2 Simulated nuclear attack pattern from an Operation Alert exercise, Federal Civil Defense Administration, 1955.

civic leaders and politicians to lead theatrical evacuations of the city for television cameras, followed by media discussions of blast damage versus fire damage versus fallout, and the expected casualty rates if the attack had been "real." In 1955, for example, the Operation Alert scenario involved sixty cities hit by a variety of atomic and hydrogen bombs, producing over eight million instant deaths and another eight million radiation victims over the coming weeks (fig. 8.2). It imagined twenty-five million homeless and fallout covering some sixty-three thousand square miles of the United States.[24] Each year Americans acted out their own incineration in this manner, with public officials cheerfully evacuating cities and evaluating emergency planning while nuclear detonations in Nevada and the South Pacific provided new images of fireballs and mushroom clouds to reinforce the concept of imminent nuclear threat. The early Cold War state sought to install a specific idea of the bomb in the American imagination through these public spectacles, creating a new psychosocial space caught between the utopian promise of American technoscience and the minute-to-minute threat of thermonuclear incineration. It sought to make mass death an intimate psychological experience, while simultaneously claiming that thermonuclear war could be planned for alongside tornados, floods, and traffic accidents. Civil Defense ultimately sought to make nuclear war a space of nation-building and thereby bring this new form of death under the control of the state.

Here is how one of the most widely circulated U.S. Civil Defense films of the 1950s, *Let's Face It*, described the problem posed by nuclear warfare.

> The tremendous effects of heat and blast on modern structures raise important questions concerning their durability and safety. Likewise, the amount of damage done to our industrial potential will have a serious effect upon our ability to recover from an atomic attack. Transportation facilities are vital to a modern city. The nation's lifeblood could be cut if its traffic arteries were severed. These questions are of great interest not only to citizens in metropolitan centers but also to those in rural areas who may be in a danger zone because of radioactive fallout from today's larger weapons. We could get many of the answers to these questions by constructing a complete city at our Nevada Proving Ground and then exploding a nuclear bomb over it. We could study the effects of damage over a wide area, under all conditions, and plan civil defense activities accordingly. But such a gigantic undertaking is not feasible.

The problem voiced here is ultimately one of scientific detail: How can the security state prepare to survive a nuclear attack if it does not know in *detail* how every aspect of American life would respond to both the effects of the bomb and the resulting social confusion? But after denying the possibility of building an entire city in Nevada simply to destroy it, the narrator of *Let's Face It* reveals that the nuclear state has, in fact, done just that.

> Instead we build representative units of a test city. With steel and stone and brick and mortar, with precision and skill—as though it were to last a thousand years. But it is a weird, fantastic city. A creation right out of science fiction. A city like no other on the face of the earth. Homes, neat and clean and completely furnished, that will never be occupied. Bridges, massive girders of steel spanning the empty desert. Railway tracks that lead to nowhere, for this is the end of the line. But every element of these tests is carefully planned in these tests as to its design and location in the area. A variety of materials and building techniques are often represented in a single structure. Every brick, beam, and board will have its story to tell. When pieced together these will give some of the answers, and some of the information we need to survive in the nuclear age.

A *weird fantastic city*. This test city was also an idealized model of the contemporary American suburb, and by publicizing its atomic destruction, the state was involved in an explicit act of psychological manipulation. The Nevada Test Site was the location of nuclear war "simulations" involving real nuclear explosions and model American cities destroyed in real time for a national audience. Each ruin in these national melodramas—each element of bombed U.S. material culture—was presented as a key to solving the "problem" of nuclear warfare, a means of cracking the code for survival in nuclear conflict. But in this effort to control a specific idea of death, the civil defense strategy also forced citizens to confront the logics of the nuclear state, allowing many to reclaim and reinvest these same ruins with a counternarrative and critique.[25] Thus, real and imagined nuclear ruins became the foundation for competing ideas of national community, producing resistance to, as well as normalization of, a militarized society. But while the early Cold War effort to produce an "atomic bomb proof" society may have failed, the psychosocial legacies of this moment continue to haunt and inform U.S. national culture.[26] In the remainder of this essay, I offer a visual history of nuclear ruins in the United States as a means both of recovering the affective coordinates of the nuclear security state, and of exploring the lasting impacts of the Cold War "emotional management" strategy on American society.

"Cue for Survival"

On 5 May 1955, a hundred million Americans watched live on television a "typical" suburban community being blown to bits by an atomic bomb.[27] Many watched from homes and apartments that were the explicit models for the test city, and they saw mannequin families posed in casual everyday moments (at the kitchen table, on the couch, in bed—or watching TV) experience the atomic blast. Operation Cue was the largest of the Civil Defense spectacles staged at the Nevada Test Site: it promised not only to demonstrate the power of the exploding bomb but also to show citizens exactly what a postnuclear American city would look like. In addition to the live television coverage, film footage was widely distributed in the years after the test, with versions shown in movie theaters and replayed on television. Some of the most powerful and enduring U.S. images of atomic destruction were crafted during Operation Cue, and remain in circulation to this day. Thus, in important ways, the broken buildings and charred rubble produced

L. A. Darling Co., civil defense mannequin family.

8.3 Mannequins used in Operation Cue, Federal Civil Defense Administration, 1955.

in Operation Cue continue to structure contemporary American perceptions of postnuclear ruins, constituting a kind of ur-text for the nuclear age.

As an experiment, Operation Cue was designed to test residences, shelter designs, utilities, mobile housing, vehicles, siren systems, as well as a variety of domestic items, under atomic blast. Linked to each of these objects was a specific test program and research team drawn from Los Alamos Scientific Laboratory, the Atomic Energy Commission, and the Federal Civil Defense Administration. A variety of Civil Defense exercises were conducted in the aftermath of the explosion as well, including rescue operations, fire control, plane evacuations, communication and sanitation efforts, and mass feeding. The test city was designed as a "representative" American community, and was made up of a variety of current building styles (ramblers, two-story brick houses, as well as trailers and mobile homes), a variety of utilities (from electronic towers to propane systems), numerous bomb shelter designs, as well as efforts to protect records (i.e., a variety of office safes). More than 150 industrial associations participated in the test, ensuring that the very latest consumer items from cars to furniture, clothing to dishware, televisions to radio, were installed in the brand-new houses. Hundreds of civilian participants were invited to inhabit not the pristine pretest city but the post-test atomic ruins: civilians were simultaneously witnesses and test subjects, serving as representative "Americans" and individuals to be tested by viewing the blast and participating in mass feeding and emergency operations. The formal inhabitants of Operation Cue were the mannequin families, dressed and theatrically posed to suggest everyday life activities, communicating through their posture and dress that the bombing was an unexpected intrusion into an intimate home space (fig. 8.3).

Operation Cue was designed to appeal to a domestic audience, and particularly to women.[28] Unlike previous civil defense films, *Operation Cue* has a female narrator—Joan Collins—who promises to see the test "through my own eyes and the eye of the average citizen."[29] In its effort to produce a "bomb proof" society, the FCDA was concerned with documenting the effects of the bomb against every detail of middle-class, white, suburban life. The media strategy involved recalibrating domestic life by turning the nuclear family into a nuclearized family, preprogrammed for life before, during, and after a nuclear war. Gender roles were reinforced by dividing up responsibility for food and security in a time of nuclear crisis between women and men. Similarly, the civil defense campaigns in public schools were designed to deploy children to educate their parents about civil defense. Normative gender roles were used to reinforce the idea that nuclear crisis was not an exceptional condition but one that could be incorporated into everyday life with minor changes in household technique and a "can do" American spirit.

Of particular concern in Operation Cue, for example, were food tests and mass feeding programs. In each of the model homes, the pantries and refrigerators were stocked with food. In her voiceover, Collins underscores the Operation Cue's address to women, announcing, "As a mother and housewife, I was particularly interested in the food test program, a test that included canned and packaged food." Additionally, food in various forms of packaging was buried along the desert test site, in order to expose it to radiation, and some of the mannequin families were posed to be involved in food preparation at the time of the detonation. Conceptually, the argument was that at any moment of the day—while enjoying one's breakfast, for example—the bomb could drop. The FCDA sought, as Laura McEnaney argues, to create a "paramilitary housewife," emotionally and materially in control of her home and thinking about postnuclear social life.[30] Formally, the FCDA was interested in whether or not food would be too contaminated in the immediate aftermath of a blast to eat, and also what kinds of techniques would be needed to feed large groups of homeless, injured, and traumatized people. Within this scheme of crisis management, food was positioned as a primary means of calming individual anxieties and establishing social authority.[31] Informally, the goal was to saturate the domestic space of the home with nuclear logics and civic obligations, to militarize men, women, and children to withstand either a very long nuclear confrontation or a very short nuclear war.

Food was flown in from Las Vegas, Chicago, and San Francisco for the test to document the state's ability to move large quantities of food around the country in a time of "emergency." The FCDA report *Effects of Nuclear Explosions on Frozen Food* concludes that "under emergency conditions similar to this exposure, frozen foods may be used for both military and civilian feeding," but this conclusion only hints at the scale of this experiment.[32] Frozen chicken pot pies were a privileged test item and were distributed through the test homes as well as buried in bulk freezers. The pies were then exposed to nuclear blast and tested for radiation, as well as for nutritional value, color, and taste. Thus, while building increasing powerful atomic and thermonuclear weapons, the security state set about demonstrating to Americans that even if the nation-state disappeared under nuclear fire, its newly developed prepared foods would still be edible (making the chicken pot pie a curious emblem of modernity in the process). Like these bomb-proof pies, all commodified aspects of American life were to be tested against nuclear blast, as the state sought to demonstrate not only that there could be a "postnuclear" moment, but that life within it could be imagined on largely familiar terms.

Indeed, documenting evidence of material survival after the atomic blast was ultimately the point of Operation Cue. The mass feeding project, for example, pulled equipment from the wreckage after the test, as well as the food from refrigerators and buried canned goods, and served them to assembled participants: this emergency meal consisted of roast beef, tomato juice, baked beans, and coffee.[33] The destruction of a model American community thus became the occasion of a giant picnic, with each item of food marked as having survived the atomic bomb, and each witness positioned as a postnuclear survivor. Additionally, the emergency rescue group pulled damaged mannequins from out of the rubble and practiced medical and evacuation techniques on them, eventually flying several charred and broken dummies to offsite hospitals by charter plane. The formal message of Operation Cue was that the postnuclear environment would be only as chaotic as citizens allowed, that resources (food, shelter, medical) would still be present, and that society—if not the nation-state—would continue. Nuclear war was ultimately presented as a state of mind that could be incorporated into one's normative reality—it was simply a matter of emotional preparation and mental discipline.

The mannequin families that were intact after the explosion were soon on a national tour, complete with tattered and scorched clothing. J.C. Penney's department store, which provided the garments, displayed these postnuclear families in its stores around the county with a sign declaring, "This could be you!" Inverting a standard advertising appeal, it was not the blue suit or polka-dot dress that was to be the focal point of viewers' identification. Rather, it was the mannequin as survivor, whose very existence seemed to illustrate that you could indeed "beat the A-bomb," as one civil defense film of the era promised. Invited to contemplate life within a postnuclear ruin as the docile mannequins of civil defense, the national audience for Operation Cue was caught in a sea of mixed messages about the power of the state to control the bomb. This kind of ritual enactment did not resolve the problem of the bomb, but rather focused citizens on emotional self-discipline through nuclear fear. It asked them to live on the knife's edge of a psychotic contradiction—an everyday life founded simultaneously in total threat and absolute normality—with the stakes being nothing less than survival itself.

Indeed, while Operation Cue was billed as a test of "the things we use in everyday life," the full intent of the test was to nationalize nuclear fear and install a new civic understanding via the contemplation of mass destruction and death. Consider the narrative of Arthur F. Landstreet, the general manager of the Hotel King Cotton in Memphis, who volunteered to crouch down in a trench at the Nevada Test Site about ten thousand feet from ground zero and experience the nuclear detonation in Operation Cue. After the explosion he explained why it was important for ordinary citizens to be tested on the front line of a nuclear detonation.

> Apparently the reason for stationing civilians at Position Baker was to find out what the actual reaction from citizens who were not schooled in the atomic field would be, and to get some idea of what the ordinary citizen might be able to endure under similar conditions. This idea was part of the total pattern to condition civilians for what they might be expected to experience in case of atomic attack. . . . Every step of the bomb burst was explained over and over from the moment of the first flash of light until the devastating blast. We were asked to make time tests from the trench to our jeeps. We did this time after time, endeavoring to create more speed and less loss of motion. We were told that this was necessary because, if the bomb exploded directly over us with practically no wind, the fallout would drop immediately downward, and we would be alerted to get out of the territory. We would have about 5 minutes to get at least 2.5 to 3 miles distant, so it was necessary that we learn every move perfectly.[34]

The total pattern to condition civilians. Physical reactions to the nuclear explosion are privileged in Landstreet's account, but a corollary project is also revealed, that of training the participants not to think but simply to act in a case of emergency. If the first project was an emotional-management effort to familiarize citizens with the exploding bomb—to psychologically inoculate them against their own apocalyptic imagination—the later effort sought simply to control those same bodies, to train and time their response to official commands.[35] The atomic bomb extended the docility of the citizen-subject to new levels, as Civil Defense sought to absorb the everyday within a new normative reality imbued with the potential for an imminent and total destruction.

This short-circuiting of the brain, and willingness to take orders under the sign of nuclear emergency, reveals the broader scope of the civil defense project: anesthetizing as well as protecting, producing docility as well as agency. The effort to document the potentialities of life in a postnuclear environment met with almost immediate resistance. In addition to the mounting scientific challenges to the claims of civil defense, a "mothers against the bomb" movement started, in 1959, when two young mothers in New York refused to participate in Operation Alert by simply taking their children to Central Park rather than to the fallout shelter.[36] The widely publicized effects of radioactive fallout in the 1950s and the move from atomic to thermonuclear weapons provided ample evidence that Operation Cue was not, in the end, a "realistic" portrait of nuclear warfare.[37] And indeed by the time the film *Operation Cue* was re-released, in 1964, the following text was added to the introduction, minimizing the claims of the film.

> The nuclear device used was comparatively small. It had an explosive force of 30 kilotons, equivalent to 30,000 tons of TNT. Whereas, some modern thermonuclear weapons are in the 20-megaton range—twenty million tons—more than 600 times as powerful as the bomb shown here, and with a much wider radius of destruction. In this test, many of the structures damaged by the 30-kiloton bomb were approximately one mile from "ground zero." With a 20–megaton blast, they probably would be obliterated, and comparable damage would occur out to a distance of at least 8.5 or 9 miles.

They probably would be obliterated. Thus, as a scientific test of "everyday objects" Operation Cue had less value over time, as the effects of blast and radiation in increasingly powerful weapons rendered Civil Defense almost immediately obsolete as a security concept. In Cold War ideology, however, the promise of nuclear ruins was deployed by the state to secure the possibility of a postnuclear remainder, and with it, the inevitable reconstitution of social order. The discourse of "obliteration" here, however, reveals the technoscientific limitations of that ideological project, as the destructive reality of thermonuclear warfare radically limits the possibility of a postnuclear United States.

After the 1963 Partial Test Ban Treaty, the visual effects of the bomb were eliminated as atomic testing went underground. The elimination of aboveground tests had two immediate effects: first, it changed the terms of the public discourse about the bomb, as the state no longer had to rationalize the constant production of mushroom clouds and the related health concerns over radioactive fallout to American society; second, it locked in place the visual record of the bomb. Thus, the visual record of the 1945–63 aboveground test program, with its deep implication in manipulating public opinions and emotions, remains the visual record of the bomb to this day. As science, Operation Cue was always questionable, but as national theater it remains a much more productive enterprise: it created an idealized consumer dream space and fused it with the bomb, creating the very vocabulary for thinking about the nuclear emergency that continues to inform American politics (fig. 8.4). Thus, the motto of Operation Cue, "Survival Is Your Business," is not an ironic moment of atomic kitsch, but rather reveals the formal project of the nuclear state, underscoring the link between the production of threat, its militarized response, and the Cold War economic program. As an emotional-management campaign, Civil Defense proved extraordinarily influential, installing within American national culture a set of ideas, images, and assumptions about nuclear weapons that continued to inform Cold War politics, and that remain powerful to this day. I turn now to two afterimages of the 1950s Civil Defense program, each set roughly a generation apart, to consider the lasting consequences of this era's emotional-management strategy, and to explore the psychosocial effects of deploying highly detailed depictions of the end of the nation-state as a means of establishing national community.

Afterimage 1: *The Day After* (1983)

> The anticipation of nuclear war (dreaded as the fantasy, or phantasm, of a re-
> mainderless destruction) installs humanity—and through all sorts of relays
> even defines the essence of modern humanity—in its rhetorical condition.
> —JACQUES DERRIDA, "No Apocalypse, Not Now"

On Sunday, 20 November 1983, a hundred million Americans tuned in to watch the United States destroyed by Soviet missiles (ICBMs) and the few survivors in Lawrence, Kansas, negotiate everyday life in a postnuclear environment (fig. 8.5). Watched by half of the adult population in the United States, *The Day After* (directed by Nicholas Meyer) was a major cultural event, one that refocused public attention on the effects of radiation, mass casualties, and life without a functioning state. Presented as a "realistic" account, the blast and radiation effects depicted in the film were supported by statements from health experts and transformed into a moment of national dialogue about the physical and biological effects of nuclear war.[38] Immediately following the broadcast, the ABC network presented a roundtable discussion of the film and the current state of nuclear emergency. Public school teachers across the country advised students to watch *The Day After* in order to discuss its implications in class, thereby nationalizing the discussion. Even President Reagan, whose arms build-up and provocative nuclear rhetoric helped instigate the film, watched along with his fellow Americans, announcing after the program aired that he, too, had been terrified by the filmic depiction of nuclear war. In synchronizing a hundred million viewing subjects, *The Day After* created a national community brought together by images of their own destruction. In doing so, it also replayed the official program of Operation Cue with uncanny precision and demonstrated the enduring national-cultural legacy of the 1950s emotional-management project.

The Day After follows several "idealized" Midwestern families, documenting their lives before nuclear war breaks out and then in a postnuclear world. The first hour of the film is devoted to everyday life in Lawrence (against the backdrop of increasing international tensions); the second hour is devoted to the brief nuclear attack and then life in a postnuclear environment. The film rehearses the lessons of Operation Cue with eerie precision: after nuclear attack, the state is absent and it is up to citizens to provide order, food, and medical care to survivors. The key difference between *The Day After* and Operation Cue has to do with the nature of "survival." While Cue argued that life was possible after nuclear attack and promoted an idea that nuclear war was simply another form of everyday risk (alongside weather, fire, and

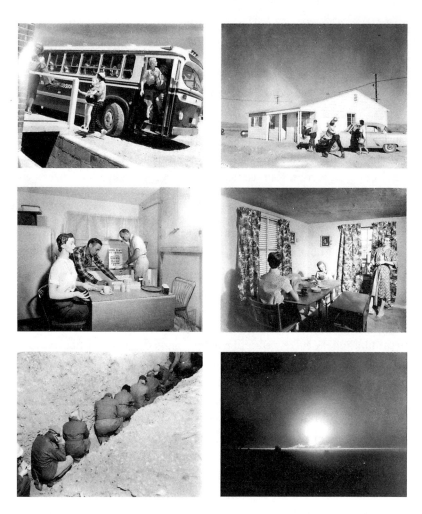

8.4 Photographic sequence of Operation Cue, 1955. Photo courtesy of the U.S. National Archives and Records Administration.

8.5 Soviet nuclear attack. Still from the television drama *The Day After*.

traffic accidents), *The Day After* questioned whether life was worth living after nuclear war.[39] The central protagonist of the story, a medical doctor played by Jason Robards, is left in the final scene dying of radiation sickness, collapsed in what might be the ruins of his former home, his wife and children dead from the attack. No triumphal narrative of survival and reinvention here. Instead, the final moment of the film issues yet another warning: "The catastrophic events you have witnessed are, in all likelihood, less severe than the destruction that would actually occur in the event of a full nuclear strike against the United States. It is hoped that the images of this film will inspire the nations of this earth, their peoples and leaders, to find the means to avert the fateful day." Thus, the "realism" of *The Day After* is revealed in the end to be a deception—just as it was in the *Operation Cue* film a generation earlier—as the filmmakers are forced to admit that the horror of nuclear war is ultimately unrepresentable.

The simulated realism of the film perfectly illustrates Derrida's claim that nuclear war is "fabulously textual" because until it happens it can only be imagined and once it happens it marks the end of the human archive.[40] As the only "remainderless event," nuclear war is thus in the realm of the sublime, ungraspable and subject only to displacements, compensations, and misrecognitions. Thus, by rehearsing nuclear war in the imagination or via civil defense, one does not master the event or its aftermath. Rather, one domesticates an image of a postnuclear world that "stands in" for the actual failure of the imagination to be able to conceive of the end. This postnuclear imagination is necessarily an arena of cultural work, as early Cold War officials immediately recognized, one which promotes an idea of order out of the sublime and often becomes a space of pure ideology. To this end, the consistency of the nuclear tropes presented in *The Day After*, as well as the nationalization of the televised event, document the multigenerational power of nuclear ruins in the American imaginary. For a full generation after Operation Cue, filmmakers could rehearse with startling specificity the entire 1950s program of Civil Defense and provoke a national conversation about life after nuclear war. The state was no longer needed to enact this national melodrama of destruction; its terms were already installed in American culture and simply subject to citation and repositioning. The entertainment industry could now provide the firestorm and fallout as "special effects," rehearsing the lessons of nuclear crisis that a live television audience first experienced in 1955 via a real atomic bomb. This time, however, the ruins were engineered not to "emotionally inoculate" Americans to nuclear war, but rather to shock them into action during the nuclear emergency of the early 1980s.

Put differently, in response to the Reagan administration's escalating arms race and talk of "winnable" nuclear wars was a cultural return to the images and logics of Operation Cue, mobilized this time as a call to political action rather than normalization.[41] Thus, while the form and content of cinematic nuclear destruction remains unchanged from 1955 to 1983, its emotional project has been inverted from promoting the docility of the citizen-subject to mobilizing a national community before the bombs fall. *The Day After* reenacted the national melodrama articulated in Operation Cue twenty-eight years earlier with remarkable precision, but it did so not to produce a "bomb proof" society, but rather as a de facto form of nuclear critique. Similarly, activist groups (including Physicians for Social Responsibility and the Nuclear Weapons Freeze Campaign) used depictions of nuclear warfare—including the targeting and blast damage maps of U.S. cities, and medical analyses of radiation injuries—to counter the escalating military budgets and nuclear tensions of the late Cold War.[42] In other words, the calibration of the emotional-management project was no longer controlled solely by the government, thus allowing counterformulations using the same texts and images that originally enabled the Cold War cultural project. Nuclear ruins are revealed here to be the very grammar of nuclear discourse

in the United States — enabling both pronuclear and antinuclear projects —
inevitably deployed to articulate the affective terms of national belonging.
For despite its implicit nuclear critique, The Day After continues to mobilize a
nuclear-bombed America as a call to community rather than as a marker of
the end of sociability itself.

Afterimage 2: Armageddon/Deep Impact (1998)

> There was a tacit agreement, equally binding on everyone, that the true state
> of material and moral ruin in which the country found itself was not to be
> described. The darkest aspects of the final act of destruction, as experienced
> by the great majority of the German population, remained under a kind of
> taboo like a shameful family secret, a secret that could not even be privately
> acknowledged.
>
> —W. G. SEBALD, On the Natural History of Destruction

Questioning the near total silence in German literature about everyday life in
the bombed-out ruins of the Second World War, W. G. Sebald finds an "extraordinary faculty for self-anesthesia shown by a community that seemed to
have emerged from a war of annihilation without any signs of psychological
impairment."[43] He attributes this absence of commentary (about life in the
ruins of Dresden and other German cities that were firebombed) to a collective understanding that it was Germany who pioneered mass bombing years
earlier in Guernica, Warsaw, and Belgrade.[44] Thus, the national repression he
interrogates is doubled — that of life in the postwar ruins and that of a prior
position as mass bomber — linking trauma and destruction as part of the
same psychosocial legacy. The United States — a country that did not itself
experience mass bombing in the Second World War, but did conduct such
bombings using both conventional and nuclear weapons — took an opposite national-cultural route in the Cold War. For while nuclear war did not
occur, rather than repress the bomb American culture proliferated its meaning and influence. The bomb became an intimate part of American popular
and political culture, a set of ideas, images, and institutions, installed in the
1950s that soon functioned outside the direct control of the national security state.[45] In other words, we live today in the world made by the Cold War,
a global project that engineered everyday life — and life itself — around the
technological means of apocalyptic destruction.[46]

What are we to make, for example, of the Hollywood films of the 1990s —
the first period in the nuclear age in which U.S. national security was not

structured in relationship to a nuclear-armed, external enemy—which none-theless repetitively enact the destruction of the nation on film? While we no longer detonate atomic bombs on fabricated cities populated with manne-quins, we do have yearly spectacles in which America's cities are reduced to smoldering ruins all in the name of fun. The Hollywood blockbuster—with its fearsome life-ending asteroids, aliens, earthquakes, floods, and wars— allows Americans to rehearse destruction of their nation-state much as their parents and grandparents did in the 1950s and 1980s. These yearly techno-aesthetic displays of finely rendered destruction are a unique form of Ameri-can expressive culture. Only U.S. cinema deploys the cutting-edge techno-logical achievements of computer-generated imagery in order to visualize the destruction of its cities, and it does so with such fetishistic glee.[47]

Consider 1998, a year in which the United States was cinematically at-tacked twice by asteroids—in Armageddon (directed by Michael Bay) and Deep Impact (directed by Mimi Leder)—the second and eighth most successful films of the year at the box office (figs. 8.6–8.7). In both cases, life on earth is threatened from outer space and saved only at the last minute by the heroics of Americans armed with nuclear weapons. While Armageddon uses the threat to the planet as a vehicle for resuscitating working-class masculinity as pro-tectors of the nation qua planet (oil riggers are sent via the space shuttle to destroy the asteroid with atomic bombs), Deep Impact is a study of civil de-fense and individual sacrifice right out of Operation Cue. In both cases, what is striking is that the destruction of the United States is presented as a form of entertainment and redemptive play. A series of summer films in the 1990s similarly rehearsed the destruction of the United States and demonstrated the necessity of U.S. nuclear weapons, suggesting that decade as a moment of psychic and cultural release from the Cold War arms race.[48] In the 1990s Hollywood could work out the details of nuclear war (and various allegorized nuclear threats) with new computer-generated precision—precisely because nuclear terror no longer had the meaning it had had for a previous genera-tion. In the immediate post–Cold War moment, in other words, life did not hang so oppressively in the nuclear balance, and thus the cinematic imagina-tion was freed to explore the end of the United States in a new way. Cold War nuclear cinema always had a moral point to make about the nuclear state of emergency: not only was nuclear war always marked as an object of distinct seriousness, but the detonation of the bomb was marked as a political, ethi-cal, and technological failure of the Cold War system. In striking contrast, post–Cold War films have no purpose other than patriotism and pleasure;

8.6–8.7 New York under attack. Stills from the films *Armageddon* and *Deep Impact*.

they seek to reinstall American identity through mass violence, suggesting that it is only threat and reactions to threat that can create national community.[49]

Regardless of form (asteroid or tsunami or alien invader), these apocalyptic spectacles function as nuclear texts because they use mass destruction as a means of mobilizing the United States as a global superpower. As allegories of nuclear war, they both reproduce the emotional language of nuclear threat (mass death as a vehicle for establishing national community) and allow a productive misrecognition of its political content. This filmic genre also inevitably reinforces through aestheticized politics the ever-present need for war and the ubiquity of external enemies with apocalyptic power. And in doing so, these texts relegitimize the need for nuclear weapons in the United States, while offering an image of the United States as a reluctant superpower forced into global military action for the greater good. As a maelstrom of meteorites devastate New York in *Armageddon*, for example, a taxi driver yells to no one in particular: "We at war! Saddam Hussein is bombing us!" This scene from 1998 prefigures the second Bush administration's successful (but fabricated) effort to link the terrorist attacks on New York and Washington in 2001 to the Iraqi government of Saddam Hussein. Naming the enemy in this way (as science fiction or state propaganda) underscores the ideological alignment between the Hollywood blockbuster and the U.S. military, which both rely on rehearsing threat as a means of stabilizing their industries.[50] Cinematic viewers, as Benjamin saw so early on, experience such ideological projects in a state of distraction, allowing both the covert habituation of ideas and a broader aestheticizing of politics in support of increasing militarization and war.[51]

One afterimage of the Cold War emotional-management campaign is found in this continued commitment to, and pleasure in, making nuclear ruins, and then searching the wreckage for signs about the collective future. The nuclear logics of the Cold War continue to haunt American society, informing how individuals experience acts of mass violence and how the federal government then engages the world. Nuclear cinema in the 1990s transforms anonymous mass death into a vehicle for individuals to demonstrate their moral character and for the nation to be regenerated through apocalyptic threat. Indeed, the pleasure of post–Cold War nuclear cinema is precisely in witnessing the destruction of the United States, then walking out of the theater into the unbroken world. Unlike viewers of Operation Cue in 1955 and of The Day After in 1983, the viewers of Armageddon and Deep Impact were not addressed as citizens who needed to demonstrate their civic virtue by performing nuclear fear. Rather, the emotional-management strategy was transformed into a form of posttraumatic play, with the destruction of the nation now presented as a diversion rather than a serious threat or opportunity for political mobilization. Nonetheless, it is important to recognize the remarkable coherence of the nuclear images from 1955 through 1998 to see the long-term effects of the Cold War emotional-management strategy. It is also important to interrogate the long-term national cultural effects of rehearsing mass violence in this manner, of repetitively producing images of destroyed U.S. cities to constitute both pleasure and national community.

Epilogue

> Facing clear evidence of peril, we cannot wait for the final proof,
> the smoking gun that could come in the form of a mushroom cloud.
> —PRESIDENT GEORGE W. BUSH, address to the nation on Iraq
> on 7 October 2002

Be prepared to be bombed. Be prepared to go back to the Stone Age.

—PRESIDENT MUSHARRAF OF PAKISTAN, reporting on a message
delivered to him from the U.S. State Department immediately after 9/11

Reclaiming the emotional history of the atomic bomb is crucial today, as nuclear fear has been amplified to enable a variety of political projects at precisely the moment American memory of the bomb has become impossibly blurred. In the United States, nuclear fear has recently been used to justify preemptive war and unlimited domestic surveillance, a worldwide system of secret prisons, and the practices of rendition, torture, and assassination. But what today do Americans actually know or remember of the bomb? We live not in the ruins produced by Soviet ICBMs, but rather in the emotional ruins of the Cold War as an intellectual and social project. The half-century-long project to install and articulate the nation through contemplating its violent end has colonized the present. The terrorist attacks on New York City and Washington in 2001 may have produced a political consensus that "the Cold War is over" and a formal declaration of a counterterrorism project.[52] But American reactions to those attacks were structured by a multigenerational state project to harness the fear of mass death to divergent political and military industrial agendas. By evoking the image of the mushroom cloud to enable the invasion of Iraq, President George W. Bush appealed directly to citizens' nuclear fear, a cultural product of the very Cold War nuclear standoff he formally disavowed in inaugurating the new counterterrorist state. The mushroom-cloud imagery, as well as the totalizing immediacy of the threat in his presentation, worked to redeploy a cultural memory of apocalyptic nuclear threat (established during the four decades of the Soviet-American nuclear arms race) as part of the new "war on terror." The new color-coded terrorist warning system (first proposed by Project East River in 1952 to deal with Soviet bombers) and the Homeland Security Administration's transformation of shampoo bottles on planes into a totalizing threat are official efforts to install and regulate fear in everyday life.[53] In this regard, the "war on terror" has been conducted largely as an emotional-management campaign in the United States, using the tropes and logics developed during the early Cold War to enable a new kind of American geopolitical project. The "war on terror" redirects but also reiterates the American assumptions about mass violence and democracy I have explored in this essay.

If the September 11 attacks on New York and Washington felt strangely familiar to many U.S. citizens, it was because American society has been imaginatively rehearsing the destruction of these cities for over three generations: in the Civil Defense campaigns of the early and late Cold War, as well as in the Hollywood blockbusters of the 1990s, which destroyed these cities each summer with increasing nuance and detail. The genealogy of this form of entertainment is traumatic; it goes back to the specific way in which the United States entered the nuclear age with the atomic bombings of Hiroshima and Nagasaki, and to the specific propaganda campaigns informing nuclear threat throughout the Cold War. Indeed, the ease with which the 9/11 attacks were nationalized as part of a nuclear discourse by the second Bush administration has much to do with this legacy.[54] Not coincidentally, the two graphic measures of nuclear blast damage most frequently used during the Cold War were the Pentagon and the New York City skyline.[55] Figures 8.8 and 8.9, for example, are taken from the U.S. Atomic Energy Commission (AEC) campaign to document the size of the first U.S. hydrogen bomb test from 1952. Fourteen true-to-scale versions of the Pentagon, identified by the AEC as the largest building in the world, are placed inside the blast crater (the former Elugelab Island) to document its size, while the New York skyline is used to demonstrate the vast horizontal and vertical scope of the detonation. The events of 9/11 were easily nationalized and transformed into a nuclear discourse precisely because our security culture had imagined and rehearsed attacks on Washington and New York for generations, and because the specific symbols in the attacks—the Pentagon and the tallest building in the New York skyline—were also used by the nuclear state for three generations as part of its emotional-management strategy. The second Bush administration, in other words, mobilized a well-established logic of nuclear attack to pursue its policy objectives, translating discrete, nonnuclear threats into the emotional equivalent of the Cold War nuclear crisis.

For a nation that constructs itself via discourses of ruination, it should not be a surprise to see the exportation of ruins on a global scale. As President Musharraf clearly understood, the "with us or against us" logics of the Bush administration in 2001 left no ambiguity about the costs of Pakistan not aligning with the sole global superpower. The threat to reduce Pakistan to a "Stone Age" ruin is the alternative, international deployment of nuclear fear, constituting a U.S. promise to reduce the country to a prenational, pretechnological state. Thus, the United States enters the twenty-first century as a nation both fascinated and traumatized by nuclear ruins. It transforms real and imagined mass death into a nationalized space, and supports a political culture that believes bombing campaigns can produce democracy abroad. It is simultaneously terrorized by nuclear weapons and threatens to use them. The U.S. military both wages preemptive war over nascent "weapons of mass

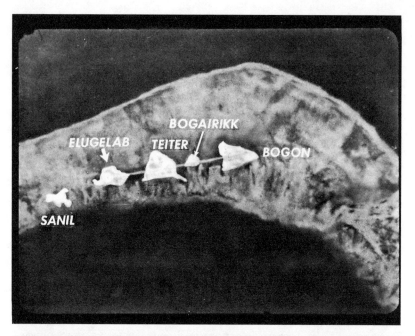

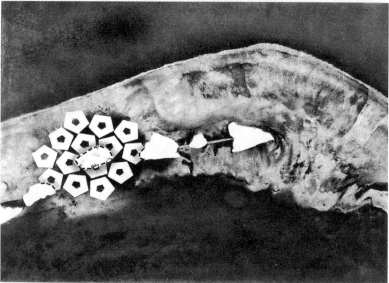

8.8 Before and after images of the first U.S. hydrogen bomb explosion, with multiple Pentagons depicted in the blast crater, 1952. Photo courtesy of the U.S. National Archives and Records Administration.

8.9 Blast radius of the first U.S. hydrogen bomb explosion set against the New York skyline, 1952. Photo courtesy of the U.S. National Archive and Records Administration.

destruction" programs and is preparing to build a new generation of U.S. nuclear weapons.[56] American society is today neither "atomic bomb proof" nor capable of engaging nuclear technologies as a global problem of governance. Instead, U.S. citizens live today in the emotional residues of the Cold War nuclear arms race, which can only address them as fearful docile bodies. Thus, even in the twenty-first century, Americans remain caught between terror and fear, trapped in the psychosocial space defined by the once and future promise of nuclear ruins.

Notes

This essay is reproduced by permission of the American Anthropological Association. It originally appeared in *Cultural Anthropology* 23, no. 2 (2008): 361–98, and cannot be used for sale or further reproduction.

Research for this essay was enabled by a Research and Writing Grant from the John D. and Catherine T. MacArthur Foundation. I am grateful to Ann Stoler for her invitation to participate in this volume, as well as for her intellectual engagement. Many thanks to Mike Fortun and Kim Fortun for their editorial care, and to Shawn Smith for her critical readings of this essay.

1. For example, see Glasstone and Dolan, *The Effects of Nuclear Weapons*; Kahn, *On Thermonuclear War*; Vanderbilt, *Survival City*.

2. The United States conducted 1,054 nuclear detonations (in addition to bombing Hiroshima and Nagasaki) from 1945 to 1992, with 928 explosions conducted at the Nevada Test Site. On the global health effects of this program, see Richards L. Miller, *Under the Cloud*; Makhijani, Hu, and Yih, *Nuclear Wastelands*; Advisory Committee on Human Radiation Experiments, *The Human Radiation Experiments*; Makhijani and Schwartz, "Victims of the Bomb"; and Masco, *The Nuclear Borderlands*.

3. See Keeney, *The Doomsday Scenario*; and Office of Technology Assessment, *The Effects of Nuclear War*, for damage assessments of a potential Soviet nuclear strike on the United States.

4. Stoler with Bond, "Refractions Off Empire."

5. My understanding of photographic "afterimages" has been developed in conversation with Shawn Michelle Smith, *American Archives*.

6. Benjamin, "The Work of Art in the Age of Mechanical Reproduction," 246. For a detailed discussion of Walter Benjamin's approach to the politics of visual culture, see Buck-Morss, *The Dialectics of Seeing*, as well as her reading of art in the years before the Cold War, Buck-Morss, *Dreamworld and Catastrophe*.

7. On the constitution of the Cold War state, see Friedberg, *In the Shadow of the Garrison State*; Leslie, *The Cold War and American Science*; Schwartz, *Atomic Audit*; and Gaddis, *Strategies of Containment*.

8. For the NSC 68 document, as well as detailed commentary, see Ernest R. May, *American Cold War Strategy*; for critical analysis, see Brands, "The Age of Vulnerability"; and for a review of the concept of "containment," see Gaddis, *Strategies of Containment*.

9. For historical and cultural analysis of the U.S. civil defense programs during the Cold War, see Oakes, *The Imaginary War*; McEnaney, *Civil Defense Begins at Home*; Garrison, *Bracing for Armageddon*; George, *Awaiting Armageddon*; Grossman, *Neither Dead Nor Red*; Krugler, *This Is Only a Test*; Scheiback, *Atomic Narratives and American Youth*.

10. Oakes, *The Imaginary War*, 34; and also George, *Awaiting Armageddon*.

11. Associated Universities, *Report of the Project East River*.

12. Oakes, *The Imaginary War*, 47.

13. See Associated Universities, *Report of the Project East River*; Oakes, *The Imaginary War*, 62–63.

14. Peterson, "Panic."

15. Osgood, *Total Cold War*; Craig, *Destroying the Village*; Hewlett and Holl, *Atoms for Peace and War*.

16. In 1956 a report published by the Panel on the Human Effects of Nuclear Weapons Development, which imagined a Soviet attack in 1959 in which ninety major cities would be destroyed and fifty million people killed, concluded: "In the event of a massive nuclear attack on the United States, of the proportions assumed above, without drastically improved preparation of the people, support of the National Government and of the war effort would be in jeopardy, and national disintegration might well result" (*Human Effects of Nuclear Weapons Development*, 9). The panel then argued

that the problem was how to incorporate the possibility of a Soviet sneak attack into the "feelings" of citizens, thus allowing atomic warfare to be naturalized as part of the everyday world (see Vandercook, "Making the Very Best of the Very Worst"). One could productively compare the early Cold War studies to recent studies of nuclear attack: see Meade and Molander, *Considering the Effects of a Catastrophic Terrorist Attack*, for example, which models a ten-kiloton nuclear explosion in Los Angeles. The study, by Rand, concludes that the effects of the blast would overwhelm all services and render a $1 trillion blow to the U.S. economy.

17. Val Peterson, the first director of the Federal Civil Defense Agency, described the media campaign for atomic civil defense as "the greatest mass educational effort" in U.S. history (quoted in Garrison, *Bracing for Armageddon*, 36). In this regard, the civil defense program was also a laboratory for exploring how to mobilize and control a mass society.

18. Federal Civil Defense Administration, *Annual Report for 1955*, 78.

19. See Braw, *The Atomic Bomb Suppressed*; Weller, *First into Nagasaki*; and the 2006 documentary film *White Light, Black Rain: The Destruction of Hiroshima and Nagasaki* (directed by Steven Okazaki), which details the history of censorship and presents some of the once prohibited film footage.

20. Janis, *Air War and Emotional Stress*, 220.

21. Martin and Latham, *Strategy for Survival*, 182.

22. Andrew Grossman has underscored how governmental, media, and industry communication explicitly sought to harmonize their civil defense messages, providing a reinforcing series of messages across the media spectrum (*Neither Dead Nor Red*, 47). This worked both to reinforce the civil defense project and to reduce the opportunities for critique; see also Keever, *News Zero*; Scheiback, *Atomic Narratives and American Youth*; and Rojecki, *Silencing the Opposition*.

23. See Oakes, *The Imaginary War*; McEnaney, *Civil Defense Begins at Home*; and Tracy D. Davis, "Between History and Event."

24. Federal Civil Defense Administration, *Annual Report for 1955*; and Krugler, *This Is Only a Test*, 126.

25. For a history of the antinuclear movement see, Rojecki, *Silencing the Opposition*; Katz, *Ban the Bomb*; as well as Wittner, *Toward Abolition*; Wittner, *Resisting the Bomb*; Wittner, *One World or None*.

26. Dee Garrison, in *Bracing for Armageddon*, argues that the civil defense programs of the Cold War should be judged as failures because no nationwide system of shelters was ever built. I would argue that the project of civil defense was about building not a new urban infrastructure, but rather an emotional one. To this end, the utilization of the civil defense was much more successful, installing a set of ideas and images about nuclear warfare that maintained public support for the nuclear state through the end of the Cold War and provided a set of ideological resources that the Bush administration relied on to initiate its "war on terror."

27. See Federal Civil Defense Administration, *Operation Cue*; and Federal Civil Defense Administration, *Annual Report for 1955*.

28. See Garrison on the Mother's Protest against the Civil Defense Project (*Bracing for Armageddon*, 94–96); Laura McEnaney's extensive conversation about the role of women and the militarization of the home, in *Civil Defense Begins at Home*; Elaine May, *Homeward Bound*, on the domestic version of "containment"; and Scheiback, *Atomic Narratives and American Youth*, on the effects of civil defense on youth culture. See Cohn, "Sex and Death in the Rational World of Defense Intellectuals," for a discussion of gender in the language of Cold War defense intellectuals; and Orr, *Panic Diaries*, for a remarkable study of "panic" in Cold War psychology and nation-building.

29. Federal Civil Defense Administration, *Operation Cue* (15-minute film), 1955, http://archive.org/details/Operatio1955.

30. McEnney, *Civil Defense Begins at Home*, 109.

31. Ibid., 111.

32. Schmitt, *Effects of Nuclear Explosions on Frozen Foods*, 3.

33. Federal Civil Defense Administration, *Operation Cue*, 67.

34. Ibid., 75.

35. The project to test the cognitive effects of witnessing an exploding atomic bomb on citizens was a small part of a larger military project, which involved thousands of troops at the Nevada Test Site. Over a series of aboveground tests, soldiers were involved in "atomic warfare" exercises. They were also tested for the cognitive effects of being exposed to the visual image of the blast. In some cases, this involved simple cognitive drills administered minutes after the explosion or timing basic military activities, like dismantling and reassembling a rifle. Thus, across a wide spectrum of public and military projects, the national security state was testing the limits of participation, and conditioning emotions and bodies to the atomic bomb.

36. Garrison, *Bracing for Armageddon*, 93–95.

37. On the politics of atmospheric fallout during aboveground nuclear testing, see Masco, *The Nuclear Borderlands*; Richards L. Miller, *Under the Cloud*; Hewlett and Holl, *Atoms for Peace and War*; Kraus, Mehling, and El-Assal, "Mass Media and the Fallout Controversy"; Bentz et al., "Some Civil Defense Problems in the Nation's Capital Following Widespread Thermonuclear Attack"; and Makhijani and Schwartz, "Victims of the Bomb."

38. Rubin and Cummings, "Nuclear War and Its Consequences on Television News."

39. Indeed, one of the most powerful voices in the renewed antinuclear movement of the 1980s was Physicians for Social Responsibility (PSR), which devoted its energies to publicizing the health effects of nuclear war by offering detailed descriptions of probable attacks on American cities. For its public-health campaign against nuclear war, PSR won the Nobel Peace Prize. In other words, PSR used the same elements of the civil defense campaigns of the 1950s, but provided more detailed information about radiation injury and casualty figures, in order to mobilize resistance to the renewed nuclear project of the Reagan administration. See Forrow and Sidel, "Medicine and Nuclear War."

40. Derrida, "No Apocalypse, Not Now."

41. See Sheer, *With Enough Shovels*.

42. In response to the Nuclear Weapons Freeze Campaign, the Reagan administration pursued a new emotional-management strategy in the form of the Strategic Defense Initiative (SDI), which promised an end to the arms race by installing a system of space-based lasers to shoot down intercontinental ballistic missiles (see FitzGerald, *Way Out There in the Blue*). Though Reagan offered SDI to the public as a near-term technological fix to the nuclear standoff with the Soviet Union—a way out of the nuclear danger—it was never a realistic proposal. Over twenty-five years and $100 billion later it has yet to hit a real-world target, but it has served the emotional needs of its constituency very well, allowing an aggressive pursuit of nuclear weapons technology and the militarization of space all the while praising the goal of disarmament. *The Day After*, the Nuclear Weapons Freeze Campaign, and SDI were all in various ways emotional-management campaigns that drew on the images of nuclear destruction produced during the aboveground testing regime to mobilize a response to the nuclear crisis of the 1980s. Rather than moving past Operation Cue, each of these project redeployed the strategies of the early Cold War state to enable their political projects: activists working for disarmament, and the state working to maintain support for the Cold War arms race.

43. Sebald, *On the Natural History of Destruction*, 11.

44. Ibid.

45. For example, see Evans, *Celluloid Mushroom Clouds*; Sontag, "The Imagination of Disaster"; Brians, *Nuclear Holocausts*.

46. See Masco, *The Nuclear Borderlands*.

47. The destruction of cities is a recurring theme in the nuclear cinema of Japan, but is not mobilized as part of a militarized nation-building campaign as it is in the United States (see Broderick, *Hibakusha Cinema*). I would also note that there is a fundamental difference between the "disaster movie" and nuclear cinema in the United States. The disaster film uses destruction as a means of establishing drama at an individual level, while nuclear cinema always nationalizes its content via a friend-enemy configuration. Thus, while a disaster movie has heroic individuals, the ultimate project of nuclear cinema is to establish and mobilize a national community through mass violence. For critical analysis of nuclear cinema, see Evans, *Celluloid Mushroom Clouds*; Sontag, "The Imagination of Disaster." See Taylor, "Nuclear Pictures and Metapictures," on nuclear photography; and Virilio, *War and Cinema*, on war and perception.

48. Compare Rogin, *Independence Day*; Doug Davis, "'A Hundred Million Hydrogen Bombs'"; and Mellor, "Colliding Worlds."

49. On the American politics of regeneration through violence, see Slotkin, *Regeneration through Violence*; Rogin, *Independence Day*; and Rogin, *Ronald Reagan, the Movie, and Other Episodes in Political Demonology*.

50. *Armageddon*, for example, was supported by NASA, as well as the Department of Defense, which allowed the producer Jerry Bruckheimer to film on location in military installations in exchange for script changes that favored the armed services. See Robb, *Operation Hollywood*, 94–95, for a discussion of the changes to the film script made in

exchange for support from the Pentagon. See also Rogin, *Ronald Reagan, the Movie, and Other Episodes in Political Demonology*, for studies in Cold War cinema, and his detailed reading (*Independence Day*) of the militarized gender and race politics in the 1996 film *Independence Day*.

51. Benjamin, "Theses on the Philosophy of History." See also Sontag, "The Imagination of Disaster."

52. The Bush doctrine of preemptive war, first articulated in 2002, formally ended the Cold War doctrines of containment and deterrence that had defined U.S. foreign policy since the 1950s (see Gaddis, *Strategies of Containment*).

53. In August 2006, after British authorities broke up a terrorist plot to smuggle explosive chemicals onto an airline, the Department of Homeland Security raised the threat level to its highest point, "red," and the Transportation Security Administration (TSA) banned fluids from domestic U.S. flights. The British plot was in the very early discussion phase and not a viable threat to passenger safety, yet the response from DHS and TSA was total (see the transcript of a press conference held on 10 August 2006, "Remarks by Homeland Security Secretary Michael Chertoff, Attorney General Alberto Gonzales, FBI Director Robert Mueller, and Assistant Secretary for TSA Kip Hawley," Transportation Security Administration website, http://www.tsa .gov/press/speeches/dhs_press_conference_08102006.shtm). This totalizing response to a fantasy threat does not make sense as a security strategy, but is an excellent illustration of the mobilization of affect and the demand for public docility that support the "war on terror." For expert security analysis of British and American reactions to the liquid explosive "plot," see Nafeez Ahmed, "Sources: August Terror Plot Is a 'Fiction' Underscoring Police Failures," *Raw Story*, 18 September 2006, http://www .rawstory.com/news/2006/Sources_August_Terror_Plot_Fiction_Underscoring _0918.html; and Bruce Schneier, "Details on the UK Liquid Terrorist Plot," Schneier on Security (blog), 6 August 2007, http://www.schneier.com/blog/archives/2007/08 /details_on_the_1.html.

54. See Kaplan, "Homeland Insecurities."

55. Compare Eden, "City on Fire."

56. In fall 2006, under directives from the Bush administration, Los Alamos National Laboratory and Lawrence Livermore National Laboratory submitted to the Department of Energy their first new nuclear weapons designs since the end of the Cold War. This was the first major step toward a return to nuclear testing, and perhaps underground nuclear testing. For a copy of the redacted 2002 Nuclear Posture Review see http://www.fas.org/blog/ssp/united_states/NPR2001re.pdf.

The Future in Ruins

Under the lowering, thundery sky, Harsud . . . [appears] like a scene out of a Mar-
quez novel . . . behind the blind buffalo, silhouetted against the sky, the bare bones
of a broken town. A town turned inside out, its privacy ravaged, its innards exposed.
Personal belongings, beds, cupboards, clothes, photographs, pots and pans lie on
the street. . . . The insides of houses lie rudely exposed. . . . Perched on the concrete frames of wrecked buildings, men, like flightless birds, are hammering, sawing,
smoking, talking. If you didn't know what was happening, you could be forgiven for
thinking that Harsud was being built, not broken. That it had been hit by an earthquake and its citizens were rebuilding it. . . . The people of Harsud are razing their
town to the ground. Themselves. The very young and the very old sit on heaps
of broken brick. The able-bodied are frantically busy. They are tearing apart their
homes, their lives, their past, their stories. . . . There is an eerie, brittle numbness
to the bustle. It masks the government's ruthlessness and people's despair.
—ARUNDHATI ROY, "The Road to Harsud"

I first encountered the village Jetprole in a sumptuously illustrated, center-
spread story about an obscure yet important archaeological project in the
Telangana region of the southern Indian state of Andhra Pradesh that appeared in a major national English-language newspaper. The project, known
widely among Indian archaeologists simply as the "salvage archaeology
project," involved the physical removal and transplantation of more than
a hundred monumental temple complexes from their original locations in

9.1 Jetprole submerged: Srisailam Dam reservoir in full spate, July 2006.
Photo by author.

village sites that had been submerged due to the construction of the Srisailam megadam, several kilometers upstream (fig. 9.1). Subsequent to their transplantation, the temples were also "revivified" by ritual reconsecration performed by priests handpicked by the Andhra Pradesh state government. By the time the article appeared, the village sites had been submerged for almost a decade beneath the dam's reservoir lake. Most of the villages had disappeared both in name and as communities; others had merged and rearranged themselves as communities in the course of resettlement. More than 150,000 people were displaced as a result of the submergence. A large number of people had left the region altogether as they lost lands, homes, the means for livelihood, and, by many accounts, the will to continue living in such close proximity to the remains of a settled, if often difficult life.

Yet the newspaper article presented this reconstruction and resettlement project as an unqualified success, and Jetprole in particular stood out as a model village—a place where a historically continuous community had resettled voluntarily and that was chosen, for that reason among others, as a site for an open-air "temple-museum" complex. The perfect convergence of modern technology with the preservation of a carefully selected and curated past received unqualified praise whenever journalists and archaeologists brought the project to the public's attention. Within a vast compound at the edge of this resettled village, the Andhra Pradesh State Department of

Archaeology and Museums had reconstructed a fifth of the "rescued" monumental temple complexes. In addition, archaeologists also removed, reconstructed, and transplanted Jetprole's own monumental temple, the Jetprole Madanagopalaswamy Temple, although they deviated from their principles by reconstructing this particular temple within the space of newly resettled village community of Jetprole, rather than in a museum compound along with temples of the same period and style. The transplanted monuments in Jetprole could therefore be placed in two different categories: first, the "archaeology temples" that were reconstructed within the temple-museum complex; second, the Jetprole temple complex, which was transplanted within the resettled village space.[1] The juxtaposition of these differently placed monuments also made Jetprole a place of special interest and a model site for showcasing both the technological transformations enabled by the modernization project and respect for the village spaces and traditions despite the destruction of their everyday material environments.

However, these archaeologically manufactured ruins, made from existing historical materials, both veiled and sur-veilled a historic and psychic landscape that was far more complicated than that implied by the successful archaeological rescue operation of the temples. Embedded within the geography of the new village are also the (in)visible remains of the old site—of homes, fields, village temples, a monumental fort, and royal palaces—that attest to Jetprole's own past as the capital of a "little kingdom," a political entity that was between a feudal estate and a princely state in its scale and political impact.[2] The old village site, which lies beneath the placid lake created by the dam for part of the year, resurfaces seasonally during the dry months, from March to July, creating a dramatic theater for the play of local imaginaries and, more practically, providing much-needed additional land for cultivation, even though cultivation of the submerged land is illegal. The reservoir and the submerged village site are both easily visible as well as just a short walk from the new site and thus are integral to the new village. The remains are always present in some way, even when they are not being used or actively traversed.

Unmaking Jetprole

What is the relationship between these remains that surface regularly and recurrently and the museum site on which the successful claims of the nation's development project rest? Arundhati Roy's image of Harsud, a town actively being broken, is a powerful reminder of the status of the material debris that remains after acts of deliberate and willful destruction, especially those undertaken in the name of the public good. Like Jetprole, Harsud, a seven-hundred-year-old town in the state of Madhya Pradesh, was slated to be submerged by the Narmada Sagar Dam, which is a part of India's largest dam system, second in scale only to China's Three Gorges project. Roy argues in the article that these images make "visible" a normally invisible relationship between development and destruction.

Since independence, projects like the Sardar Sarovar (of which the Narmada Sagar Dam is a part) and Srisailam have displaced nearly thirty-five million people. From the state's point of view, Harsud's material destruction appears only as a stepping-stone to "development" and "progress." One could be forgiven for thinking that this was a town being built, not broken, as Roy puts it. For the state, the material processes of destruction and the remains they leave in their wake are willfully acknowledged not as ruins, but simply as the costs of development. Bland and neutral categories like "resettlement," "rehabilitation," and "project-affected person" come to be used both officially and casually when referring to displaced persons and processes of forced resettlement. For the first time in postcolonial history, the story of towns like Harsud also makes visible the longer and deeper history of the costs of development paid by places like Jetprole, as social movements protesting the dams over the River Narmada in the mid- to late 1990s have made development projects a major political issue, contesting the rights of the state to trample citizens' rights at will.

This essay is an ethnographic exploration of the particular predicament of Jetprole—what it would mean to acknowledge the remains of the old village as ruins, or as the debris of a sustained and protracted process of destruction undertaken in the name of progress and modernization. When I was doing fieldwork in Jetprole, more than two decades after the completion of the dam, modernization remained an elusive goal. The archaeological salvage operation was the one concrete sign of the achievements of modern technologies, aside from the dam itself. But its benefits for the villagers were ambiguous at best. Despite the evident grandeur of these resurrected ruins, Jetprole and its people remain remote and unconnected to the circuits of development, heritage tourism, and investment. Their isolation and desperation is all the more evident thirty years after the dam, as the region is now an active node in a Maoist war against the iniquitous policies of the nation-state and its political technologies. Yet the dam itself and the damage it has wrought on this region are accepted matter-of-factly in everyday conversations.

But the silence surrounding the remains of the old village is a veil. As people moved in and out and around these ruins, their keen understanding of the effects of the dam became increasingly articulated both in quotidian conversations with me and in a special repertoire of poetic and musical narratives still performed on ritual occasions in the village. In these articulations, a sharp contrast emerged between a modernist sense of the future, expressed implicitly in the hopes of progress and modernization through development projects on the one hand and, on the other, in a sense of being arrested or imprisoned in a space that was neither progressive nor evidently continuous with their past. This modernist sense of the future however was clearly tied, through the archaeological project, to the equally significant work of "taming" or containing the past so as to limit any deleterious and feudal pull it might exert on the future. I focus on the persistent thread presented by these articulations about the future in the midst of ruins. The proximity of the abandoned and the rescued, the contrast between the abject poverty of the villages and the grandiose claims of heritage bring together two very different projects and the different senses of the future they engender into a "relational history."[3]

Such schizophrenic landscapes of modernist development are neither particular to India nor unique to Jetprole. The drama created by this village's particular geography resonates with similar, arresting images across the world where modernist constructions or ancient sites reclaimed as national heritage stand in an analogous relation to erased local histories and the material tokens of those histories. But here in Jetprole, the juxtaposition between the abandoned and the rescued provides a particularly vivid context within which to explore the texture of material traces and their enduring distribution within everyday life, within the space of that which is left behind and apparently intact. By contrasting these traces, not officially recognized as marks of ruination, with the care provided for the ruins that signify vestiges of national history, we can track certain complicities between the colonial project of archaeology, its contemporary practice in India, and the political technologies of the nation-state's agenda for development, modernization, and attracting transnational investment capital.

These complicities and the entanglements between colonial practices such as archaeology and modernist ones of development, committed to a project of modernization at all costs, raise questions about the straightforward mapping of the effects of colonial history on a postcolonial landscape. The expectations postcolonial nation-states have of transcending the effects of colonial history have been entangled, from the very beginning, with these modernist agendas. What name could capture these convergences, which, however, exceed both colonial effects and modernist agendas within the bounded sovereignties of postcolonial national states? The term *postcolony*, as conceptualized by Achille Mbembe, designates a structure of such convergences that subvert and challenge temporal conceptualizations of the postcolonial as a node of dislocations of modernity that dream of transcending colonial effects or of reversing the hierarchical, ontological relationship between colonialism and its progeny.

Yet this structural account seems incomplete, especially in relation to the powerful imaginaries of the future exerted by projects of modernization, their ongoing and constantly deferred temporal effects and the ways in which these effects continue to be vividly entangled with the colonial and precolonial past. Ann Stoler conceptualizes such temporal effects—of promises deferred as the only ways of fulfilling "expectations of modernity"—as specific to what she calls "imperial formations" or forms of political sovereignty and power that simultaneously *exceed and concatenate* what scholars have conceived of as colonial, postcolonial, and modern. In this essay I explore the specificity of such imperial effects by focusing on a place whose relationship with both the colonial past and the nation-state has been historically oblique and complicated by the political dominance of native elites as intermediaries. How do dreams of modernity and aspirations for modernization play out in a place like Jetprole, in the shadow of a ruthless and obliterating development machine? What does listening carefully to the silences around the remains of the old village tell us about contemporary political technologies and their relationship to historical antecedents? What new vectors of accountability might emerge from this exercise and what are the ethicopolitical consequences of exploring the effects of these new vectors of accountability?

After Submergence

When I first arrived in Jetprole, people used the phrase "after Srisailam" a great deal, expecting me to translate Srisailam as I wished: as a dam that was constructed at Srisailam; as a traumatic event in their collective history; as an evocative metaphor for their present condition of being left unmoored, without land, water, and livelihoods. The phrase covered a variety of conditions—both material and psychic—and was often coupled with assertions that in fact, nothing had changed from how they had lived their lives in the village before submergence. This assertion was made time and again despite the fact that the villagers were now living in a space that was utterly transformed by the temple-museum at the edge of the village. Despite the huge shadow cast by the "archaeology temples," their presence was largely ignored. A single priest, paid by the state's Hindu Religious and Charitable Endowments Department, looked after all the temples, opening them up each day, cleaning them, and making ritual offerings to the deities. The priest was an outsider, appointed by the local endowments department officials, and was often absent from his job. The archaeology temples were therefore falling into neglect and disrepair within a few years of reconstruction.

Although evidently magnificent from a distance, the archaeology temples — or "group temples" (mukalla gudlu) as villagers called them — presented a very strange sight up close. Each stone of every temple had been marked indelibly with a code to enable archaeologists to determine its right position for reconstruction. These marks were still visible after decades, despite the Archaeology Department's efforts to cover them up with a coat of saffron paint. Up close, the temples resembled pieces of a giant puzzle rather than sacred monuments. The sole rescued temple that was in active, daily use was the Madanagopalaswamy Temple that had stood at the center of the old village of Jetprole and had served as the family temple of the Rajas of Jetprole since the sixteenth century.

In order to translate "after Srisailam" and to connect it with the common, sometimes emphatic assertion that nothing had changed, I had to undertake a historical ethnography to understand how the pasts of this village — which had little connection to either colonial governance or the nation-state — came to be connected with a particular form of postcolonial political technology that is enacted through the willful destruction of material life and the persistent exposure of social relations to the deconstructive gaze of postcolonial law. The marginal space of the archaeology temples, rescued and enshrined as vestiges of the past, is an important part of that puzzle.

Rebuilding Jetprole involved an active, everyday, and material engagement with the submerged village site. On the one hand, villagers had been forced to contest the state in courts to gain recognition of their claims over the submerged lands. The ownership of these lands was actively entangled with forms of tenure that diverged radically from the private-property paradigm, and the legal battle that ensued over recognition of claims lasted for nearly two decades. The effects of this legal drama resonate to this day. On the other hand, within a few years of submergence, villagers had to begin using their old fields during the dry season, when the dam's reservoir emptied, because they were unable to secure enough land with the meager cash compensations they were offered by the state. These incursions into the submergence zone were fraught, both because of the fear of state reprisal, since the agricultural activity in the submergence zone was a threat to the dam, and because of the villagers' haunting confrontation with their past. The movements in and out of the abandoned village site—which was just a short walk from the new village—created new ways of relating materially and mnemonically to the past as well as to the future.

While every place may be composed of a palimpsest of material forms—some in active use, others abandoned or more ambivalent in terms of their contemporary influence—in Jetprole after submergence, there was an active call to relate to these remainders of the Srisailam project. The archaeology temples are familiar to a modernist sensibility, signifying structures abandoned by time yet recoverable within an enchanted and linear national history, attesting to the past glory and achievements of the nation. The salvage archaeology project was thus suffused with the "redemptive satisfaction of chronicling loss," a sentiment that was amply evident in my conversations with various archaeologists involved in the project.[4] But it was significant that the archaeology temples, while admired by the villagers, remained largely invisible in the broader narratives surrounding their own displacement, remaining hidden under other layers of the palimpsest that was Jetprole. The submerged village, on the other hand, exerted a much more ambivalent, psychic pressure on villagers. It marked a deep sense of loss, but one that could not be mourned as such. Recovering the village as a material resource was an important reason why the engagement with the submerged site—the houses, monuments, and fields—felt current and contemporary rather than like an encounter with a forgotten space from the past.

For the residents of Jetprole, the work of rebuilding the village coincided with their being interpellated, perhaps for the first time in their history, by the institutions of the nation-state. Like many regions of what is now India, Jetprole was never under direct British colonial rule, but rather was governed by Rajas who were themselves the vassals of the princely state of Hyderabad, the largest indirectly ruled territory in the subcontinent. The state of Hyderabad was itself integrated into the territory of the Republic of India only after a short but brutal military action one year after the Indian independence from British rule. Yet, like many other territories that were formerly princely states in British India, the state of Hyderabad was poorly interpellated into the structures and institutions of the newly independent nation. A separate bureaucracy was created for abolishing *jagirs*, or landed estates like Jetprole, within the state of Hyderabad, but the complexities of land-tenure arrangements were hard to untangle and existing arrangements continued to prevail until the dam's construction was announced.

In the early 1970s, when Revenue Department officials from the capital of Andhra Pradesh came to Jetprole to decide on land claims and to apportion cash compensations for lands about to be submerged, issues of ownership, private property, tenancy arrangements, and the lifeways that went with them came to the fore with visceral force. Those who could not prove their status as holders of ownership titles or as protected tenants of "legitimate" landowners were cut off altogether from receiving compensation. What ensued were long battles with the state over legitimacy of rights and material claims as well as over the amounts of cash that were handed out as compensation.

This contestation took place through the court system of Andhra Pradesh, with the active participation of dozens of lawyers from nearby towns, who moved quickly into the submergence villages to offer legal advice and help. Their goals, of course, were neither altruistic nor calculated to expose the state to critique through the practice of law. As hundreds of thousands of people were receiving compensations in cash, the customary fee of 10 percent was a major attraction to these mofussil lawyers, some of whom had familial connections to the villages. In these courtroom dramas, the entanglements of the past with the present became sharply visible. As well, the legal cases had crucial bearing on the future lives of the villagers, for many of those who were forced to go to court were precisely those whose claims to landholding were denied by the state. In denying these claims, the state was refusing to acknowledge the particular history of places like Jetprole.

The Pasts of a "Little Kingdom"

Like many of the other submerged villages, Jetprole lay in a region between the two important and historic Saiva pilgrimage centers of Srisailam and Alampur.[5] For several centuries, this region was a frontier over which successive South Indian kingdoms fought for dominion. The rich monumental legacy of the villages was a result of these battles, as each successive kingdom consolidated its powers by building and endowing monumental temples, monasteries, palaces, wells, and travelers' shelters as signs of power and status. By the mid-seventeenth century, Jetprole had become the official seat of an eponymous "little kingdom," known in Telugu as *samsthanam*, ruled by the Surabhi family.[6]

In multiple ways, the submerged village site reflected the social life of the "little kingdom." A massive stone fort, several monumental temple complexes, and the palace of the Rajas of Jetprole formed the spatial and political heart of the now submerged village site. Although the seat of government was moved in the mid-nineteenth century to another village (Kollapur), Jetprole continued to be of special importance due to the Madanagopala-swamy Temple, a monumental sixteenth-century SriVaishnava temple that was at the geographic center of the submerged village and served as the royal temple even though Jetprole was no longer the capital of the Samsthanam.[7]

In the nineteenth century, the Rajas of Jetprole, who controlled around a hundred and fifty villages, became vassals of the Nizam monarchy of the princely state of Hyderabad, paying tribute in exchange for control over revenue, autonomous policing, and administration of justice within the Samsthanam. Unlike much of British India, there was little reliance on land revenue to generate tax income, and much of the land was in fact governed by complicated tenurial practices involving hereditary squatting rights over land in exchange for certain forms of labor. Such services were rendered either personally for the royal family or to the temples in the direct control of the Raja's family. These land tenure arrangements were referred to as *inams*, conceived as variations on forms of gift-exchange, exchanging labor for rights to land use across multiple generations. Each specific type of grant, or inam, had a particular name, depending on the extent to which taxes were waived or the type of service for which the tax waiver or tenurial rights were granted.[8]

Importantly, the arrangements governing the control of land were not merely administrative but modes of subjectification as well, for they enmeshed generations of villagers in complex social, political, moral, and economic relations with the governing authorities.[9] The dam interrupted these relations while also making visible their deep, structural links to village life. The remains of the submerged village thus evoke this deep history of subjectification as well. The ruins of monuments, fields, and homes each tell a story of a particular community within the village and their relation to the moral centers of authority—the palace and the temple. The spatial organization of the village, too, divided into caste-based neighborhoods, or *geris*, provides important clues to understanding the social relations between communities.

Formally, these arrangements continued until 1948, when, after independence, Hyderabad (the largest princely state in British India) was annexed into independent India. Many of the complicated land-revenue grant arrangements between the Raja of Jetprole and his subjects continued de facto well into the 1970s, even though various land-reform acts had been passed in the 1950s rationalizing and redistributing land according to socialist principles of land to the tiller. The persistence of historic arrangements in the face of land reform rendered issues of ownership and compensation immensely problematic, postsubmergence. The tenuous yet real authority of the "little kingdom," which rested on this patchwork of landed arrangements between ruler and subjects, came into direct contact with regimes of modernization and with the nation-state itself after the dam. During my own research in Jetprole, I interacted extensively with two groups of villagers, belonging to the largest caste-groups in the village—the *tenugu bhoyas* and the *dalits*—and on many occasions I also visited with Muslim families in the village. Both the Hindu groups had crucial relations to the Jetprole Madanagopalaswamy Temple, and the reconstruction of the temple impacted each group in a critical though different way.

The history I recount here is embedded and compressed into local imaginaries of the tenugus and the dalits surrounding the aftermath of "Srisailam." The state's refusal to acknowledge these microrelations of power, moral authority, and forms of social structuration stood in sharp contract with their willingness to rescue the temples around which these social relations were constructed and to reconstruct those temples as objects cast in a new historical light. Thus the archaeological practice of salvage actively rearranged relations both between people and things as well as among people. Yet villagers felt deeply ambivalent about the relations that had been displaced in the course of their forced resettlement even as the ongoing engagement with the submerged village site seemed to block a complete disengagement with those relations. This active, ongoing demand to inhabit and engage with the remains of a life that had not entirely ebbed away while anticipating the modernization of those social relations through the new laws and structures of the state translated into a refusal on the part of many residents to acknowledge the extraordinary transformation of the landscape of their village. When this transformation was acknowledged, it often came up swiftly and suddenly, in moments of distraction, marked by a profusion of what Walter Benjamin has called *memoire involuntaire*, a state that was closer to forgetting, but nonetheless tethered to recollection.

An Ungraspable Event

In everyday conversations about the dam project and its effects, many villagers spoke about their relationship with the state in terms of a division in time—between a time of promised but deferred development and a time of deliberate abandonment. The contrast between the time of deferred development, before the dam, and of deliberate abandonment, after the dam, described the space within which a relationship to the sustained political project of neglect and disregard, precipitated by the development project, could be located. After the dam was sanctioned, in the late 1960s, the government stopped all investment in public works in the region on the grounds that the villages were slated for submergence anyway.

As an example, older residents recounted memories of a destructive flood that might have been prevented if a small earthen dam had been constructed at the right time. This period before Srisailam is remembered as a time of suspension due to the deliberate deferral of even such minor public works. After the Srisailam dam's completion however, villagers found that their situation had not improved, but perhaps had worsened. The future promised by the state had arrived, arrested in a form that was unexpected. Ironically, the "future" converged, visually and materially, with the monumental "past," as the village became partially a museum. For the state, the vision of this region as an ongoing zone of modernization ended with the completion of the archaeology project, thus contributing to the villagers' sense that their expectations for the future had been somehow petrified and forever "arrested."[10]

The "time of suspension" that many villagers spoke of seemed to stretch indefinitely over the dozen years that it took for the dam to be completed and even beyond, as it became clear later on, years after the dam was completed. During this period, many residents said that they lost faith in the project, hardly even believing that the dam was actually being constructed. Four years before submergence, revenue officials started touring throughout the submergence zone, studying land records and deciding on amounts to be paid as cash compensations for houses and agricultural lands. At the same time, archaeologists began intensifying their operations in these villages. The extended bureaucratic scrutiny of the revenue officials produced one of the most extraordinary legal battles against the State in contemporary India as lawyers rushed into the scene and instructed thousands of villagers to accept cash compensations "under protest." By accepting the cash amounts "under protest," villagers were retaining their rights to bring suit against the State, contesting various aspects of their forced resettlement, including the amount of compensation. The meager amounts paid set an extremely low value on the lives and livelihoods of the displaced and the lack of a postsubmergence resettlement plan rendered their situation particularly precarious.[11]

In March 1981, when the dam construction was finally completed, many of the villagers spoke of being rudely awakened from this time of suspension to a nightmarish reality. Not believing the rumors that the dam was nearly complete, most villagers had not made any plans for the impending move. Finally, they had to be forcibly evicted from their homes by the police through a campaign officially labeled Operation Demolition.[12] With no alternative plans, many residents described camping out on the rocky high ground overlooking the reservoir that had submerged their homes and fields as they watched. Several people spoke of feeling like castaways, completely unmoored from the social and moral contexts of their lives. This liminal period lasted a few years, but there was very little willingness to recall what things had been like during that time. On numerous occasions, however, I was directed to talk to a man named Sayalu, from the Madiga community (one of the two major dalit communities in this village) to better understand Srisailam, an event whose dimensions were yet to be grasped. When I finally met him, he was with a large group of his kinsmen when they came to consult a lawyer from Mahbubnagar town (the district headquarters) whose parents lived in Jetprole. In response to my request for an interview, they invited me to a ritual performance in their geri (neighborhood) the same evening.

A number of men from the community were performing a ritual hagiography of Brahmamgaru, a saintly figure known for his apocalyptic prophesies. Through this ritual performance, Sayalu and his kinsmen, like hundreds of other devotees across the region, hoped to prepare themselves for the ephemeral nature of human life and its everyday attachments by reminding themselves of imminent apocalypse. In between two acts of this performance, Sayalu picked up his single-string drone and started singing alone, a very different kind of a song. It was a song he had composed just after the villagers were brutally evicted, looking down on the reservoir and all that it had swallowed. Sayalu's song, and its affective and melancholic quality, was known throughout the village as a repository for their collective feelings about the event. Even though it was an individual's composition without any ritual significance—a secular song—it had achieved a measure of fame not only in Jetprole but elsewhere in the submergence zone as well.

The song comes out of a local tradition of spontaneous poetry called kai *kattu*, mostly composed in the fields to pass time during work. Kai kattu's distinguishing feature is its context-sensitive nature. Songs in this genre often refer to current events, rumors, and local gossip. After Srisailam, Sayalu's song and a few other such songs referring directly or obliquely to the experience of dislocation came into circulation, but they were rarely performed. Many of the other songs and poems about Srisailam were incorporated into ritual performances on various festive occasions throughout the year. While performing a mythic poem about a divine figure or a hagiographic song, a group of song leaders would incorporate a remembered scene or a story relating to Srisailam into the ongoing song by introducing a refrain about Srisailam. The other singers would then use the opportunity to add their own, spontaneously composed recollections. Such spontaneous interjection about actual historical events or contemporary happenings was not uncommon, and villagers who performed regularly on these festive occasions had come to expect these interjections as part of the song's routine. Yet when Srisailam was mentioned during such performances, it always appeared to surprise both the singers and their audience as an unexpected punctuation into the space of the everyday. Sayalu's song about Srisailam was different because it was carried only by a singular voice and was not tied to any particular ritual occasion.

As if addressing the unknown, an abyss, not expecting an answer, Sayalu structured the first lines of his song—also the recurring refrain—in the form of a rhetorical question: "Where is this Srisailam? Who built these projects?" The refrain operates as a door to each stanza—which is preceded by and returns to this lament—opening onto a scene or a space indicated by the name of a vanished place (see the appendix for the full text of the song). While the song is also descriptive, its centerpiece is a lamenting rendition of the names of villages, many of them in the vicinity of Jetprole, which vanished in the aftermath of Srisailam.[13] With dense movement around these names, the poet suggests that the only thing that can be grasped about Srisailam is what has vanished, not what has remained. The names themselves stand in for the communities, and Sayalu's song makes clear that these social forms are gone yet he structures the entire song around the refrain—"Where did this Srisailam come from?" or "What is this Srisailam?"—unable to grasp its effects entirely.

The song ends with the image of people pulling themselves up to the edge of another land, an image suggesting something beyond the sudden and inexplicable disappearance of everything that makes life possible—the fields of millet and peanuts in full crop, for example. But the image is not a hopeful one. And the song stopped everyone short, coming as it did in the middle of another performance about theodicy and apocalypse. The remains of Srisailam are its ongoing effects, but as Sayalu's song suggests, understanding these effects remains out of reach, except for that moment in which everything disappeared for a while.

Ruins and Recollections

Soon after I started living in Jetprole, in early March after the last full moon of winter, marked by the Festival of Colors and winter bonfires, and before the festival of Ugadi (New Year), the reservoir ran dry. I was struck immediately by the extraordinary spectacle of the remains. Most of the villagers I was working with were going into the submergence zone to clear their old fields of mud and detritus to start planting their peanut and millet crops, as they had in the old days. They felt lucky that they could harvest an extra crop from the submerged lands. After submergence, most villagers in Jetprole had only managed to lease lands from neighboring villages for one crop every year. Without the second crop harvested from the old fields, many said that they would be perilously close to starving. I hesitated to follow them into the fields knowing that they would be very busy with work. However, on the night of the full moon, just before the reservoir had fully dried up, Ramulu—the Jetprole temple watchman—and a few other people offered me a tour of the old fort that the Surabhi Rajas had built and their palace, which was now reduced to a foundation with a single, free-standing, winding staircase in the middle.

We wandered among those places, with Ramulu telling us stories about the Rajas, about hidden treasures and treasure hunters. All these stories, while interesting, were simply partial representations of a very complex field of social relations. Such stories generically tie history with the sublime aesthetic experience of landscapes considered representative of the past. As such, they are closer to the experiences that archaeologists and museologists sought to produce in viewers and consumers of national history. And this turned out to be just the first of many trips into that submergence zone. An outsider might expect this dramatic front of mythic stories and rumors to be played out against the backdrop of the monumental fort and palace, as happens at many sites of historical tourism all over India. My subsequent trips with different groups of villagers, however, were dedicated to more mundane pursuits. In retrospect they could be conceived as mapping exercises through which I was being circuitously led to understand the effects of Srisailam. We looked for the foundations of houses and neighborhoods (geris), for the original location of the Jetprole temple, marking all the shrines to the minor village deities and other divine beings that were left behind with their habitations. I followed people as they worked their fields and listened to the songs they composed and sang in the fields.

Several months later, just before the reservoir filled up again, I accompanied a group of dalit women to the shrine of a locally famous Muslim pir (saint) called Darvesh Kadri. Unlike the monumental stone temples that were rescued by archaeologists, the dargah, or the tomb-shrine, of Darvesh Kadri could not be moved. Nevertheless, it was clearly not abandoned. Each year, before the annual festival of the saint (the urs), the villagers—both Hindu and Muslim—still crossed the muddy remains to clean the dargah and to whitewash its walls, preparing for the urs as before. Even before they began to reclaim their fields on a regular basis, this annual ritual drew them into the zone of submergence without fear or hesitation. When I started my research, almost two decades had passed since the submergence. The visit to the dargah was the first invitation for me to personally cross into that zone, which remained unspoken in my daily conversations with many of the villagers.

Until that moment, my insistent questions about "what had changed" were often met with the cryptic response that "nothing had changed." This was incomprehensible to me, particularly in the light of the ruptures visible in the material landscape that appeared so clearly, albeit only to me. If I had expected a neat division of time and space into the old and the new, the past and the present, I was, of course, constantly confounded by the assertion that "nothing had changed." That claim, however, had little to do with the continuity of the monumental past represented by the various reconstructed and resurrected temples, as I understood from the conversations that developed on the way to the dargah.

In response to my persistent question about how life was different after Srisailam, Lakshmamma, an outspoken Madiga woman and a group of her friends, asked me, "Do you know what happens when we go back to our old fields to work?" "In the fields," they said, their children ask, "Where is home?"[14] "We take them there, we point out—there's the granary, there are the pots, there are the sleeping quarters, there we are—all this was ours." "We swallow our sorrow and we move on, we peek into other people's houses. There's Balaiah's house and there's Rosaiah's house." They then spoke as if transfixed, "We think of our own condition. At our age, our grandfathers had everything, but we, we are already drowned."

The stillness of the air as we wandered through the muddy paths of the old village to get to the dargah perfectly matched the stillborn quality of the lives that the women were describing to their children. They were speaking of their lives, post-Srisailam, as if they were already dead, and yet we were all forcefully aware that they were speaking about their present, about the village and the life from which we had walked the short distance to the dargah. But in that distance, they had conveyed to me a sense of despair about change. Forced to abandon a life with all its trappings of settled domesticity and intergenerational ties, the women worried that their future was already prophesied in the life that they were now living, in the village they had put together using bits and pieces of their old homes—door frames, wooden beams, and other objects. That future was suffused with a feeling of going nowhere, of being rooted and arrested in an unchanging scenario.

The women were viscerally aware that even this cobbled-together foundation for their futures and those of their children was inherently precarious. On another day, standing at the edge of the reservoir, when it was full and they could no longer see their old homes, Lakshmamma and others said to me, "We wonder when the day will come for us to destroy even this hearth. We wait for the day when a catastrophe will befall us again. One day when we are asleep we wonder if the flood will drown us and move on. Like those villages, which were washed away in the flood three years ago. Crops, goats, sheep, cattle, cots, jars, clocks, thresholds of houses—the flood tossed them our way. We saw those things, we saw the big wardrobe marooned in the mud at the edge of the reservoir. We grieved for ourselves as we grieved for those who had drowned there."

Built on promises of a better future in exchange for the sacrifice of their homes and lands and livelihoods for the sake of the public good, the expectations of these women for a stable, secure, and indeed modern future were constantly dashed by the realities of living amid the ruins produced by the modernization project in the form of the archaeology temples and among the silences surrounding the ruination of the social and material ecologies of their old lives. The deterioration of intergenerational relations, competition among kinsmen for scarce land, and strained relations with their natal homes over new laws granting equal property rights to women were often mentioned as among the intangible hardships engendered by Srisailam. If there was a sense that mere abandonment of their old lives—the recognition of those ecologies as ruins whose place was in the past—could allow people to move on with their lives, the situation they found themselves in was an intolerable one. They could neither move forward nor step back fully into what they had lost. Their engagement with these forms of ruination was an on-going process, traced in their daily movements between the new village and the old, between new kinds of social relations and the persistence of older structures of oppression and power.

However, living in this zone of abandonment and reconstruction obliquely conditioned their expectations of the future. What was there made clear what was missing: there were archaeology temples, but no factories or even tourists; there was the dam, but no electricity for illumination or for irrigation; there were houses, but no land. Everything was incomplete and therefore precarious. These observations, shared by many of the villagers, were critical of the modernization project, but specifically through the rec-ognition that the deleterious effects of Srisailam were distributed not just by the dam at a distance, but by the very presence of the archaeology temples, close at hand. These impotent markers of modernization, mute, abandoned by both villagers and tourists, were routinely ignored in daily life and con-versation — but therein also lay their power and hold over local imaginaries of suffering.

Living Monuments, Dead Pasts

The archaeological project began nearly a decade after the dam was ap-proved. In the mid-1970s, a "high-power committee" consisting of repre-sentatives of the Ministries of Irrigation, Archaeology and Museums, and Tourism, as well as of various experts, sanctioned the massive project, which competes in scale with the famous monument salvage project undertaken by UNESCO in Egypt.[15] Archaeologists, technicians, and armies of laborers were involved in the project. The temples to be moved were first identified based on their historical importance and the feasibility of moving them. Their stones were marked with indelible ink to identify their location, and then the temples were dismantled. The stones were transported to the new locations for reconstruction. In case the temples had been actively "in use" prior to submergence, the idols were removed to a temporary sanctuary after elaborate rituals, justified by reference to ancient texts, were performed. Similarly, after reconstruction, the state of Andhra Pradesh facilitated the performance of equally elaborate reconsecration rituals for all the trans-planted temples, thus "resurrecting" the temples for worship while also turning them into national monuments (see fig. 9.2).

By the late 1990s, when I was doing research in the area, the salvage ar-chaeology project was nearly complete, with just a few "disputed" temples

9.2 Temple museum compound at Jetprole crossroads, July 2006. Photo by author.

remaining to be reconstructed. The decision to remove the temples from their original village contexts had caused problems in cases where village-level attachments to the particular shrines had to be reckoned with politically. In the case of Jetprole, an important exception was made to accommodate the interests of the Raja of Jetprole, then living in the city of Hyderabad. At his request, the monumental Madanagopalaswamy Temple of Jetprole was removed and transplanted to a site that would become the geographic center of the reconstructed village, rather than into a museum with other temples from the same period or built in the same style. Like most of the submerged villages, a part of Jetprole's territory remained outside the submergence zone and this remainder was appropriated for the reconstruction of the Madanagopalaswamy Temple. The new village grew around this transplanted temple since its reconstruction was already in progress when the dam was completed and the residents displaced. In addition, Jetprole was chosen as a site for a temple-museum, given its prior historical importance.

It is important to note, however, that the Jetprole temple was the proprietary temple of the Surabhi family, in which the Surabhi Raja's family and their invited guests enjoyed exclusive rights of worship.[16] Apart from high-caste families, the village public rarely participated in the temple rituals, and many, especially the untouchable communities in the village, saw the deity only when specially made procession idols (*utsava vigrahalu*) were taken out into the streets of the village during festivals. The two main communities in the village, the tenugus and the dalits, had intimate yet different relations to this temple. While the former experienced a form of intimate inclusion, performing various services in the temple, the latter experienced a form of intimate exclusion in which the temple featured prominently because they were not allowed to enter the temple at all.[17] Moreover, the remainder of Jetprole village's official revenue territory, which was appropriated for transplanting the Jetprole temple, was being used by certain dalit families who claimed hereditary squatting rights to the land as an inam for serving the Rajas of Jetprole for various personal needs not involving the temple. Their dispossession was emblematic of the complex forms of displacement that took place after Srisailam. These groups formed the main population of the village, while the remaining groups—mostly upper-caste farming families—had largely moved out of the social life of the village after submergence, since many had homes in district towns even though they continued to maintain homes and farms in Jetprole.

From 1968, when the dam's construction began, to the late 1990s, the entire submergence zone was being incorporated into national geography in new ways. Already known for being major suppliers of labor to construction sites all over India, these districts were seen by the state as hopelessly underdeveloped and remote. Yet the interventions into the region brought many outsiders into the region including state officials, ambulance-chasing lawyers who enabled villagers to contest the compensations being paid to them, and construction laborers working on archaeological sites. The remoteness of these villages should be understood in the phenomenological sense, experienced, perceived, and evoked by villagers in their stories about the development project.

The project brought new relations to the world, but at the same time the proximity of the past in its material forms drew the place into other lived times and spaces. These development-driven interventions had juxtaposed the large-scale ruin-making capacities of the state, the willful and calculated disregard for how people would survive without land or water, with the loving care the state extended to the temples that it chose to rescue as vestiges of a glorious, precolonial national past. The sense of neglect experienced by the people of these villages was evidenced by comments that they made about archaeologists being the only agents of the state that they saw with any regularity both before and after the submergence. This sense was also conveyed to me by many archaeologists who felt uncomfortable with the role they occupied as agents of a neglectful and indeed irresponsible state as they witnessed, at very close quarters, the hardships experienced by the villagers throughout the process of displacement.

Yet the archaeologists were both motivated and even excited by the historical and aesthetic opportunities afforded by the project. Postreconstruction, the monuments manufactured by the salvage process occupied a very particular kind of past tense, the past perfect. The archaeologists whom I interviewed over the course of my research were clear about the role of archaeology in rescuing the "relics" of the past. They viewed these monuments as tokens of a bygone era, even those temples, such as the Madanagopalaswamy Temple of Jetprole, that clearly continued to play a complex role in the social, economic, and political life of the villages in which they were located. The formal and aesthetic aspects of these monumental temples were what most interested the archaeologists, since style, according to their analytic, signified period of construction and thereby allowed them to draw historical conclusions about precolonial South Indian polities.

As in many countries, archaeology in India is tied intimately to the state. The archaeologists involved in the salvage project were, first and foremost, civil servants, rather than university-based research archaeologists. The latter were able to undertake field research only in collaboration with state-employed archaeologists. Another important feature of archaeological practice in post-independence India is precisely its intimate connection to the development regime. As the then director of the Andhra Pradesh state department of Archaeology and Museums, who supervised much of the Srisailam salvage project, stated in a written report on this project, "These salvage operations have become a catalyst for even the 'normal' work of archaeology in a country lacking in the resources for expanded archaeological activities, causing archaeologists to move from one scene of submergence to the next, excavating and choosing remains destined for museums."[18] The sense that the rescued temples were remains, leftovers, from a past that was decisively separate from the (modern) present was dominant, at least among this particular community of archaeologists.

This melancholic but redemptive understanding of the ruin as the decayed remnant of a vanished past is certainly modernist, but at the same time the archaeological ruin is not found but made. The salvage operation is but an extreme practice in a genealogy of practices that actively constitute relations between history and identity through material artifacts, rather than merely reflecting a preexisting relation between history and identity.[19] Recent histories of archaeology in India trace the continuities between the institutions of postcolonial archaeology and their colonial predecessors.[20] In particular, the distinction, made by colonial archaeologists, between "living" and "dead" monuments, or between monuments in active use and abandoned or disused monuments, continues to animate the concerns of contemporary archaeologists. A large number of the historic monuments tended to by archaeologists in India are also actively occupied and therefore objects of contest between the state and the occupants, or between different communities with competing claims over these monuments.

The distinction between the "living" and the "dead" monument is significant to understanding how and why the material trace of the past has come to assume such a contentious position in debates about national identity in recent years. Combined with archaeological methods of excavation, the "proper" positioning of material remains has proved, as it has in so many other places, to be a volatile practice in contemporary India where the more temporally recent layers have been interpreted to embed signs of iconoclasm and desecration. The violent debates over the Babri Mosque in northern India, which was claimed by both Muslims and Hindus as a holy site, for example, have animated a virulent, exclusionary identity politics for over two decades. The passage of the mosque into the trusteeship of the state after independence contributed to an imaginary of its being a "dead monument," while the claims of Hindu nationalist politicians and archaeologists, aligned by their mutual contention that the foundations of the mosque lay on top of the foundations of a destroyed temple, contributed to a fierce debate over the site itself, which culminated in the physical destruction of the mosque by armies of youth members of the Vishwa Hindu Parishad and other, similar, xenophobic Hindu nationalist groups.

The salvage archaeology project highlights similar processes of history-making by aligning layers of spatial forms to the temporal ideologies of historical periods. More important, by transplanting the temples and reorganizing their relations to one another as evocative ruins within the open-air museum compounds, the salvage archaeology project follows a modernist aesthetic attitude, both in terms of its organization of time and in terms of its organization of individual sensory experience.[21] Such an organization of time foregrounds a particular emphasis on understanding the past as a completed process, as "history outside of lived reality."[22] As Jacques Rancière elaborates in his recent work, the aesthetic focus on particular objects, considered to fall solely within the sphere of art, attempts to fundamentally affect the "redistribution of the relations between the forms of sensory experience."[23] Yet the archaeology temples are caught in a paradoxical ontological bind: the salvage process turns them into objects of an aesthetic regime of recognition, while at the same time the reconsecration ceremonies attempt to bring them into a different order of time, to reconstruct their qualities as "living" monuments.

The archaeologist's work, tied to the modernization project, is central to a politics of dislocation as well as to an apportioning of risks.[24] The state and its allies envision development as a normative project whose overall benefits are not blunted by the costs borne by some populations. The sustained disregard for the lives of people in the submergence zones of dams, in the forests being extracted for resources, or in the shadows of the high-rise buildings of globalizing cities is recast as a necessary cost of "progress." But the state is well aware that acknowledgment of the large-scale ruin-making required by the project of modernization is not enough to justify these processes. Other, more calculated projects — such as the salvage archaeology project and other schemes of "compensation" — are in fact required to supplement and substantiate the necessity of development. Such schemes and schemas trace the continuity between imperial pedagogic projects that projected natives as children in need of an education and the policies of postcolonial states.[25] These schemas also recast the ruination of life, opportunities, and aspirations by cutting off specific material ecologies from the flow of time and pushing the ways of life associated with these ecologies into the sphere of "history outside of lived reality." Yet this cordoning off of space and time hardly stems the flow of history or the seepage of these very material ecologies into the political imaginaries of the present as people struggle with the ambivalence of letting go of an oppressive past in the context of a hopeless present.

The salvage archaeology project struggles to contain these imaginaries, restricting the understanding of the past to the loss documented, archived, and aesthetically repackaged by the project. This imperialist nostalgia, however, is called into question when that which is destroyed demands to be recognized as having an influence on the imaginaries and possibilities of the future. The archaeological refusal to establish a relationship to the destroyed is turned on its head by the villagers, who in turn refuse to acknowledge the transformative, aesthetic effect of the salvaged temples. Through the salvage archaeology project — in the attention to the material trace of history, in its relocation and repositioning as an evocative ruin — an evasive history of empire reappears and is joined to a sustained biopolitical project to disregard the agency of particular populations, populations already rendered vulnerable by hurts that can be traced back through time.

The Disappearance of Jetprole

If modernization projects have a particular relation to that which they lay waste to—viewing the pasts of villages they submerge or the spaces of slums that they redevelop or the depths of mines and forests that they extract resources from as necessary and inevitable waste—then projects like the salvage archaeology project pick up that waste and attempt to curate and control its effects.[26] The salvage archaeology project cultivates a particular, modernist sensibility of the past as a space that can be cordoned off from the flow of time and whose symbolic effects on the present and the future can be carefully controlled through the control of the material objects representing the past. Yet this process of control gives rise to unexpected, critical encounters that reveal new possibilities for grounding processes of re-composing lives. In this concluding section, I turn to narratives surrounding the relocation of the Jetprole Madanagopalaswamy Temple to explore these encounters.

The archaeological relocation of Jetprole's monumental temple provided an important element of physical continuity between the old village and the new. But it also proved temporally disorienting to the villagers because, after reconstruction, worship was resumed in the temple but with very different vectors of authority since the management of the temple had been radically transformed. Although the Raja of Jetprole retained rights of worship and other kinds of honors as the hereditary trustee, the temple was now fully managed by the Religious Endowments Department of the Andhra Pradesh government, which controlled everything from the budget to appointments of temple servants. This situation particularly affected the many families—both tenugu and dalit—attached to the temple through rights of use over temple lands. These lands—numbering hundreds of acres—had been endowed to the temple by the Rajas of Jetprole over the course of four centuries. Rights of use over these temple lands were, in turn granted to different families in the village in exchange for specific services: pouring oil into the lamps, supplying flowers for daily worship, washing vessels, bearing the processionary idol, and, of course, priestly duties among numerous other major and minor duties.[27]

After the reconstruction of the temple, the cash compensations paid for these lands were collected by the Hindu Religious and Charitable Endowments (HRCE) Department and deposited in a bank account from which salaries were paid to a few villagers for taking care of the daily operations of the temple. The staff was reduced to a priest, a watchman, a sweeper, and a gardener, who struggled to maintain the huge, magnificent temple complex. They spent their days in the temple gossiping and waiting for the very occasional visitor to drop by. Villagers still refrained from going into the temple without a specific reason for doing so because it remained tied, in their memories and in reality, to the family of the Raja of Jetprole, who now resided in Hyderabad city and visited the village only on rare occasions.

Other families, who had served in the temple until it was dismantled and who had cultivated the temple lands, were locked up in a legal battle with the state, arguing that they, and not the HRCE Department, should rightfully receive the cash compensation for the temple lands. For these families, there was a deep sense of disappointment; they were no longer servants of the temple, nor were the rights accrued from their previous position serving the temple recognized after the submergence. The legal battle and the forms of testimony required by these families required them to relive memories of particular forms of oppression and humiliation that they had suffered for the rights to cultivate the temple's fields. This, coupled with the fact that the dam project had failed to materialize a radical transformation in their living conditions, contributed to their repeated assertions about the fact that "nothing had changed," despite the extraordinary incursions into their everyday life by the dam, the reconstruction of the temples, the lawyers, and the courts.

Not surprisingly, however, the temple formed a central motif in the poetic language in which experiences of displacement often resurfaced. A story sung about the transplantation of the Jetprole temple provided an extended canvas on which to observe these ideas at play. I first heard the song performed during the celebration of Ugadi, the Telugu New Year, which coincides with the harvest in midsummer. On the day of Ugadi, there were typically celebrations and entertainments in all the different neighborhoods of the village. In the tenugu neighborhood, a woman named Savaramma gathered a group of her kinswomen to sing a long and moving song about the process of dislocation, transplantation, and reconsecration of the temple. The song was reputed to be Savaramma's original composition, which came to her in a moment of possession by the deity himself. Such moments of possession led men and women to start singing stories and legends about deities, especially caste and family deities. That the Jetprole *gopalaswamy*, as the deity was affectionately called by the villagers, should possess someone was somewhat incongruous, given his status as a "high" god, removed from everyday life and worshiped only by the highest castes. But the events of the submergence had rendered him available to treatments similar to those of the caste, family, and village deities, including practices of storytelling into which events from everyday life were woven.

Prior to submergence, Savaramma's family was intimately associated with the temple. Men from her family carried the processional idols around the village during festivals. During its reconstruction, she was employed as a laborer on the construction site. She was deeply moved by the experience of witnessing the deity removed from his place, being taken away to a temporary shrine in the neighboring village, and his return to Jetprole, many years later. Savaramma's song referenced the special relations that her family and community enjoyed with the deity and the Jetprole temple. She was quite wary of performing the song too frequently, afraid of becoming possessed as she had been when she first composed the song, but the song itself had migrated to other neighborhoods and other singers took up the basic story, weaving in their own stories of displacement. All versions of this song, regardless of who performed them, turned on a trope of death. They recounted the scene of the deity leaving the village as a corpse, drained of his life by the elaborate deconsecration ceremonies. The touch of this corpse turned the old village site into a ghostly space that people waited to flee, but they had nowhere to go until they were forcibly evicted, years later. And yet, Savaramma's song suggested, they were unsure that the condition of being ghosts, of being between life and death, had ended when the village was rebuilt and the temple reconstructed.

Later, on the same Ugadi day, I heard another version of this song, performed by Lakshmamma, the dalit woman whom I had accompanied into the old village. Her version of the song told the story of her community's dispossession from the lands they were cultivating under the decree of the Raja of Jetprole. These lands, which were appropriated for rebuilding the Jetprole temple, assumed a symbolic charge as the only part of village territory that was not submerged. Reconstructing the temple on these grounds meant that the temple would retain its ancient connection to the village. But, as the song explained, the Madigas who cultivated those lands had no idea what was in store.[28] They assumed that the land was *charayi* (common land, typically used for grazing) to which the Raja had gifted them squatting rights on his authority. Yet they discovered that these rights could be taken away just as arbitrarily. The temple therefore stood as the emblem of a very particular kind of history in the memory of Lakshmamma and her kinswomen who sang with her.

Her song was not a direct indictment of the state or the Raja but something more. Lakshmamma's song and her story provide an exploration of the impermanence and mutability of the relations of care and attachment across generations. While such arbitrary dispossessions may have been part of historical memory, the labor needed to resitutate the vanished into the order of lived time was new. For the vanished objects of intergenerational transmission, like the landed ties of their inam, marked the difference, for these women, between life and death, between being corpses and becoming ghosts. The song decried the foolishness of their elders, who in their ignorance had given away their land to gopalaswamy, and it contemplated the women's own futures as elders to their children, wondering what would become of them and how they would be remembered. Both in its structure and its affect, the song exhibited a deep concern with the recognition that the future, which they were so worried about, might already have arrived, in a form that could not be changed.[29] Their understanding of the future contrasted distinctly from their aspirations for a life in which their children would have greater opportunities than themselves.

Many of the women recounted, for example, how they had obliquely become aware of the equal property rights that the government of Andhra Pradesh's laws had bestowed on women. They only become aware of this right, they said, when their brothers from other villages in the submergence zone requested that they sign away their rights to compensation for their shares in the family property. The women did so, they said, in order to maintain their visiting rights to their natal homes and their rights to receive turmeric and vermillion on ritual occasions. Thus dispossessed many times over, Lakshmamma and her kinswomen struggled to account for the vanished and the appearance of a stillborn future into their everyday experience. The Jetprole Madanagopalaswamy Temple became both an emblem of ruination and a token of the capacity to constitute a meaningful understanding of this experience.

Encountering Srisailam: Modernist Ruins and Imperial Debris

To encounter Srisailam, the project, and to trace its location is to encounter this complex terrain of ruins and debris generated by the project of modernization. The resituation of these traces of the vanished—like the moral geographies of entitlements that are passed along generations—into the order of lived time required the sustained work of confronting the material remains of this event, of resignifying their status as emblems of progress or as the wasted matter left over by the project of development or as the materials with which to rebuild their lives. The "verification" of these claims and entitlements is an extremely complicated process, as the legal cases make clear. I focus here on the claims that are made in the songs specifically because my informants and I were never able to discuss their land claims directly. The larger work of which this essay is a part looks into the ways in which postcolonial law deals with customary claims as well as into the broader problematic made visible by different narrative styles of introducing claims. Claims made in the everyday and poetic speech of ordinary villagers adversely affected by the dam project stand in sharp contrast to the rationalizing discourses of the law which were deployed both by the lawyers that I worked with and by literate, upper-caste villagers conversant with the legal framing of displacement and compensation issues. If the latter narratives foreground verification and verifiability, the former are more concerned with affective framing of the spaces and materials that remain and with the contextualization of claims over these spaces in relation to forms of authority that continue to operate without being visible to the law.

In this ethnographic exploration, I have marked the ways in which the language and practice of contemporary political activism has been critical in making visible the connection between public works and evasive histories of imperial formations in the contexts of large-scale development projects. In mapping the effects of development on formerly colonized societies, scholars have offered us a rich array of accounts situated in multiple localities. As many of the accounts make clear, modernization projected above all a biopolitics directed toward remaking the normative conditions of subjected societies. Development constituted an ideology of hope, deeply linked to the aspiration for modernity itself.[30] At the same time, such projects also embedded the experience of violence and catastrophe within the life-worlds of people and fostered a politics of protest and identity formation.[31] Several accounts have paid close attention to the question of scale, spatiality, and sovereignty in the formation of such politics of protest and identity.[32] Yet other accounts look at the effects of the violence of development on the constitution of memory and subjectivity and the recovery of everyday life from such catastrophic experiences that are visited by purely exogenous factors.[33]

Most accounts, however, do not focus on the relations between subjects and the material ecologies of remains, leftovers, and the debris among which those subjects must lead their daily lives. To encounter Srisailam—the project—and to trace its location is to encounter a complex terrain of ruins, as traces of the vanished as well as the specter of the future in the form of the phantom debris of the project of modernization. Paradoxically, the archaeology temples serve as the only concrete signs of a modernization project and its promised future, which has come and gone. The temples stand as the relics and ruins of progress, and they act as "fossils of the future," to use the English writer J. G. Ballard's evocative expression. In so doing, they offer a rearview-mirror look at the future in the absence of any hopeful, redemptive visions of progress in this space of disappearance, dereliction, and vanishing. Yet, viewed alongside the recurrently reappearing village, these relics of destruction and construction together open a space in which it is possible to witness the intertwining of different senses of temporality and historical consciousness and, in general, different levels of saturation and investment in debris.

Within a logic of modernization, the memorialization of fragments of the past as heritage by the archaeological salvage operation takes place by denying the contemporaneity of these fragments. A utopian notion of the future is connected to understanding these fragments of the past as a form of waste, inevitably produced by modernization, permanently withdrawn from time. In this understanding, waste is material that has no duration, only durability, for which the passage of time is irrelevant. From this perspective of waste as durable substance without temporality, the utopian products of modernization and modernism—whether cities like Brasilia and Chandigarh or the temples rescued by the salvage archaeology project—are thus waste from the outset, but as examples of perfection. Such a notion of waste reconfigures the utopian futures of modernization as a future already in ruins, albeit permanent and aesthetically perfect or correct ruins.

By contrast, an exploration focusing on the material remains that people are left with in the wake of development projects adds to the literature on development in one significant way. It brings to the fore some of the historical vectors through which postcolonial regimes of national development achieve their goals. In the Jetprole case, I have explored in depth the positioning and repositioning of the different categories of monuments manufactured by the salvage archaeology project and placed them in relation to the remains of the submerged village that are invisible yet viscerally connected to the everyday life of the villagers. This intersection between a still-colonial practice of archaeology, saturated with an imperialist nostalgia for resurrecting a glorious past, and the biopolitics of the development and modernization process that actively disregards and neglects the economic and social welfare of the villagers suggests the persistent relevance of colonial effects. Yet it also scrambles any sense of analytic neatness in finding temporal convergences between colonialism and imperial forms of the modern, on the one hand, and postcolonialism and utopian forms of modernism on the other—or, in other words, between political technologies and forms of power, on the one hand, and aesthetic and subjective experiences on the other. It is urgent to recognize the persistent relevance of colonial effects not in order to absolve postcolonial regimes, but in order to recognize the histories through which they work and that are at work through them. At the same time, it is necessary to recognize the disjunctive and persistent relations between colonial practices and effects and the modern practices that Ann Stoler provocatively captures through the term "imperial formations."

Certainly, life in Jetprole does go on and new forces are at work within the village. A more meaningful monument appearing openly in this landscape these days is the memorial marker topped off by the sickle and hammer erected in memory of comrades slain in the extrajudicial "encounters" between the police and the Maoist revolutionary guerrillas who constitute the most active political force in this region today. Yet the scars and wounds of Srisailam, the "ecologies of remains," are precisely the signs whose presence concretely ties this geography of despair to a larger canvas of colonial privilege and its distribution of the vulnerabilities that continue to play an active role in the politics of the present.

In Jetprole these material remains are hardly forms of waste in the modernist sense. Rather, they are actively morphing, changing, and being recycled in local imaginaries around displacement, suffering, and life-making. The active and ironic disregard that the people of Jetprole and other villages show, in everyday conversation, to the archaeology temples and their museological settings and the deployment of all forms of remains in their poetic narratives about displacement are both significant ways in which villagers grapple with the ongoing effects of Srisailam. These veiled and oblique attempts to grasp at the event and to situate its effects point not to a passive acceptance of their fates, but rather to an active and ongoing engagement with ruins, not as remains to be feared for what they predict about their future or as intimations of loss, but as sites from which to direct and sharpen "political and affective states of sustained resentment that redirect what will be in ruins and who will be living in them."[34] An exploration of those active forms of political resentment being played out today through sustained everyday insurrections and insurgencies across India today is beyond the scope of this essay. However, to understand the specificity of new forms of action, visibly symbolized by new memorial markers such as those of slain Maoist cadres, it is necessary to follow the traces of histories embedded in these scarred landscapes.

Appendix: Sayalu's Song

"Where is this Srisailam? Who built these projects?"

"Land, like the mother who bore me,
vanished from the sight of my eye.
Fields, full of standing crops,
drowned in the water."

"Where is this Srisailam? Who built these projects?"

"For destroying cultivated land,
they gave us money.
For destroying cultivation,
the government gave us money.
One part for the loser's soil,
another for the lawyer's bribe.
Six thousand apiece,
six thousand a head,
six thousand a portion of land.
Six thousand they promised,
but not even three can be accounted for."

"Where is this Srisailam? Who built these projects?"
"Land, like the mother who bore me, vanished from the sight of my
    eye."

(Lament on names of disappeared villages)
: Kurramu, Bollaram, O Brother, Amaragiri, Marugocche . . .
Drowned, mingled in the waters . . .

"Where is this Srisailam? Who built these projects?"

(Lament on names of disappeared villages)
: Kurramu, Bollaram, O Brother, Amaragiri, Marugocche . . .
: Siddheswaram, Malleswaram
Mingled in the waters . . .
: Malleswaram, Sangameswaram
Drowned . . .
But Koppunuru and Jetprole, they sank without a trace . . .

"Where is this Srisailam? Who built these projects?"

(Lament of names)

: Peddamarur, Chinnamarur, Kanuru, Erupalle
Disappeared . . .

: Sangameswaram, Kudavelli [important pilgrimage centers, at the
     confluence of several rivers, that were submerged by the reservoir]
Sealed up and drowned . . .

"Where is this Srisailam? Who built these projects?"
"Land, like the mother who bore me, vanished from the sight of my
     eye . . ."

"Fields in which young peanuts ripened,
fields in which young millet ripened,
lie engulfed in the middle of waters . . ."

"Our lives drained,
we've taken refuge on these rocky shores,
we pulled ourselves to the edge of disappearing,
we reached the edge of another land . . ."

Notes

I gratefully acknowledge the assistance offered by the Surabhi family and the support
of my extended family in Hyderabad. My late father-in-law, Dr. P. V. R. Bhaskar Rao,
especially encouraged me through the most difficult periods of my research with his
warmth, affection, and practical advice. My research was funded by a grant from the
American Institute of Indian Studies. I am deeply grateful to Ann Stoler for inviting
me to consider parts of my dissertation under the rubric of imperial debris, which allowed me to highlight the singular theoretical significance of material landscapes in
accounting for postcolonial development regimes.

1. The location of these reconstructed monuments mattered greatly to their influence on local imaginaries and on accounts of the development project.

2. The term "little kingdom" is used by Nicholas Dirks in his book, *The Hollow Crown*,
a historical ethnography of a minor political entity in southern India. Dirks argues
that the concept of the "little kingdom"—which symbolically perpetuated the sump-
tuary practices central to precolonial tactics of power, while itself being eviscerated of
"real" power—is crucial to understanding the British colonial rule of South Asia. Such
vassal states worked by maintaining their rulers' symbolic power while real political
authority was ceded to the British.

3. See Coronil, "Editor's Column."

4. See Stoler's essay in this volume.

5. See Bruno Dagens's *Entre Alampur et Srisailam*, an archaeological survey of his-

torical artifacts and monuments in the presubmergence villages. Dagens, a French indologist, suggests, from his survey of inscriptions and types of monuments that his team found and classified in each village, that the submersible zone appeared to have an identity, not so much through any recognizable essence like language or religion, but in fact as the place that many successive southern Indian empires sought to control in order to secure their access to these two major pilgrimage towns. While this might be a highly simplified characterization of the social history of these villages, it can nevertheless be used as a shorthand for understanding the wealth of monumental remains—both sacred and secular—in these villages. As I showed in my unpublished master's thesis, "Itinerant Temples and Monumental Ruins," the construction and endowment of temples, mosques, monasteries, and other similar institutions was essential to the consolidation of imperial powers, especially in frontier zones, for these institutions performed vital economic functions by redistributing agricultural surplus and by providing local employment on the lands endowed to these religious institutions. See also Appadurai, *Worship and Conflict under Colonial Rule*; and Talbot, *Precolonial India in Practice*.

6. The following account of Jetprole's history is compiled from various sources, including interviews with the Surabhi family head, S. V. K. V. Aditya Lakshma Rao; Bhattara Srinivasacharya's "Jetprole Samsthanam Pariseelana," an M.Phil. thesis in history submitted to Telugu University, Srisailam; interviews with M. R. Sarma of Osmania University; and local accounts. There is little written material apart from Srinivasacharya's thesis and a few manuscripts relating to royal history.

7. See Appadurai, *Worship and Conflict under Colonial Rule*, for a detailed history and sociology of the SriVaishnava sect and their religious institutions. Here it is sufficient to note that the SriVaishnavas exclusively worshipped different physical forms and manifestations of the deity Lord Vishnu.

8. For a detailed analysis of the system of inams and the roles that such arrangements played both in direct rule and indirect rule in the colonial period, see Dirks, *The Hollow Crown*; and Frykenberg, "The Silent Settlement in South India."

9. Numerous local accounts make reference to these relations as if they were social facts, well understood even though they are not officially recorded in revenue documents and other official forms of post-independence recordkeeping.

10. I thank Ann Stoler for referring me to the work of Carol McGranahan on "arrested histories," on which I build this notion of an arrested future.

11. There is a rich literature on rehabilitation and resettlement: Chatterjee, *The Politics of the Governed*; Fernandes and Thukral, *Development, Displacement and Rehabilitation*; Kaushik Ghosh, "Between Global Flows and Local Dams"; *Economic and Political Weekly* (June 1996), special issue on "Development, Displacement and Rehabilitation"; McCully, *Silenced Rivers*.

12. "The evacuation of the villages was carried out with brutal insensitivity towards the feelings of the villagers who, not unnaturally, were bewildered and distressed at being forced out of their homes. The villagers were not properly informed about the details of the evacuation: some did not even know where to go once they had been

ordered to move. Many villagers did not take government announcements about the evacuation seriously. 'The government is always announcing things which it never carries out,' they told us. Some refused to believe that their villages would be submerged—or thought that, at worst, their lands would only be flooded when the Tungabhadra and Krishna rivers were in spate. Still others delayed moving either because they had no money to do so or because they had failed to find alternative housing and employment. The evacuation programme was so rushed that few villagers had enough time to move all their belongings to the resettlement sites. Worse still, when the villagers reached the new sites, they found them lacking in basic amenities—including proper housing.

"During the last week of March 1981, the government announced—for the first time—that all villagers had to leave their homes. Two months later, convinced that the villagers would not move whilst their houses and huts were still standing, the authorities launched 'Operation Demolition.' Under heavy police guard, officers and staff from the Departments of Revenue and Irrigation and Power, accompanied by hired labourers from the towns, set about demolishing those villages which were to be flooded. Some twenty thousand houses and huts were destroyed—leaving a hundred thousand people (twenty-one thousand families) homeless. The houses were either knocked down or dismantled by removing doorframes, window frames and roofs. Demolition work on the huts was carried out with much vigour and zeal. Utensils and other belongings were thrown out on to the streets, cattle were let loose and entire families were unceremoniously driven out of their homes. The operation was carried out without any regard for the villagers, who were already in a state of shock. An old woman in Rolampad village reported that her ankle and the bone of her right hand were broken when she was dragged by the police from her hut. Not surprisingly, the villagers are still bitterly resentful of the behaviour of the authorities" (Fact-Finding Committee on the Srisailam Project, "Srisailam Resettlement Experience," 258, 259).

13. D. Venkat Rao, writing about a similar tradition of rural and revolutionary song-making, notes that "the tune or the refrain . . . works as a trace, as an already glimmering grapheme. The source of the trace is in other people's voices" ("Writing Orally," 256).

14. Dalit which literally means "oppressed" is the political term used by the formerly untouchable communities to identify themselves. It emerged as a term of contrast and confrontation with the term harijan ("children of god"), which was coined by Gandhi. Arguing that harijan glossed over a highly oppressive history, the former untouchables preferred dalit as a label for self-identification. Many of my older informants, however, preferred to refer to themselves as harijan. I worked with both the main dalit communities in the village—Malas and Madigas—who had little contact with each other and largely behaved like autonomous caste groups.

15. The project came close on the heels of a similar initiative, on a much smaller scale, to rescue and museumize Buddhist relics that were discovered in Andhra during the construction of the Nagarjuna Sagar dam.

16. The Madanagopalaswamy Temple was likely constructed during the period of

the Vijayanagara empire (circa sixteenth century CE) and was dedicated to an unusual form of Vishnu known as Madanagopalaswamy, affectionately called Gopalaswamy by the villagers. This iconographic form is extremely rare, making the temple an exceptional monument.

17. The Muslims of the village also had an interesting relationship to the Jetprole temple. According to local legends, the deity Madanagopalaswamy regularly played chess with the Muslim pir Darvesh Khadri, and during the annual urs of the saint, the temple sent sandalwood to the dargah as a birthday gift from the deity. The sandalwood gift was reciprocated during the annual temple festival in the summer season.

18. Sastri, "Salvage Archaeological Operations under Srisailam Project."

19. See Abu el-Haj, *Facts on the Ground*.

20. See especially Chakrabarti, *A History of Indian Archaeology*.

21. As Jacques Rancière puts it in his recent book, *Aesthetics and Its Discontents*, "Aesthetics . . . is a form for identifying the specificity of art and a redistribution of the relations between the forms of sensory experience. . . . [A] regime for identifying art [that] is linked to the promise of an art that would be no more than an art or would no longer be art. . . . The stake here does not only concern those objects that fall within the sphere of art, but also the ways in which, today, our world is given to perceiving itself and in which the powers that be assert their legitimacy" (14–15).

22. See S. Stewart, *On Longing*.

23. Rancière, *Aesthetics and Its Discontents*.

24. See Stoler's essay in this volume.

25. Mehta, *Liberalism and Empire*; Cooper and Packard, *International Development and the Social Sciences*.

26. See Bauman, *Wasted Lives*, for a development of the relationship between modernity and waste. Bauman's implicit understanding of waste as substance withdrawn from time is politically salient for his establishing a relationship between waste and modernity.

27. These services were also encoded into the names of the fields themselves, which in turn were an important mnemonic device within local narratives about the submerged village.

28. The Madigas, as explained above, are a subgroup of the larger dalit community.

29. In this understanding, the future has none of the positive instability attributed to it by various theorists of modernity, including Marx and Reinhardt Koselleck, among others, who write of this instability as central to modern historicity.

30. See Sivaramakrishnan and Agrawal, *Regional Modernities*; Ferguson, *Expectations of Modernity*.

31. See Das, *Remaking a World*; and Kaushik Ghosh, "Between Global Flows and Local Dams."

32. See especially Chatterjee, *The Politics of the Governed*; Gupta, *Post-colonial Developments*; and Kaushik Ghosh, "Between Global Flows and Local Dams."

33. Das, *Remaking a World*; Ferguson, *Expectations of Modernity*.

34. See Stoler's essay in this volume.

BIBLIOGRAPHY

Abélès, Marc. *The Politics of Survival*. Trans. Julie Kleinman. Durham: Duke University Press, 2009.

Abu El-Haj, Nadia. *Facts on the Ground: Archaeological Practice and Territorial Self-Fashioning in Israeli Society*. Chicago: Chicago University Press, 2001.

Adhikari, Mohamed. *Not White Enough, Not Black Enough: Racial Identity in the South African Coloured Community*. Athens: Ohio University Press, 2005.

Adorno, Theodor. *Negative Dialectics*. New York: Continuum, 1973 [1966].

Advisory Committee on Human Radiation Experiments. *The Human Radiation Experiments: Final Report of the President's Advisory Committee*. New York: Oxford University Press, 1996.

Agamben, Giorgio. *Homo Sacer: Sovereign Power and Bare Life*. Trans. Daniel Heller-Roazen. Stanford: Stanford University Press, 1998.

———. *Remnants of Auschwitz: The Witness and the Archive*. Trans. Daniel Heller-Roazen. New York: Zone, 1999.

———. *State of Exception*. Trans. Kevin Attell. Chicago: University of Chicago Press, 2006.

Agee, James, and Walker Evans. *Let Us Now Praise Famous Men*. Boston: Houghton Mifflin, 1988 [1939].

Allard, Robert. "Contribution gynécologique à l'étude de la stérilité chez les mongo de Befale." *Annales de la Société Belge de la Médecine Tropicale* 35 (1955): 631–48.

Alonso, Ana Maria. "Conforming Disconformity: 'Mestizaje,' Hybridity, and the Aesthetics of Mexican Nationalism." *Cultural Anthropology* 19, no. 4 (November 2004): 459–90.

Alumni, José. *El Chaco: Figuras y hechos de su pasado*. Resistencia, Argentina: Talleres Gráficos Juan Moro, 1951.

———. *Nuestra Sra. de los Dolores y Santiago de la Cangayé (Apuntes Históricos)*. Resistencia, Argentina: Talleres Gráficos Juan Moro, 1948.

Appadurai, Arjun. "The Capacity to Aspire." *Culture and Public Action*, eds. Vijayendra Rao and Michael Walton, 59–84. Stanford: Stanford Social Sciences, 2004.

———. "The Globalization of Archaeology and Heritage: A Discussion with Arjun Appadurai." *Journal of Social Archaeology* 1, no. 1 (1981): 35–49.

———. "The Past as a Scarce Resource." *Man* 16, no. 2 (1981): 201–19.

———. "Putting Hierarchy in Its Place." *Cultural Anthropology* 3, no. 1 (February 1988): 36–49.

———. *Worship and Conflict under Colonial Rule: A South Indian Case*. Cambridge: Cambridge University Press, 1981.

Aráoz, Guillermo. *Navegación del Río Bermejo y viajes al Gran Chaco*. Buenos Aires: Imprenta Europa, 1884.

———. *Río Bermejo: Itinerario de viaje del vapor Sol Argentino*. Buenos Aires: Imprenta de la Unión, 1872.

Arendt, Hannah. *The Human Condition*. Chicago: University of Chicago Press, 1958.

———. *On Violence*. New York: Harcourt and Brace, 1969.

———. "The Rights of Man—What Are They?" *Modern Review* 3, no. 1 (summer 1949): 24–37.

Aretxaga, Begoña. "Dirty Protest: Symbolic Overdetermination and Gender in Northern Ireland Ethnic Violence." *Ethos* 23 (1995): 123–48.

Arnaud, Leopoldo. *Del Timbó al Tartagal: Impresiones de un viaje a través del Gran Chaco*. Buenos Aires: Imprenta del Río de la Plata, 1889.

Associated Universities. *Report of the Project East River*. New York: Associated Universities, 1952.

Azoulay, Ariella. *Atto di stato: Palestina-Israele, 1967–2007; Storia fotografica dell'occupazione*. Milan: Bruno Mondadori, 2008.

———. *Civil Imagination: A Political Ontology of Photography*. New York: Verso, 2011.

———. *From Palestine to Israel: A Photographic Record of Destruction and State Formation, 1947–1950*. London: Pluto, 2011.

———. "Has Anyone Ever Seen a Photograph of a Rape?" *The Civil Contract with Photography*, 217–87. New York: Zone, 2008.

Azoulay, Ariella, and Adi Ophir. *This Regime Which Is Not One: Occupation and Democracy between the Sea and the River (1967–)*. Stanford: Stanford University Press, 2011.

Badiou, Alain. *Deleuze: The Clamor of Being*. Minneapolis: University of Minnesota Press, 2000.

Baker, John R. "The Sinharaja Rain-Forest Ceylon." *Geographical Journal* 89, no. 6 (1937): 544–47.

Balibar, Étienne. "Uprisings in the 'Banlieues.'" *Constellations* 14, no. 1 (March 2007): 47–72.

Ballard, Richard, and Gareth Jones. "Natural Neighbors: Indigenous Landscapes and

Eco-Estates in Durban, South Africa." *Annals of the Association of American Geographers* 101, no. 1 (2011): 131–48.

Bancel, Nicolas, Pascal Blanchard, and François Verges, eds. *La République Coloniale.* Paris: Hachette, 2003.

Bandarage, Asoka. *Colonialism in Sri Lanka.* Berlin: Walter de Gruyter, 1983.

Barchiesi, Franco. "Classes, Multitudes and the Politics of Community Movements in Post-apartheid South Africa." *Challenging Hegemony: Social Movements and the Quest for a New Humanism in South Africa*, ed. Nigel Gibson, 161–94. Trenton, N.J.: Africa World Press, 2006.

Barthes, Roland. "Shock-Photos." *The Eiffel Tower and Other Mythologies*, trans. Richard Howard, 71–73. New York: Hill and Wang, 1979.

Basualdo, Victoria. "Complicidad patronal-militar en la última dictadura argentina: Los casos de Acindar, Astarsa, Dálmine Siderca, Ford, Ledesma y Mercedes Benz." *Revista Engranajes* no. 5 (March 2006): 1–21.

Bataille, Georges. "Writings on Laughter, Sacrifice, Nietzsche, Unknowing." *October* 36 (1986): 3–110.

Bate, Peter, dir. *Congo: White King, Red Rubber, Black Death.* 90 min. Video recording. New York: Periscope Productions in co-production with the BBC, ArtMattan Productions, 2004.

Baucom, Ian. *Out of Place: Englishness, Empire, and the Locations of Identity.* Princeton: Princeton University Press, 1999.

Baudelaire, Charles. "De l'essence du rire et généralement du comique dans les arts plastiques." *Oeuvres complètes de Baudelaire*, ed. Claude Pichois, 975–93. Paris: Gallimard, 1961.

Baugh, Edward. *Derek Walcott.* New York: Cambridge University Press, 2006.

Bauman, Zygmunt. *Wasted Lives: Modernity and Its Outcasts.* Cambridge: Polity, 2004.

Bayart, Jean-François. *Les études postcoloniales: Un carnaval academique.* Paris: Karthala, 2010.

———. "Les très fâché(e)s des études postcoloniales." *Sociétés Politques Comparées* 23 (March 2010): 1–12.

Bear, Laura. "Ruins and Ghosts." *Lines of the Nation: Indian Railway Workers, Bureaucracy, and the Intimate Historical Self*, ed. Laura Bear, 257–84. New York: Columbia University Press, 2007.

Beasley-Murray, Jon. Comments to "Ships Stranded in the Forest: Debris of Progress on a Phantom River," by Gastón Gordillo. *Current Anthropology* 52, no. 2 (2011): 160.

———. "Interrupted Pasts and Futures." Paper presented at the "Ruins of Modernity" conference, University of Michigan, March 2005.

———. "Vilcashuamán: Telling Stories in Ruins." *Ruins of Modernity*, ed. Julia Hell and Andreas Schönle, 212–31. Durham: Duke University Press, 2010.

Becher, Bernd, and Hilla Becher. *Typologies of Industrial Buildings.* Cambridge: Massachusetts Institute of Technology Press, 2004.

Beinart, William, and Lotte Hughes. *Environment and Empire.* New York: Oxford University Press, 2007.

Benjamin, Walter. *The Arcades Project*. Trans. Howard Eiland and Kevin McLaughlin. Cambridge: Harvard University Press, 1999.

———. *Illuminations: Essays and Reflections*. Ed. Hannah Arendt. New York: Schocken, 1985 [1935].

———. *One-Way Street and Other Writings*. Trans. Edmund Jephcott and Kingsley Shorter. London: Verso, 1992 [1974–76].

———. "On the Concept of History." *Selected Writings, Vol. 4: 1938–1940*, ed. Howard Eiland and Michael W. Jennings, 389–400. Cambridge: Harvard University Press, 2003.

———. *The Origin of the German Tragic Drama*. Trans. John Osborne. London: Verso 1998 [1928].

———. "Paralipomena to 'On the Concept of History.'" *Selected Writings, Vol. 4: 1938–1940*, eds. Howard Eiland and Michael W. Jennings, 401–11. Cambridge: Harvard University Press, 2003.

———. *Selected Writings, Vol. 3: 1935–1938*. Ed. Howard Eiland and Michael W. Jennings. Cambridge: Harvard University Press, 2006.

———. "Theses on the Philosophy of History." *Illuminations: Essays and Reflections*, ed. Hannah Arendt, 253–65. New York: Schocken, 1969.

———. "The Work of Art in the Age of Mechanical Reproduction." *Illuminations: Essays and Reflections*, ed. Hannah Arendt, 217–51. New York: Schocken, 1969.

Bentz, Richard, et al. "Some Civil Defense Problems in the Nation's Capital Following Widespread Thermonuclear Attack." *Operations Research* 5, no. 3 (1957): 319–50.

Bernardot, Marc. *Loger les immigrés: La Sonacotra, 1956–2006*. Paris: Éditions du Croquant, 2008.

Bhattar, Srinivasacharya. "Jetprole Samsthanamu Pariseelana" (in Telugu). M.Phil thesis, Department of History and Culture, Telugu University (Srisailam), 1989.

Biehl, João. "Pharmaceutical Governance." *Global Pharmaceuticals: Ethics, Markets, Practices*, ed. Adriana Petryna, Andrew Lakoff, and Arthur Kleinman, 206–39. Durham: Duke University Press, 2006.

———. *Vita: Life in a Zone of Social Abandonment*. Berkeley: University of California, 2005.

———. "Will to Live: AIDS Drugs and Local Economies of Salvation." *Public Culture* 18, no. 3 (2006): 457–72.

———. *Will to Live: AIDS Therapies and the Politics of Survival*. Berkeley: University of California Press, 2007.

Bissell, William Cunningham. "Engaging Colonial Nostalgia." *Cultural Anthropology* 20, no. 2 (May 2005): 215–48.

Blake, Casey Nelson. "The Usable Past, the Comfortable Past, and the Civic Past: Memory in Contemporary America." *Cultural Anthropology* 14, no. 3 (August 1999): 423–35.

Blanchard, Pascal, Nicolas Bancel, and Sandrine Lemaire, eds. *La fracture coloniale: La société française au prisme de l'héritage colonial*. Paris: La Découverte, 2005.

Blanchot, Maurice. *The Writing of the Disaster*. Trans. Ann Smock. Lincoln: University of Nebraska Press, 1995.

Boelaert, Edmond, Honoré Vinck, and Charles Lonkama. "Arrivée des Blancs sur les bords des rivières équatoriales." *Annales Aequatoria* (1995) 16: 13–134; 17: 7–415.

Boiteau, Pierre. *Contribution à l'histoire de la Nation Malgache.* Paris: Editions Sociales, 1958.

Brands, H. W. "The Age of Vulnerability: Eisenhower and the National Insecurity State." *American Historical Review* 94, no. 4 (1989): 963–89.

Braw, Monica. *The Atomic Bomb Suppressed: American Censorship in Occupied Japan.* Armonk, N.Y.: M. E. Sharpe, 1997.

Breckenridge, Keith. "The Biometric Obsession: Trans-Atlantic Progressivism and the Making of the South African State." First Network workshop, "The Documentation of Individual Identity: Historical, Comparative and Transnational Perspectives since 1500," University of Oxford, 26–27 September 2008. http://www.history.ox.ac.uk/identinet/documents/PositionPaperBreckenridge.pdf.

———. "Verwoerd's Bureau of Proof: Total Information in the Making of Apartheid." *History Workshop Journal* 59 (2005): 83–108.

Brians, Paul. *Nuclear Holocausts: Atomic War in Fiction.* http://www.wsu.edu/~brians/nuclear/index.htm.

Briggs, Charles. *Stories in the Time of Cholera: Racial Profiling during a Medical Nightmare.* Berkeley: University of California Press, 2004.

Brinkley, Douglas. *Wheels for the World: Henry Ford, His Company, and a Century of Progress, 1903–2003.* New York: Viking, 2003.

Broch-Due, Vigdis. "Violence and Belonging: Analytical Reflections." *Violence and Belonging: The Quest for Identity in Post-colonial Africa,* ed. Vigdis Broch-Due, 1–40. London: Routledge, 2005.

Broderick, Mick, ed. *Hibakusha Cinema: Hiroshima, Nagasaki and the Nuclear Image in Japanese Film.* New York: Kegan Paul, 1996.

Brook, Daniel. "Environmental Genocide: Native Americans and Toxic Waste." *American Journal of Economics and Sociology* 57, no. 1 (January 1998): 105–13.

Brown, Wendy. "Wounded Attachments." *Political Theory* 21, no. 3 (1993): 390–410.

Browning, Frank, and Dorothy Forman, eds. *The Wasted Nation.* New York: Harper and Row, 1972.

Bruckner, Pascal. *La tyrannie de la penitence: Essai sur le masochisme occidental.* Paris: Bernard Grasset, 2006.

Bruner, Edward. *Culture on Tour: Ethnographies of Travel.* Chicago: Chicago University Press, 2004.

Buckley, Liam. "Objects of Love and Decay: Colonial Photographs in a Postcolonial Archive." *Cultural Anthropology* 20, no. 2 (May 2005): 249–70.

Buck-Morss, Susan. *The Dialectics of Seeing: Walter Benjamin and the Arcades Project.* Cambridge: Massachusetts Institute of Technology Press. 1991.

———. *Dreamworld and Catastrophe: The Passing of Mass Utopia in East and West.* Cambridge: Massachusetts Institute of Technology Press, 2000.

Burbank, Jane, and Frederick Cooper. "Review of Marc Ferro's *Le livre noir du colonia-*

lisme: 16–21 Siécle: De l'Extermination à la Repentance." *Cahiers d'études Africaines* 44, no. 1–2 (2004): 455–63.

Butler, Declan. "U.S. Abandons Health Study on Agent Orange." *Nature* 434, no. 7034 (April 2005): 687.

Butler, Mark, and David Hallowes. *The groundWork Report 2003: Forging the Future: Industrial Strategy and the Making of Environmental Injustice in South Africa.* Pietermaritzburg: groundWork, 2003. http://www.groundwork.org.za/Publications/Reports.

Butler, Mark, and David Hallowes, with Chris Albertyn, Gillian Watkins, and Rory O'Connor. *The groundWork Report 2002: Corporate Accountability in South Africa: The Petrochemical Industry and Air Pollution.* Pietermaritzburg: groundWork, 2002. http://www.groundwork.org.za/Publications/Reports.

Caldeira, Teresa, and James Holston. "State and Urban Space in Brazil: From Modernist Planning to Democratic Interventions." *Global Assemblages: Technology, Politics, and Ethics as Anthropological Problems,* ed. Aihwa Ong and Stephen Collier, 393–416. Malden: Blackwell, 2005.

Calhoun, Craig, Frederick Cooper, and Kevin W. Moore, eds. *Lessons of Empire: Imperial Histories and American Power.* New York: New Press, 2006.

Campos, Daniel, and Antonio Quijarro. *De Tarija a la Asunción: Expedicion boliviana de 1883.* Buenos Aires: Imprenta de Jacobo Peuser, 1888.

Carranza, Angel Justiniano. *Expedición al Gran Chaco Austral, bajo el comando del gobernador de estos territorios, Coronel Francisco B. Bosch (1883).* Buenos Aires: Imprenta Europa, 1884.

Carruthers, David V., ed. *Environmental Justice in Latin America.* Cambridge: Massachusetts Institute of Technology Press, 2008.

Caruth, Cathy. *Unclaimed Experience: Trauma, Narrative, and History.* Baltimore: Johns Hopkins University Press, 1996.

Castro Boedo, Emilio. *Estudios sobre la navegación del Bermejo y la colonización del Chaco.* San Salvador de Jujuy, Argentina: Universidad Nacional de Jujuy, 1995 [1872].

Caton, Steven. "Coetzee, Agamben, and the Passion of Abu Ghraib." *American Anthropologist* 108, no. 1 (2006): 114–23.

Caton, Steven, and Bernardo Zacka. "Abu Ghraib, the Security Apparatus, and the Performativity of Power." *American Ethnologist* 37, no. 2 (2010): 203–11.

Césaire, Aimé. *Discourse on Colonialism.* New York: Monthly Review Press, 2000.

Chakrabarti, Dilip K. *A History of Indian Archaeology: From the Beginning to 1947.* New Delhi: Munshiram Manoharlal Publishers, 2001.

Chambers, Michael Margrave. "Lomako: A Zairian Journey." Montreal: printed typescript, 1993.

Chance, Kerry. "Living Politics: Practices and Protests of 'the Poor' in Democratic South Africa." Unpublished manuscript, Department of Anthropology, University of Chicago, 2008.

Chari, Sharad. "The Antinomies of Political Evidence in Post-apartheid Durban, South Africa." *Journal of the Royal Anthropological Institute* (Special Issue 2008): S61–76.

———. "How Do Activists Act? Conceiving Counterhegemony in Durban." *Counterhe-*

gemony in the Colony and Postcolony, ed. John Chalcraft and Yaseen Noorani, 252–74. Basingstoke: Palgrave Macmillan, 2007.

———. "Photographing Dispossession, Forgetting Solidarity: Waiting for Social Justice in Wentworth, South Africa." Transactions of the Institute of British Geographers 34, no. 4 (2009): 521–40.

———. "Post-apartheid Livelihood Struggles in Wentworth, South Durban." The Development Decade? Economic and Social Change in South Africa, 1994–2004, ed. Vishnu Padayachee, 397–412. Cape Town: HSRC Press, 2006.

———. "Silencing the Present: Planning, Habitation, Opposition." Paper presented at the "Markets and Modernities" seminar, University of Toronto, 24 October 2008.

———. "State Racism and Biopolitical Struggle: The Evasive Commons in Twentieth Century Durban, South Africa." Radical History Review 108 (2010): 73–90.

———. "Subalternities That Matter in Times of Crisis." The Wiley-Blackwell Companion to Economic Geography, ed. Trevor J. Barnes, Jamie Peck, and Eric Sheppard, 501–14. London: Wiley-Blackwell, 2012.

Chatterjee, Partha. "Empire and Nation Revisited: 50 Years after Bandung." Inter-Asia Cultural Studies 6, no. 4 (2005): 487–96.

———. Nationalist Thought and the Colonial World: A Derivative Discourse? London: Zed Books for the United Nations University, 2001.

———. The Politics of the Governed: Reflections on Popular Politics in Most of the World. New York: Columbia University Press, 2004.

Chipkin, Ivor. Do South Africans Exist? Nationalism, Democracy and the Identity of the People. Johannesburg: Witwatersrand University Press, 2007.

Cliff, Michelle. No Telephone to Heaven. New York: Vintage, 1989.

Clifford, James, and George E. Marcus. Writing Culture: The Poetics and Politics of Ethnography. A School of American Research Advanced Seminar. Berkeley: University of California Press, 1986.

Coghlan, B., et al. "Mortality in the Democratic Republic of Congo: A Nationwide Survey." Lancet 367, no. 9504 (2006): 44–51.

Cohen, Shaul Ephraim. The Politics of Planting: Israeli-Palestinian Competition for Control of Land in the Jerusalem Periphery. Chicago: University of Chicago Press, 1995.

Cohn, Carol. "Sex and Death in the Rational World of Defense Intellectuals." Signs 12, no. 4 (1987): 687–718.

Collier, Stephen. "Topologies of Power: Foucault's Study of Political Government beyond 'Governmentality.'" Theory, Culture, and Society 26, no. 6 (2009): 1–31.

Collins, John. "'But What If I Should Need to Defecate in Your Neighborhood, Madame?': Empire, Redemption and the 'Tradition of the Oppressed' in a Brazilian Historical Center." Cultural Anthropology 23, no. 2 (2008): 279–328.

———. "Culture, Content, and the Enclosure of Human Being: UNESCO's 'Intangible' Heritage in the New Millennium." Radical History Review, no. 109 (winter): 121–35.

———. "Patrimony, Public Health, and National Culture: The Commodification and Redemption of Origins in Neoliberal Brazil." *Critique of Anthropology* 28, no. 2 (2008): 237–55.

———. *The Revolt of the Saints: Memory and Redemption in the Twilight of Brazilian "Racial Democracy."* Durham: Duke University Press, forthcoming.

———. " 'X Marks the Future of Brazil': Racial Politics, Bedeviling Mixtures and Protestant Ethics in a Brazilian Cultural Heritage Center." *Off Stage / On Display: Intimacies and Ethnographies in the Age of Public Culture*, ed. Andrew Shryock, 191–224. Stanford: Stanford University Press, 2004.

Comaroff, Jean. "Beyond Bare Life: AIDS, (Bio)Politics, and the Neoliberal Order." *Public Culture* 19, no. 1 (2007): 197–219.

Comaroff, Jean, and John L. Comaroff. "Occult Economies and the Violence of Abstraction: Notes from the South African Postcolony." *American Ethnologist* 26, no. 3 (1999): 279–301.

———. "Millennial Capitalism: First Thoughts on Second Coming." *Public Culture* 12, no. 2 (2000): 291–343.

Congo Reform Association. "Treatment of Women and Children in the Congo State, 1895–1904: An Appeal to the Women of the United States of America." Boston: Congo Reform Association, 1904.

Cooper, Frederick. "Decolonizing Situations: The Rise, Fall, and Rise of Colonial Studies, 1951–2001." *French Politics, Culture, and Society* 20, no. 2 (2002): 47–76.

Cooper, Frederick, and Randall Packard, eds. *International Development and the Social Sciences*. Berkeley: University of California Press, 2004.

Cooper, Frederick, and Ann L. Stoler, eds. *Tensions of Empire: Colonial Cultures in a Bourgeois World*. Berkeley: University of California Press, 1997.

Coronil, Fernando. "Editor's Column: The End of Postcolonial Theory?" *Publications of the Modern Language Association* 122, no. 3 (2007): 645.

Cosby, Alfred. *Ecological Imperialism: The Biological Expansion of Europe, 900–1900*. New York: Cambridge University Press, 1986.

Craig, Campbell. *Destroying the Village: Eisenhower and Thermonuclear War*. New York: Columbia University Press, 1998.

Crapanzano, Vincent. *Waiting: The Whites of South Africa*. New York: Random House, 1985.

Csete, Joanne, and Julianne Kippenberg. *The War within the War: Sexual Violence against Women and Girls in Eastern Congo*. New York: Human Rights Watch, 2002.

da Cunha, Euclides. *The Amazon: Land without History*. Trans. R. Sousa. New York: Oxford University Press, 2006.

———. *Rebellion in the Backlands*. Trans. S. Putnam. Chicago: University of Chicago Press, 1944.

Dagens, Bruno. *Entre Alampur et Srisailam: Recherches archéologiques en Andhra Pradesh*. Pondichéry: Institut Français D'Indologie, 1984.

Daniel, E. Valentine. *Charred Lullabies*. Princeton: Princeton University Press, 1996.

———. "The Coolie." *Cultural Anthropology* 23, no. 2 (2008): 254–78.

————. *Fluid Signs: Being a Person the Tamil Way*. Berkeley: University of California Press, 1984.

Daniel, E. Valentine, and Jan Breman. "The Making of a Coolie." *Plantations, Proletarians, and Peasants in Colonial Asia*, ed. E. V. Daniel and Henry Tom Brass, 268–95. London: F. Cass, 1992.

Das, Veena. "Dislocation and Rehabilitation: Defining a Field." *Economic and Political Weekly* 31, no. 24 (1996): 1509–14.

————. *Life and Words: Violence and the Descent into the Ordinary*. Berkeley: University of California Press, 2007.

————. *Remaking a World: Violence, Social Suffering and Recovery*. Berkeley: University of California Press, 2001.

Davis, Doug. " 'A Hundred Million Hydrogen Bombs': Total War in the Fossil Record." *Configurations* 9 (2001): 461–508.

Davis, Tracy D. "Between History and Event: Rehearsing Nuclear War Survival." *Drama Review* 46, no. 4 (2002): 11–45.

de Brizuela, Blas Joaquín. "Diario de Matorras." *"Entradas" al Chaco*, ed. P. De Angelis, 135–53. San Salvador de Jujuy, Argentina: Universidad Nacional de Jujuy, 1989 [1774].

de Genova, Nicolas. "The Stakes of an Anthropology of the United States." *New Centennial Review* 7, no. 2 (2007): 231–77.

de la Serna, Gerónimo. *1,500 kilómetros a lomo de mula: Expedición victorica al Chaco, 1884–1885*. Buenos Aires: Imprenta López, 1930.

Delathuy, A. M. *De Geheime documentatie van de Onderzoekcommissie in de Kongostaat*. Berchem, Belgium: EPO, 1988.

Deleuze, Gilles, and Felix Guattari. *A Thousand Plateaus: Capitalism and Schizophrenia*. Trans. Brian Massumi. New York: Continuum, 1987.

Derrida, Jacques. "No Apocalypse, Not Now (Full Speed Ahead, Seven Missiles, Seven Missives)." *Diacritics* 20 (1984): 20–31.

Desai, Ashwin. *We Are the Poors: Community Struggles in Post-apartheid South Africa*. New York: Monthly Review Press, 2002.

de Silva, G. P. S. H. "Beginnings of Commercial Road-Passenger Transportation in Sri Lanka." *Journal of the Ceylon Branch of the Royal Asiatic Society* 36 (1991–92): 96–107.

Dirks, Nicholas. *The Hollow Crown*. Cambridge: Cambridge University Press, 1987.

Dirlik, Arif. "Historical Colonialism in Contemporary Perspective." *Public Culture* 14, no. 3 (2002): 611–15.

Dobrizhoffer, Martin. *An Account of the Abipones, an Equestrian People of Paraguay*. New York: Johnson Reprint Corporation, 1970 [1784].

Donham, Donald L. "Freeing South Africa: The 'Modernization' of Male-Male Sexuality in Soweto." *Cultural Anthropology* 13, no. 1 (February 1998): 3–21.

Drèze, Jean, Meera Samson, and Satyajit Singh, eds. *The Dam and the Nation: Displacement and Resettlement in the Narmada Valley*. Delhi: Oxford University Press, 1997.

Dubois, Laurent. *A Colony of Citizens*. Chapel Hill: University of North Carolina Press, 2004.

Eagleton, Terry. *After Theory*. New York: Basic, 2003.

——. *Holy Terror*. Oxford: Oxford University Press, 2005.

Eden, Lynn. "City of Fire." *Bulletin of the Atomic Scientists* (January–February 2004): 33–42.

Edensor, Tom. *Industrial Ruins: Space, Aesthetics and Materiality*. New York: Berg, 2005.

Emizet, Kisangani N. F. "The Massacre of Refugees in Congo: A Case of UN Peacekeeping Failure and International Law." *Journal of Modern African Studies* 38, no. 2 (2000): 163–202.

Erasmus, Zimitri. "Introduction: Re-imagining Coloured Identities in Post-apartheid South Africa." *Coloured by History, Shaped by Place: New Perspectives on Coloured Identities in Cape Town*, ed. Zimitri Erasmus, 13–28. Cape Town: Kwela Books/South African History Online, 2001.

Evans, Joyce A. *Celluloid Mushroom Clouds: Hollywood and the Atomic Bomb*. Boulder: Westview, 1998.

Fact-Finding Committee on the Srisailam Project. "Srisailam Resettlement Experience: The Untold Story." *The Social and Environmental Effects of Large Dams, Vol 2: Case Studies*, ed. Edward Goldsmith and Nicholas Hildyard, 255–60. Cornwall: Wadebridge Ecological Centre, 1986.

Fanon, Frantz. *The Wretched of the Earth*. New York: Grove, 1963.

Farred, Grant. "The Not-Yet Counterpartisan: A New Politics of Oppositionality." *South Atlantic Quarterly* 103, no. 4 (2004): 589–605.

——. "Where Does the Rainbow Nation End? Colouredness and Citizenship in Post-apartheid South Africa." *New Centennial Review* 1, no. 1 (2001): 175–99.

Fassin, Didier. *When Bodies Remember: Experiences and Politics of AIDS in South Africa*. Berkeley: University of California Press, 2007.

Fassin, Didier, and Paula Vasquez. "Humanitarian Exception as the Rule: The Political Theology of the 1999 *Tragedia* in Venezuela." *American Ethnologist* 32, no. 3 (2005): 389–405.

Federal Civil Defense Administration. *Annual Report for 1955*. Washington: Government Printing Office, 1956.

——. *Operation Cue: The Atomic Test Program*. Washington: Government Printing Office, 1955.

Feldman, Allen. *Formations of Violence: The Narrative of the Body and Political Terror in Northern Ireland*. Chicago: University of Chicago Press, 1991.

Feldman, Ilana. *Governing Gaza: Bureaucracy, Authority, and the Work of Rule, 1917–1967*. Durham: Duke University Press, 2008.

Ferguson, James. *Expectations of Modernity: Myths and Meanings of Urban Life on the Zambian Copperbelt*. Berkeley: University of California Press, 1999.

——. "Seeing Like an Oil Company: Space, Security, and Global Capital in Neoliberal Africa." *American Anthropologist* 107, no. 3 (2005): 377–82.

Fernandes, Walter, and E. G. Thukral, eds. *Development, Displacement and Rehabilitation*. New Delhi: Indian Social Institute, 1989.

Fernández Cornejo, Adrián. "Diario de la expedición de Cornejo al Chaco." *Colección* de obras y documentos relativos a la historia antigua y moderna de las provincias del Río de la Plata, ed. Pedro de Angelis, 459–509. Buenos Aires: Plus Ultra, 1970 [1790].

Figlan, Lindela, Rev Mavuso, Busi Ngema, Zodwa Nsibande, Sihle Sibisi, and Sbu Zikode. *Living Learning*. Abahali baseMjondolo, 3 October 2009. http://abahlali .org/node/5843.

Filho, Godofredo. *Irmã poesia: Seleção de poemas, 1923–1986*. Salvador: Secretaria da Educação e Cultura da Bahia, Academia de Letras da Bahia, 1987.

Fine, Ben, and Zavareh Rustomjee. *The Political Economy of South Africa: From Minerals-Energy Complex to Industrialisation*. London: C. Hurst, 1996.

Fine-Dare, Kathleen S. *Grave Injustice: The American Indian Repatriation Movement and NAGPRA*. Lincoln: University of Nebraska Press, 2002.

Finn, Janet. *Tracing the Veins: Of Copper, Culture, and Community from Butte to Chuquicamata*. Berkeley: University of California Press, 1998.

FitzGerald, Frances. *Way Out There in the Blue: Reagan, Star Wars, and the End of the Cold War*. New York: Simon and Schuster, 2000.

Fontana, Luis Jorge. *El Gran Chaco*. Buenos Aires: Solar-Hachette, 1977 [1881].

Fontein, Joost. *The Silence of Great Zimbabwe: Contested Landscape and the Power of Heritage*. London: University College London Press, 2006.

Forrow, Lachlan, and Victor Sidel. "Medicine and Nuclear War." *Journal of the American Medical Association* 280, no. 5 (1998): 456–61.

Foucault, Michel. *The Archaeology of Knowledge and the Discourse on Language*. Trans. A. M. Sheridan Smith. New York: Pantheon, 1972.

———. *The Birth of Biopolitics: Lectures and the Collège de France, 1978–1979*. Basingstoke: Palgrave Macmillan, 2008.

———. *Discipline and Punish: The Birth of the Prison*. Trans. Alan Sheridan. New York: Vintage, 1979.

———. *The History of Sexuality, Volume 1: An Introduction*. New York: Vintage, 1980.

———. *"Society Must Be Defended": Lectures and the Collège de France, 1975–1976*. New York: Picador, 2003.

Fox, Diane. "Chemical Politics and the Hazards of Modern Warfare: Agent Orange." *Synthetic Planet: Chemical Politics and the Hazards of Modern Warfare*, ed. Monica Casper, 73–89. New York: Routledge, 2003.

———. "One Significant Ghost: Agent Orange: Narratives of Trauma, Survival, and Responsibility." Ph.D. diss., Department of Anthropology, University of Washington, 2007.

French, Jan. "Buried Alive: Imagining Africa in the Brazilian Northeast." *American Ethnologist* 33, no. 3 (2006): 340–60.

Freund, Bill, and Vishnu Padayachee, eds. *(D)urban Vortex: South African City in Transition*. Pietermaritzburg: University of Natal Press, 2002.

Freyre, Gilberto. *The Masters and the Slaves: A Study in the Development of Brazilian Civilization*. Trans. S. Putnam. Berkeley: University of California Press, 1986.

Friedberg, Aaron L. *In the Shadow of the Garrison State: America's Anti-statism and Its Cold War Grand Strategy*. Princeton: Princeton University Press, 2000.

Frykenberg, Robert. "The Silent Settlement in South India, 1793–1853: An Analysis of the Role of Inams in the Rise of the Indian Imperial System." *Land Tenure and Peasant in South Asia*, ed. Robert Frykenberg, 37–53. New Delhi: Orient Longman, 1977.

Furlong, Guillermo. *Cartografía jesuítica del Río de la Plata*. Buenos Aires: Jacobo Peuser, 1936.

———. *Entre los Vilelas de Salta*. Buenos Aires: Academia Literaria del Plata, 1939.

Gaddis, John Lewis. *Strategies of Containment: A Critical Appraisal of Postwar American National Security Policy*. Oxford: Oxford University Press, 1982.

Garmendia, José. "Diario del Coronel Garmendia." *Campaña del Chaco*, 84–152. Buenos Aires: Imprenta Europa, 1885.

Garrison, Dee. *Bracing for Armageddon: Why Civil Defense Never Worked*. Oxford: Oxford University Press, 2006.

George, Alice. *Awaiting Armageddon: How Americans Faced the Cuban Missile Crisis*. Chapel Hill: University of North Carolina Press, 2003.

Geurts, Kathryn Linn. *Culture and the Senses: Bodily Ways of Knowing in an African Community*. Berkeley: University of California Press, 2002.

Ghosh, Amitav. "The Global Reservation: Notes toward an Ethnography of International Peacekeeping." *Cultural Anthropology* 9, no. 3 (August 1994): 412–22.

Ghosh, Kaushik. "Between Global Flows and Local Dams: Indigenousness, Locality and the Transnational Sphere in Jharkhand, India." *Cultural Anthropology* 21, no. 4 (2006): 501–33.

Gibbon, Edward, and D. M. Low. *The History of the Decline and Fall of the Roman Empire*. New York: Harcourt, Brace, 1960 [1776–88].

Gibson, Nigel C. "Calling Everything into Question: Broken Promises, Social Movements and Emergent Intellectual Currents in Post-apartheid South Africa." *Challenging Hegemony: Social Movements and the Quest for a New Humanism in Post-apartheid South Africa*, ed. Nigel C. Gibson, 1–54. Trenton, N.J.: Africa World Press, 2006.

———, ed. *Challenging Hegemony: Social Movements and the Quest for a New Humanism in Post-apartheid South Africa*. Trenton, N.J.: Africa World Press, 2006.

———. "What Happened to the 'Promised Land?' A Fanonian Perspective on Post-apartheid South Afric." *Antipode* 44, no. 1 (2012): 51–73.

Gilroy, Paul. *Against Race: Imagining Political Culture Beyond the Color-Line*. Cambridge: Belknap Press of Harvard University Press, 2000.

Ginsberg, Robert. *The Aesthetics of Ruins*. Amsterdam: Rodopi, 2004.

Glaser, Clive. *Bo-Tsotsi: The Youth Gangs of Soweto, 1935–1976*. Portsmouth: Heinemann, 2000.

———. "Swines, Hazels and the Dirty Dozen: Masculinity, Territoriality and the Youth Gangs of Soweto, 1960–1976." *Journal of Southern African Studies* 24, no. 4 (1998): 719–36.

Glasstone, Samuel, and Philip J. Dolan, eds. *The Effects of Nuclear Weapons*. 3d edn. Washington: U.S. Department of Defense / U.S. Department of Energy, 1977.

Glissant, Edouard. *Caribbean Discourse: Selected Essays*. Charlottesville: University of Virginia Press, 1989.

Goldstein, Donna. *Laughter Out of Place: Race, Class, Violence, and Sexuality in a Rio Shanty-town*. Berkeley: University of California Press, 2003.

Good, Mary-Jo DelVecchio, Sandra Teresa Hyde, Sarah Pinto, and Bryon Good, eds. *Postcolonial Disorders*. Berkeley: University of California Press, 2008.

Gordillo, Gastón R. *The Afterlife of Places: Ruins and the Destruction of Space*. Durham: Duke University Press, forthcoming.

———. *Landscapes of Devils: Tensions of Place and Memory in the Argentinean Chaco*. Durham: Duke University Press, 2004.

———. "Ships Stranded in the Forest: Debris and Memories of Progress on a Phantom River." *Current Anthropology* 52, no. 2 (2011): 141–67.

Gorostiaga, Máxima. *El misterio de Esteco*. Santiago del Estero: Editorial El Liberal, 1986.

Govender, Pregs. *Love and Courage: A Story of Insubordination*. Cape Town: Jacana, 2008.

Government of South Africa. *Constitution of the Republic of South Africa, 1996*. Chapter 2: Bill of Rights, section 24: Environment. South Africa Government Information. Last updated 19 August 2009. http://www.info.gov.za/documents/constitution/1996/96cons2.htm.

Grandin, Greg. *Empire's Workshop: Latin America, the United States, and the Rise of the New Imperialism*. New York: Metropolitan, 2005.

———. *Fordlandia: The Rise and Fall of Henry Ford's Forgotten Jungle City*. New York: Metropolitan, 2009.

———. "Touring Empire's Ruin: From Detroit to the Amazon." *Nation*, 23 June 2009. http://www.thenation.com/article/touring-empires-ruins-detroit-amazon.

Grant, Kevin. *A Civilised Savagery: Britain and the New Slaveries in Africa, 1884–1926*. New York: Routledge, 2005.

Griffiths, Philip Jones. *Agent Orange: "Collateral Damager" in Viet Nam*. London: Trolley Limited, 2003.

Grinde, Donald, and Bruce Johansen, eds. *Ecocide of Native America: Environmental Destruction of Indian Lands and People*. Santa Fe: Clear Light, 1995.

Grossman, Andrew. *Neither Dead Nor Red: Civilian Defense and American Political Development during the Early Cold War*. New York: Routledge, 2001.

Grosz, Elizabeth A. *The Nick of Time: Politics, Evolution, and the Untimely*. Durham: Duke University Press, 2004.

———. "A Politics of Imperceptibility: A Response to 'Anti-racism, Multiculturalism and the Ethics of Identification.'" *Philosophy and Social Criticism* 28, no. 4 (2002): 463–72.

Grove, Richard H. *Green Imperialism: Colonial Expansion, Tropical Island Edens and the Origins of Environmentalism*. New York: Cambridge University Press, 1995.

Gueye, Khalil, dir. *Les âmes brisées: Dans l'enfer des femmes, filles, et petites filles victimes des viols sexuels en RDC*. Kinshasa: UNFPA, 2006.

Guha, Ranajit. *A Rule of Property for Bengal: An Essay on the Idea of Permanent Settlement*. Foreword by Amartya Sen. Durham: Duke University Press, 1996.

Gullón Abao, Alberto. *La frontera del Chaco en la gobernación del Tucumán 1750–1810*. Cádiz: Universidad de Cádiz, 1993.

Gunasekara, Tisaranee. *Sri Lanka in Crisis: A Lost Generation: The Untold Story*. Colombo, Sri Lanka: S. Gadage and Brothers, 1998.

Gupta, Akhil. *Postcolonial Developments: Agriculture in the Making of Modern India*. Durham: Duke University Press, 1998.

Hale, Charles. "Does Multiculturalism Menace? Governance, Cultural Rights, and the Politics of Identity in Guatemala." *Journal of Latin American Anthropology* 2, no. 1 (2002): 34–61.

———. *Más que un Indio / More Than an Indian: Racial Ambivalence and Neoliberal Multiculturalism in Guatemala*. Santa Fe: School for Advanced Research Press, 2006.

Hall, Stuart, "Race, Articulation and Society Structured in Difference." *Sociological Theories: Race and Colonialism*, ed. UNESCO, 304–45. Paris: UNESCO, 1980.

Hallowes, David, and Victor Munnik. *The groundWork Report 2006: Poisoned Spaces: Manufacturing Wealth, Producing Poverty*. Pietermaritzburg: groundWork, 2006. http://www.groundwork.org.za/Publications/Reports.

Halperín Donghi, Julio. *Una nación para el desierto argentino*. Buenos Aires: Prometeo, 2006.

Hamilton, Carolyn, Verne Harris, Jane Taylor, Michele Pickover, Graeme Reid, and Razia Saleh, eds. *Refiguring the Archive*. Cape Town: David Philip, 2002.

Handel, Ariel. "Chronology of the Occupation Regime, 1967–2007." *The Power of Inclusive Exclusion: Anatomy of the Israeli Rule in the Occupied Palestinian Territories*, ed. Adi Ophir, Michal Givoni, and Sari Hanafi, 603–34. Cambridge, Mass.: Zone, 2009.

Handler, Richard, and Eric Gable. *The New History in an Old Museum: Creating the Past at Colonial Williamsburg*. Durham: Duke University Press, 1997.

Hansen, Thomas Blom. "Melancholia of Freedom: Humour and Nostalgia among Indians in South Africa." *Modern Drama* 48, no. 2 (summer 2005): 297–315.

———. "Sounds of Freedom: Music, Taxis, and Racial Imagination in Urban South Africa." *Public Culture* 18, no. 1 (2006): 185–208.

Hardt, Michael, and Antonio Negri. *Empire*. Cambridge: Harvard University Press, 2000.

Harms, Robert. "The End of Red Rubber: A Reassessment." *Journal of African History* 16 (1975): 73–88.

———. "The World ABIR Made: The Maringa-Lopori Basin, 1885–1903." *African Economic History* 12 (1983): 125–39.

Harootunian, Harry. "The Benjamin Effect: Modernism, Repetition, and the Path to Different Cultural Imaginaries." *Walter Benjamin and the Demands of History*, ed. Michael P. Steinberg, 62–87. Ithaca: Cornell University Press, 1996.

———. "Some Thoughts on Comparability and the Space-Time Problem." *boundary 2*, no. 32 (2005): 23–52.

Harrington, Carol. "Governing Peacekeeping: The Role of Authority and Expertise in the Case of Sexual Violence and Trauma." *Economy and Society* 35, no. 3 (2006): 346–80.

Hart, Gillian. "Changing Concepts of Articulation: Political Stakes in South Africa Today." *Review of African Political Economy* 111 (March 2007): 85–101.

———. *Disabling Globalization: Places of Power in Post-apartheid South Africa.* Berkeley: University of California Press, 2002.

———. "The Provocations of Neo-liberalism: Contesting the Nation and Liberation after Apartheid." *Antipode* 40, no. 4 (2008): 678–705.

Harvey, David. *The New Imperialism.* New York: Oxford University Press, 2005.

Hasty, Jennifer. "The Pleasures of Corruption: Desire and Discipline in Ghanaian Political Culture." *Cultural Anthropology* 20, no. 2 (May 2005): 271–301.

Heather, Peter. *Empires and Barbarians: The Fall of Rome and the Birth of Europe.* New York: Oxford University Press, 2010.

Hell, Julia, and Andreas Schönle. "Ruins of Modernity: Introduction." *Ruins of Modernity,* ed. Julia Hell and Andreas Schönle, 1–16. Durham: Duke University Press, 2010.

Hewlett, Richard G., and Jack M. Holl. *Atoms for Peace and War, 1953–1961: Eisenhower and the Atomic Energy Commission.* Berkeley: University of California Press, 1989.

Hochschild, Adam. *King Leopold's Ghost: A Story of Greed, Terror, and Heroism in Colonial Africa.* Boston: Houghton Mifflin, 1998.

Hodges, Sarah. "Chennai's Biotrash Chronicles: Chasing the Neo-liberal Syringe." Garnet Working Paper no. 44/08.

Hoffman, Daniel Lee. "The City as Barracks: Freetown, Monrovia, and the Organization of Violence in Postcolonial African Cities." *Cultural Anthropology* 22, no. 3 (November 2010): 400–428.

Hollup, Oddvar. *Bonded Labour: Caste and Cultural Identity among Tamil Plantation Workers in Sri Lanka.* New Delhi: Sterling, 1994.

Holston, James. *The Modernist City.* Chicago: University of Chicago Press, 1989.

Hooks, Gregory, and Chad L. Smith. "The Treadmill of Destruction: National Sacrifice Areas and Native Americans." *American Sociological Review* 69, no. 4 (August 2004): 558–75.

Hoole, Rajan. *Sri Lanka: The Arrogance of Power: Myths, Decadence and Murder.* Jaffna, Sri Lanka: University Teachers for Human Rights, 2001.

Host, Francisco. "Informe del Comandante Host." *Campaña del Chaco,* 640–711. Buenos Aires: Imprenta Europa, 1885.

Hunt, Nancy Rose. " 'Le bébé en brousse': European Women, African Birth Spacing and Colonial Intervention in Breast Feeding in the Belgian Congo." *International Journal of African Historical Studies* 21 (1988): 401–32.

———. *A Colonial Lexicon of Birth Ritual, Medicalization, and Mobility in the Congo.* Durham: Duke University Press, 1999.

———. "Colonial Medical Anthropology and the Making of the Central African Infertility Belt." *Ordering Africa: Anthropology, European Imperialism, and the Politics of Knowledge,* ed. Helen Tilley with Robert J. Gordon, 252–81. Manchester: Manchester University Press, 2007.

———. "Hommes et femmes, sujets du Congo colonial." *La mémoire du Congo: Le temps colonial,* ed. Jean-Luc Vellut, 50–57. Tervuren, Belgium: Musée royal de l'Afrique centrale, 2005.

————. *A Nervous State: Violence, Remedies, and Reverie in Colonial Congo*. Durham: Duke University Press, forthcoming.

————. "Tintin and the Interruptions of Congolese Comics." *Images and Empires: Visuality in Colonial and Postcolonial Africa*, ed. Paul S. Landau and Deborah Kaspin, 90–123. Berkeley: University of California Press, 2002.

Initiative Conjointe de Lutte contres les Violences Sexuelles Faites aux Femmes et aux Enfants en RDC. "Rapport de mission à Mbandaka, Kisangani, Kindu, Kalemie, Bukavu, Goma, Kinshasa, du 4 au 21 aout 2003." Kinshasa: unpublished typescript, 2003.

Integrated Regional Information Networks. "Democratic Republic of Congo (DRC): New Cases of Rape and Abuse by Police in Equateur." IRIN, 7 September 2007. http://www.irinnews.org/report.aspx?reportid=60830.

Ismond, Patricia. *Abandoning Dead Metaphors: The Caribbean Phase of Derek Walcott's Poetry*. Barbados: University of the West Indies Press, 2001.

Jackson, Stephen. "Making a Killing: Criminality and Coping in the Kivu War Economy." *Review of African Political Economy* 93–94 (2002): 517–36.

Jaguaribe, Beatriz. "Modernist Ruins: National Narratives and Architectural Forms." *Public Culture* 11, no. 1 (winter 1999): 294–312.

Jain, S. Lochlann. "Cancer Butch." *Cultural Anthropology* 22, no. 4 (November 2007): 501–38.

Jakobson, Roman. *Six Lectures on Sound and Meaning*. Cambridge: Massachusetts Institute of Technology Press, 1978.

Janis, Irving L. *Air War and Emotional Stress: Psychological Studies of Bombing and Civilian Defense*. New York: McGraw-Hill, 1951.

Jarosz, Lucy. "Defining and Explaining Tropical Deforestation: Shifting Cultivation and Population Growth in Colonial Madagascar (1896–1940)." *Economic Geography* 69, no. 4 (October 1993): 366–79.

Johnson, Chalmers. *The Sorrows of Empire: Militarism, Secrecy, and the End of the Republic*. New York: Metropolitan Books, 2004.

Kabha, Mustafa, and Guy Raz, eds. *Remembering a Place: A Photographic History of Wadi 'Ara, 1903–2008*. Umm el-Fahm, Israel: Umm el-Fahm Art Gallery, Alsabar, 2008.

Kahn, Herman. *On Thermonuclear War*. Princeton: Princeton University Press, 1960.

Kahn, Paul W. *Sacred Violence: Torture, Terror, and Sovereignty*. Ann Arbor: University of Michigan Press, 2008.

Kaplan, Amy. "Homeland Insecurities: Reflection on Language and Space." *Radical History Review* 85 (winter 2003): 82–93.

Katz, Milton. *Ban the Bomb: A History of SANE, the Committee for a Sane Nuclear Policy, 1957–1985*. New York: Greenwood, 1986.

Keeney, L. Douglas. *The Doomsday Scenario*. St. Paul: MBI Publishing, 2002.

Keever, Beverly Ann Deepe. *News Zero: The New York Times and the Bomb*. Monroe, Maine: Common Courage Press, 2004.

Khalidi, Rashid. *Resurrecting Empire: Western Footprints and America's Perilous Path in the Middle East*. Boston: Beacon, 2004.

Khalidi, Walid. *All That Remains: The Palestinian Villages Occupied and Depopulated by Israel in 1948*. Washington: Institute for Palestine Studies, 1992.

Kincaid, Jamaica. *A Small Place*. New York: Farrar, Straus and Giroux, 1988.

Klawiter, Marin. *Biopolitics of Breast Cancer: Changing Cultures of Disease and Activism*. Minneapolis: University of Minnesota Press, 2008.

Klein, Naomi. *The Shock Doctrine: The Rise of Disaster Capitalism*. New York: Holt, 2007.

Falk, Richard A., Gabriel Kolko, and Robert Jay Lifton, eds. *Crimes of War: A Legal, Political-Documentary, and Psychological Inquiry into the Responsibility of Leaders, Citizens, and Soldiers for Criminal Acts in Wars*. New York: Random House, 1971.

Kosek, Jake. *Understories: The Political Life of Forests in Northern New Mexico*. Durham: Duke University Press, 2006.

Koselleck, Reinhardt. *Futures Past: On the Semantics of Historical Time*. Trans. Keith Tribe. Cambridge: Massachusetts Institute of Technology Press, 1985.

Kramer, Paul. *The Blood of Government: Race, Empire, the United States and the Philippines*. Chapel Hill: University of North Carolina Press, 2006.

Kraus, Sidney, Reuben Mehling, and Elaine El-Assal. "Mass Media and the Fallout Controversy." *Public Opinion Quarterly* 27, no. 2 (1963): 191–205.

Krugler, David F. *This Is Only a Test: How Washington DC Prepared for Nuclear War*. New York: Palgrave, 2006.

Kuklick, Henrika. "Contested Monuments: The Politics of Archeology in Southern Africa." *Colonial Situations: Essays on the Contextualization of Ethnographic Knowledge*, ed. George Stocking Jr., 135–69. Madison: University of Wisconsin Press, 1991.

Kuletz, Valerie. "Cold War Nuclear and Militarized Landscapes." *Violent Environments*, ed. Nancy Lee Peluso and Michael Watts, 237–60. Ithaca: Cornell University Press, 2001.

———. *The Tainted Desert: Environment and Social Ruin in the American West*. New York: Routledge, 1998.

Kull, Christian. *Isle of Fire: The Political Ecology of Landscape Burning in Madagascar*. Chicago: University of Chicago Press, 1995.

Lambek, Michael. *The Weight of the Past: Living with History in Mahajanga, Madagscar*. New York: Palgrave, 2002.

Lampert, Lawrence. *Nietzsche's Teaching: An Interpretation of Zarathustra*. New Haven: Yale University Press, 1986.

Langguth, A. J. *Hidden Terrors*. New York: Pantheon, 1978.

Latour, Bruno. *Reassembling the Social: An Introduction to Actor-Network-Theory*. Cambridge: Cambridge University Press, 2005.

Lazarus, Neil. "Postcolonial Studies after the Invasion of Iraq." *New Formations* 59 (2006): 10–22.

Lazreg, Marnia. *Twilight of Empire: From Algiers to Baghdad*. Princeton: Princeton University Press, 2008.

Lazzara, Michael, and Vicky Unruh, eds. *Telling Ruins in Latin America*. New York: Palgrave, 2009.

Leary, John Patrick. "Detroitism." *Guernica*, 15 January 2011. http://www.guernicamag
.com/features/2281/leary_1_15_11.

Le Cour Grandmaison, Olivier. *La République impériale*. Paris: La Découverte, 2009.

Lefebvre, Henri. *The Production of Space*. Oxford: Blackwell, 2001 [1974].

———. *Writings on Cities*. Oxford: Blackwell, 1996.

Lefeuvre, Daniel. *Pour en finir avec la repentance colonial*. Paris: Flammarion, 2006.

Legassick, Martin. "South Africa: Forced Labor, Industrialization and Racial Differentiation." *The Political Economy of Africa*, ed. R. Harris, 229–70. New York: Halsted
Press, 1975.

Leslie, Stuart W. *The Cold War and American Science: The Military-Industrial Academic Complex
at MIT and Stanford*. New York: Columbia University Press, 1993.

Lévi-Strauss, Claude. *The Savage Mind*. Chicago: University of Chicago Press, 1966.

———. *Tristes Tropiques*. New York: Atheneum, 1964.

———. *Tristes Tropiques*. New York: Atheneum, 1981.

Lev-Tov, Boaz. "Cultural Relations between Jews and Arabs in Palestine during the
Late Ottoman Period." *Zmanim* 110 (spring 2010): 42–55.

Li, Tania Murray. "Beyond 'the State' and Failed Schemes." *American Anthropologist* 107,
no. 3 (2005): 383–94.

———. "To Make Live or Let Die? Rural Dispossession and the Protection of Surplus
Populations." *Antipode* 14, no. 6 (2009): 1208–35.

———. *The Will to Improve: Governmentality, Development, and the Practice of Politics*. Durham: Duke University Press, 2007.

Lloyd, David. "Ruination: Partition and the Expectation of Violence (on Allan de-
Souza's Irish Photography)." *Social Identities* 9, no. 4 (2003): 475–509. Online, ac-
cessed 8 September 2010.

Locke, John. *The Second Treatise of Government and a Letter Concerning Toleration*. Mineola,
N.Y.: Dover, 2002.

Lockman, Zachary. *Comrades and Enemies: Arab and Jewish Workers in Palestine, 1906–1948*.
Berkeley: University of California Press, 1996.

Lottering, Agnes. *Winnifred and Agnes: The True Story of Two Women*. Cape Town: Kwela
Books, 2002.

Lozano, Pedro. *Descripción corográfica del Gran Chaco Gualamba*. San Miguel de Tucumán,
Argentina: Universidad Nacional de Tucumán, 1989 [1733].

Lussy, P. J., and K. I. Matemo. "La violence sexuelle des jeunes filles à Goma: À pro-
pos de 91 cas reçus au Docs Heal Africa." *Congo Medical* 14, no. 8 (2006): 703–9.

Lutz, Katherine. "Empire Is in the Details." *American Ethnologist* 33, no. 4 (2006): 593–
611.

MacCannell, Dean. *The Tourist: A New Theory of the Leisure Class*. Berkeley: University of
California Press, 1999.

MacDonald, Andrew. "Durban-Bound: Chinese Miners, Colonial Medicine and the
Floating Compounds of the Indian Ocean, 1904–7." *Journal of Natal and Zulu History* 23 (2005): 94–128.

Magis, P. "Consultations de stérilité à l'hôpital de Boende." Unpublished Examen B manuscript, Institute of Tropical Medicine, Antwerp, 1958.

Makhijani, Arjun, Howard Hu, and Katherine Yih, eds. *Nuclear Wastelands: A Global Guide to Nuclear Weapons Production and Its Health and Environmental Effects*. Cambridge: Massachusetts Institute of Technology Press, 1995.

Makhijani, Arjun, and Stephen I. Schwartz. "Victims of the Bomb." *Atomic Audit: The Costs and Consequences of U.S. Nuclear Weapons since 1940*, ed. Stephen I. Schwartz, 395–431. Washington: Brookings Institution Press, 1998.

Malkki, Lisa H. "Speechless Emissaries: Refugees, Humanitarianism, and Dehistoricization." *Cultural Anthropology* 11, no. 3: 377–404.

Mangcu, Xolela. "Liberating Race from Apartheid." *Transformation* 47 (2001): 18–27.

Mann, Gregory. "Locating Colonial Histories: Between France and West Africa." *American Historical Review* 110, no. 2 (April 2005). http://www.historycooperative .org/journals/ahr/110.2/mann.html.

Marais, Hein. *South Africa, Limits to Change: The Political Economy of Transformation*. Cape Town: University of Cape Town Press, 1998.

Marchal, Jules. *E. D. Morel contre Léopold II*. Paris: l'Harmattan, 1996.

Marchand, Yves, and Romain Meffre. *The Ruins of Detroit*. London: Steidl, 2011.

Marcus, George E., and Michael M. J. Fischer. *Anthropology as Cultural Critique: An Experimental Moment in the Human Sciences*. Chicago: University of Chicago Press, 1999.

Martin, Thomas J., and Donald C. Latham. *Strategy for Survival*. Tucson: University of Arizona Press, 1963.

Masco, Joseph. *The Nuclear Borderlands: The Manhattan Project in Post–Cold War New Mexico*. Princeton: Princeton University Press, 2006.

May, Elaine. *Homeward Bound: American Families in the Cold War Era*. New York: Basic, 1990.

May, Ernest R., ed. *American Cold War Strategy: Interpreting NSC 68*. New York: Bedford/ St. Martin's, 1993.

Mbembe, Achille. "Necropolitics." *Public Culture* 15, no. 1 (2003): 11–40.

———. "Nicolas Sarkozy's Africa." *Africultures*, 8 August 2007. http://www.afri cultures.com/php/index.php?nav=article&no=6816.

———. *On the Postcolony*. Berkeley: University of California Press, 2001.

McCaffrey, Katherine T. "The Struggle for Environmental Justice in Vieques, Puerto Rico." *Environmental Justice in Latin America*, ed. David V. Carruthers, 263–86. Cambridge: Massachusetts Institute of Technology Press, 2008.

McCoy, Alfred W. *Policing America's Empire: The United States, the Philippines, and the Rise of the Surveillance State*. Madison: University of Wisconsin Press, 2009.

McCulloch, Jock. *Asbestos Blues: Labour, Capital, Physicians and the State in South Africa*. Oxford: James Currey, 2002.

McCully, Patrick. *Silenced Rivers: The Ecology and Politics of Large Dams*. Hyderabad: Orient Longman, 1997.

McDonald, Charles A. "The Eye of the Storm: Hurricane Hugo and Imperial Debris in 'America's Paradise.'" Paper presented at the "Colonial and Postcolonial Disorder" workshop, New School for Social Research, New York City, December 2010.

McEnaney, Laura. *Civil Defense Begins at Home: Militarization Meets Everyday Life in the Fifties*. Princeton: Princeton University Press, 2000.

McGovern, Dan. *The Capo Indian Landfill War: The Fight for Gold in California's Garbage*. Norman: University of Oklahoma Press, 1995.

McGranahan, Carole. "Arrested Histories: Between Empire and Exile in Twentieth Century Tibet." Ph.D. diss., Program in Anthropology and History, University of Michigan, 2001.

———. *Arrested Histories: Tibet, the CIA, and Memories of a Forgotten War*. Durham: Duke University Press, 2010.

———. "Empire Out of Bounds: Tibet in the Era of Decolonization." *Imperial Formations*, ed. Ann Laura Stoler, Carole McGranahan, and Peter C. Perdue, 173–210. Santa Fe: School for Advanced Research, 2007.

———. "Truth, Fear, and Lies: Exile Politics and Arrested Histories of the Tibetan Resistance." *Cultural Anthropology* 20, no. 4 (November 2005): 570–600.

McKenzie, Peter. "Vying Posie: Photographs by Peter McKenzie." Indepth Art News, AbsoluteArts.com, 10 May 2005. http://www.absolutearts.com/artsnews/2005/05/11/32995.html.

McKenzie, Peter, and Sylvie Peyre, dirs. *What Kind?* Video. South Africa and France, 2007.

Meade, Charles, and Roger C. Molander. *Considering the Effects of a Catastrophic Terrorist Attack*. Santa Monica, Calif.: RAND Corporation, 2006.

Mehta, Uday Singh. *Liberalism and Empire: A Study in Nineteenth-Century British Liberal Thought*. Chicago: University of Chicago Press, 1999.

Meixner, Seth. "Cambodia: Ghosts and Grandeur." Iafrica.com, 8 March 2007. http://travel.iafrica.com/destin/asia/655247.htm.

Mellor, Felicity. "Colliding Worlds: Asteroid Research and the Legitimization of War in Space." *Social Studies of Science* 37, no. 4 (2007): 499–531.

Miller, Daniel. "Introduction." *Materiality*, ed. Daniel Miller, 1–50. Durham: Duke University Press, 2005.

Miller, Perry. *Errand into the Wilderness*. Cambridge: Harvard University Press, 1956.

Miller, Richards L. *Under the Cloud: The Decades of Nuclear Testing*. New York: Free Press, 1986.

Mintz, Sidney. *Sweetness and Power: The Place of Sugar in Modern History*. New York: Viking, 1985.

Morel, E. D. *King Leopold's Rule in Africa*. London: William Heinemann, 1904.

———. *Red Rubber*. London: T. Fisher Unwin, 1907.

Morresi, Eldo. *Las ruinas del km. 75 y Concepción del Bermejo*. Resistencia, Argentina: Editorial de la Universidad Nacional del Nordeste, 1971.

Morris, Rosalind C. *Can the Subaltern Speak? Reflections on the History of an Idea*. New York: Columbia University Press, 2010.

Mountmorres, Viscount. *The Congo Independent State: A Report on a Voyage of Enquiry*. London: Williams and Norgate, 1906.

Muehlmann, Shaylih. *Where the River Ends: Environmental Conflict and Contested Identities in the Colorado Delta*. Durham: Duke University Press, forthcoming.

Murphy, Cullen. *Are We Rome? The Fall of an Empire and the Fate of America*. New York: Houghton Mifflin, 2007.

Musharraf, Pervez. *In the Line of Fire: A Memoir*. New York: Simon and Schuster, 2006.

Navaro-Yashin, Yael. "Abjected Spaces: Political Debris and the Affects It Engenders." Paper presented at the "Affect in Political Life" conference, Cambridge University, Cambridge, 7–8 April 2006.

Neumann, Roderick. *Imposing Wilderness: Struggles over Livelihood and Nature Preservation in Africa*. Berkeley: University of California Press, 1998.

Nevins, Allan, and Frank Ernest Hill. *Ford: Expansion and Challenge, 1915–1933*. New York: Scribner, 1954.

Newell, Samuel. "What a Field Is Here for Missionary Exertions." *Images of Sri Lanka through American Eyes*, ed. H. A. I. Goonetilake, 2–15. Colombo, Sri Lanka: U.S. Information Service, 1983 [1815].

Nietzsche, Friedrich. *The Will to Power*. Trans. Walter Kaufmann and R. J. Hollingdale. New York: Random House/Vintage, 1968.

Nixon, Rob. "Slow Violence, Gender, and the Environmentalism of the Poor." *Journal of Commonwealth and Postcolonial Studies*. 13, no. 1 (2006): 14–37.

Noys, Benjamin. *The Persistence of the Negative: A Critique of Contemporary Continental Philosophy* Edinburgh: Edinburgh University Press, 2010.

Nuttall, Sarah, and Carli Coetzee, eds. *Negotiating the Past: The Making of Memory in South Africa*. Cape Town: Oxford University Press, 1998.

Nuttall, Sarah, and Achille Mbembe, eds. *Johannesburg: The Elusive Metropolis*. Johannesburg: Witwatersrand University Press, 2008.

Oakes, Guy. *The Imaginary War: Civil Defense and American Cold War Culture*. New York: Oxford University Press, 1994.

Office of Technology Assessment. *The Effects of Nuclear War*. Washington: Congress of the United States, 1980.

Okazaki, Steven, dir. *White Light, Back Rain: The Destruction of Hiroshima and Nagasaki*. 86 min. Video recording. New York: HBO Documentaries, 2007.

Olascoaga, Manuel. "Instrucciones que Deben Cumplir los Ingenieros, Jefes y Ayudantes de las Comisiones Organizadas para el Estudio y Levantamiento Topográfico de la Región del Gran Chaco." *Campaña del Chaco*, 31–37. Buenos Aires: Imprenta Europa, 1885.

Ong, Aihwa. *Neoliberalism as Exception: Mutations in Citizenship and Sovereignty*. Durham: Duke University Press, 2006.

Orr, Jackie. *Panic Diaries: A Genealogy of Panic Disorder*. Durham: Duke University Press, 2006.

Orta, Andrew. "Burying the Past: Locality, Lived History, and Death in an Aymara Ritual of Remembrance." *Cultural Anthropology* 17, no. 4 (2002): 471–511.

Osgood, Kenneth. *Total Cold War: Eisenhower's Secret Propaganda Battle at Home and Abroad*. Lawrence: University Press of Kansas, 2006.

Padayachee, Vishnu. "Development Discourses in Post-apartheid South Africa." *The Development Decade: Economic and Social Change in South Africa 1994–2004*, ed. Vishnu Padayachee, 1–32. Cape Town: HSRC Press, 2006.

Pandolfo, Stefania. *Impasse of Angels: Scenes from a Moroccan Space of Memory*. Chicago: University of Chicago Press, 1997.

Panel on the Human Effects of Nuclear Weapons Development. *Human Effects of Nuclear Weapons Development*. A Report to the President and the National Security Council. Washington: Federal Civil Defense Administration, 1956.

Parmentier, Richard. *The Sacred Remains: Myth, History and Polity in Belau*. Chicago: University of Chicago Press, 1987.

Parnell, Sue. "Creating Racial Privilege: The Origins of South African Public Health and Town Planning Legislation." *Journal of Southern African Studies* 19 (1993): 1–18.

Peebles, Patrick. *The Plantation Tamils of Ceylon*. New York: Leicester University Press, 2001.

Peek, Sven (Bobby). "Doublespeak in Durban: Mondi, Waste Management, and the Struggles of the South Durban Community Environmental Alliance." *Environmental Justice in South Africa*, ed. David McDonald, 202–19. Athens: Ohio University Press, 2002.

Peirce, Charles S. *Collected Papers*. Cambridge: Belknap Press of Harvard University Press, 1960.

Pelleschi, Giovani. *Eight Months on the Gran Chaco of the Argentine Republic*. London: Sampson Low, Martson, Searle and Rivington, 1886.

Peluso, Nancy Lee, and Michael Watts, eds. *Violent Environments*. Ithaca: Cornell University Press, 2001.

Pemberton, John. "The Ghost in the Machine." *Photographies East: The Camera and Its Histories in East and Southeast Asia*, ed. Rosalind C. Morris, 29–56. Durham: Duke University Press, 2009.

Peterson, Val. "Panic: The Ultimate Weapon?" *Collier's*, 21 August 1953, 99–109.

Petryna, Adriana. *Life Exposed: Biological Citizens after Chernobyl*. Princeton: Princeton University Press, 2002.

Pithouse, Richard. "Burning Message to the State in the Fire of Poor's Rebellion." *Business Day*, 29 July 2009. http://www.bdlive.co.za/articles/2009/07/23/burning-message-to-the-state-in-the-fire-of-poor-s-rebellion.

———. "Solidarity, Co-optation and Assimilation: The Necessity, Promises and Pitfalls of Global Linkages for South African Movements." *Challenging Hegemony: Social Movements and the Quest for a New Humanism in Post-apartheid South Africa*, ed. Nigel C. Gibson, 247–86. Trenton, N.J.: Africa World Press, 2006.

Posel, Deborah. "What's in a Name? Racial Categorisations under Apartheid and Their Afterlife." *Transformation* 47 (2001): 50–74.

Pottier, Johan. "Roadblock Ethnography: Negotiating Humanitarian Access in Ituri, Eastern DR Congo, 1999–2004." *Africa* 76 (2006): 151–79.

Price, Richard. "An Absence of Ruins? Seeking Caribbean Historical Consciousness." *Caribbean Review* 14, no. 3 (1985): 24–30.

————. *The Convict and the Colonel: A Story of Colonialism and Resistance in the Caribbean.* Durham: Duke University Press, 2006.

Puechguirbal, Nadine. "Women and War in the Democratic Republic of the Congo." *Signs* 28, no. 4 (2003): 1271–80.

Ramanujan, A. K. *Poems of Love and War.* New York: Columbia University Press, 1985.

Rancière, Jacques. *Aesthetics and Its Discontents.* Cambridge: Polity, 2009.

————. *Disagreement: Politics and Philosophy.* Trans. Julie Rose. Minneapolis: University of Minnesota Press, 1999.

————. *The Nights of Labor: The Workers' Dream in Nineteenth-Century France.* Trans. John Drury. Philadelphia: Temple University Press, 1989.

Rao, D. Venkat. "Writing Orally: Decolonization from Below." *Positions* 7, no. 1 (1999): 253–67.

Rao, Vyjayanthi. "Itinerant Temples and Monumental Ruins." Master's thesis, Department of Anthropology, University of Chicago, 1992.

————. "Ruins and Recollections: On the Subjects of Displacement." Ph.D. diss., Department of Anthropology, University of Chicago, 2002.

Reddy, Thiven. "The Politics of Naming: The Constitution of Coloured Subjects in South Africa." *Coloured by History, Shaped by Place: New Perspectives on Coloured Identities in Cape Town,* ed. Zimitri Erasmus, 64–79. Cape Town: Kwela Books/South African History Online, 2001.

Redfield, Peter. "Doctors, Borders and Life in Crisis." *Cultural Anthropology* 20, no. 3 (2005): 328–61.

————. "A Less Modest Witness: Collective Advocacy and Motivated Truth in a Medical Humanitarian Movement." *American Ethnologist* 33, no. 1 (November 2009): 3–26.

Reyes Gajardo, Carlos. *La ciudad de Esteco y su leyenda.* San Miguel de Tucumán, Argentina: Universidad Nacional de Tucumán, 1968.

Richman, Paula, ed. *Many Ramayanas.* Berkeley: University of California Press, 1991.

Robb, David L. *Operation Hollywood: How the Pentagon Shapes and Censors the Movies.* Amherst: Prometheus, 2004.

Robert, Karen. "The Case against Ford." Unpublished manuscript, 3 June 2006. In possession of the editor.

————. "The Falcon Remembered." "The Diaspora Strikes Back: The Politics of Race and Globalization, Part 3," NACLA *Report on the Americas* 39, no. 3 (November–December 2005): 12–15.

Robins, Steve. "From 'Rights' to 'Ritual': AIDS Activism in South Africa." *American Anthropologist* 108, no. 2 (2008): 312–23.

Robinson, Jennifer. "(Im)mobilising Space—Dreaming (of) Change." In *Blank___: Architecture, Apartheid and After,* ed. Hilton Judin and Ivan Vladislavic, D7. Rotterdam: NAI, 1998.

————. *The Power of Apartheid: State, Power and Space in South African Cities.* London: Butterworth-Heinemann, 1996.

Rodriguez, José E. *Campañas del desierto (Expediciones premiadas)*. Buenos Aires: Imprenta López, 1927.

Rogin, Michael. *Independence Day*. London: British Film Institute, 1998.

———. *Ronald Reagan, the Movie, and Other Episodes in Political Demonology*. Berkeley: University of California Press, 1987.

Rojecki, Andrew. *Silencing the Opposition: Antinuclear Movements and the Media in the Cold War*. Champaign: University of Illinois Press, 1999.

Romaniuk, Anatole. "The Demography of the Democratic Republic of Congo." *The Demography of Tropical Africa*, ed. William Brass, 241–341. Princeton: Princeton University Press, 1968.

———. "Infertility in Tropical Africa." *The Population of Tropical Africa*, ed. John C. Caldwell and Chukuka Okonjo, 212–24. London: Longman, 1968.

Ronell, Avital. *Stupidity*. Urbana: University of Illinois Press, 2002.

Rosaldo, Renato. "Imperial Nostalgia." *Culture and Truth*, 68–87. Boston: Beacon, 1989.

Rosas, Gilberto. "Illiberal Technologies and Liberal Societies." Paper presented at "BIOS: Life, Death, Politics" at the Unit for Criticism and Interpretive Theory, and the Holocaust, Genocide and Memory Studies Initiative, University of Illinois, Urbana-Champaign, 30 April–1 May 2010. Kritik (public blog), 4 May 2010. http://unitcrit.blogspot.com/2010/05/bios-life-death-politics-closing.html.

Rotbard, Sharon. *White City, Black City: Architecture and War in Tel Aviv and Jaffa*. Tel Aviv: Babel, 2005.

Roy, Arundhati. *The Greater Common Good*. Delhi: India Book Distributors, 1999.

———. "The Road to Harsud: The Death of a Town." *Outlook India*, 19 July 2004, http://www.outlookindia.com/article.aspx?224596.

Rubin, David M., and Constance Cummings. "Nuclear War and Its Consequences on Television News." *Journal of Communication* 39, no. 1 (1989): 39–58.

Rutherford, Blair. "Desired Publics, Domestic Government, and Entangled Fears: On the Anthropology of Civil Society, Farm Workers, and White Farmers in Zimbabwe." *Cultural Anthropology* 19, no. 1 (February 2004): 122–53.

Rybczynski, Witold. "Incredible Hulks." *Slate*, 18 March 2009. http://www.slate.com/articles/arts/architecture/2009/03/incredible_hulks.html.

Saldanha, Arun. "Re-ontologising Race: The Machinic Geography of Phenotype." *Environment and Planning D: Society and Space* 24, no. 1 (2006): 9–24.

Salgado, Sebastião. *Workers: An Archaeology of the Industrial Age*. New York: Aperture, 2005.

Santner, Eric L. *On Creaturely Life*. Chicago: University of Chicago Press, 2006.

Sarma, I. Karthikeya. "Report on the Antiquarian Remains in the Submersible Area under Srisailam Hydro-Electric Project." Unpublished report, Andhra Pradesh State Department of Archaeology and Museums, n.d.

———. "Some Aspects of Salvage Archaeology in Andhra Pradesh." *Itihas* 14 (January 1988): 95–101.

Sarma, M. Radhakrishna. *A Case for Salvage Archaeology: Area under Srisailam Project to Be*

Submerged. Hyderabad: Osmania University Department of Publication and Press, 1974.

Sastri, V. V. Krishna. "Salvage Archaeological Operations under Srisailam Project." Unpublished report, Andhra Pradesh State Department of Archaeology and Museums, n.d.

Saunders, Mark. *Ambiguities of Witnessing: Law and Literature in the Time of a Truth Commission.* Palo Alto: Stanford University Press, 2007.

Scheiback, Michael. *Atomic Narratives and American Youth: Coming of Age with the Atom, 1945–1955.* Jefferson, N.C.: McFarland, 2003.

Schmitt, H. P. *Effects of Nuclear Explosions on Frozen Foods.* Project 32.5 of Operation Teapot. Washington: Government Printing Office, 1956.

Schuck, Peter H. *Agent Orange on Trial: Mass Toxic Disasters in the Courts.* Cambridge: Harvard University Press, 1986.

Schwartz, Stephen, ed. *Atomic Audit: The Costs and Consequences of U.S. Nuclear Weapons since 1940.* Washington: Brookings Institution Press, 1998.

Scott, David. *Conscripts of Modernity: The Tragedy of Colonial Enlightenment.* Durham: Duke University Press, 2004.

Scott, Dianne. "Communal Space Construction: The Rise and Fall of Clairwood and District." Ph.D. diss., Department of Geography, University of Natal, Durban, South Africa, 1994.

Scott, James. *The Art of Not Being Governed: An Anarchist History of Upland Southeast Asia.* New Haven: Yale University Press, 2009.

Sebald, W. G. *The Emigrants.* New York: New Directions, 1992.

———. *On the Natural History of Destruction.* New York: Random House, 2003.

———. *The Rings of Saturn.* New York: New Directions, 1998.

Seed, Patricia. *Ceremonies of Possession in Europe's Conquest of the New World, 1492–1640.* Cambridge: Cambridge University Press, 1995.

Sela, Rona. *Photography in Palestine / Eretz Yisrael in the 1930s and 1940s.* Herzlia Museum of Art and Co-existence. Tel Aviv: HaKibbutz Hameukhad, 2001.

Senga Kossy, Raymonde. "Kinshasa abrite le 9ème Congrès de la Société Africaine Gynécologie Obstétrique." *Le Potentiel* 4114 (4 September 2007): 24.

Seremetakis, C. Nadia, ed. *The Senses Still: Perception and Memory as Material Culture in Modernity.* Chicago: University of Chicago Press, 1996.

Sharma, Aradhana. "Crossbreeding Institutions, Breeding Struggle: Women's Empowerment, Neoliberal Governmentality, and State (Re)Formation in India." *Cultural Anthropology* 21, no. 1 (2006): 60–95.

Shatrugna, M. "Unrehabilitated Poor of Srisailam Project." *Economic and Political Weekly,* 26 December 1981, 2123–26.

Shaw, Rosalind. "Displacing Violence: Making Pentecostal Memory in Postwar Sierra Leone." *Cultural Anthropology* 22, no. 1 (February 2007): 66–93.

Sheer, Robert. *With Enough Shovels: Reagan, Bush, and Nuclear War.* New York: Random House, 1982.

Sheriff, Robin. *Dreaming Equality: Color, Race, and Racism in Urban Brazil*. New Brunswick: Rutgers University Press, 2001.

Showers, Kate B. *Imperial Gullies: Soil Erosion and Conservation in Lesotho*. Athens: Ohio University Press, 2005.

Shumpeter, Joseph. *Capitalism, Socialism, and Democracy*. New York: Harper Brothers, 1950 [1942].

Simmel, Georg. "The Ruin." *Essays on Sociology, Philosophy and Aesthetics*, ed. Kurt H. Wolff, 259–66. New York: Harper and Row, 1965.

Simon, Steven L., Andre Bouville, Charles E. Land, and Harold L. Beck. "Radiation Doses and Cancer Risks in the Marshall Islands Associated with Exposure to Radioactive Fallout from Bikini and Enewetak Nuclear Weapons Tests: Summary." *Pediatric Radiology* 36, supplement 2 (September 2006): 159–62.

Síocháin, Séamas O., and Michael Sullivan, eds. *The Eyes of Another Race: Roger Casement's Congo Report and 1903 Diary*. Dublin: University College Dublin Press, 2003.

Sivaramakrishnan, K., and Arun Agrawal, eds. *Regional Modernities: The Cultural Politics of Development in India*. New Delhi: Oxford University Press, 2003.

Skidmore, Thomas. *Black into White: Race and Nationality in Brazilian Thought*. New York: Oxford University Press, 1974.

Sliwkinski, Sharon. "The Childhood of Human Rights: The Kodak on the Congo." *Visual Culture* 5, no. 3 (2006): 333–63.

Slotkin, Louis. *Regeneration through Violence: The Mythology of the American Frontier, 1600–1860*. New York: Harper Perennial, 1996.

Smith, Neil. *American Empire: Roosevelt's Geography and the Prelude to Globalization*. Berkeley: University of California Press, 2003.

Smith, Shawn Michelle. *American Archives: Gender, Race and Class in Visual Culture*. Princeton: Princeton University Press, 1999.

Snow, Keith Harmon. "Three Cheers for Eve Ensler? Propaganda, White Collar Crime, and Sexual Atrocities in Eastern Congo." *Z Magazine*, 24 October 2007. http://towardfreedom.com/home/content/view/1201/1/.

Sodikoff, Genese. "Forced and Forest Labor in Colonial Madagascar, 1926–1936." *Ethnohistory* 52, no. 2 (2005): 407–35.

Solís, José. *Ensayo sobre la historia natural del Gran Chaco*. Resistencia, Argentina: Universidad Nacional del Nordeste, 1972 [1789].

Solnit, Rebecca. *A Paradise Built in Hell: The Extraordinary Communities that Arise in Disaster*. New York: Viking, 2009.

Sommer, Doris. *Proceed with Caution: When Engaged with Minority Writing in the Americas*. Cambridge: Harvard University Press, 1999.

Sontag, Susan. "The Imagination of Disaster." *Against Interpretation, and Other Essays*, 209–25. New York: Farrar, Straus and Giroux, 1966.

———. *Regarding the Pain of Others*. New York: Picador, 2003.

Sparks, Stephen. "Civic Culture, 'Environmentalism' and Pollution in South Durban: The Case of the Wentworth Refinery." History and African Studies Seminar, Department of Historical Studies, University of KwaZulu-Natal, Durban, South

Africa, 19 April 2005. History Department at UKZN. http://www.history.ukzn
.ac.za/?q=node/611.

———. "'Playing at Public Health': The Search for Control in South Durban 1860–
1932." History and African Studies Seminar, Department of Historical Studies,
University of KwaZulu-Natal, Durban, South Africa, 25 March 2003. History Department at UKZN. http://www.history.ukzn.ac.za/?q=node/557.

———. "'Stink, maar uit die verkeerde rigting': Pollution, Politics and Petroleum Refining in South Africa, 1948–1960." History and African Studies Seminar, Department of Historical Studies, University of KwaZulu-Natal, Durban, South Africa, 27 April 2004. History Department at UKZN. http://www.history.ukzn.ac
.za/?q=node/587.

Statistics South Africa. *Census 2001*. Pretoria: Statistics South Africa, 2001. http://www
.statssa.gov.za/census01/html/default.asp.

Steedman, Carolyn Kay. *Landscape for a Good Woman*. New Brunswick: Rutgers University Press, 1987.

Steinmetz, George. "Colonial Melancholy and Fordist Nostalgia: The Ruinscapes of
Namibia and Detroit." *Ruins of Modernity*, ed. Julia Hell and Andreas Schoenle,
294–320. Durham: Duke University Press, 2010.

———. "Detroit: A Tale of Two Crises." *Society and Space: Environment and Planning* 27
(2009): 761–70.

———. "Harrowed Landscapes: White Ruingazers in Namibia and Detroit and the
Cultivation of Memory." *Visual Studies* 23, no. 3 (2008): 211–37.

Stellman, Jeanne. "The Extent and Patterns of Usage of Agent Orange and Other Herbicides in Vietnam." *Nature* 422, no. 17 (April 2003): 681–87.

Stepan, Nancy. *"The Hour of Eugenics": Race, Gender and Nation in Latin America*. Ithaca: Cornell University Press, 1991.

Stewart, Kathleen. *A Space on the Side of the Road: Cultural Poetics in an "Other" America*.
Princeton: Princeton University Press, 1996.

Stewart, Susan. *On Longing: Narratives of the Miniature, the Gigantic, the Souvenir, the Collection*. Durham: Duke University Press, 1993.

Stoler, Ann Laura. *Along the Archival Grain: Epistemic Anxieties and Colonial Common Sense*.
Princeton: Princeton University Press, 2010.

———. "The Carceral Archipelago of Empire." Keynote address for "The Political Life
of Documents" conference, University of Cambridge, 16 January 2010.

———. *Carnal Knowledge and Imperial Power: Race and the Intimate in Colonial Rule*. Berkeley: University of California Press, 2002.

———. "Colonial Aphasia: Race and Disabled Histories in France." *Public Culture* 23,
no. 1 (2011): 121–56.

———. "Imperial Debris: Reflections on Ruins and Ruination." *Cultural Anthropology*
23, no. 2 (2008): 191–219.

———. "Introduction: Intimidations of Empire: Predicaments of the Tactile and the
Unseen." *Haunted by Empire: Geographies of Intimacy in North American History*, ed. Ann
Laura Stoler, 1–22. Durham: Duke University Press, 2006.

————. "On Degrees of Imperial Sovereignty." *Public Culture* 18, no. 1 (2006): 125–46.

————. *Race and the Education of Desire: Foucault's History of Sexuality and the Colonial Order of Things*. Durham: Duke University Press, 1995.

————. "Racial Histories and Their Regimes of Truth." *Political Power and Social Theory* 11 (1997): 183–206.

————. "Sexual Affronts and Racial Frontiers: European Identities and the Politics of Exclusion in Colonial Southeast Asia." *Comparative Studies in Society and History* 34, no. 3 (1992): 514–51.

————, ed. *Haunted by Empire: Geographies of Intimacy in North American History*. Durham: Duke University Press, 2006.

Stoler, Ann Laura, with David Bond. "Refractions Off Empire: Untimely Comparisons in Harsh Times." *Radical History Review* 95 (spring 2006): 93–107.

Stoler, Ann Laura, and Carole McGranahan. "Introduction: Refiguring Imperial Terrains." *Imperial Formations*, ed. Ann Stoler, Carole McGranahan, and Peter Purdue, 3–42. Santa Fe: School for Advanced Research Press, 2007.

Stoler, Ann Laura, Carole McGranahan, and Peter C. Perdue, eds. *Imperial Formations*. Santa Fe: School for Advanced Research Press, 2007.

Stora, Benjamin. *Le transfert d'une mémoire: De "l'Algérie française" au racisme anti-arabe*. Paris: La D'ecouverte, 1999.

Sugrue, Thomas. *The Origins of the Urban Crisis: Race and Inequality in Postwar Detroit*. Princeton: Princeton University Press, 2005.

Swanson, Maynard. "The Sanitation Syndrome: Bubonic Plague and Urban Native Policy in the Cape Colony, 1900–1909." *Journal of African History* 18 (1977): 387–410.

Szmagalska-Follis, Karolina. "Repossession: Notes on Restoration and Redemption in Ukraine's Western Borderland." *Cultural Anthropology* 23, no. 2 (2008): 329–60.

Talbot, Cynthia. *Precolonial India in Practice: Society, Region and Identity in Medieval Andhra*. New Delhi: Oxford University Press, 2001.

Tatz, Colin, Alan Cass, John Condon, and George Tippet. "Aborigines and Uranium: Monitoring the Health Hazards." AIATSIS Research Discussion Paper 20, December 2006.

Taussig, Michael. *The Nervous System*. New York: Routledge, 1992.

————. *Shamanism, Colonialism and the Wild Man: A Study in Terror and Healing*. Chicago: University of Chicago Press, 1987.

Taylor, Bryan C. "Nuclear Pictures and Metapictures." *American Literary History* 9, no. 3 (1997): 567–97.

Teruel, Ana. *Misiones, economía y sociedad: La frontera chaqueña del Noroeste Argentino en el siglo 19*. Buenos Aires: Universidad Nacional de Quilmes, 2005.

Thomas, Martin. *Empires of Intelligence: Security Services and Colonial Disorder after 1914*. Berkeley: University of California Press, 2008.

Tomas de Matorras, Gerónimo. "Diario de Arias." *"Entradas" al Chaco*, ed. P. De Angelis, 381–411. San Salvador de Jujuy, Argentina: Universidad Nacional de Jujuy, 1989 [1780].

Tomasini, Alfredo, and Ricardo Alonso. *Esteco, el Viejo: Breve historia y localización de Nuestra Señora de Talavera, 1566–1609.* Salta, Argentina: Gofica Editora, 2001.

Tommasini, Gabriel. *La civilización cristiana del Chaco: 1554–1810.* Buenos Aires: Biblioteca de Doctrina Católica, 1937.

Torre Revelo, José. *Esteco y Concepción del Bermejo, dos ciudades desaparecidas.* Buenos Aires: Talleres Casa Peuser, 1943.

Trouillot, Michel-Rolph. *Silencing the Past: Power and the Production of History.* Boston: Beacon, 1995.

Tully, James. *An Approach to Political Philosophy: Locke in Contexts.* Cambridge: Cambridge University Press, 1993.

Twain, Mark. *King Leopold's Soliloquy: A Defense of His Congo Rule.* Boston: P. R. Warren, 1905.

United Nations Mission to the Congo (MONUC). "MONUC Expresses Its Satisfaction about the Verdict of the Songo Mboyo Case." 13 April 2006. http://allafrica.com /stories/200604130799.html.

———. "South Kivu: 4,500 Sexual Violence Cases in the First Six Months of This Year Alone." Press release, 30 July 2007. http://www.unhchr.ch/huricane/huricane .nsf/o/B5D0053875B01B8CC1257328003A8FEE?opendocument.

United Nations Panel of Inquiry. "Final Report of the Panel of Experts on the Illegal Exploitation of Natural Resources and Other Forms of Wealth of the Democratic Republic of the Congo." UN Security Council Document S/2001/357, 12 April 2001. Geneva: United Nations Panel of Inquiry.

United States of America. *The National Security Strategy of the United States of America.* Washington: Government Printing Office, 2002.

Vanden Driessen, Ian H. *The Long Walk: Indian Plantation Labor in Sri Lanka in the Nineteenth Century.* New Delhi: Prestige Books, 1997.

Vanderbilt, Tom. *Survival City: Adventures among the Ruins of Atomic America.* New York: Princeton Architectural Press, 2002.

Vandercook, Wm. F. "Making the Very Best of the Very Worst: The 'Human Effects of Nuclear Weapons' Report of 1956." *International Security* 11, no. 1 (1986): 184–95.

Vangroenweghe, Daniel. *Du sang sur les lianes: Léopold II et son Congo.* Brussels: Didier Hatier, 1986.

Van Herp, Michel, Veronique Parqué, Edward Rackley, and Nathan Ford. "Mortality, Violence and Lack of Access to Health-Care in the Democratic Republic of the Congo." *Disasters* 27, no. 2 (2003): 141–53.

Van Riel, J., and R. Allard. *Contribution à l'étude de la dénatalité dans l'ethnie mongo.* Brussels: Institut Royal Colonial Belge, 1953.

Veitch, Jonathan. "Colossus in Ruins: Remembering Pittsburgh's Industrial Past." *Public Culture* 10, no. 1 (1997): 115–34.

Vellut, Jean-Luc. "La Violence Armée dans l'Etat Indépendant du Congo." *Cultures et Développement* 16, nos. 3–4 (1984): 671–707.

Victorica, Benjamín. "Correspondencia telegráfica del General en Jefe con el Presidente de la República." *Campaña del Chaco*, 153–85. Buenos Aires: Imprenta Europa, 1885.

———. "Proclama del General en Jefe en la ceremonia de la inauguración del Puerto Presidencia Roca." *Campaña del Chaco*, 73–76. Buenos Aires: Imprenta Europa, 1885.

Vine, David. *Island of Shame: The Secret History of the U.S. Military Base on Diego Garcia*. Princeton: Princeton University Press, 2009.

Virilio, Paul. *War and Cinema: The Logistics of Perception*. London: Verso, 1989.

Vlassenroot, Koen, and Timothy Raeymaekers. "Citizenship, Identity Formation, and Conflict in South Kivu: The Case of the Banyamulenge." *Review of African Political Economy* 93–94 (2002): 499–516.

———. "The Politics of Rebellion and Intervention in Ituri: The Emergence of a New Political Complex?" *African Affairs* 103, no. 412 (2004): 385–412.

Voas, David. "Subfertility and Disruption in the Congo Basin." *African Historical Demography*, 2:777–99. Edinburgh: Centre of African Studies, University of Edinburgh, 1981.

Walcott, Derek. "The Antilles: Fragments of Epic Memory." Nobel Lecture, 7 December 1992. Nobelprize.org. http://nobelprize.org.

———. *Collected Poems 1948–1984*. New York: Farrar, Straus and Giroux, 1987.

———. "A Dilemma Faces W[est] I[ndian] Artists." *Sunday Guardian*, 12 January 1964, 3.

Walley, Christine J. "Searching for 'Voices': Feminism, Anthropology, and the Global Debate over Female Genital Operations." *Cultural Anthropology* 12, no. 3 (August 1997): 405–38.

Warner, Marina. *Phantasmagoria: Spirit Visions, Metaphors, and Media in the Twenty-First Century*. Oxford: Oxford University Press, 2006.

Watts, Michael. *Silent Violence: Food, Famine, and Peasantry in Northern Nigeria*. Berkeley: University of California Press, 1983.

———, ed. *Curse of the Black Gold: Fifty Years of Oil in the Niger Delta*. Photographs by Ed Kashi. Brooklyn: Powerhouse, 2008.

Webb, James L. A. *Tropical Pioneers: Human Agency and Ecological Change in the Highlands of Sri Lanka, 1800–1900*. Athens: Ohio University Press, 2002.

Weisberg, Barry. *Ecocide in Indochina: The Ecology of War*. San Francisco: Canfield Press, 1970.

Weizman, Eyal. *Hollow Land: Israel's Architecture of Occupation*. London: Verso, 2007.

———. "Lawfare in Gaza: Legislative Attack." openDemocracy, 1 March 2009. http://www.opendemocracy.net/article/legislative-attack.

Weller, George. *First into Nagasaki*. New York: Crown, 2006.

White, Hylton. "The Dwelling of Culture." Unpublished manuscript, Department of Anthropology, New School for Social Research, n.d.

Whiteside, Thomas. *The Withering Rain: America's Herbicidal Folly*. New York: E. P. Dutton, 1971.

Willett, John, and Ralph Manheim, eds. *The Rise and Fall of the City of Mahagonny: And, the Seven Deadly Sins of the Petty Bourgeoisie*. New York: Arcade, 1996.

Williams, Raymond. *The Country and the City*. New York: Oxford University Press, 1973.

———. *Marxism and Literature*. New York: Oxford University Press, 1978.

Wittner, Lawrence S. *One World of None: A History of the World Nuclear Disarmament Movement through 1953*. Stanford: Stanford University Press, 1993.

———. *Resisting the Bomb: A History of the World Nuclear Disarmament Movement, 1954–1970*. Stanford: Stanford University Press, 1997.

———. *Toward Abolition: A History of the World Nuclear Disarmament Movement 1971 to the Present*. Stanford: Stanford University Press, 2003.

Wolpe, Harold. "Capitalism and Cheap Labour-Power in South Africa: From Segregation to Apartheid." *Economy and Society* 1, no. 4 (1972): 425–56.

Woodward, Christopher. *In Ruins: A Journey through History, Art, and Literature*. New York: Vintage, 2001.

Wright, Beverly. "Living and Dying in Louisiana's 'Cancer Alley.'" *The Quest for Environmental Justice: Human Rights and the Politics of Pollution*, ed. Robert Bullard, 87–107. San Francisco: Sierra Club Books, 2005.

Wright, Pablo. "El desierto del Chaco: Geografías de la alteridad y el estado." *Pasado y presente de un mundo postergado*, ed. Ana Teruel and Omar Jerez, 35–56. San Salvador de Jujuy, Argentina: Universidad Nacional de Jujuy, 1998.

Yahav, Dan. *Paths of Coexistence and the Joint Arab-Jewish Economic and Social Struggle, 1930–2008*. Printed by author, 2009.

Zapata Gollan, Agustín. *El Chaco Gualamba y la ciudad de Concepción del Bermejo*. Santa Fe: Departamento de Estudios Coloniales / Editorial Castellví, 1966.

CONTRIBUTORS

ARIELLA AZOULAY is a writer, curator, and filmmaker. She is the author of *Civil Imagination: The Political Ontology of Photography* (2011), *From Palestine to Israel: A Photographic Record of Destruction and State Formation, 1947–1950* (2011), and *The Civil Contract of Photography* (2008).

SHARAD CHARI is an associate professor at the Centre for Indian Studies in Africa, and the anthropology department at the University of the Witwatersrand in South Africa. He is the author of *Fraternal Capital* (2004), *The Development Reader* (2008), and articles in *Comparative Studies in Society and History, Radical History Review, South Atlantic Quarterly,* and other journals. He is currently completing a monograph titled *Apartheid Remains*.

JOHN COLLINS is an associate professor of anthropology at Queens College and the Graduate Center, City University of New York. His *Revolt of the Saints: Memory and Redemption in the Twilight of Brazilian "Racial Democracy,"* a study of the making of a Brazilian World Heritage site in the ruins of the Portuguese South Atlantic, is forthcoming from Duke. He is currently conducting fieldwork for a new project on hunters of white-tailed deer in central New Jersey.

E. VALENTINE DANIEL is a professor of anthropology at Columbia University in the City of New York.

GASTÓN GORDILLO is an associate professor of anthropology at the University of British Columbia. He is the author of *Landscapes of Devils: Tensions of Place and Memory in the Argentinean Chaco* (Duke, 2004) and the forthcoming *The Afterlife of Things: Ruins and the Destruction of Space*, also with Duke.

GREG GRANDIN is a professor of history at New York University and a member of the American Academy of Arts and Sciences. He is the author of *Fordlandia* (2009), a finalist for the Pulitzer Prize, the National Book Award, and the National Book Critics Circle Award; *Empire's Workshop: The United States, Latin America, and the Rise of the New Imperialism* (2006); *The Last Colonial Massacre: Latin America in the Cold War* (2004); and *The Blood of Guatemala: A History of Race and Nation* (Duke, 2000), winner of the Latin American Studies Association's Bryce Wood Award. He is coeditor, with Gilbert Joseph, of *A Century of Revolution: Insurgent and Counterinsurgent Violence during Latin America's Long Cold War* (2010). He is currently writing a book on Herman Melville and free and unfree labor in the Americas during the Age of Revolution.

NANCY ROSE HUNT is a professor of history at the University of Michigan and was a Wissenschaftskolleg zu Berlin fellow in 2010–11. She received the Herskovits Prize for her *A Colonial Lexicon* (Duke, 1999). *A Nervous State* is forthcoming, also from Duke.

JOSEPH MASCO is an associate professor of anthropology at the University of Chicago. He is the author of *The Nuclear Borderlands: The Manhattan Project in Post Cold War New Mexico* (2006).

VYJAYANTHI RAO is an assistant professor of anthropology at the New School for Social Research.

ANN LAURA STOLER is Willy Brandt Distinguished University Professor of Anthropology and Historical Studies at the New School for Social Research. Her publications include *Along the Archival Grain: Epistemic Anxieties and Colonial Common Sense* (2009); *Imperial Formations*, with Carole McGranahan and Peter Perdue (2007); *Haunted by Empire: Geographies of Intimacy in North American History* (Duke, 2006); *Carnal Knowledge and Imperial Power: Race and the Intimate in Colonial Rule* (2002); *Tensions of Empire: Colonial Cultures in a Bourgeois World* (1997), with Frederick Cooper; *Race and the Education of Desire: Foucault's History of Sexuality and the Colonial Order of Things* (Duke, 1995); and *Capitalism and Confrontation in Sumatra's Plantation Belt, 1870–1979* (1985; 1995).

INDEX

Arias, Francisco, 235, 239–40
Armageddon, 274–77, 285n50
Arnaud, Leopoldo, 237–38, 240
arrested futures, 21–22, 291, 298, 303, 319n10
"arrested histories," 4, 319n10. See also arrested futures
Atget, Eugène, 149
atomic bomb, 252–53, 257, 262, 265, 267, 273, 275, 278–79, 281, 284n35
Atomic Energy Commission (AEC), 263, 279
Australia, 6, 24
auto industry, 117, 125

Badiou, Alain, 228
Bakhtin, Mikhail, 51
Ballard, J. G., 315
Bataille, Georges, 51–52, 64n80
Baucom, Ian, 27–28
Baudelaire, Charles, 51
Bauman, Zygmunt, 23–24, 321n26
Beasley-Murray, Jon, 245
Belgian Congo. See Democratic Republic of the Congo
Bemba, Jean-Pierre, 39, 54
Benjamin, Walter, ix, 9, 22, 71, 131, 133–35, 149, 245, 247, 254, 277, 282n6, 297; "Paris," 131, 149, 247
Biehl, João, 23, 190n10, 190n20; Vita: Life in a Zone of Social Abandonment, 23
Bikini Atoll, 13, 22
biopolitical sovereignty, 137, 143, 154–56
biopolitics, 23, 136, 182, 314–15; of refusal, 131–56. See also biopolitical sovereignty
Blanchot, Maurice, The Writing of the Disaster, 254
Blumberger, Hans, x
Boali, 40–44, 57–59
Bolivia, 241
Bonaparte, Napoleon, 15, 176
Bosnia, 55
Brazil, 2–3, 23, 27, 118–24; as imperial

exception, 162–89; race and, 191n29, 192n49
Brazil (Terry Gilliam), 247
Brecht, Bertolt, 116, 156; Rise and Fall of the City of Mahagonny, 116
Britain, 41–42, 59, 68, 117. See also England
British, the: Ceylon's independence from, 107n12; colonization, 181, 294–95, 318n2; imperial legacy of, 212–13; imperial pursuits, 4; public, 41; state policies, 23
British South Africa Company, 16
Brown, Wendy, 10
Brussels, 43
Buck-Morss, Susan, ix
Buenos Aires, 124, 235–36
Burgher, 91–92, 112n67
Bush, George W., 277–79, 286n52, 286n56

Cambodia, 9, 15, 117
Cape Town, 16, 149
capitalism: Adorno and, 228; American, 117; apartheid and, 138; "Cold War consensus" and, 255; colonial, 70–71; "creative construction," 115; empire and, 23, 118, 227–28, 247; financial, 45, 125; industrialization and, 115–16, 120, 123, 126; modernity and, 24, 236; relationship to ruin, 115; territorial expansion of, 235; welfare, 46
"carceral archipelago of empire," the, 22
Caribbean, the, 14–15, 167
Carranza, Angel, 239–40
Caruth, Cathy, 41
Casement, Roger, 17, 43–45, 47–52, 55
caste: India, 296–97, 305–6, 311–12, 314, 320n14; Sri Lanka, 73, 86, 92, 111nn55–57, 112n60, 112n62
Catholic Church, 15, 242, 245–46
Center for Studies and Therapy of Drug Abuse (CETAD), 162, 166, 168, 178–84, 189, 191n36

Cesaire, Aimé, 10
Ceylon, 67, 78, 91, 107n12, 113n81. *See also* Sri Lanka
Chatterjee, Partha, 139, 165, 189n9
Chemical, Engineering and Industrial Workers Union (CEIWU), 140, 142
Chile, 15, 23, 123–24
Christianity, 231, 234–35, 239–40
civil defense, 252–64, 266–68, 273, 275, 279, 282n9, 283n17, 283n22, 283n26
civil discourse, 202, 207–8, 217–19
Clichy-Sous-Bois, 28–29
Cliff, Michelle, 19, 33n68
Cold War, the, 21, 117, 252–60, 262, 268, 273–79, 281, 282n7
colonialism, x, 6, 15–16, 26, 28, 30n9, 70, 134, 163–65, 183, 292, 315–16
colonial studies, 7, 12, 29, 186
Comaroff, Jean, 136
Concepción del Bermejo, 227, 229–30, 234–37, 241–42, 245, 248n1
concepts, x, 4, 12, 133
Congo. *See* Democratic Republic of the Congo
Congo Free State, the, 39–40, 43–44, 54. *See also* Democratic Republic of the Congo
Congo Reform Association (CRA), 40–43
Conrad, Joseph, 47, 53
coolies, 26, 67–70, 73, 75, 77, 79–81, 83, 93–94, 100, 106n2, 108n19, 112n75, 113n83
Cooper, Frederick, 7
Coronil, Fernando, 24
Crapanzano, Vincent, 150–51
cultural heritage. *See* heritage: cultural
Cycle of Violence, The, 146–48, 152–53

da Cunha, Euclides, 174–76; *Rebellion in the Backlands*, 175–76
Day After, The, 269, 272–74, 277
Deep Impact, 274–77
de la Serna, Gerónimo, 237–41, 243
Deleuze, Gilles, 90, 228

Democratic Republic of the Congo (DRC), 3, 17, 22, 26, 39–60, 60n1, 65n99; gender relations in, 57–58; rape and, 39–60, 65n99; visual narratives of, 39–43, 48, 58–60
Department of Homeland Security, 11–12, 278, 286n53. *See also* United States: national security
Derrida, Jacques, 269, 272
Detroit, 18, 32n51, 115–27, 128n8, 135, 158n17
Detropia (Heidi Ewing and Rachel Grady), 116
development, 145, 154, 155, 165, 290–92, 298, 307, 309, 314–15; costs of, 290; critique of, 22; modernist, 291; national, 15, 22, 174, 315; policies, 21; projects, 22, 27, 183, 289–91, 298, 306, 313–15
Devji, Faisal, 28, 149
Dialectics of Seeing, The (Walter Benjamin), ix
Diderot, Denis, 15
Dow Chemicals, 26–27
Drake, Sir Francis, 1, 2
Dresden, 25, 274
Durban, 17–18, 131–56

Eagleton, Terry, 7
Eastwood, Clint, *Gran Torino*, 117
Egypt, 15, 198, 304
Eisenhower, Dwight D., 117, 255–56
emotional management, 262, 267–69, 273, 277–79, 285n42
empire: edges of, 227–29, 246–47; ethnographic engagements with, 186–87; labor and, 78–83; Roman, 30n2, 126; Spanish, 229, 235, 240, 242, 244–45; studies of, 2–6, 12, 23–24, 29; temporality of, 1–4, 5–7, 10, 23–24, 29, 163–64, 184, 186
England, 27–28, 102, 126
environmentalism, 133, 136–37, 155
environmental racism, 11–12, 143. *See also* ruins: environment and

Homeland Security Administration, 11, 278, 286n53
humanitarianism, 4, 40, 43, 57
Hyderabad, 294–97, 305, 311

imperial debris: allocation of, 7–8; Benjamin and, 9, 71; definition of, x–xi; gender and, 16–17; modernist ruins and, 313–16; nature of, 31n21, 134; race and, 24–27; toxic, 40
imperial formations, 31n21, 138, 144, 149, 165, 185, 186, 195, 228, 292, 314, 316; definition of, 2–3, 5, 8–10, 12, 19, 24, 29
imperialism. *See* empire
imperial ruins, ix, 13, 15–16, 22, 229, 241, 245
India, 7, 13, 17, 21–22, 27, 111n55
Indonesia, 14
Institute for Artistic and Cultural Patrimony (IPAC), 166, 168, 170–73, 180–85
Iraq, 3, 4, 9, 19, 113, 123, 164, 277–78
Iron Mountain, 119
Israel, 3, 6, 13, 17, 19–20, 195–96, 198–99, 201, 208–9, 212, 214, 217–18, 221
Israeli Defense Forces (IDF), 194
Ivory Coast, 24

Jamaica, 19–20
Japan, 6, 257
Java, 13, 25. *See also* Indonesia
Jayyus, 199
Jesuits, 229–30, 232–33, 241, 244–45
Jetprole, 287–97, 299–302, 305–7, 310–13, 315–17, 319n6
Jews, 211, 213–16

Kabila, Joseph, 39–40, 57
Kahn, Albert, 119
Kennedy, John F., 117
Kincaid, Jamaica, 15
King Leopold, 17, 26, 39–43, 45, 47, 58–59. *See also* Leopold's Congo
King Leopold's Ghost (Adam Hochschild), 41, 52

Kinshasa, 40, 54, 57
Klein, Naomi, *The Shock Doctrine*, 23
Korengal Valley, 247
Kuklick, Henrietta, 16, 20
Kuletz, Valerie, 12

Lacangayé (Santiago de Lacangayé), 234–37, 241–43, 246
Lahore, 13, 27
Lajee Children's Center, 20–21
Laos, 117
Latham, Donald C., *Strategy for Survival*, 258–59
Latin America, 122, 124–25, 175–76, 185, 246
Latour, Bruno, 187
laughter, 17, 44, 48, 50–54, 64n80
Law of Conquest, the, 78, 109n31
Law of Nature (John Locke), 78
Leary, John Patrick, 115–16, 125, 127n3
Lefebvre, Henri, 134, 148
Leopold's Congo, 17, 40–41, 47, 53, 55, 57–58. *See also* Democratic Republic of the Congo; King Leopold
Les âmes brisées (Khalil Gueye), 54, 56
Let's Face It, 261
Let Us Now Praise Famous Men (James Agee), 24–25
Lévi-Strauss, Claude, 13, 22, 27–28, 81
Lloyd, David, 23
Locke, John, 78, 109nn29–30; *Law of Nature*, 78
Los Alamos Scientific Laboratory, 263

Machu Picchu, 230, 246
Manaus, 121–23, 126–27
Mandela, Nelson, 140
Marcus, George, 67
Martin, Thomas J., *Strategy for Survival*, 258–59
Mbeki, Thabo, 133, 136
Mbembe, Achille, 4–5, 64n80, 292
Mbweni Ruins Hotel, 15–16
McEnaney, Laura, 264, 284n28
McKenzie, Peter, 149–53, 155

McNamara, Robert, 117, 124
Merebank, 131, 134, 138–39, 141, 157n2
metaphors, x, 1–2, 10, 12, 22, 28, 30n1,
    46, 90, 181, 184–85, 292
Middle East, 4
militarization, 254, 277, 284n28, 285n42
Miller, Daniel, 5
Miller, Perry, 125–26
missionaries, 48–49, 57, 229–31, 233,
    235, 239–40
Mobutu, Joseph Désiré, 44
modernity: alternate, 175; Argentine, 124;
    capitalist, 236; colonialism and, 292;
    future and, 314, 321n29; reproductive,
    46; ruins and, 15, 21, 24, 134, 291, 303,
    308; waste and, 321n26
modernization, 18, 120, 289–92, 297–98,
    303–4, 309–10, 313–15
Mojave Desert National Preserve, 24
Mongo, the, 45–46
Monsanto, 26–27
MONUC, 40
Morel, E. D., 40, 41, 42–43, 53, 59, 61n7.
    See also rubber: "red rubber"
Musharraf, Pervez, 278
Muslims, 297, 302, 308
mutilation, 3, 17, 40–42, 44, 47, 55;
    photographs, 3, 40–41

Nagasaki, 257, 279
Naipaul, V. S., 27–28
national heritage, 22, 164–65, 172–73,
    291
National Key Points Act, 142, 144
negativity, 228, 230–31, 240, 244, 246–
    47. See also positivity
neoliberalism, 123–25, 136, 142–43, 185–
    86, 190n10
Netherlands Indies, 13, 15. See also Indo-
    nesia
New York City, 20, 164, 254, 259, 267,
    276–79, 281
Nietzsche, Friedrich Wilhelm, x, 107n13,
    113n80
9/11, 3, 278–79

Nixon, Rob, 23
North Africa, 4, 28
Noys, Benjamin, *The Persistence of the Nega-
    tive*, 247
NSC 68: A Report from the National Security
    Council, 255, 282n8
Nsongo Mboyo, 39–40, 54–56
nuclear ruins, 21, 253, 254, 256, 262, 268,
    273, 277, 279, 281
nuclear war, 21, 252–59, 261–62, 264–65,
    267, 269, 272–76
nuclear weapons, 12–13, 22, 24, 252–81,
    282nn1–2, 282n16, 285n42, 286n56

Ochagavia Hospital, 21
oil refineries, 18, 131, 133, 139–40, 142–
    45, 148, 153–54
oil spills, 24, 34n89
On the Natural History of Destruction (W. G.
    Sebald), 22–23
Operation Alert, 260, 267
Operation Cue, 262–70, 272–73, 275,
    277
Operation Demolition, 299, 319n12
Oslo Accords, 216

Pakistan, 278–79
Palestine, 19–23, 208, 211–12
Palestinian Authority, 216, 221
Palestinians: dispossession of, 3, 13;
    expulsion of, 23
Palestinian villages, 20, 214
Paraguay, 241
Paris, 131, 149, 247; 2005 riots, 28–29
"Paris" (Walter Benjamin), 131, 149, 247
Parmentier, Richard, 163
Partial Test Ban Treaty, 268
partition: Ireland, 23; Palestine, 23, 212,
    214
patrimonialization, 167, 172, 176. See also
    heritage
patrimony. See heritage
peasants, 83, 110n43, 175, 185
Peirce, Charles Sanders, 106n4
Pelourinho, 163–74, 177–87